CHINESE BUSINESS UNDER SOCIALISM

This volume is sponsored by
THE CENTER FOR CHINESE STUDIES
University of California, Berkeley

Chinese Business Under Socialism

The Politics of Domestic Commerce, 1949–1980

Dorothy J. Solinger

University of California Press

Berkeley   Los Angeles   London

University of California Press
Berkeley and Los Angeles, California
University of California Press, Ltd.
London, England
© 1984 by
The Regents of the University of California
Printed in the United States of America

1 2 3 4 5 6 7 8 9

Library of Congress Cataloging in Publication Data
Solinger, Dorothy J.
Chinese business under socialism.

Bibliography: p.
Includes index.
1. China—Commercial policy.   2. Socialism—China.
I. Title.
HF1604.S64   1984   381'.3'0951   83-17930
ISBN 0-520-04975-6

CONTENTS

FIGURES AND TABLES

FIGURES

TABLES

ACKNOWLEDGMENTS

It is now some six years since I first noticed that my fascination with the phenomenon the Chinese call "socialist commerce" was taking me beyond the scope of an article-length study. In these six years I have watched the Chinese leadership experiment with forms of trading that touched on practices more typically connected with capitalism; I have also seen these leaders return, in time, to the structures and procedures long in place. This book delineates the system formed by those structures and procedures and details the politics that surround it.

This critical feature of economic and social life in the People's Republic has, oddly enough, received scant scholarly attention until now. Thus, the present study should address an important need, for surely the procurement and the distribution of the goods of daily use affects every resident of the country. An array of issues revolve around the market in this poor and populous nation as its political elite strains to realize a socialist society. These range from the basic matter of living standards to the distribution of economic power among various social groups and classes to the more theoretical question whether buying and selling is appropriate in a genuinely socialist setting.

My own journey through thirty years of Chinese commercial policy and politics has satisfied me that I now understand the substance of the phrase "socialist commerce," that I grasp how it works, and that I have found a framework to explain the forces that shape it. I hope this book, the product of my journey, will clarify for others the nature of this commercial system. It aims to do so through analyzing the effect on the system of three key factors: the socialist planned economy, political conflict among a socialist elite, and technological underdevelopment.

A number of people have helped me by reading and commenting on individual chapters, and I have tried to take their remarks into account in my revisions. They are David Bachman, Susan Mann, Richard Curt Kraus, Nicholas Lardy, Ramon Myers, Michel Oksenberg, William Parish, Donald Sutton, Steven Thorpe, Peter Van Ness, Andrew Walder, Carl Walter, and Fred Whelan. I appreciate very much their good advice.

In addition, four others each gave the manuscript as a whole a careful and thorough reading, and offered a number of thoughtful suggestions, both editorial and substantive. Here I must thank Charles E. Lindblom, Mark Selden, Susan Shirk, and Vivienne Shue. Mark's efforts in particular went far beyond the usual duties of a reader for the Press, as he noted from one to as many as six critical comments or questions on almost every page. His and Susan's probing queries challenged some of my basic assumptions, forcing me to rethink my approach toward a number of central issues raised by this study. Charles Lindblom's remarks helped me to put some of my ideas into a larger, more comparative perspective, and Vivienne raised valuable points about the structure of individual chapters. I feel very fortunate that all four of these people gave me the benefit of their insights and of their time.

Two individuals named above contributed to this work in ways other than simply by criticizing the written page, each during a different phase of the work. Richard C. Kraus was an invaluable colleague in the early years, when I first conceived the study and as my ideas initially began to take shape. His interest helped to spark my enthusiasm as we discussed the thoughts I formed while reading the Chinese press and as he recommended references. My bibliography and my understanding of the Chinese political system are both much richer because of his friendship then.

At a later stage, after I had begun to write the book, the sharp editorial eye of Ramon Myers enabled me to pick out the patterns in the material I was describing and so to give structure to the presentation. It is difficult to underline adequately the significance of his help in honing the analysis and clarifying the overall argument. Both Dick and Ramon, each at different times, also gave me the kind of support and encouragement that continually shores up one's conviction that the job is worth the effort. For their company in this labor, many thanks.

Gordon Bennett, John Wilson Lewis, Evelyn Sakakida Rawski, Thomas G. Rawski, Alberta Sbragia, and Donald Sutton each helped by suggesting references and by talking about my ideas with me at different points throughout my research and writing. I am grateful for their interest in my project. Also, the nearly flawless typing of Polly Tooker and Kendall Stanley facilitated the final preparation immensely.

A last group of individuals assisted in the preparation of this study. These are the informants I spoke with in Hong Kong and in China, people who have worked or are still working in the Chinese commercial sector. These people helped by supplying details about how marketing actually occurs in the PRC.

The research for this book was done at three institutions: the Hoover Institution, the Universities Service Centre in Hong Kong, and the East Asian Library of the Hillman Library at the University of Pittsburgh. In each case, I wish to thank the director of the collection concerned—Mark Tam, John Dolfin, and Thomas Kuo, respectively—and his staff for generosity with their time and for bibliographic assistance.

Financial support for this project came from three sources, each at different times in the work. The Joint Committee on Contemporary China of the Social Science Research Council and the American Council of Learned Societies funded two conferences for which I prepared papers on commercial affairs (on Southwest China, 1975; on the Pursuit of Political Interest in the People's Republic, 1977). These early pieces of research primed me for this present endeavor, and the paper at the second of these eventually became chapter three of this study.

The University of Pittsburgh financed the major portion of one of my several summer visits to the Hoover Institution, my two trips to China (1978, 1979), and my time in Hong Kong (autumn 1979) when I carried out a good deal of the research for this volume. The grants from the University were awarded by the Provost's Development Fund and by the small-grants fund of the Asian Studies Program. The Hoover Institution's National Fellows program hosted me during the 1981–1982 academic year, when I was finishing the manuscript. The opportunity that year to work full time on my writing and to discuss my ideas with other scholars was very precious.

Parts of chapters one and two appear in my article in the book *State and Society in Contemporary China,* edited by Victor Nee and David Mozingo. I appreciate Cornell University Press's permission to use this material.

A somewhat different form of chapter three was published in the journal *Comparative Studies in Society and History,* and I thank that journal for allowing me to draw on that essay for this book.

Two passages from *Commerce and Society in Sung China* by Shiba

Yoshinobu, translated by Mark Elvin, Michigan Abstracts of Chinese and Japanese Works on Chinese History no. 2, p. 145 (copyright 1970), are reprinted by permission of The University of Michigan Center for Chinese Studies. All of the photographs in this volume, except for those from the nineteenth century (p. 126), are the work of the author.

It is wonderful to have had the benefit of this assistance from so many quarters. Whether I could have asked for even more help or better used the help I received can become clear only with time.

D. J. S.
Pittsburgh

ABBREVIATIONS

AS	*Asian Survey*
BJGS	*Beijing Gongshe* (Beijing Commune)
BR	*Beijing Review*
CASS	Chinese Academy of Social Sciences
CB	*Current Background*
CJRB	*Changjiang ribao* (Yangtze Daily)
CJYJ	*Caijing yanjiu* (Financial Research)
CNA	*China News Analysis*
CQ	*China Quarterly*
DGB	*Da Gong Bao* (Impartial Daily)
DX	*Dongxiang* (Trend)
DXF	*Dongxifang* (East and West)
ECMM	*Extracts from China Mainland Magazines*
FBIS	*Foreign Broadcast Information Service* (U.S.)
GCJ	*Guanchajia* (Observer)
GJJ	*Guang jiaojing* (Wide Angle)
GMRB	*Guangming ribao* (Bright Daily)
GRRB	*Gongren ribao* (Workers' Daily)
GXRB	*Guangxi ribao* (Guangxi Daily)

HQ	*Hong Qi* (Red Flag)
I&S	*Issues and Studies*
JAS	*Journal of Asian Studies*
JB	*Jing bao* (Mirror)
JHJJ	*Jihua jingji* (Planned Economy)
JJYJ	*Jingji yanjiu* (Economic Studies)
JPRS	*Joint Publications Research Service*
JXRB	*Jiangxi ribao* (Jiangxi Daily)
MC	*Modern China*
NCEA	*New China's Economic Achievements*
NFRB	*Nanfang ribao* (Southern Daily)
PR	*Peking Review*
PRC	People's Republic of China
RGP	*Red Guard Publications*
RMRB	*Renmin ribao* (People's Daily)
SC	*Shichang* (Market)
SCMM	*Selections from China Mainland Magazines*
SCMP	*Survey of the China Mainland Press*
SCMPS	*Survey of the China Mainland Press-Supplement*
SCRB	*Sichuan ribao* (Sichuan Daily)
SMC	Supply and marketing cooperative
SPRCM	*Selections from People's Republic of China Magazines*
SPRCP	*Survey of the People's Republic of China Press*
XGS	*Xin Gong Shang* (New Industry and Commerce)
XHBYK	*Xinhua banyuekan* (New China Semimonthly)
XHRB	*Xinhua ribao* (New China Daily)
XHYB	*Xinhua yuebao* (New China Monthly)
XX	*Xuexi* (Study)
XXYPP	*Xuexi yu pipan* (Study and Criticism)
YCWB	*Yangcheng wanbao* (Yangcheng Evening News)
ZM	*Zheng Ming* (Contend)

Introduction

Over many centuries, local Chinese marketplaces lent color and lilt to the countryside, as their observers chronicled:

> The small market—
> People with their bundles of tea or salt,
> Chickens cackling, dogs barking,
> Firewood being exchanged for rice,
> Fishes being bartered for wine.[1]

In more urbanized settings, the market town was similarly lively:

> The lodges and stores are countless as the clouds.
> They bring linen fabrics and paper-mulberry paper,
> Or drive pullets and sucking pigs ahead of them.
> Brushes and dustpans are piled this way and that—
> Too many domestic trifles to list them all.[2]

1. From verses by the thirteenth-century literatus Chou Mi, quoted in Mark Elvin, *The Pattern of the Chinese Past*, p. 169.
2. Ibid. From a poem by the eleventh-century poet Tao-ch'ien.

What has happened to this animated exchange, and to the consumer goods that were its substance, under the People's Republic? Soon after the establishment of the new socialist regime in China, its rulers chose to sweep away the brisk business of private producers, scenes of which are evoked by these verses, in the interest of ensuring a distribution pattern consistent with socialist goals. In its stead, the leadership inserted regulated markets, to be run by state-owned offices charged with meeting planned quotas for their trade.

From many angles, one must question this choice. Consider, for example, the several virtues that a noted sociologist attributed to a local market he investigated in a North China community in the 1930s:

> The excitement of the market contrasts with the monotony of the peasantry. Here, itinerary merchants from distant provinces stop, bringing products, articles and ideas that are foreign to the local community. Here, the magicians, the story-tellers, and the medicine peddlers and quack doctors make their unwonted appearance, attract gazing eyes and listening ears, and spread strange talks, news and ideas through the surrounding villages. Here, above all, the neighboring villages come together to exchange products, to dispose of one's surplus for one's need, thus making life richer than any single individual, family or village can accomplish alone. . . . Unwittingly, [the individual] cooperates with outsiders, most of whom are totally strange to him, for a common end. Through the market, the sphere of communal cooperation is enlarged beyond the family, the neighborhood and the village.[3]

According to this account, markets bring excitement, afford both cultural and material enrichment, and lend a spirit of cooperation to the life of the village-bound peasant. For its author, Adam Smith's invisible hand is clearly carrying the wares from producer to consumer.

And yet three caveats are in order, for the observations of other scholars force one, in appraising the benefits of commerce, to pose the questions where, when, and for whom. Thus, some regions of China, blessed with favorable geographical conditions (navigable waterways, relatively flat terrain), low transport costs, fertile soil, and mild climates, were sites of active exchange, as they offered conveniently located, frequent, and well-stocked, versatile bazaars. But there was a wide varia-

---

3. Ching-kun Yang, *A North China Local Market Economy*, p. 1. For a broader statement of the benefits of markets, see Ramon Myers, "Customary Law, Markets, and Resource Transactions in Late Imperial China." Myers makes the point that competitive markets permitted resource exchange, production, and distribution to flourish everywhere in the empire (p. 275).

tion across the landscape of China even into modern times—in numbers of marketplaces per county, in the sorts of goods available for purchase, in the distance one had to travel to market, and in the frequency with which local markets met.[4]

The question of when points to the uncertainty under which marketers labored, dependent on favorable weather and calm politics. One economist took note of the fact that farmers were often reluctant to market more of their produce than was absolutely necessary, because of the danger that too great a reliance on the market for one's grain supply could spell starvation.[5] Uncertain natural conditions limited specialization and encouraged self-sufficiency in many areas.

Any one of a number of adverse political conditions had their effect as well. During the late 1930s and 1940s, a battery of these worked together to cut back to almost total inactivity a previously flourishing exchange on the North China Plain.[6] At that time, guerrilla warfare, plus Japanese forays into the countryside to seize stocks of grain, halted the flow of goods. This flow had been curtailed in earlier decades by another political factor—the fighting between warlords, which had disrupted traffic on the railways.

The inroads into the rural market made by foreign economic penetration constituted another political factor that created disadvantages for those who used markets. Again taking the case of North China, a study of central Hebei province in the early twentieth century illustrated how land hunger forced peasants then to become linked into trading systems centered on treaty ports. Such systems drained the rural surplus out of the hinterland while offering little in return.[7] Some farmers turned to a

4. On this point, see Yang, p. 3 (Yang states here that intervals of two to six days marked the time between fairs in different communities in the 1930s); and Kung-ch'üan Hsiao, *Rural China*, pp. 21–23. Also, contrast the description of the active marketing community in the North China community of Dingxian given in Sidney D. Gamble, *Ting Hsien: A North China Rural Community*, pp. 277–82, with the one of trading conditions in Yunnan and Guizhou provinces in the topographically forbidding Southwest at just the same time, in Dorothy J. Solinger, *Regional Government and Political Integration in Southwest China, 1949–1954*, pp. 67–71. The classic exposition of marketing structure, scheduling, and functions, and of the sizes of marketing areas in traditional China is G. William Skinner's "Marketing and Social Structure in Rural China, Part I." Also on the structure of markets in late traditional China, see Gilbert Rozman, *Urban Networks in Ch'ing China and Tokugawa Japan*.

5. Dwight H. Perkins, *Agricultural Development in China 1368–1968*, p. 116.

6. Ramon H. Myers, *The Chinese Peasant Economy: Agricultural Development in Hopei and Shantung, 1890–1949*, pp. 277–281.

7. Linda Grove, "Treaty Port and Hinterland: Revolution in a Semi-Colonial Society," pp. 16–19. Dani Rodrik, in "Rural Transformation and Peasant Political Orientations in Egypt and Turkey," pp. 424 and 428, discusses the insecurity, vulnerability to exploitation, and unpredictability visited upon the Egyptian fellah once he turned from subsistence farming to cash-cropping, a transition Rodrik terms "quite painful."

monocultural production, which made them vulnerable to local depressions whenever foreign demand faltered. In other cases peasants obtained from the treaty ports only the semiprocessed goods to be used as raw materials for their handicraft exports. Meanwhile, they went on consuming the rough grains and vegetables produced on their own land.

Finally, the question of for whom introduces the central issues of class and polarization that have particularly engaged the attention of the socialist rulers of the PRC. Problems of market-induced polarization were especially pertinent in areas where treacherous topography cut off the poor, pole-carrying peasant from easy access to markets. Such lack of access often caused the less well-off to be ignorant of competitive prices in surrounding areas, to pay excessive costs for conveyance, and to sell wholesale at a loss. Alternatively, they had to depend on layers of middlemen, each of whom took a cut.

Natural disaster also fell disproportionately on the poor, as in times of shortage the rich refused to sell their stocks locally, either hoarding grain or shipping it to other districts where it might fetch a better price.[8] As a local man of learning and wealth in southwest Hunan province wrote, in commenting on food riots in 1832:

> Those who are causing trouble in the area are the rich who protect their grain. They resist till death lowering their prices. They believe they can control goods through monopoly. . . . The crime belongs to the riotous people, but the situation is really due to the rich non-benevolent people who name their own prices.[9]

Some economists have even suggested that commercialization itself can be a cause of increased impoverishment and undernourishment for some. For it brings in its wake a more skewed distribution of income, which in turn means that a substantial segment of the population is likely to suffer nutritionally.[10] One study of food riots during the Qing dynasty found, too, that as a heightened degree of market exchange expanded the numbers of people relying on common food supplies, the wealthy were at the same time provided with a wider and more profitable arena in which to sell their grain. In pursuing these new opportunities, men of means often ignored needy local marketers. In addition, when greater amounts of grain went into trading channels, grain was drawn away from the customary

8. R. Bin Wong, "Food Riots in the Qing Dynasty," p. 767.
9. Cited in ibid., p. 776.
10. Lillian M. Li, "Introduction" to "Food, Famine, and the Chinese State—A Symposium," p. 695.

(largely charitable) circulation of the past.[11] In these ways the rich clearly gained at the expense of the indigent.

These several considerations—of spatial variation, temporal unpredictability, and social inequity—constitute the backdrop for the decision of the elite in the PRC to replace the structure of localized, uncontrolled bazaars of pre-1949 China with a state-managed, national market.

But the politicians who made this decision have been unable to rest with its consequences. As commercial activity ebbed and state markets failed to serve as an adequate substitute, a long-term debate within the elite has surfaced on several occasions. The heart of the disagreement lies in the determination of how much to permit spontaneously operating markets again to allocate goods, how much to continue to impose state-designed procedures on the circulation of commodities.

This question was never conclusively answered in the first three decades of PRC history. As a result, the pattern of policy toward the commercial sector has continually been one of rotating strategies and frequent reversals of policy. This book examines the process and the politics of state domination of the marketing of consumer goods in China over three decades. It also seeks to explain the reasons behind the constant shifts and adjustments in policy that have marked that effort of control.

The study will analyze these vacillations in policy in a framework of political economy. Simply put, three givens, or independent variables—the planned economy, policy conflict among the leadership, and economic underdevelopment—have determined the shape of policies toward the three central facets of Chinese commercial policy: the treatment of the private sector, the disposal of the products of light industry, and free markets for agricultural produce.

Like any socialist developing nation, the PRC has gone through the process of nationalizing and collectivizing private business, and must cope with the effects of that process. It has had to design methods for purchasing the output of factories which can permit the state to determine the means of apportionment of this output among the populace. And it has wrestled with the trade-offs involved in allowing the peasants to decide for themselves how to handle their surplus product, as opposed to directing state-owned cooperatives to procure the bulk of rural produce. The book uncovers the circumscribed scope for liberalization

11. Wong, "Food Riots," p. 784. Also see p. 769 on "customary circulation," which Wong defines as "largely the local wealthy selling or lending grain received as rents or obtained through purchase to the local poor."

in each of these areas which elite commitment to the planned economy and leadership disagreements have created in this economy of scarcity.

Each of the three independent variables places the discussion within a context broader than the immediate subject at hand. For they refer, respectively, to three general areas of social science inquiry: the political economy of socialist societies, public policy analysis, and development. Thus, though the book concentrates on one sector in one country, its implications are far greater. The effects of these three factors on trading in China can be alluded to briefly here, in preview.

The first variable is the state plan, which organizes trade through the use of state-managed organs and enterprises, and which directs these units to procure and allocate goods in accord with annual targets for sales turnover dictated by offices in Beijing. The obligations this arrangement imposes to meet quotas for business create rivalries among all units—whether state-owned or private—engaged in commerce. These rivalries in turn complicate the process of delivering commodities as a range of contenders fight for power over goods and their disposal. This competition caused by the plan applies to socialist states generally.

In addition, conflict over public policy among the Chinese elite is a second element shaping domestic trade. Disagreement in this sector revolves around the question of the proper scope for the market under socialism, a question that has engaged socialist politicians and theoreticians internationally throughout the twentieth century. As chapter two will make clear, this controversy has its roots in conflicting ideals within the philosophy of Marxism, each of which is relatively more important to some members of the elite than to others. Specifically, adherents to three distinct values stress, respectively, equitable distribution, order and state control, and productivity, goals that in practice cannot all be realized at the same time.

Put in different terms, the leaders of socialist regimes have argued over how to balance the issues of restructuring class relations and benefits (distribution), ensuring the discipline of the plan (order), and using material incentives (productivity). These questions of public policy go beyond socialist politics, as discussion of the same three themes underlies debates over budget and programmatic design in any modern state. In the Chinese case, the repeated reorganizations of the processes for handling consumer goods is in large part the product of sharp clashes among the elite over the priorities in these values.

The third variable, economic underdevelopment and scarcity, here discussed principally in terms of its influence on the infrastructure for marketing, is obviously the central obstacle faced by the nations of the

Third World. This book highlights the difficulties of circulating fresh and varied commodities nationally in the face of the Chinese domestic market's dependence on climate, the regional disparities in resource endowment of the country, and the still inadequate storage and transport facilities that support trading. The job of realizing state control over distribution, a job undertaken by the governments of many developing nations, is greatly magnified under these conditions.

This book is organized into two parts. In the first part, one chapter is devoted to each of these three key variables. Chapter one examines the dominating structure of the state economic plan. Chapter two analyzes ideological and political conflicts among decision makers over the role of the market and uses six specific cases of controversy as examples. And chapter three focuses on the nature of the technological environment for marketing. Each of these first three chapters explicates the several dimensions of the variable that is its focus. Each also shows how that variable has affected the institutions, practice, and policy toward commercial activity in the PRC over three decades.

In the second part, chapters four, five, and six each deal with one of the three central issues in the management of socialist commerce: the treatment of the private sector (chapter four), the disposal of the products of light industry (chapter five), and the "free" markets for rural produce (chapter six). As each chapter presents its issue, it stresses the effect that the three independent variables of chapters one through three have had on the state's handling of that issue. At the same time, each chapter also contains case studies of historical instances of policy conflict among the elite over that issue; local-level implementation of policy; and, where possible, mass reaction to policy, interpreted in light of the social interests of different groups within the population.

I have chosen to arrange the material here in topical, issue-oriented chapters instead of presenting a chronological unfolding of policy development. I have done so because my interest throughout the course of this study has been to ferret out and emphasize persisting themes, recurring strategies of the leadership, and remittent strains over time in the relationship between state and society in the People's Republic with regard to the circulation of goods among the populace. Thus my purpose is not to detail a history per se. Rather, I will refer to history only when this can help to reveal continuities or learning among the elite in the Chinese leadership's efforts to install a commercial sector informed by socialist principles, and in their battles over the most workable proportions of public versus private activity in this realm.

Also, instead of attempting to cover every period of PRC history in equal depth, I have opted in the second part of the book to focus most of my attention on the episodes of economic liberalization—in 1956–1957, the early 1960s, and 1978–1980—by studying the policies toward the private sector, the products of light industry, and free markets promulgated in those eras. For this is a book about business, and it is in the examination of practices in these times that the most incisive insights into the state's handling of commercial activity can be garnered. This means that the Great Leap Forward (1958–1960) and the Cultural Revolution (1966–1976) receive short shrift; but there are descriptions of the sort of business that existed in those periods and the efforts by radicals to cut it back.

Three subjects related to the substance of this book have not been included in it. These are foreign trade; the industrial distribution network (which manages the allocation of the supplies for and the products of heavy industry); and big businessmen, those capitalists known in China as the "bureaucratic capitalists" (made up of "feudal," comprador, and state-monopoly capitalists). Instead, the volume concentrates solely on the field of domestic buying and selling, on the exchange of the kinds of products that are handled by the Ministry of Commerce and its departments and enterprises (i.e., agricultural products, light industrial goods for daily use, and sundry handicraft items);[12] and on the trading that takes place in the daily lives of ordinary urban consumers, peasants, and petty merchants. Though each of these other topics has a bearing on the conduct of commerce within the PRC, their treatment must be left to other studies.

As this volume reaches toward an understanding of the institution of socialist commerce in China, and of the role of the market in this socialist society, it will become evident that certain inescapable features that mark business in a capitalist setting have not been, and cannot be, eliminated in the PRC. But it will also be clear that three central explanatory factors—the framework for this trading imposed on it by the state plan, the sorts of ideological conflicts that structure policies toward commerce, and the technological foundation for marketing—each skews the shape that sales and purchases have taken in the People's Republic.

12. According to *Renmin ribao* [People's Daily] (Beijing), July 1, 1982, p. 5, the state commercial network and its organs handles over 90 percent of the products of the light and textile industries and the "majority" of the rural products of the country. The same article states that the state manages over 90 percent of the wholesale trade in the country and about 70 percent of the retail trade. Tong-eng Wang, in *Economic Policies and Price Stability in China*, on p. 96, notes that the socialist market network controls the dominant portion of commodity distribution, or more than 80 percent of China's total retail sales in early 1962 and about 92.5 percent in the early 1970s.

PART ONE

The Framework for Commerce in the People's Republic

The Planned Economy and Competition for Goods

Chinese trade in the centrally planned, state-directed economy remains a competitive activity. But the fact of the plan, with its dictates to each commercial unit—wholesale and retail, at various levels, and in different localities—to fulfill targets for profits and sales, has restructured the simple rivalry of firm against firm that characterizes the capitalist marketplace. Other features of Chinese society—its socialist morality and generalized economic scarcity—combine, along with the plan's commands, to restrict much money-based exchange.

In this context, Chinese business under socialism has one basic outstanding characteristic: commodities often substitute for currency as a medium of exchange among units and so, like money under capitalism, are treated as a tool of power and as an object of contention. Informal exchange between individuals as well is often carried out through the use of goods, rather than with money alone. Trade in China is largely a game of competition for control over goods, and goods themselves are frequently used in its practice.

This chapter first delineates the overall social framework within which commerce occurs in the People's Republic, and it does so by highlighting the several factors that cause commodities to replace cash. The second half of the chapter outlines the structure of the commercial bureaucracy, and then shows how exchange—among various agencies in the state commercial bureaucracy, between state and private sectors, and within the populace—plays out this conflict over goods. In the struggle for command, it is power and not possession alone that counts, a power to dump goods as well as a power to obtain and distribute them.

Structural Factors:
The Context for Commercial Activity
and the Centrality of Goods

Several features of Chinese society in the People's Republic form the context in which the circulation of commodities occurs. They do so in a way that places more emphasis on power over goods than on money and its use, or on the accumulation of capital. Central among these features are the ideological underpinnings of Chinese culture, both traditional and contemporary; economically, investment patterns over the first three decades of the PRC, and the omnipresence of scarcity; and organizationally, the structure and regulations that make up the totality of the planned economy. Each of these elements has worked to limit free marketing activity and, in the process, to force traders toward barter forms of business.

IDEOLOGICAL

Marxist views on marketing mesh neatly with a strain in traditional Chinese thought. Both valued the production of social wealth and took for granted the necessity for producers to exchange their output to meet social needs. At the same time, though, neither Marx nor the classical Chinese philosophers thought well of profit taking. Illustrating this ambivalence toward market activities which has been present in China historically, one writer noted:

China's Thucydides, Ssu-ma Ch'ien . . . on the one hand . . . praised as natural the free flow of the market unhampered by state restrictions. On the other, he sighed that Mencius' warning against the pursuit of *li* (profits, material advantages) was very right and added: "From the son of heaven to the common people, how is there any difference in the troubles that come from liking *li*!" Wang Fu (ca. 100 A.D.) condemned trade in "useless" articles but regarded trade in needed commodities by merchants as vital.[1]

The same author added that "merchants often were vehemently criticized for corrupt machinations even while their services were regarded as essential."[2]

Similarly, Marx took an ambiguous position on the role of commerce in society, linking it with capitalism, which he expected to vanish in time. Marx, like the Confucians, put a premium on the promotion of social wealth and evaluated trading activity primarily in light of its contribution to that end. Thus, he recognized that merchant capital expands the market; promotes the productivity of industrial capital and adds to its accumulation; shortens the time of circulation of productive capital; and reduces industry's expenditure of energy, thereby setting time free for more production.[3] However, most relevant for our purposes here is Marx's assessment that no value is produced in the process of circulation, that is, no new wealth is created for society, so that the surplus value (essentially, profit) that it appropriates is actually merely a portion of the surplus value already yielded by productive (industrial) capital.[4] Buying and selling, then, partook of parasitism for Marx.[5]

Marx, at one point terming at least part of commerce "unproductive exploitation," did draw a distinction between "supplemental" costs in commerce—which grew from activities that continued the productive process and added to the value of the product (including packaging, storing, and transport)—and "pure" costs, which arise only because of the process of purchase and sale. It is these latter costs—for accounting, marketing, bookkeeping, correspondence, and advertising—which grow out of what he saw as a worthless transfer of title of ownership (among wholesalers, speculative buyers, and other commission agents) which Marx felt to be especially unworthy.[6]

A different way of putting this same point appears in Marx's concepts

1. Thomas A. Metzger, "The State and Commerce in Imperial China," p. 29.

2. Ibid., p. 30. See chapter 3 for more on this point.

3. Karl Marx, *Capital*, vol. 3, bk. 3, pp. 275, 298; bk. 2, p. 131.

4. Ibid., pp. 274, 277. See Ernest Mandel, *Marxist Economic Theory*, vol. 1, p. 84.

5. Jere L. Felker, *Soviet Economic Controversies: The Emerging Marketing Concept and Changes in Planning, 1960–1965*, p. 17.

6. Marshall I. Goldman, *Soviet Marketing: Distribution in a Controlled Economy*, p. 3; and Felker, pp. 16–17; Marx, p. 284.

of "use-value" and "exchange-value" (or simply "value"). The former relates to the utility of a product, that is, its ability to fulfill a particular human need, and depends on the totality of its physical qualities. The latter, value, concerns the product's relation to other goods on the market, and is established, according to Marx, by the amount of labor time socially necessary to produce it. This is to say that on the market the exchange-values of goods are based on the number of hours necessary to make a given object at the average conditions of productivity present in a society at a given time.[7]

Marx saw this concept of value, which forms the core of his labor theory of value, as being the principal factor determining the price of a commodity. Thus it was to obtain only in capitalist societies, where markets and money were present. Indeed, one analyst concludes, it seems that Marx emphasized labor-unit bookkeeping in socialist society, after the proletarian revolution had brought capitalism to an end.[8] Whereas Marx was not altogether clear here, Engels was far more explicit, as in this much-cited passage:

> From the moment society enters into the possession of the means of production and uses them in direct association for production, the labor of each individual becomes social labor . . . the quantities of labor put into products would then be expressed in their natural, absolute measure, time . . . at that point, society will not assign values to products.[9]

Explicating this point further, Ernest Mandel interprets Marx to have meant to say that "in socialist society the products of human labor have a directly social character, and thus have no value . . . they are not commodities [that is, products created for the purpose of being sold], but use-values, produced for the satisfaction of human needs." Mandel holds that all of Marx's "economic categories"—commodities, value, money, price, wages, profit—would cease to exist in a true socialist society. In this view, the fully developed socialist economy was to be capable of producing an abundance of use-values, so that distribution might be done directly. It would then no longer be based on a monied market exchange, as the economy ensured each member of society the satisfac-

7. A clear presentation of the definitions of these terms is found in Ernest Mandel, *An Introduction to Marxist Economic Theory*, 2d ed., pp. 9–10; also see Mandel, *Marxist Economic Theory*, chap. 2.

8. Deborah D. Milenkovitch, *Plan and Market in Yugoslav Economic Thought*, pp. 21–24.

9. Frederick Engels, *Anti-Dühring*, pp. 401–2.

tion of his or her basic needs.[10] Thus, the future society that Marx predicted and preferred would be one in which products reached those needing to use them, but did so without the mediation of money.

Followers of Marx shared his vision of a form of social organization that would operate without commercial activity, but were less sanguine about the ease of realizing such a society. After the Russian revolution, it became apparent to Lenin and later to Stalin that the market would not immediately die out with the nationalization of industry. Lenin justified its continuation by pointing to the still-present small-scale peasant sector in the Soviet Union and the low level of industrialization.[11]

Stalin and, building on Stalin's logic, Mandel, Bettelheim, and Mao have specified that Marx's phase of direct distribution must wait for a total socialization of the entire economy—a time when state ownership would adhere in all industrial firms and in agriculture as well. At such a time, there was to be but one all-encompassing productive sector, which would work through a system of "products-exchange." That development was to render commodity circulation obsolete, along with its concomitant money economy. All four socialists have recognized, too, that until this is possible, commodity production, commodity exchange, and money, along with the other "economic categories" would persist, even into socialist society.[12]

These writers all drew the same distinction between market-based, monetary exchange, on the one hand, which they hoped would expire as society progresses toward communism; and a simple exchange of necessities on the other, which they viewed as positive. Thus, Bettelheim tells us that "in a fully developed, socialist economy, products, not being commodities [in the Marxist definition, goods produced for the purpose of exchange], do not have prices."[13] Mandel foresees an increasing "substitution of money of account for fiduciary money" as socialization of the means of production occurs, and as planning comes to guide all exchange,

---

10. Mandel, *Marxist Economic Theory*, pp. 10, 565–67. See also Alec Nove, *The Soviet Economic System*, p. 257; Milenkovitch, p. 14.

11. Wlodzimierz Brus, *The Market in a Socialist Economy*, p. 24.

12. Joseph Stalin, *Economic Problems of Socialism in the U.S.S.R.*, pp. 16, 22; Ota Šik, *Plan and Market Under Socialism*, p. 25; Mandel, *Theory*, p. 567; Charles Bettelheim, *The Transition to Socialist Economy*, pp. 40–41, 107; Mao Tse-tung, *A Critique of Soviet Economics*, pp. 130, 132, 140; Milenkovitch, *Plan and Market*, chap. 3 on the history of debates on socialism in the Soviet Union and the role of commodities (and thus implicitly the market) in socialist society. Also, Alec Nove and D. M. Nuti, eds., *Socialist Economics: Selected Readings*, pp. 11 and 12, for the views of Bukharin, Lange, and others on these points.

13. Charles Bettelheim, *Economic Calculation and Forms of Property: An Essay on the Transition between Capitalism and Socialism*, p. 47. See also Branko Horvat, *The Yugoslav Economic System*, p. 10.

during the transition between capitalism and socialism.[14] This vision reinforces Marx's prediction of eventual payment of producers in paper checks, rather than in circulating money, under communism.[15]

Thus, Marx and his followers saw profit and money as part and parcel of each other, both of which were negative features of the capitalist market economy. Though they entertained different views about when along the road toward communism these categories would disappear, each expected their demise to be followed by simple barter and finally by a direct distribution of goods. Disapproval of the exploitative tendencies and the unproductive nature of the market, combined with a faith in the efficacy of the socialist planned economy, fueled a vision for them all of a very different future society. In that dream not only would money not dirty anyone's hands, but the products of society's labor were to be distributed on grounds other than that of the differential financial power that various consumers command. In China this theory supplemented traditional ideas with which it fitted nicely on this theme. Together, this set of ideological influences sets the context for and also contributes to a tendency in China to eschew the use of cash and to celebrate instead an exchange of goods outside a market.

ECONOMIC

The Chinese economy and its structure buttress this intellectual bias to minimize buying and selling activity. Here the relevant factors are the historically inherited agricultural base of the economy, along with an emphasis on heavy industry in the investment pattern chosen over nearly three decades by planners in the PRC. Behind these structural factors lies economic scarcity, which has an important influence as well.

As throughout centuries of history, the foundation of the Chinese economy continues to be agricultural. In this society where even today 80 percent of the population still lives on the land, the degree of self-sufficiency has often been high, and produce has traditionally served as a kind of currency. That these features persisted well into the twentieth century is clear in the results of surveys in the countryside in the 1920s and 1930s. These studies documented that on the average only 38 to 58 percent of a typical peasant income was in cash.[16]

14. Mandel, *Theory*, p. 667.
15. P. J. D. Wiles, *The Political Economy of Communism*, pp. 333, 345, 348.
16. Dwight H. Perkins, *Agricultural Development in China 1368–1968*, p. 114. G. William Skinner, in "Marketing and Social Structure in Rural China, Part I," p. 11, makes the point that "general poverty, a value emphasis on frugality and traditional consumption

An article written in China in the 1950s refers to rural peddlers who "make purchases and sales by barter in the countryside, in line with the people's customs."[17] In a modern-day variant, peasants trade one rationed good for another (such as a certain quantity of oil for some amount of grain).[18] Thus, historical habit predisposes consumers in the countryside toward subsistence agriculture and exchange in goods, at least for a portion of their needs.

Besides the agricultural base, the investment pattern in the PRC has helped to diminish the role of marketing and the quantity of marketable goods. That is, an emphasis on heavy industry often worked to the detriment of the other sectors of the economy. During the First Five Year Plan (1953–1957) investment in heavy industry was 38.7 percent of total investment; during the period from 1958 to 1978 the proportion rose to 52.8 percent. "We one-sidedly sought the production of primary and intermediate products of heavy industry and neglected the production of ultimate consumer goods, with the result that various consumer goods, especially consumer durables, urgently needed by the people, were for a long time in a state of short supply," ran a reassessment written in 1981.[19] Shortage of goods, then, has put a premium on them.

Not only has Chinese industry turned out fewer consumer goods than the market demanded, but the formal mechanisms for circulating the commodities that do exist have long been inadequate. For the commercial as well as the light industrial sector has suffered from a lack of investment. According to one account, during the First Five Year Plan only 1.58 percent of state investment in basic construction went to the commercial system; by 1978, that proportion had dwindled to 0.46 percent.[20] As that sector attained greater legitimacy in the less doctrinaire mood of the late 1970s, a section of the Ministry of Commerce lobbied in the press for its interests, beginning its plaint with a quotation from Mao at the end of the 1950s:

---

norms all contributed to a minimal definition of subsistence needs in the peasant household." He goes on to note: "These needs in considerable part were supplied without recourse to marketing, for the peasant household produced (or received through wages in kind) much of what it consumed; self-sufficiency was a virtue."

17. *Da Gong Bao* [Impartial Daily] (Beijing) (*DGB*), March 3, 1956.

18. Interviews in Hong Kong, September 7 and November 12, 1979. B. Michael Frolic, *Mao's People*, pp. 151 and 187, has examples of people trading food and clothing coupons for tickets to cultural programs, and sugar for pork coupons.

19. This summary in U.S. *Foreign Broadcast Information Service* (*FBIS*), August 12, 1981, pp. K14–K15, is one example of many such analyses in the press after late 1978. See also Christopher Howe, *China's Economy: A Basic Reader*, pp. xxv and 95–96, for a Western economist's view, based on Chinese data released before 1978.

20. *Renmin ribao* [People's Daily] (Beijing) (*RMRB*), June 23, 1980, p. 5.

> In the past several years there's been a problem in construction . . . we've paid attention only to the "bones" and not to the "meat"; factory building and machinery have both been done well, but urban administration and measures of a service nature have not been done correspondingly well.

The problem of accommodating the needs of urban populations, though, instead of being attended to at that time, grew over the years, according to these authors, while insufficient funding led to crowded shops, reductions in the number of vegetable markets, and long queues.[21] Flaws in storage installations and in transport facilities were not corrected; and sanitation, displays, and working hours remained problems as well.[22] Thus the effect of a set of interrelated choices for investment was to discriminate against business throughout most of a twenty-year period.

Behind the agricultural base and the several decades of inattention to light industry and the tertiary sector, and adding to the effect of both of these factors, is the relative poverty of the Chinese economy and of the overwhelming bulk of the populace. Thus, not only shortages of goods and services but also low salaries and a lack of cash have caused consumers to fall back on a substitution of some kind of goods over which they have control, in order to effect a bribe, when possible. In the Soviet Union, by contrast, the exchange by barter in the 1950s and earlier has gradually been replaced over the past two decades by monetary palm-greasing. One analyst attributes this shift to the increasing affluence of Soviet society.[23]

Thus, peasant habits, sectoral imbalances, and indigence add a set of economic factors to the ideological ones discussed above, creating a context in which commodities themselves often act as money.

21. *Hong Qi* [Red Flag] (*HQ*), no. 7 (1978), pp. 74–78.

22. *Guangming ribao* [Bright Daily] (Beijing), February 9, 1980, which states that the number of urban "commercial points" (retail stores, food and drink shops, and other service centers) was reduced by 82% after 1957, from one million in that year to 180,000 in 1978; and that the personnel working in such points represented 3.57% of urban population in 1957, but fell to only 2.34% on the average by 1978, and was even as low as 2% in some cities by that later date. Also, according to *RMRB*, February 15, 1980, p. 5, in 1957 there were ten retail stores for every one thousand persons (1:100), while in 1979 there was only one shop per 10,000 persons. By the end of 1980, there were 13,960,000 persons working in all service industries, which includes those in restaurants and repair and service trades such as barbers, as well as commercial personnel (New China News Agency, June 19, 1981, reported in *New York Times*, June 20, 1981).

23. Hedrick Smith, *The Russians*, p. 115. Although this replacement of barter by cash bribery may be the general trend, vodka still serves as a unit of exchange in the Soviet Union today, according to Gregory Grossman, as stated in a lecture at the University of Illinois, October 27, 1980.

BUREAUCRATIC

Superimposed on this backdrop of ideological ambivalence and economic limitation, forming yet another key component of the milieu in which marketing occurs, is the central plan. In explaining the influence of planning on the circulation of commodities, Western scholars have focused on its inefficiencies—its tendency to produce goods not in demand and to deliver unwanted commodities to the wrong place or at the wrong time. Stockpiling, deterioration, shortages, and queuing are the oft-bemoaned results.[24]

The analysis here takes a different tack. In line with the discussion to this point, this section will show how the totality of the planned economy, in eschewing economic methods of management, discourages the use of money. The outcome, once again, has been to enhance the value of goods, thereby laying the groundwork for a battle over their control, among the bureaucratic units that manage them and within the population at large. To make this point will involve a consideration of a broad set of features that make up the planning system, and that go beyond the distribution sector itself. The description that follows presents that system as it existed from the mid-1950s through 1980.

24. The Chinese themselves made this point, as long ago as 1956, at the Eighth Congress of the Chinese Communist Party, where Zeng Shan, soon to be dismissed from his post as minister of commerce, offered what amounted to a self-criticism on behalf of his unit. He admitted to "shortcomings in our work," including products not supplied on time, varieties and patterns not meeting the requirements of the buyer, the same stocks accumulating in some areas but sold out in others, allocations from units higher in the hierarchy ignorant of local demands, and lower-level sales agents thus unable to distribute goods in accord with need. See *Extracts from China Mainland Magazines* (*ECMM*), no. 423 (1956), pp. 1–7. More recently, a prominent Chinese economist noted: "Planning itself explains why goods accumulate in one place while they are sold out in another—because the law of value is not used" (Xue Muqiao, "Liyung jiazhi guilu wei jingji jianshe shiye fuwu" [Use the law of value to serve economic construction], *HQ*, no. 1 (1979), p. 64. This phenomenon has frequently been the subject of critiques of the planned economy in other socialist systems. For example, Smith, on p. 132, blames the excessive regulations in the Soviet economy for the "second economy," and on p. 112 states that "corruption and illegal private enterprises . . . grow out of the very nature of the Soviet economy and its inefficiencies—shortages, poor quality goods, terrible delays in service." Benjamin N. Ward, *The Soviet Economy*, p. 179, says that extra-plan exchanges are tolerated because they are useful for minor corrections that result from bad planning. Gregory Grossman, in "The 'Second Economy' of the USSR," p. 29, cites maldistribution and shortages as providing opportunities for black marketing. Goldman, *Soviet Marketing*, p. 62, speaks of the lack of precision in planning, and of the faulty distribution of consumer goods in Russia as being due to planning inflexibilities and human misallocation, as well as other factors. On p. 70 Goldman blames mistakes in planning for gluts and deficits. Charles E. Lindblom, in chapter 5 of *Politics and Markets*, says that economic inefficiency occurs because of the nature of "central authoritative coordination," with its problems of communication, internal control, distortions connected with conflicts among targets, and its uncertain incentives.

Planned economy, copying the example of the Soviet Union, has dominated the administrative implementation of socialism and the effort to achieve an equitable handling of economic scarcity in the PRC over most of three decades. Under the plan, the allocation of resources is based principally on political decisions, and not on a pricing system. Within the state-owned sector, money can be used only in accord with the plan's dictates. While it acts as a signal, money is not used as an adjuster, that is, it does not function to invoke responses or to correct movement away from equilibrium prices.[25] As one Chinese commentator put it:

> For the economy of the state ownership, an attempt was made to adopt a highly planned system which limited commodity relations. . . . Though, in reality, it was impossible to altogether abolish commodities and money, their role and the role of value were very limited.[26]

Planners' intentions are realized through a number of administrative mechanisms. Perhaps the best known of these operate within the industrial sector, where output targets for production are written in terms of physical units (such as tons); and raw materials, machinery, and other supplies (inputs) are assigned on a quota basis to firms without charge, in accord with the production target a given firm is to meet. Other aspects of this system include the centralization of financial transactions within the state-run People's Bank; taxation of the countryside in grain, coupled with large compulsory purchase deliveries of grain (and other goods, such as cotton and oil) to the state, which remove much of this principal commodity from the free market; a significant portion of rural remuneration for labor done in kind not cash; the rationing of scarce and vital consumer items; and the administration of state-set prices, along with price controls to keep inflation in check. Although many of these features of the economic system came under discussion and even attack beginning in 1978 and 1979, with the exception of the devolution of economic decision making to the household level in the countryside and the charging of users' fees on fixed capital, both of which began in 1979 and 1980, no basic changes altered this overall structure in the period under review.[27]

25. G. Garvy, "The Monetary System and the Payments Flow," pp. 275–93.
26. *Beijing Review (BR)*, no. 34 (1981), p. 15.
27. The first major critique of the system in the post-Mao period was Hu Qiaomu's seminal article on observing economic laws, in *RMRB*, October 6, 1978. Another article of import in that paper was one by Xue Muqiao on June 15, 1979. The journal *Jingji yanjiu* [Economic Studies] (*JJYJ*) printed a number of articles after 1978 calling for reforms, too numerous to list here. Among the first were Liu Guoguang and Zhao Renwei, "Shehui zhuyi jingji zhong jihua yu shichang de guanxi" [The relation between plan and market in the socialist economy], *JJYJ*, no. 5 (1979), pp. 46–55, which calls for loosening the controls of the plan; and Sun Shangqing, Chen Jiyuan, and Zhang Er, "Shehui shuyi jingji de

In the industrial sector, planning began in the early 1950s and has operated there—with greater or lesser consistency—ever since.[28] Central planners draw up the plan in Beijing, in light of production and consumption data supplied by industrial firms. Their final document relies on a system of "material balances," whereby the inputs are assigned to firms gratis in light of what is available, and an attempt is made to account for all resources.[29] Allocation amounts to a transferral of goods between producing and consuming ministries, without any money being used. A recent critique, written in favor of market reforms, claims that "because the enterprises are not required to pay for the supplies, they have frantically stockpiled goods, whether or not the goods are of any use to them. Some factories have stocks that could last more than ten years."[30]

This allocating and accounting in terms of physical units, along with pressures on factory managers to expand their production, has often induced managers in China, as in other systems based on the Soviet economic model, to concentrate most of their attention on the physical quantity of output.[31] Similarly, in agriculture, though the peasantry are

---

jihuaxing yu shichangxing xiang jiehe de jige lilun wenti" [Several theoretical questions in the combination of planning and market in the socialist economy], *JJYJ*, no. 5 (1979), pp. 56–67, which, on p. 61, suggests changing the method of allocation of production materials to one of commodity circulation (that is, through supply-and-demand determined prices) and on p. 67 speaks of using floating not fixed prices for nonessential goods. The experiments based on these and other suggestions are discussed in *China News Analysis* (CNA), no. 1165 (October 12, 1979). For the Party line several years later, see *BR*, no. 41 (1982), p. 23, which has a defense of the planned economy, one which refutes most of the attacks on planning of the several preceding years.

28. See Dorothy J. Solinger, "Some Speculations on the Return of the Regions: Parallels with the Past," on the history of planning in China, 1949–1977; p. 633 surveys the changing use of targets. Also, Cyril Chihren Lin, "The Reinstatement of Economics in China Today."

29. J. M. Montias, "Planning with Material Balances in Soviet-Type Economies," describes the institution of material balances on pp. 275–277. Also, see Lindblom, *Politics and Markets*, p. 292. Unified distribution of key raw materials and major equipment began in China in 1950. See Perkins, *Agricultural Development*, p. 100; Yu-min Chou, "Wholesaling in Communist China," pp. 259–60, which describes the operation of the direct allocation system; and Audrey Donnithorne, *China's Economic System*, chaps. 6 and 17.

30. *Zheng Ming* [Contend] (Hong Kong), no. 19 (May, 1979), pp. 9–13. An article from the mid-1950s explains the disjunction between the prices and the allocation of producer goods. "Since the production tasks of the enterprises are determined by the state, the quantity of producer goods needed by the enterprise is allocated by the state according to the plan. Therefore, the level of prices for producer goods does not regulate the quantity of producer goods required by the enterprise." This statement is taken from Ch'en Hsi-jun, "Chia-ko chi-hua" [Price planning], *Chi-hua Ching-Chi* [Planned Economy], no. 7 (1956), pp. 30–33, translated in Nicholas R. Lardy, *Chinese Economic Planning*, p. 95.

31. Goldman, *Soviet Marketing*, p. 135; Perkins, *Agricultural Development*, pp. 119–20; Nove, *Soviet Economic System*, p. 258. Since the Chinese system drew heavily on the Soviet model, insights into its workings can be gleaned from studies of socialist Russia.

responsive to price and income incentives, lower-level cadres have preferred to direct their energies to crash programs to increase production
of key crops, in order to overfulfill targets, and they commanded the
peasants to perform accordingly.[32] In both industry and agriculture,
then, physical targets for production of goods and produce have often
been more decisive than price in determining the quantity of output.

Another mechanism that contributes to material-mindedness and
not money-mindedness is the mediation of much exchange through the
People's Bank. Chinese radicals have explained that this system was instituted expressly to avoid allowing cash to pass through people's hands:

> To close loopholes in the flow of currency, we have adopted a series of
> restrictive measures. Transactions between enterprises of more than thirty
> yuan should all be settled through bank transfers. This prevents people
> from using money to make illegal deals.[33]

In the Soviet Union, which uses the same banking system, it has been
estimated that about 90 percent of the financial transactions among enterprises take place through clearinghouse adjustments, mediated
through Gosbank.[34]

Also, the extensive practice of exchange under contract in the classical Soviet system has this same effect of causing the contracting parties
to focus more on the goods involved than on their costs, as the major
part of the flow of goods in and out of enterprises is simply matched in
each case by an opposite flow of credit from the other party. Through
these procedures, the People's Bank is able to act as overseer and guaran-
tor of the planned use of resources.[35]

In the commercial sector as well, management of interorgan transactions through the Bank obviates the use of currency. According to the
initial directive establishing a state-run trading system in 1950:

> Currency may not be used for payment in the allocation of materials
> among state trade organs, for those between the state trade organs and the
> state enterprises, and for transportation between the state trade organs

---

32. Dwight H. Perkins, *Market Control and Planning in Communist China*, pp. 65–67,
explains that planning was attempted in agriculture as early as 1951, but was largely
abandoned by mid-1958. On pp. 67–68 he notes cadre pressures for increased output.

33. *Selections from China Mainland Magazines*, no. 822 (1975), p. 22.

34. Goldman, pp. 116–17.

35. Ward, *Soviet Economy*, p. 178; Svetozar Pejovich, "The End of Planning: The Soviet
Union and East European Experiences," p. 103.

and the national transportation organs. Payment shall be made in drafts, to be cleared through the Bank.[36]

Furthermore, the Bank's rigid control over capital generally is reinforced in the commercial sector by its being the sole authority that can extend short-term credit, as between wholesale and retail trade organs. For transactions outside a circumscribed locality, all expenditures must be approved through the Bank office where the buyer's credit is deposited, and all credit must be used only for the purpose specified. These regulations, while written to ensure close supervision over interunit business dealings, also have the effect of limiting the amount of cash that trading units may use.[37]

In the agricultural sector, free marketing of grain ended in 1953. Here again, the Chinese followed the Soviet example of abolishing the market for major crops (grain in 1953; cotton and oil-bearing crops in 1954) and substituting a system of fixed-price compulsory procurement by the state, coupled with distribution by rationing.[38] Only in brief periods of liberalization have these controlled commodities been allowed on open markets, and then only after state delivery quotas have been met.[39]

Both countries initiated this system in response to what were viewed by planners as the same imperatives: voluntary marketings proved insufficient to feed the city populations and meet state export needs; state-controlled grain, in fulfilling these demands, could thereby fuel the big industrialization drives which began in both countries concurrently with the institution of compulsory purchase.[40] As grain has not legally been an item of sale throughout much of the period of communist rule in

36. Government Administrative Council, "Decisions on the procedures governing the unification of state-operated trade in the nation," March 10, 1950, in Chao Kuo-chün, *Economic Planning and Organization in Mainland China: A Documentary Study (1949–1957)*, vol. 2, pp. 20–23. Kenneth Lieberthal, in "Beijing's Consumer Market," p. 38, says that transactions of less than ten yuan may be made in cash.

37. Chou, "Wholesaling," pp. 267–68. More material on the Bank's role in commerce can be found in Donnithorne, *China's Economic System*, p. 316.

38. Perkins, *Market Control*, pp. 50 ff. Beginning in 1955, the earlier system, "planned purchase, planned supply," for these three rationed crops was supplemented by a system entitled "unified purchase," by which quotas were set for delivery to the state of a wide range of other agricultural products whose supply was not rationed.

39. Beginning in late 1978, surplus grain (after state delivery quotas were met) was permitted on free markets. The first indication of this is in *New China News Agency* (Beijing), November 11, 1978. See chapter 6.

40. Felker, *Economic Controversies*, p. 29; Naum Jasny, *The Socialized Agriculture of the U.S.S.R.: Plans and Performance*, pp. 31, 223; Charles Bettelheim, *Class Struggles in the U.S.S.R.: First Period: 1917–1923*, pp. 204–6; Vivienne Shue, "Reorganizing Rural Trade: Unified Purchase and Socialist Transformation"; Perkins, *Market Control*, p. 184.

China, the role of money and the market in the countryside has correspondingly diminished.

Assessing and collecting rural taxes in grain is yet another way in which the financial system in the planned economy acts to preclude monetary exchanges in the countryside. By the 1960s (and ever since) the portion of the grain harvest requisitioned as a tax in kind had been fixed at about 5 percent of gross production-team income.[41] Taxes continued to be taken in kind, in traditional fashion, by the new government in 1949 when the state needed grain, at a time when prices and currency systems were all in a chaotic state; no change was made thereafter.[42]

Thus, both the procurement and the taxation systems are so designed that the peasantry uses less money than it would if free marketing in grain and other key products were permitted.[43] This effect was reinforced by the collectivization of agriculture, by which, from 1955 (to 1979–80), most peasants received from their work units the major portion of the payment for their labor in kind (in the form of grain, oil, cotton, vegetables, and services).[44] Moreover, recompense in the countryside, both in kind and in cash, was made only after the harvest, so that when a peasant family's cash ran out, its members fell back on the customary practice of barter.[45] In all these ways, the socialist state in China has built financial and commercial systems that curtail the flow of cash between rural hands.

41. Donnithorne, *Economic System*, p. 273; see also her chap. 13. The workings of the procurement and taxation system in the Guangdong countryside in the mid-1970s are described in William L. Parish and Martin King Whyte, *Village and Family in Contemporary China*, pp. 48–51. After 1980, the "production responsibility system," essentially household-based farming through share-cropping, taxed households, not teams. See *BR*, no. 48 (1983), pp. 19, 21.

42. Perkins, *Market Control*, pp. 43–44. Taxes were taken in grain in the civil war period in the late 1940s. See Ramon H. Myers, *Chinese Peasant Economy*, p. 286.

43. Even during periods when free marketing has been legalized and even encouraged by the government (1956–57, the early 1960s, and after 1978), grain, cotton, and oil have either been banned from the markets or permitted there only after state delivery quotas have been met. See chapter 6.

44. According to Wortzel, on the basis of interviews in China, "An important factor in agricultural wage mechanisms is the use of a combination of cash and in-kind payments to equal the basic wage. Thus, a peasant earning 30 yuan per month may receive only a small portion of it (8–10 yuan) in cash, while the remainder is provided in grain, vegetables, meat, and charcoal" (Larry M. Wortzel, "Incentive Mechanisms and Policies of the Eleventh Central Committee," p. 962). Also, Fox Butterfield, in *China: Alive in the Bitter Sea*, p. 238, reports: "More important to peasants than monetary figures is the amount of grain they receive for their work, for on most production teams peasants actually get the bulk of their income directly in kind." Mark Selden noted in a private communication that this is more the case for poor than for rich areas. Household-based farming in and after 1980 changed this system.

45. Interview in Hong Kong, November 27, 1979. See Gordon Bennett, *Huadong: The Story of a Chinese People's Commune*, pp. 96–97, on disposal of the collective income in the countryside. Also, Margery Wolf reported, on the basis of 1981 observations in Shan-

The rationing of scarce and vital items is one more planning device that elevates the value of goods in themselves, at the same time making money rather less useful than it could be were there no restrictions on its use. The system of formal rationing began with the institution of compulsory purchase quotas,[46] to which it is linked: produce requisitioned from the rural areas is distributed through ration coupons in the cities. This form of allocation has often made it possible to avoid using inflation to cut back on demand; has enabled the regime to enforce a fair measure of population control in most periods; and serves socialist goals of equity.[47]

A Chinese economist's defense of this system pointed out that high prices could instead have been used to limit the sales of scarce consumer goods. The effect of this, however, would have been that those with higher incomes would enjoy relatively unlimited access to such goods, while those whose incomes were low might be unable even to satisfy their most basic needs, he explained.[48] Another purpose of rationing has been to prevent speculation and stockpiling; in fact, however, a lively trade in ration tickets themselves somewhat circumvents the system.

When they are used legally, ration tickets are worthless in the marketplace by themselves, as they must be combined with money for the purchase of rationed items.[49] In fact, however, these papers have become a kind of currency in China, collected and exchanged through a variety of strategies. For example, poverty-stricken petty "speculators" (*touji daoba*) peddle eggs at people's doors in Beijing, in the hopes of exchang-

---

dong, Shanxi, and Fujian, that commune members sign a chit against work-points for vegetables, meat, grain, and even house payments as their need for these arises. Their year-end distribution is made after deductions for these expenses.

46. Perkins, *Market Control*, on pp. 177 and 191, distinguishes between "formal" and "de facto" rationing. The latter refers to the fact that for many items supply falls short of demand, and where desire runs particularly high (as in the case of bicycles, radios, and more recently, television sets), waiting lists informally enforce a type of rationing. Both formal and de facto rationing take the place of a market distribution. See appendix A for the procedures used in rationing.

47. Perkins, *Market Control*, pp. 192, 197.

48. This analysis was offered by Xue Muqiao in *HQ*, no. 10 (1959) (reprinted in *Xinhua banyuekan* [New China Semimonthly], no. 10 [1959], p. 167). Years later, in an era when the entire Chinese economic system came under scrutiny, Xue changed his approach. Then he argued instead for floating prices and against rations. See note 27, above.

49. The rationing system as formally designed is discussed in Donnithorne, *Economic System*, pp. 310–12; Christopher Howe, *China's Economy*, pp. 180–84; Dennis L. Chinn, "Research Note: Basic Commodity Distribution in the People's Republic of China," pp. 745–49; and Jan S. Prybyla, "Key Issues in the Chinese Economy," pp. 929–31. G. William Skinner, "Vegetable Supply and Marketing in Chinese Cities," p. 769, has a footnote on rationed items in different cities. See also appendix A.

ing eggs for grain tickets, which they might sell later. Less vital but still scarce goods are acquired, not with tickets, but by having a chart-like certificate checked off at the time of purchase. If the official doing the checking happens to be one's friend or relative, it is possible to obtain produce without having the certificate checked. The chart can be reused elsewhere or later to procure a second batch of goods.[50] A notice posted in Tianjin in December 1978 openly railed against a black market in coupons, whereby people were exchanging subsidiary agricultural produce for grain coupons, which they then bartered for grain. Their final move was to sell the excess grain on the black market. According to one account, simply buying and not bartering prized products on the free market is too costly for many.[51]

The rationing system does entail the use of money, and irregularities in this system are sometimes aimed at acquiring money (but sometimes, too, simply at acquiring more goods). Still, the fact of rationing—the regulated right to only a set, limited quantity—puts an extra premium on scarce goods, since merely having more money does not make it easy to obtain a surfeit of supplies.

All the features of the Chinese planned economic system outlined above entail exchange in which money and markets barely come into play. Nevertheless, prices do have a definite role in the Chinese economy. But prices too are largely designed and utilized so as to minimize the role of the market. This is so because at the macro level a principal function of price has been to enhance state economic control and to facilitate capital redistribution by the government.

Over the years there has been a recurrent debate in China on the problem of relating the market and prices to the state plan. Most discussions have been complicated by a tension between trying to subordinate prices to the dictates of state-planned economic goals, on the one hand, and allowing prices to have a certain incentive effect, on the other. For example, an article from 1963 states: "In socialist society, commodities' production and distribution are based on the plan, and price, too, is decided by the plan." Within a few pages, however, this same article also informs the reader that "prices should be good at developing production

---

50. Interviews in Hong Kong, October 22 and 23, 1979. An official source described this practice in discussing the situation in commerce in Sichuan in 1972. Market management was lax, according to the account, and one result was that coupons were traded for goods. See *Quanguo caimao xue daqing xue dazhai huiyi dianxing cailiao xuanbian* [A collection of models from the National Finance and Trade Conference to Study Daqing and Dazhai], p. 278.

51. That notice is reproduced here on p. 35. See also Frolic, *Mao's People*, p. 129.

and exchange."[52] Thus, prices have been fixed in line with the aims of the authorities as stated in plans, although they have been expected to have some limited directing role as well, especially in agriculture.

The effect of state pricing policies has been twofold: most retail prices (except for those in free peasant markets in the countryside) have been set by the state at various administrative levels; and price stability and thus rigid controls on prices over time have been major cornerstones of policy.

State-set prices in the Chinese system (as in other Soviet-type systems) serve more as writs of calculation for planners than as scarcity indicators in the market—that is, they are meant to direct physical planning rather than to guide supply to meet demand.[53] Since the 1950s efforts have been made in all Eastern European states to increase the flexibility of prices, but, with exceptions in Yugoslavia and to a certain extent in Hungary, the reforms have remained within a system of state-administered price fixing.[54] In China, too, discussions on loosening price control took place three times—in the mid-1950s, the early 1960s, and after 1978. In the latter period, this was accompanied by experimentation with "negotiated prices" in retail sales, in which ceilings were set by the state, but which permitted some flexibility to account for market forces.[55] But the ultimate decision has always been to leave the overall price system intact, thereby diverting attention from cost accounting and the market, as prices have neither reflected nor controlled the relationship of supply and demand.

Prices of those consumer goods controlled by the state in China (as in all command economies) are set in accord with the rate at which planners hope to dispose of the goods. Here again, then, supply has little to do with market pressures. In the face of the shortages and repressed inflation which inevitably result, consumers in what are essentially sellers' markets must submit to queues and informal rationing, and they often have money for which there is no outlet.[56] One effect documented by a Western

52. Xue Muqiao, "Jiazhi guilu he women de jaige zhengce" [The law of value and our price policy], *HQ*, no. 7–8 (1963), pp. 1, 3.

53. Lindblom, *Politics and Markets*, p. 303; Wiles, *Political Economy*, p. 115; Hans-Hermann Höhmann, Michael Kaser, Karl C. Thalheim, eds., *The New Economic Systems of Eastern Europe*, p. 279; Perkins, *Market Control*, p. 198.

54. Höhmann et al., p. 297. See also Alec Nove, "Economic Reforms in the USSR and Hungary, a Study in Contrasts."

55. Dorothy J. Solinger, "Economic Reform via Reformulation: Where Do Rightist Ideas Come From?" and Lin, "Reinstatement of Economics." Negotiated prices are discussed in *RMRB*, May 6, 1980, p. 2.

56. Lindblom, *Politics and Markets*, p. 303; Philip Hanson, *Advertising and Socialism*, pp. 7 and 81; Grossman, "'Second Economy' of the USSR," p. 39; Nove, *Soviet Economic System*, p. 257.

journalist, reporting from the Chinese countryside in the late 1970s, was that money itself was nearly meaningless: "There isn't much point in working to save money if there is nothing to spend the money on."[57]

Prices in China are by no means set arbitrarily, however. A careful hierarchy of authority dictates which types of goods may be priced at which levels;[58] and an effort is made to weigh many factors in determining the overall structure of prices across the country.[59] At a theoretical and aggregate level, these include the balance at any given time between the entire social purchasing power across the country, on the one hand, and the supply of all commodities available at that time, on the other; the relative gains and losses a given change in retail sales prices or state purchase prices will cause for the peasantry, the state's income, and the urban population; and the effect a price change will have on the span in urban-rural, interdistrict, and interseasonal price differentials, respectively. Ultimate state aims have been to reduce somewhat urban-rural differentials while still adding to the state treasury, and to diminish the seasonal and regional differentials that have facilitated speculative activity in China for centuries.

57. Ross Munro, "Why China's Peasants Don't Want to Work," *San Francisco Chronicle*, July 29, 1977.

58. This is true in the Soviet Union as well. See Goldman, *Soviet Marketing*, p. 96. For some examples of Chinese regulations on this matter, see "Regulations of the Chinese Communist Party Central Committee and the State Council on Graded Control of Market Prices," September 24, 1958, in Union Research Institute, *Documents of the Chinese Communist Party Central Committee September 1956–April 1969*, vol. 1 (Hong Kong, 1971), pp. 609–11; and "Guowuyuan guanyu gedi bu de zidong tigao guojia tonggou he shougou de nongfu chanpin shougou jiage de zhishi" (November 14, 1956) [State Council Directive Forbidding Various Places from Autonomously Raising the Purchase Prices of Agricultural and Subsidiary Products under Unified Purchase and Procurement by the State] in *Zhonghua renmin gongheguo fagui huibian* [Chinese People's Republic Compendium of Laws and Regulations] (Beijing, 1956), p. 333, which states that provinces may not raise the prices of produce purchased by quota by the state without central approval. Generally speaking, only the prices of a few vital and centrally rationed goods are set in Beijing, or require central approval for changes. The prices of ordinary consumer retail goods and vegetables are set at the municipal level in urban areas, though generally with reference to a centrally set standard price for that commodity (see Lieberthal, "Beijing's Consumer Market," pp. 37–38; Richman, *Industrial Society in Communist China*, pp. 889–90; Chinn, "Research Note," pp. 749–51; and Skinner, "Vegetable Supply," p. 786). In the countryside, prices for "general goods," which are daily consumer items, are set by the county, and those for nonstaple agricultural produce are also legally supposed to be set at this level. In fact, communes and even brigades do set produce prices, especially for easily spoiled goods (data from interviews in Hong Kong, September 7, November 27, November 29, and December 11, 1979). According to an early 1980 article (*BR*, no. 3, p. 30), urban state-owned shops are allowed to set their own prices, within certain limits, for such things as fresh vegetables, live poultry, and fish.

59. Zhang Yifei, "Guojia guiding shangpin shichang jiage de genzhu" [The basis for state-set commodity market prices], *JJYJ*, no. 4 (1958), pp. 53, 57, 59; and Donnithorne,

Other factors that, at least ideally, are said to have a bearing on the price set for specific goods include the Marxian notion of value (that the cost of a given item is determined by the average cost of producing that item for the entire industry), conditions of supply and demand, the needs of planned and proportional development of the national economy, and the division of the national income between savings and consumption.

More concretely, for a given consumer good, the final retail price is based on its ex-factory price (determined by average cost of production plus the industrial-commercial tax paid by the factory), to which is added the wholesale charges (transport costs, a markup of about 8 percent, and an additional percentage reflecting circulation expenses for this link), and finally the retail markup of about 13 percent (based on retail-shop expenses, a business tax of 3 percent on gross sales, and re-tail-circulation expenses).[60]

For agricultural products, the policy has been for the central government to maintain most state purchase prices for key crops over a long term and to raise those for selected individual products on occasion, to encourage the production of a particular crop.[61] If one locality wishes to raise the procurement price of some less essential crop over which it has jurisdiction, its pricing officials must give consideration to the effects this may have on the prices of other local crops, the prices of the same or

---

p. 436 and chap. 16 as a whole. See also Ch'en Hsi-jun (n. 30 above), pp. 92–93, for the factors involved in pricing industrial products; Chou, "Wholesaling," pp. 268–69, where he explains that the wholesale margin, or the difference between the ex-factory and the wholesale price, arises from a combination of circulation costs and profits, and lists the factors taken into account in setting wholesale prices (the state's view of a given commodity's importance to the people's livelihood, supply and demand, and the availability of necessary raw materials) and agricultural products' prices (historical prices, costs of production, and importance of the product to the national economy and the people's livelihood); *Survey of the China Mainland Press (SCMP)*, no. 1528 (1957), pp. 13–17, for the factors taken into account in raising the sales (or market price) after an earlier increase in procurement price; *ECMM*, no. 12 (1955), p. 42, on how rural prices are set by supply and marketing cooperatives (considering, among others, factors governing production, transportation and sale, the volume of production, comparative prices of allied commodities in the locality, market conditions, and historical background); *ECMM*, no. 74 (1957), on consumer goods' prices; and Yao Yilin, "Shi nian lai de shangye" [Ten Years of Commerce] in *Jian guo shi nian 1949–1959* [10 Years of National Construction] (Hong Kong: Jiwen chubanshe, 1959), vol. 1, p. 272, on the elements that go into the state sales price of grain (expenditures for business operations, safekeeping and depletion, and taxes).

60. Lieberthal, "Beijing's Consumer Market," p. 37.

61. Perkins, *Market Control*, p. 162. In March 1979 state procurement prices for a number of agricultural products were raised at one time. All pricing at local levels is done by the local vegetable company, according to grade, and adjusted with seasonal fluctuations (Skinner, "Vegetable Supply," p. 786).

similar crops in neighboring areas, retail sales prices, and the people's livelihood.[62]

The enormous complexity of fixing prices on a national basis in a socialist state helps to account for the fact that price changes in China are infrequent.[63] Rather, the state's policy for consumer goods has been to rely on enterprise turnover taxes to absorb cost increases, rather than risk losing mass political support for the regime by allowing inflation to occur.[64] There is also a tendency in orthodox socialist economies to adjust gross quantities of output rather than to alter individual prices, in order to reach an equilibrium in particular markets. This practice, which probably occurs in China too, once again focuses attention on goods not money.[65] "Supply and demand are constantly changing," explained one commercial bureaucrat. "The state cannot follow each such change," he went on, "or there would be no [price] stability in people's lives, and this would also destroy the foundation of the state's planned economic construction."[66]

Thus, this combination of prices set by state planners who take the supply-demand relationship as only one factor among many in their calculations, along with long-term freezes in these prices, gives money an ambiguous role to play on the state market. When demand does not regulate production, and desired goods are not available in any event, people must be concerned more about finding sources of goods, whether licitly or illicitly, and less about their monetary values.

In a vision that would have pleased many Confucian scholars, Marx predicted that a regulated, planned economy would one day be the vehicle for the distribution of necessities, thereby replacing the market,

62. Gordon A. Bennett, "Activists and Professionals: China's Revolution in Bureaucracy, 1959–1965, A Case Study of the Finance-Trade System," p. 100.

63. In contrast, Richard M. Cyert, James G. March, A Behavioral Theory of the Firm, state on pp. 153–54 that individual business firms in capitalist societies determine prices merely by adjusting the present price in the face of feedback on the firm's goals, the product's costs, and competitors' behavior.

64. Perkins, Market Control, p. 212. The salience of inflation as a political issue—and the regime's efforts to avoid it—grow in large part from the ruinous price rises of the 1940s, which helped to bring down the Nationalist government. On this, see Suzanne Pepper, Civil War in China, chap. 4. Price inflation did occur in periods of free marketing, and most notably of late in 1979 and 1980. This point about turnover taxes is made in Perkins's book without further elaboration. According to Audrey Donnithorne, Centre-Provincial Economic Relations in China, p. 5, the turnover tax is the industrial and commercial tax. It is payable by all enterprises engaged in industrial production, in the purchase of certain agricultural products, in the import of goods, in retail trade, in transportation, and in the communication and service trades.

65. Hanson, Advertising and Socialism, p. 49.

66. Zhang Yifei, p. 53 (n. 59 above). As opposed to state-set prices, those on the peasant free markets do respond much more to supply and demand.

money, and the commodities that money purchases. What he did not foresee, however, was that still poor socialist states, enticed by his teachings, would rush to install the trappings of a nonmarket, nonmonetized economy—such as a plan laid out largely in physical units, direct allocation of production materials, and rationed consumer goods—before Marx's prerequisite of plenty could render trade truly obsolete. So trade has continued to exist in China, but its medium is not always money. The second half of this chapter examines the implications that the ideological, economic, and bureaucratic context sketched out above has had for commercial exchange in China.

Commercial Practice, Conflict over Commodities, and Commodities as Exchange Medium

In this system where commodities are a kind of currency in their own right, it is not surprising that a battle for their control lies at the heart of much commercial activity. This conflict characterizes each pair of institutional relationships within which commercial exchange occurs—between public and private sectors, upper and lower bureaucratic levels, region and region, wholesale and retail units. Furthermore, among individuals, when needed goods or supplies prove difficult to obtain, people resort more often to the use of informal personal ties and to gift giving than to bribery with money to secure what they need. Their ability to do so, of course, depends on their power to barter with valued goods under their own control. Chinese sources written by radicals drew upon this sort of analysis to describe the phenomenon:

> Under the influence of the commodity economy, it is possible to make the means of production in state enterprises into the capital of certain individuals or groups, to be utilized for exploitation, as in barter between industrial and agricultural units by their leaders.[67]

Similarly, using the term "capital" quite loosely, these sources claimed:

> Commodities supplied by the commercial departments are for the workers, peasants, and soldiers, but some people make them "capital." They

67. Guangdong Sheng zhexue shehui kexue yanjiuso, jingji yanjiu shi bian [Guangdong Province Philosophical Social Science Research Institute, Economic Research Office, ed.], *Shangpin zhidu he huabi jiaohuan* [Commodity system and monetary exchange] (hereafter Guangdong Sheng), p. 94.

begrudge selling [these goods] and hoard them as rare commodities; some are even piled up in warehouses deteriorating [and spoiling], while the market lacks goods.[68]

In short, access to valued goods, as well as the authority to distribute these, lies at the heart of control in Chinese commerce.[69]

A large part of the motivation behind hoarding and manipulating goods, then, derives from the fact that control over them represents power because they are used as currency. A second and equally significant factor accounting for this conflict for command lies in the structure which state ownership of the economy has imposed on Chinese commerce. The nationalization of private firms in the early years after the takeover brought business into the state bureaucracy, as the partners to most dealings each came to be units within the public sector. Furthermore, with the development of a national plan, each unit involved in the state-directed circulation of commodities was charged with fulfilling annual profit and sales quotas, specified in terms of volume of turnover, as part of its tasks assigned by the state plan.[70]

Although the great bulk of enterprise profits in the planned economy are remitted to the state, the unit that remits more profits will be in a position to elicit more state investment funds in future budgetary allocations. In the case of commercial units, profits are derived and costs are covered from various price margins or differentials on the specific goods in which they deal—for example, from the differences between agricultural purchase (or industrial ex-factory) and rural market (or retail sales) prices, or those between region and region, or between brisk and slack seasons.[71] Thus, each separate commercial unit has its own organizational stake in handling a larger number of commodities, as is explicit in this remark by a cadre working in a state-owned warehouse: "If no-

68. *Xuexi yu pipan* [Study and Criticism] (Shanghai), no. 12 (1975), p. 39. Both these sources are the products of the radical campaign against "bourgeois rights" of 1975.

69. Smith, *The Russians*, pp. 114–15. Guangdong Sheng, p. 95. Bettelheim, *Class Struggles: First Period*, pp. 204–5, notes that in the late 1920s in the Soviet Union, the heads of state trade organs boosted the role and importance of the organs in which they worked by arranging for the maximum quantity of goods to be handled by these organs.

70. As of 1976, commercial enterprises drafted and followed plans for commodity circulation, wages, transportation, and finance (which includes a profit plan). See *Shangye kuaiji* bian xie zu [The compilation group for *Commercial Accountant*], *Shangye kuaiji* [*Commercial Accountant*], pp. 316–19, 336, and 358.

71. Donnithorne, pp. 314–15; *SCMP*, no. 2783 (1962), p. 10. See Lieberthal, "Beijing's Consumer Market," pp. 37, 40, 41, for a discussion of how profits are derived in wholesale and retail trade.

body stores goods in our godown, with what means are we supposed to increase our profit?"[72]

Besides having a concern with managing more merchandise, agencies in charge of trading also vie to secure marketable varieties of goods in quantities that meet demand, so that their sales quotas may be met, and so that they can avoid tying up capital in accumulated stocks of unwanted items.

The battle for control over goods, then, is linked to the desire to demonstrate power and to derive profit. This is a rivalry not just for obtaining infinite quantities, but for a right of disposal and for handling the particular goods of one's choosing. How is this conflict played out throughout the supply bureaucracy?

THE BASIS FOR CONFLICT WITHIN
THE COMMERCIAL BUREAUCRACY: ORGANIZATION

Before one looks at the conflicts that characterize the commercial bureaucracy, it is necessary to examine first the structure within which they occur—the principal commercial organs, and the prescribed routes for goods as they flow between these organs. This will lay the foundation for an understanding of the tensions that develop among commercial units in their respective efforts to gain control over that flow and over the goods in it.

Atop all domestic commercial activity in China sit two central organs, each heading a separate administrative-cum-geographic hierarchy of units. These are the Ministry of Commerce and the All-China Federation of Supply and Marketing Cooperatives, both of which are subordinate to the State Council, and both of which have gone through periods of reorganization over the years.[73] These govern commerce in the state

72. *DGB*, April 18, 1963. Writers on the Soviet economy have noted two sorts of financial arrangements that induce a given commercial organ to increase the amount of commodities it handles. One is a kickback or "rebate" based on the ruble turnover of the goods they manage (see Goldman, pp. 97, 109). The other is the depletion norm. Such norms are highly elastic, and at various points in the supply and distribution systems they can be used to derive excess funds from goods in transit. Thus, for example, if one-tenth of one percent is the rate of expected normal loss for sugar in transit by rail, a loss in this amount can safely be reported and the funds for it pocketed, whether it has actually occurred or not (Charles A. Schwartz, "Corruption and Political Development in the U.S.S.R.," p. 436). Reference to these arrangements has not been located in the Chinese literature, but given the Soviet influence on the Chinese economic system, they may be present there.

73. From 1949 to 1954, the Government Administrative Council's Finance and Economic Commission supervised commercial work; with the end of that Council and the creation of the State Council to replace it in 1954, the Fifth Staff Office of the State Council

and cooperative sectors, respectively. On the whole, these organs together manage the distribution of agricultural products and light industrial products. Most raw materials and machinery for heavy industrial
production are supplied through the industrial, not the commercial, bureaucracy, in the form of planned allocation, and are not available to the
populace in the marketplace.

The duties of the Ministry of Commerce were set down in a governmental directive in March 1950 and have remained basically unchanged
in nature, if greatly expanded in scope, ever since. These duties include
drafting and executing plans in trade, supervising the operations of the
state monopoly companies under it, managing funds and inventories,
setting wholesale prices at major markets for controlled commodities,

---

was given specific responsibilities for finance and trade work (until 1959). After September
1959 this body became the State Council's Finance and Trade Office. This coordinating
body was dismantled in the Cultural Revolution, and it was not until May 1978 (*RMRB*,
May 22) that a reference appeared to a Finance and Trade Group under the State Council.
In July 1979, a Finance and Economic Commission was set up under the State Council.
Within the Party bureaucracy, the Central Committee had a Finance and Trade Work Department and, beginning in 1964, a Finance and Trade Political Department. No such
bodies have been reported since the Cultural Revolution. At the time of Communist takeover, a Ministry of Trade was established to control both domestic and foreign trade, but in
1952 these functions were divided, and the Ministry of Commerce was created for handling domestic trade. In the 1950s, a Ministry for the Purchase of Agricultural Produce
and one of Urban Services each existed briefly; and, for some months in 1958, two central
Ministries of Commerce, a First and a Second, shared the management of state trade, until
they were merged late in the year. See Donnithorne, *China's Economic System*, pp. 274–
75. During the Cultural Revolution, the Ministry of Commerce absorbed part of the
former Ministry of Food and part of the old Finance and Trade Office of the State Council.
The All-China Federation of Supply and Marketing Cooperatives was christened in mid-
1954, having been created from the Provisional Board of the All-China Federation of Cooperatives. During the Great Leap Forward (late 1958 until about 1961), the local units of
supply and marketing cooperatives (SMCs) were merged into the local commune organizations, and probably the central controlling body was inactive, if not abolished (*CNA*,
no. 391 [1961], p. 6). During the Cultural Revolution, too, the Federation was disbanded,
not to reappear until April 1976. In at least one Guangdong special district the district-
level organ for coordinating the SMCs was merged into the commercial bureau (Hong
Kong, interview, October 25, 1979), to be separated again only in 1976. Also, in the early
course of the Cultural Revolution, according to *RMRB*, November 8, 1968, p. 2, in a
Guangdong county the commercial bureau, the SMCs, and various state commercial companies were merged into one unified leadership group. The reasons behind these tamper-
ings with the SMCs include the facts that in periods of radical upheaval bureaucratic simplification has always been a goal, and commerce, seen as capitalistic, is a favored target;
and that there has always been some debate around the question of whether these co-ops
are truly socialist organs, and so they are suspect (see, for example, Bo Yun, "Wo guo
gongxiaoshe de shehui zhuyi xingzhi" [The socialist nature of my country's SMCs], *JJYJ*,
no. 5 [1956], pp. 53–68). In the Leap, in particular, when some radical politicians hoped to
speed China on its path toward communism, what seemed to be vestiges of a semisocialist
era had to go. In March 1982 a new Ministry of Commerce was created, combining the
original ministry of that name with the Ministry of Grain and the All-China Federation of
SMCs. See *RMRB*, March 12, 1982, p. 1.

Poster dated December 1, 1978, in Tianjin. A "Public
Notice of the City's Industrial Commercial
Administrative Management Bureau, on Strictly
Forbidding Illicit Sales of Ration Coupons."

and overseeing the work of the trade departments at lower levels.[74] Provincial, prefectural (special district or district), city, and county levels all house governmental bureaucracies that include a unit responsible for state commerce and one for cooperative commerce work.[75]

Originally, six state companies were created, each to deal in one or a set of related commodities on the domestic market: one each for grain, cotton, "general goods" (department store types of daily-use items), salt, coal and building materials, and native (local, special) products. In later years additional companies were added for other products. Companies focus their direct marketing activity on the cities and on the outputs of industry. For the procurement of agricultural produce, they rely on supply and marketing cooperatives, which act as intermediaries between the companies and the rural areas.

At the time of their creation, the companies placed orders for processing and manufacturing with private industrial firms, and then purchased the entire output, or else underwrote the sales. Initially, this method was designed to gain state control over the source of goods, thereby edging out capitalist wholesalers. Purchase and allocation plans approved by the state dictated the planned distribution of goods from a given state wholesaling company to the state-owned retail enterprises dealing in the same line of goods within its geographical jurisdiction.

After the protracted process of socialist transformation was completed in 1956, state companies continued to be charged by the state plan with procuring and disposing of the entire output of factories, even as all the supplying factories came under state ownership and control. This arrangement repeatedly leads to conflict between industrial and marketing departments, as factories try to fulfill numerical production quotas while commercial units are forced by the plan to buy up products, including those that may be defective or lack market demand. In such cases, the commercial units find it difficult to meet their own sales targets.

In terms of management, each company is an independent accounting unit, as are its subordinate companies at lower administrative levels. These lower-level branches are supervised on two levels: by their parent company at a higher echelon and by the government office for commercial work at their respective administrative levels as well. Each company

74. Translated in Chao Kuo-chün, *Economic Planning*, pp. 20–23.
75. Bennett, "Activists and Professionals," pp. 66–74, has excellent and thorough charts detailing commercial organization and the organs engaged in this work at a variety of levels, from central to county.

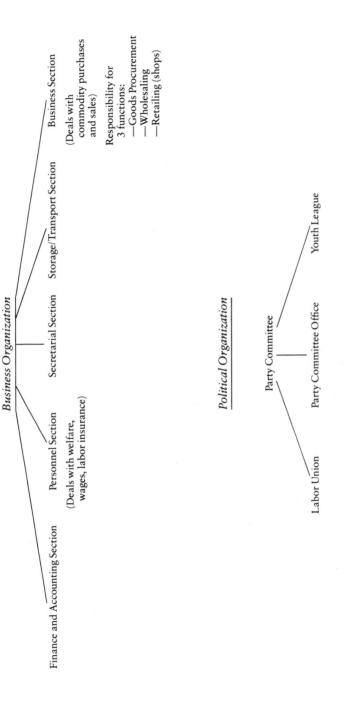

Business Organization

Finance and Accounting Section

Personnel Section

(Deals with welfare, wages, labor insurance)

Secretarial Section

Storage/Transport Section

Business Section

(Deals with commodity purchases and sales)

Responsibility for 3 functions:
—Goods Procurement
—Wholesaling
—Retailing (shops)

Political Organization

Labor Union

Party Committee

Party Committee Office

Youth League

FIGURE 1. Organization of a State General Goods Company

SOURCE: Interviews in Guilin with City Commercial Bureau official, November 1979; and in Hong Kong with an ex-commercial representative of a special district-level state company from Guangdong Province, October 1979.

drafts and implements its own plans and regulates its own funds.[76] The organization of the companies follows the lines of the political administrative hierarchy,[77] with the national-level offices of the companies governing first-grade wholesale depots; provincial-level companies directing second-grade depots at the prefectural level; and, at the county level, grade-three depots beneath them.[78]

Each company encompasses, within itself, the functions of procurement from production units, wholesaling, and retailing. The normal routing of general goods, for example, is from factory through procurement organs of the company to wholesale depot or warehouse to retail shop. Although the three functions are housed in one body, wholesale and retail activities are each carried out by a distinct chain of units, the shops led by a general store at each bureaucratic level, the wholesaling led by the depot.

Complexity characterizes retailing in Chinese cities. First, retail stores are generally subject to dual control: they are responsible to the municipal commercial bureau in personnel and welfare matters and for pricing, but are under their respective state companies for other matters. In the larger cities there are two commercial bureaus, one for manufactured consumer goods and the other for foodstuffs. Moreover, a municipal-level commercial bureau is subject to the city people's council (specifically, its finance and trade office) for some matters and to its provincial-level commercial bureau (which is then under the central Ministry of Commerce) for others.[79]

76. Chao; Donnithorne, *Economic System*, p. 276. State companies and their local units were also abolished once, in late 1957. In 1962 these were restored. See Donnithorne, p. 288.

77. *RMRB*, June 7, 1955. G. William Skinner, "Marketing and Social Structure in Rural China, Part III," pp. 363, 364, 379–80, claims that there has been a continuity of traditional marketing relationships and functions according to natural, economically based (and thus not administratively routed) trade channels. This will be discussed further below and in chapter 6.

78. See Donnithorne, *Economic System*, p. 277; Barry Richman, *Industrial Society in Communist China*, pp. 878–80; and "Guowuyuan guanyu shangye bu xitong huifu he jianli geji zhuanye gongsi de jueding" [State Council decision on restoring and establishing various levels of state specialized companies in the commercial system], in Guowuyuan faze bian zuan weiyuanhui [State Council Laws and Regulations Compilation Committee], *Zhonghua renmin gongheguo faze huibian* [Chinese People's Republic Compilation of Laws and Regulations] (Beijing: Falu chubanshe, 1962), pp. 138–40; Chou. Information was also derived from interviews with municipal commercial officials in Guilin, November 1979, and in Hong Kong, October 25, 1979.

79. For urban retailing, see Richman, *Industrial Society*, pp. 878–82; Donnithorne, *Economic System*, pp. 309–10; Lieberthal, "Market," pp. 36–41; and Skinner, "Vegetable Supply." See also table 1 for a listing of miscellaneous types of city shops in Guangzhou, Guilin, and Changsha.

FIGURE 2. Organization of a District-Level Commercial Bureau

SOURCE: Interview with ex-commercial representative of a special district-level state company from Guangdong Province, October 1979.

NOTE: Kenneth Lieberthal, in "Beijing's Consumer Market," *China Business Review*, September–October 1981, p. 37, lists these additional departments under the City-level First Commercial Bureau in Beijing: planning, basic construction, enterprise management, labor organization, and propaganda.

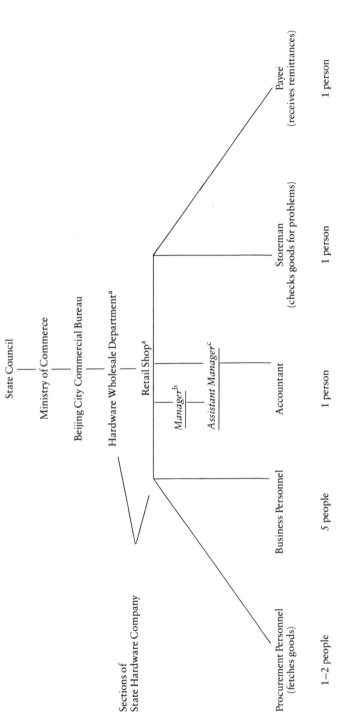

FIGURE 3. Hierarchy of Authority for and Organization of a Beijing Hardware (*wu jin*) Shop

SOURCE: Interviews with personnel at a small Beijing hardware shop, December 1978, and with a former Beijing commercial accountant, in Hong Kong in September 1979.

[a]Hardware Wholesale Department and Retail Shop are co-equal in status, but personnel from the shop obtain their goods from the department.

[b]Manager is often a party member who was a worker or salesperson before 1949.

[c]Assistant manager was generally a capitalist before 1956.

Official urban market, late 1978, Shanghai.

State-operated urban retailing is done mainly through small state-owned specialty shops, organized along product lines, and except in the largest cities, only one or two department stores for general goods. The state commercial companies—such as for textiles, hardware, clothing, stationery, general goods, and hats and shoes—for which these stores serve as retail outlets, supply the goods to them through the wholesale depots and collect a large portion of the stores' profits. When commodities are in short supply, as is often the case, the companies must allocate the goods they have in stock among those retailers in various sections of their city who deal in their line of item. They do so according to fixed percentage shares that were set for each district in the mid-1950s. Use of these dated allotment procedures is one important reason why there is frequently a poor fit between current market demand in various urban areas and the quota of goods distributed to them.

Besides this more regular arrangement, an array of anomalous management patterns characterize the store scene in urban areas. Different cities have their own peculiarities in this regard. In Guangzhou, for example, "cooperative shops" are far more common than stores that are part of the state-owned system. These shops are the smaller ones that were neither taken over outright by the state in the early 1950s (as were large private department stores), nor "bought out" by the state during the socialist transformation of the mid-1950s (as were middle-sized shops, whose owners received dividends from the state from 1956 to 1966 and again after 1979). Rather, these are small enterprises which were allowed for a time after 1956 to operate with responsibility for their own profits and losses.

By late 1979 the workers in some of these shops claimed still to be operating on that basis; most, however, said that at different times after 1956 they had become a part of the state system, obtaining capital from and remitting profits to the state, and paying their workers according to wage scales fixed by the state. They also receive their supplies from the state companies. As one PRC publication put it, as of the early 1980s, the "so-called cooperative shops and teams are a form of collective ownership in name only. . . . They really are equivalent to a branch of state-operated commerce."[80]

Another type of shop, many of which dot Changsha's streets, are the retail outlets (*menshibu*) for factories belonging to industrial companies under the city's Bureau of Light Industry. Such places sometimes do repairs and test new products; or they market cheaply goods that have small imperfections (*chuli shangpin*), or that were produced in excess of the state plan. When factories wish to sell products at other than state-set prices they must obtain permission from the local commercial bureau.[81]

A last type of store outside the regular supply channels is the commission shop, a sort of pawnshop where people may bring old and used items and bargain over their sales price. The Changsha store receives an 8 percent commission, most of which it hands over to its superior unit, the city's General Goods Company. If the seller chooses to take the money before the good has been sold, he or she will receive less money (actually, the store's commission will be higher) than if he or she can wait.[82]

80. Gao Dichen, "On the Objective Basis for the Existence of Various Commercial Forms," *JJYJ*, no. 6 (1981), p. 58. Also, see Wan Dianwu, "Several Questions in Understanding the Implementation of the Operations Responsibility System in Commerce," *HQ*, no. 14 (1982), p. 26, which notes that collective commerce basically used fixed wages after 1958. Other cities also have such shops, but Guangzhou seems to have more than most. This type of shop (*hezuo dian*) is different from the private "collective" (*jiti*) shops noted at the end of this section.

81. Interview in Hong Kong, October 23, 1979. Perhaps this changed after 1979.

82. Information obtained in a *wuze diaoji* (goods adjustment) store in Changsha, November 1979. Goldman, *Soviet Marketing*, pp. 16–17, mentions that the Soviet system also has such shops. An informant from Guangzhou referred to *shougou* (purchase) and *xintuo* (trust) shops with the same function (October 31, 1979). *Weituo* (trust) and *xintuo* are the names used in Beijing, I observed on the street. The informant from Guangzhou described a rather different procedure: the commission paid to the store increases with the length of time the item remains, unsold, in the store.

TABLE I A Sampling of Shops Outside the
Usual Commercial System Channels
in Three Cities (Changsha, Guilin, Guangzhou)

City	Name of Shop	Function and Bureaucratic Position
Changsha	Special Store for Retail Sales of the Changsha General Goods Station Changsha Baihuozhan Lingshou (Zhuan) Dian	Wholesaler for the City General Goods Company; stores and ordinary customers can both buy here; under the local Bureau of Commerce.
	Products Service Unit of the Changsha Second Bureau of Light Industry Changsha Erqinggongyeju Chanpin Fuwubu	Retail outlet of this industrial bureau, allowed to sell new commodities on a trial basis on its own; various factories under this bureau sell products here (umbrellas, shoes, hats); these commodities do not enter the commercial system.
	Scientific and Technical Retail Outlet of the New China Bookstore Xinhua Shudian Keji Menshibu	Bookstores are under the local Bureau of Propaganda rather than of Commerce.
	Central Retail Outlet of the 4th Clothing Factory Disi Fuzhuangchang Zhongxin Menshibu	Retail outlet of a clothing factory; under a local bureau of light industry.
Guilin	Guilin Municipal Grain and Oil Supply Company Guilinshi Liangyou Gongying Gongsi	This company is under the local Bureau of Grain, rather than of Commerce. (This changed in March 1982 when the Ministry of Grain was merged with the Ministry of Commerce. See chapter 1, n. 73.)
	Zhengyang Retail Outlet of a Commission Shop of the Guilin Municipal Sugar, Tobacco, and Wine Company Guilinshi Tangyanjiu Gongsi Daixiaodian Zhengyang Menshibu	"Collective" shop, responsible for its own profits and losses; obtains goods from the state-run company, and gets a commission on sales for the company.
	Central Retail Outlet of the Supply and Marketing Cooperative of Guilin Municipality's Suburban District, Chuanshan Guilinshi Jiaoqu Chuanshan Gongxiaoshe Zhongxin Menshibu	Retail outlet for the City General Goods Company; is not responsible for own profits and losses and receives no commission; gives its profits to the Company.

TABLE I (Continued)

City	Name of Shop	Function and Bureaucratic Position
	Medical Products Commission Sales Shop Yiyao Daixiaodian	Commission shop, existing on own profits and losses.
Guangzhou	Shop One of "Build-the-New" Fruits Cooperative Jianxin Guopin Hezuo Yidian	Collective fruit shop, responsible for its own profits and losses.
	Branch Shop Nine of the Rongchang Sugar, Tobacco, and Wine Cooperative Rongchang Tangyanjiu Hezuo Jiufendian	Workers there claim this is a "collective (jiti) shop," but that their own wages are fixed by the state, not dependent on the profits and losses of the shop.
	Beijing Road Overseas Chinese Commodities Supply Store Beijinglu Huaqiao Shangpin Gongying Shangdian	Sells special products exclusively to overseas Chinese resident in or visiting the PRC.

SOURCE: Personal observations and interviews with shopworkers in these three cities; interview with an official in the Guilin Municipal Commercial Bureau, November 1979.

This local diversity in types of stores has struck other observers, one of whom reflected thus:

> All in all, it seems that China's domestic trade sector is indeed organizationally very complex. I must admit that even after interviewing several Chinese commercial and retail executives I am still quite hazy. . . . This is the chief reason why I have not even attempted to draw organization charts for this sector.[83]

Even commercial cadres in China have occasion to be confused. An incident in Changsha in late 1979 illustrates this point. Two commercial officials sent from Kirin to buy tobacco arrived at a sugar wholesale depot in Changsha. Coming from the north, where sugar, wine, and tobacco are managed by one company, they had not realized that in Changsha, where the climate is mild and much sugar is grown, a separate company had

83. Richman, *Industrial Society*, p. 880.

been created for sugar some years before. Officials at the depot had to send them on to the local tobacco warehouse with a letter of introduction.[84] G. William Skinner's detailed 1978 report on vegetable marketing illustrates this same complexity and variation in the different supply channels and organizational structures and relationships used by a number of cities in vegetable procurement and sales.[85]

Rural marketing is the business of the supply and marketing cooperatives (SMCs, or co-ops),[86] collective bodies in name, which originally drew at least part of their capital from voluntary investments by peasant members. In 1958 these co-ops started remitting the major share of their profits to the state.[87] Their role is to purchase agricultural products from local peasants for state company branches in their area, and to market industrial goods (both production materials and daily consumer items) in the countryside.

Although both are state-controlled enterprises, the relationship between companies and co-ops is an ordinary business one.[88] The company's county-level wholesale depots sell goods to the wholesaling agencies of the co-ops in that region at state-set wholesale prices. Each commune also has a wholesale department, which obtains its goods from its county's SMC.[89] The commune wholesale department then sells these goods to retail stores at commune, brigade, and team levels.

---

84. I witnessed this incident in Changsha in November 1979.

85. Skinner, "Vegetable Supply," pp. 767–81. This valuable article details the procedures used by state urban vegetable companies for procuring agricultural supplies from the countryside, for distributing these through an urban marketing network, for pricing, and for planning.

86. For a report on the first Congress of the All-China Federation of Cooperatives, where the constitution of the All-China Federation of SMCs was passed, see *SCMP*, no. 868 (1954), pp. 18–20. The Statute of the Federation appeared in *Xinhua yuebao* [New China Monthly] (XHYB), no. 12 (1954), pp. 174–76. See also Vivienne Shue, *Peasant China in Transition: The Dynamics of Development Toward Socialism, 1949–1956*, pp. 203–14, for a discussion of the organization and functions of the SMCs.

87. Donnithorne, *Economic System*, pp. 277–79, 315.

88. Material on the operation of rural commerce was obtained through interviews with ex-SMC workers in Hong Kong, November and December 1979. One was an accountant, one a purchaser of local products, and one a procurement agent. Also, discussions at Zhengzhou University and at a commune outside Zhengzhou in January 1979 were helpful. There seems to be some local variation in whether teams always have their own SMC stores or (more typically, I think) simply have branch outposts of the brigade SMC store.

89. Whether the sales organ at the county level is a state company wholesale depot or a branch of the SMC may depend on the item involved. *Shichang* [Market] (*SC*), no. 11 (March 10, 1980), p. 7, says that fertilizer travels from the factory to the county-level SMC, and from there to the communes. Talks with ex-SMC workers, however, led me to understand that general goods are obtained at the county wholesale depot of the state company, where the commune wholesale workers procure them. The commune wholesale depart-

Meanwhile, the SMC, which has done the wholesaling, remits the difference between wholesale and retail prices to brigade-level credit co-operatives, at least for much of Guangdong province, where the brigade is the usual unit for SMC management. The credit co-op then hands over the bulk of this differential (actually profit) to the state, but keeps some for salaries, depletion, and other circulation expenses. The SMC also makes a profit in selling to the company the agricultural produce it collects from the peasants, but must pay a business tax to the state on this produce. Despite state ownership of the SMCs, a close link between this co-op and the collective agricultural unit is clear, not only in that the trade's profits go to the brigade, but also in the fact that some SMC workers are paid in work-points, from the brigade's collective harvest.[90]

Besides the state commercial organs and the SMCs, a private sector still exists in Chinese commerce. Essentially private exchange, unorganized by the state, occurs in the urban "collective" and individual enterprises promoted in the late 1970s to cope with problems of unemployment and scarcity of services in the cities. Such exchange also takes place in the free produce markets treated leniently and even encouraged during three eras since socialist transformation was completed: 1956–1957, 1961–1965, and after 1978. A fair degree of freedom was granted to private vendors and handicraftsmen in the same years.[91]

This brief outline suggests the cracks in the system along which conflict can flow: the partners in each pair—state trade and cooperative trade, wholesale and retail units, the state and private sectors, respectively—each compete to do a better business than its mate, and thus vie over goods and how goods are allocated. In addition, the complexity and overlappings in the urban network leave room for irregularities and also create additional opportunities for rivalry among types of shops

---

ment then sells the goods to the retail stores (which are branches of the SMCs) in the commune. In a commune on the outskirts of Zhengzhou, a brigade-level SMC procures its general goods directly from the Zhengzhou company's wholesale department. Despite the nature of their business relationship, the SMC store sees itself as a retail outlet for the state company.

90. Some SMC workers receive work-points (this seems to have applied mainly to sent-down educated youth in the rustification program during the Cultural Revolution); others, more permanently employed by the co-op, are paid a salary. For more, and slightly different, information on the organization of rural state-run trade, and on the supply planning and procurement procedures used by the supply and marketing cooperatives, see Steven Bailey Butler, "Conflict and Decision-Making in China's Rural Administration, 1969–1976," Ph.D. dissertation, Columbia University, 1979, chap. 8, "Rural Retailing," especially pp. 333–34, 336, 338 ff., and 345 ff.

91. See chapters 4 and 6 on these less official and unofficial forms of trading.

and sectors. Finally, the existence of a small but not insignificant private sector is a clear threat to state organs which are striving for their own maximum procurement and sales. More specific material below will indicate the nature of the conflicts that develop.

CONFLICT OVER COMMODITIES WITHIN THE
STATE COMMERCIAL BUREAUCRACY

Wholesalers versus retailers

Constant friction has marked the relations between state trade companies, which act as distributors, and supply and marketing cooperatives, which are their retailers in the countryside. This is so despite the fact that co-ops are often described as the "helping hand of the companies," and are meant to operate under company leadership.[92] In the earliest days just after communist takeover, co-ops were given favorable treatment by the companies, to stimulate their business. This included permitting them to buy goods from the distributing companies at lower prices than could the private merchants, who were still retailing in the countryside in large numbers. The rates of bank interest and taxation charged the co-ops were also set at terms better than those for the private merchants.

At that time, however, some co-ops took advantage of these preferential conditions by buying from the companies at the cheaper prices, only to sell the goods on the free market, rather than to their own membership, as regulations stipulated. The lower-priced items, then, became a means for co-op workers to enrich themselves, instead of being used to divert trade away from the private-sector competition, in accord with state goals.[93]

Another issue between the two types of units in the early years was their contention over industrial products. The problem eventually led to the creation of a formal division of labor between the two, by which only the state companies were to manage the wholesale business in industrial goods, while the wholesaling of handicraft products and retailing in general became the province of the co-ops. Fighting over goods seems to have led to some small price wars, as the decision on drawing this division of labor noted that this change would stabilize prices.[94]

92. On December 2, 1953, a governmental decision dictated that the co-ops were to act primarily as rural agents of state companies, buying all their nonagricultural merchandise from them, which they then sold in the countryside.

93. *XHYB*, 3, no. 4 (1951); pp. 827–29. See Shue, *Peasant China*, pp. 208–9, on mistrust and direct competition between companies and co-ops in the early years.

94. *RMRB*, December 21, 1953.

More than a decade later, tensions over the allocation of goods between the two types of units continued to be reported in the press. In one article, a county-level unit of a state company berated its local co-op for "shopping around in other counties" for goods instead of helping its own county's company to unload its stocks, according to regular administrative procedures.[95] In retaliation, the company withheld or cut back on its supply of various popular items to the SMC.[96] This enraged the co-op workers, who had already found the company's stocks to be inferior and had originally gone elsewhere for that reason. This conflict illustrates the tendency of the supplier to dump goods in disregard of the purchasing units' needs to meet sales targets; this is one common form of contention over items in demand under socialism.

In another article from the same period, consumers in a southern Shanxi district blamed the local company office for being interested only in receiving and dealing in fast-selling, larger commodities. Company cadres, however, located the problem in the SMCs, which, they said, refused to accept from the company batches of small items that tended to earn less profit, even if the company had these in stock. In the end, the company's office managers admitted their disinclination to take in new wares out of fear that merchandise would pile up and tie up capital.[97] In these battles over goods, it is not always clear where the power lies; each side has strategies at its command in its efforts to obtain what it wants or to avoid being dumped on.[98]

The difficulties between companies and co-ops arise from tensions between, on the one hand, a supplier charged by the plan with unloading a set amount of goods it has been compelled to purchase from given factories, and, on the other, the recipient of those goods, laboring under its own

95. *DGB*, December 27, 1964. Such behavior was no longer considered in error in early 1980, when, as part of the experiment in liberalization of economic policy, retail stores were encouraged to replenish their stocks by going to wholesale depots in other areas. See *SC*, no. 9 (February 10, 1980), p. 1.

96. Donnithorne, *Economic System*, p. 306, notes that state wholesaling bodies have regularly been criticized for reluctance to supply industrial goods to the countryside, even hiding popular articles when SMC workers come to purchase. This niggardliness on the part of the companies may explain the search behavior undertaken by the co-op workers.

97. *DGB*, April 29, 1965.

98. A former SMC worker related in Hong Kong (October 19, 1979), when asked whether he knew of conflicts between his SMC and the companies: "The state companies have power—you must be good to them or they won't give you things." In his view, then, his SMC had merely to submit.

plan's orders to dispose of goods on the rural market.[99] Relations between cadres in the procurement stations, wholesale depots, and retail shops of the companies in the cities are equally tense, for the same reason. Writers on the Soviet economy have pinpointed the key issues: wholesalers, seeing their primary function as distributional and not commercial, do not pay adequate attention to the market; the result is their dispersal to the retailers of unwanted goods, which accumulate, unsold.[100]

Two accounts relate cases of three-way "departmentalism" among the units that procure from factories, the wholesalers, and the retailing units. One tells how the amount, colors, varieties, and time of allocation of goods have all been the basis for "contradictions" among these units. The story is told in the form of a self-criticism by the procurement station, whose workers admitted to thinking that they themselves were in charge, since they stood in command of the overall acquisition of varieties of goods and their distribution. The wholesalers were criticized for concentrating their efforts on gaining control over the sources of goods, while the retailers were attacked for focusing only on obtaining popular goods.[101]

In the other report, a procurement station refused to release all of its popular goods as requested by the other two units, while the wholesalers and retail stores arbitrarily demanded large quantities of these items, without paying much heed to the current state of the market. Moreover, each party, acting as if in competition with the others, treated its own market data as if they were "classified." To smooth the tensions and improve cooperative efforts, the three signed an agreement, according to which the station consented to supply what the market needed. At the same time, its two opponents promised to adjust their stocks and to promote the sale especially of those goods that were in excess at the station. This they would do in large part through the use of "propa-

99. *ECMM*, no. 140 (1958), p. 43. Bennett, "Activists and Professionals," p. 211, notes that in the supply crisis attendant upon the Great Leap Forward, "some wholesale suppliers took advantage of their dominant position vis-à-vis procuring retail stores to demand that the latter buy hard-to-move merchandise they really did not want—unpopular package deals known as 'accompanying one kind of commodity with another.'" The phenomenon he describes has occurred routinely in China. See Lieberthal, "Market," p. 38, for a more detailed description of the procedures that govern the distribution of goods between wholesale companies and their retail outlets in China. Goldman, *Soviet Marketing*, p. 11, discusses competition between retailers and wholesalers in the Soviet Union.

100. Nove, p. 255; Felker, *Soviet Economic Controversies*, p. 143.

101. Shanghai Shi shangye gongzuo huiyi bian [Shanghai Municipality commercial work conference, ed.], *Shangye zhanxian qixiang xin* [A new atmosphere on the commercial front] (hereafter Shanghai Shi shangye) (Shanghai: Renmin chubanshe, 1974), pp. 7–12.

ganda" (advertising,[102] in effect).[103] "The three are friendly on the surface," warned one analysis, "but resentment lurks beneath."[104]

Conflicts structured by bureaucratic relationships

While the distinct duties of wholesalers and retailers in fulfilling their respective plans cause them to battle for mastery over goods, localities, levels, and regions also strive one against another for control over a larger share of coveted commodities.

Thus, regional distributing units charged with allocating choice items over a larger area often favor their own home ground, by delivering better assortments there in larger quantities and by doing so in a more timely fashion.[105] Complaints on this score surfaced especially in the Cultural Revolution literature. According to one critique, a Party official in Guangzhou (Canton)'s Bureau of Commerce was told by his superior to omit from a report to Beijing the fact that the bureau had in stock 410 tons of sugar and 360 tons of gasoline. His commands were to prepare two different accounts, one for internal departmental use and one for reference in preparing reports to the capital. "We give only if we receive," the chief was quoted as instructing, and "we must get more and better commodities in return.... We must not do a losing business."[106] Here the tendency is to perceive one's geographical space and its products to be private preserves, despite the actual public ownership of the capital involved.

Between hierarchical echelons similar possessiveness obstructs exchange. Instead of cooperation, with each level of the bureaucracy working with the levels above and below it to expedite the flow of goods, friction is common between echelons, each striving to increase the goods it can control. Most typically, goods in demand accumulate at the county level, while shelves are bare in the basic villages.[107] The county departments, like well-endowed localities and like the wholesaling organs, relish their right to distribute varieties and amounts in accord with their own best interest.

---

102. Hanson, *Advertising and Socialism*, pp. 30–31, 63, tells how advertising in planned economies is typically initiated in the commercial sector (not the industrial sector), to help dispose of goods they have stocked in excess of the centrally planned distributive stock norms.

103. *DGB*, April 2, 1958.

104. Shanghai Shi shangye, p. 8.

105. Richman, *Industrial Society*, p. 892, mentions a large department store in Beijing with this problem. The same phenomenon is reported in studies of the Russian commercial system. See Felker, p. 143, and Nove, pp. 254–55.

106. *SCMM*, no. 628 (1968), p. 19.

107. *RMRB*, March 15, 1955, is one example among many.

A special case of jurisdictional conflict was the effort from 1962 to 1965 to reorient the framework for shipping goods away from administratively defined sites and regions to a circulation pattern based on historically proven channels and traditional market towns in "economic regions."[108] Much difficulty was associated with the effort to effect this reform, because of the intense bureaucratic battles it incited. The different sites that would receive and transfer goods according to the two competing arrangements each fought for these rights—in part to profit from the interregional price differentials that accrue to the units that handle goods in transit,[109] and in part to obtain the spoils associated with the operation of commercial units, such as staffing offices and managing funds, in particular.[110]

In one case, the originally powerful second-level wholesale stations, set up at the politically demarcated prefecture level, "competed for power and goods" with the companies of the city (which was favored by the proposed reform), although as of 1965 the stations had lost out.[111] However, the conflict over control was never settled decisively, as this 1978 broadcast pleading in favor of an organization by economic regions illustrates:

> When the flow of commodities is organized according to economic zones, we can no longer control the commodities—this is the true thinking of those who want to organize the flow of commodities according to administrative zones. Indeed, if the flow of commodities is organized according to economic zones, some localities will lose part of their controls over commodities. But the loss of these unnecessary controls . . . will help develop the economy and ensure supplies.[112]

108. This effort was largely a response to the attempt of the Great Leap Forward (1958–1961) expressly to reorganize trade to follow politically drawn channels (see Skinner, "Marketing . . . Part III," pp. 374–75). However, much earlier administrative regions had already been used as the basis for wholesale machinery, and the arrangement was criticized as early as 1955. See *RMRB*, June 7, 1955.

109. *SCMP*, no. 2783 (1962), p. 10.

110. *DGB*, April 8, 1965. See also John Wilson Lewis, "Commerce, Education and Political Development in Tangshan, 1956–1969," p. 161. Also see *RMRB*, May 14, 1965, which tells how a county in Guangxi province that served as a transit point for salt supply each month used two million yuan and more than 200 workers, plus warehouse space for 10,000 tons, for handling salt alone. A few unwieldy compromise attempts were made to satisfy both sides: fixing target areas by administrative district and distributing supplies by economic district (*DGB*, February 24, 1963), and distributing principal commodities by administrative unit, but ordinary supplies by economic division (*DGB*, March 13, 1963). It is difficult to imagine how the bureaucracy might have managed such complicated arrangements.

111. *DGB*, April 8, 1965.

112. Beijing Radio, August 12, 1978.

Manpower, transport and storage facilities, and funds are all econo-mized, and depletion is minimized, when goods follow more geographi-cally feasible and time-tested routes of circulation. But officials in administratively designed units, with their links to the planning bu-reaucracy, have been able to impede a rerouting of goods away from their domains.

CONFLICT OVER COMMODITIES BETWEEN
STATE AND PRIVATE COMMERCIAL ACTORS

Alongside the battles for commodities within the state trade bureauc-racy, there has often been explicit rivalry between this bureaucracy, on one side, and whatever remnant of private business has existed at any given time, on the other. In fact, just as Lenin and Bukharin were advo-cating at about the same point in Soviet history, supply and marketing cooperatives were initially created in communist-controlled base areas in 1928 to place in the rural districts a Party-managed organ that would compete with private merchants for a share of the local market.[113]

Once the People's Republic was established, the new government used a variety of techniques to counter the private sector's control over the rural market. For example, in the countryside before 1953, SMCs used "advance-purchase" contracts to ensure that the peasantry sold the required quantity of key goods, particularly cotton, to the state. The system amounted to giving the peasants a generous down payment on their product, which bound them to sell their crop to the state.[114] As was noted earlier, the institution in 1953 and 1954 of state monopoly pur-chase of grain, cotton, and oil cut off the private trader from any dealing in these goods.

In the urban areas, as early as 1950, various techniques began the transferral of power over goods away from private hands. Just after communist takeover, when the new government formed state compa-nies, at the same time it set state-fixed prices, allocated supplies to private commercial concerns only under contract, and then employed these concerns as commission agents for the state companies.[115] This

113. Peter Schran, *Guerrilla Economy*, pp. 50, 53, states that the Sixth Party Congress of the Chinese Communist Party in 1928 first called for the organization of the SMCs; Mark Selden, *The Yenan Way*, p. 240, says that the model Nan-chü co-op was set up before 1940 to compete with local merchants. On Bukharin, see Moshe Lewin, *Political Under-currents in Soviet Economic Debates*, p. 46. On Lenin, see Alec Nove, *Political Economy and Soviet Socialism*, p. 93.

114. Alexander Eckstein, *China's Economic Revolution*, p. 113; Perkins, *Market Con-trol*, discusses this system in detail in chapter 3.

115. Li Choh-ming, *The Economic Development of Communist China*, pp. 12 ff., and articles by Hsueh Mu-ch'iao in *Peking Review*, nos. 49–52 (1977). In Russia also in the late 1920s, heads of state enterprises saw "the reduction or elimination of the private

process of substituting state for private control culminated in the massive takeovers and mergers of private firms in the 1956 "socialist transformation." While this process will be described in detail in a later chapter, it is important to note here that at its crux lay an increasing domination by the state over what were once privately operated channels of commodity circulation.

In later years, especially in periods when radical politicians were able to ban free markets, such leaders urged the SMCs to buy up even small, miscellaneous native products. Their purpose lay in denying these trivial goods to possibly existing peasant speculators, who were painted as ready to "jump at the chance" to raise prices and get high profits from this petty trade.[116]

In the Soviet Union, where kolkhoz (collective farm) markets are the main competitive force among the three Soviet trade networks,[117] a series of regulations restricts their sales volume, in an effort to limit the flow of goods away from state coffers. Even in times when free marketing has been permitted, the Chinese have adopted the same measures to limit private activity. These include a rule that for goods sold by quota to the state, only those produced in excess of target amounts may be traded freely; the exclusion altogether of cotton; and attempts to diminish the extent of price fluctuation in the fairs.

Also, officials in local branches of state commercial organs in the Chinese countryside have tried from time to time to get permission to raise state purchase prices for rural produce, in order to draw goods away from the popular, freer fairs and into their own procurement nets.[118] State food purchase depots can manipulate the market through pricing in other ways as well. For example, in times of plenty, their cadres buy up large stocks of pork so that they may later corner the market by offering the pork at reasonable prices in times of high demand.[119] Fairs, too, will be treated in more depth in a later chapter; here the point is simply that the term "free" in "free market" lends a somewhat false impression, in light of usual state schemes to vie for the products they offer.

A last case of conflict between state organs and what are essentially private enterprises is the contest waged by the wholesale departments of state trade companies against the "collective" and "individual enterprises" that the central government promoted in the cities beginning in

---

sector . . . [as] a way of enabling [them] to take over resources possessed by private industrialists and traders" (Bettelheim, *Class Struggles: 1917–1923*, p. 206).

116. One example is *DGB*, December 11, 1964.

117. Goldman, *Soviet Marketing*, p. 50, also, pp. 42–43; and Karl-Eugen Wädekin, *The Private Sector in Soviet Agriculture*, pp. 137, 169, 170, 177.

118. Bennett, "Activists and Professionals," p. 100.

119. Interview in Hong Kong, December 11, 1979.

1979. By mid-1982 these enterprises accounted for nearly one quarter of the country's urban employment. Official state policy was to encourage the growth of these small concerns, which are responsible for their own profits and losses, to solve problems of urban unemployment and to rectify the shortage of city services. However, state distributors and shopworkers resent the stealing of their business by these collectives, since this makes it difficult for the state organs to meet their own sales targets.

Competition grows out of the fact that workers in the collectives, forced to support themselves and not bound by state-set operating procedures, provide better service to customers and work longer hours. To nip these young enterprises in the bud, the state companies, which are their main suppliers, often give them slow-selling products, surplus foods that state shops can no longer sell, or spoiled fruit.[120] In this case, state wholesale and retail units have managed to cooperate for the purpose of cutting down a more threatening rival that is outside the usual state system.

Because goods serve as a currency in the Chinese economy, each unit charged with implementing state-designated plans fights for control over a quantity and a type of goods that will increase its leverage in the bureaucracy and that will guarantee its ability to meet its planned commitments. This battle for command over goods often results in the diversion of goods from their designated routes. And this in turn encourages and even forces shopworkers and the populace to loosen their reliance on proper procedures of procurement, and to turn instead to semi-licit forms of exchange.

INFORMAL EXCHANGE
AND COMMAND OVER GOODS

A de-emphasis on and distaste for money, along with scarcity of goods in China, has contributed to an informal network of exchange that again stresses command over goods. Workers in units in charge of circulation

---

120. *Gongren ribao* [Workers' Daily] (Beijing), August 19, 1979, corroborated by interview in Hong Kong, November 29, 1979. Even two years after these collectives were first promoted, these problems continued. See *RMRB*, July 5, 1981, pp. 1 and 5. The data from 1982 are in *FBIS*, October 1, 1982, p. K15, which claims that these enterprises give jobs to 25.88 million workers, who account for "23.6 percent of the country's total [urban] employment."

engage in "indirect theft" of goods from their place of work,[121] for their own personal pleasure, for simple barter or bargaining, and sometimes for outright bribery. It is often the case in socialist, planned economies that a downgrading of market exchange elevates the importance of non-market dealings, but this is especially so in China, where *guanxi* (personal connections) has traditionally facilitated trading.[122]

The least complicated way to benefit from one's position as a dealer in goods is to obtain a portion of whatever prized items one's shop or unit has to offer.[123] A few examples will indicate the ways in which this can be done.[124] In one case, the knitwear wholesale department in a department store in Handan City, Hebei province, had charge of a large shipment of socks. Before putting these on the market, store staff were allowed to purchase socks in accord with their ranks: cadres were permitted to buy five pairs each, and each group leader could purchase twenty-five pairs. But the biggest chief of all, the head of the department's party consolidation and rectification leading group, was given the right to buy eighty pairs. This measurement of power through pairs of socks is a vivid illustration of the importance of goods in China.

A second example comes from a department store in Hangzhou City. Here a wholesale department in a state company managing communications, power, and chemical industries equipment distributed television sets to the store. First, the chief of the wholesale department's telecommunications group made secret arrangements with the head of the store's radio department, allowing him to keep six televisions for himself. Then the Party branch secretary and others in the store radio department divided up supply coupons for the sets among themselves even before the televisions were delivered. By the time customers learned that televisions were for sale, all the supply coupons were already in the hands of the shop personnel. Also, in general, "store leaders can get anything they want by trading goods with other store leaders," an ex-shopworker revealed.[125] Once they obtain the excess goods, workers keep

121. Schwartz, "Corruption and Political Development in the U.S.S.R.," p. 437, used this term to describe the way enterprise officials in the USSR use state money or goods to obtain preferential treatment in the distribution of goods in short supply or in the delivery of a better assortment of goods to retail stores.

122. A Lawrence Chickering, "The God that Cannot Fail," in *The Politics of Planning* (San Francisco, 1976), on p. 353, states that "price controls . . . favor people who do well in non-price competition: . . . relatives, friends."

123. For examples of the same behavior in the Soviet Union, see Grossman, "'Second Economy,'" p. 29; and Smith, *The Russians*, pp. 117–18.

124. Shijiazhuang Radio, March 14, 1978; Hangzhou Radio, March 31, 1978.

125. Hong Kong interview, November 29, 1979. According to Frolic, *Mao's People*, p. 221, "All medical personnel stole medicine and equipment . . . sold drugs or traded it for food or other favors." See also William L. Parish, "Egalitarianism in Chinese Society," pp.

them, give them to friends and relatives, or sometimes use them for illegal exchange.[126]

The lines between barter, bargain, and bribery with goods obtained from one's work unit are hard to draw. According to a refugee account, "if you have a supply of any commodity, you head for the back door (*hou men*) to get ... whatever you want to bargain for."[127] Particularly well placed for barter are workers who deal in the "three treasures." This term refers to three forms of services especially in demand—medical, transport, and food. Room in crowded urban hospitals and Western medicines are both difficult to obtain without giving presents to a well-placed doctor; private transport of materials is impossible without a driver in one's debt in this society where no one owns motor vehicles; and those who deal in foodstuffs can sometimes slip out extras. Another prized item is cigarettes: in one instance, a provincial sugar, tobacco, and wine company "squeezed out" 580,000 packs of them in one year to use in "smoothing relations" with other units.[128]

Beyond the individual level, SMCs have been accused of bartering among themselves when in need of key supplies. This is a "queer way of trading," according to one criticism, that "fosters shortages." In the instance reported, the deal involved exchanging two hundred piculs of melon seeds for four hundred piculs of preserved lichee, hardly the stuff of large-scale swindle![129] The proper channels for state-run rural trade are vertical ones—through higher levels and the companies—not horizontal.

Shop managers also engage in barter business with factory officials. Department store heads or cadres in state-owned hardware trading companies, for example, change raw materials under their control for manufactured goods from the industrial plants. Units with no raw materials in stock may sometimes be unable to get needed manufactured items. In such cases, to comply with the demands of the production units they must purchase raw materials on the market at high prices.[130] Sometimes, too, the exchange goes in the other direction: factories have been

43–44, where Parish notes that "the distribution system may have been subverted more by sales workers than by any design of the new administrative elite ... sales clerks were doing as well as, or better than, administrative officials in the distribution system."

126. *SCMM*, no. 822 (1975), pp. 22–27.

127. Frolic, p. 129.

128. Fox Butterfield, *China*, p. 95; *RMRB*, June 13, 1981, p. 1.

129. *RMRB*, December 30, 1956. The picul is equal to fifty kilograms. See Butler (n. 90 above), pp. 338–44, on the buying agents attached to the supply and marketing cooperatives, who procure items not included in the distribution plans of the state system. Both barter and *guanxi* (see text, following) play a large role in their work, according to Butler.

130. *DGB*, March 21, 1957.

warned against trading their products for foodstuffs and manufactured consumer goods from stores.[131]

Barter, in which each of the two sides to the deal offers something the other needs, shades into bribery when one party is desperately enough in need of some service or commodity to supply whatever the other party demands. In socialist China, after decades of indoctrination in anticapitalist morality, people bribe with gifts more often than with cash. "There was nothing wrong: no money changed hands," Chinese in Beijing told an American journalist in the late 1970s, in discussing their petty embezzling activities.[132] Additional evidence of this proclivity to eschew the use of currency in influencing others is a State Council circular from 1981 that forbade "all enterprises giving their purchasing and sales personnel money for buying gifts or inviting people to dinner to get things done."[133] The directive makes it clear that the extortion itself is usually not carried out through the use of money.

This form of bribery through gift-giving is especially essential in commercial workers' efforts to obtain scarce, popular, or specialized goods. According to one informant, the system involved is popularly known in southern China as *ceng ceng sung li* (present a gift at every level). Hard-to-find goods often cannot be obtained without a host of middlemen or -women; and each intermediary wants at least a token in thanks for expediting the procurement.

This practice also comes into play when supplies delivered through the planning system are inadequate, in variety or amount. In such cases rural commercial cadres working near a city can go directly to a store or a factory in that city to find a necessary spare part or an extra accessory. "But they won't sell you the thing or produce it for you specially without a gift," one informant explained. His commune offered peanuts and chickens in exchange for sought-after popular goods from the city. Such gifts accompany payment at state-set prices.[134]

Many of the same factors that make goods (in the form of gifts) the currency for bribery also act to reinforce the traditional reliance of Chinese people on personal connections, or *guanxi*. That is, since money and goods are scarce, prices are controlled, and rationing, both formal and informal, dictates the legal distribution of key goods and services, informal social relationships help to circumvent the restrictiveness of

---

131. *Yangcheng wanbao* [Yangcheng Evening News] (Canton), August 22, 1962.

132. Butterfield, p. 94, and "In China, Austerity Is Less Austere If One Has Friends in Right Places," *New York Times*, December 11, 1977.

133. *BR*, no. 37 (1981), p. 7.

134. Interview in Hong Kong, October 19, 1979.

marketing regulations. The Russian concept of *blat*—influence, connections, pulling strings—plays an analogous role in the Soviet economy. One author has listed *blat* among what he calls "white" forms of bribery, those which involve no real material or monetary gain for either party, but which serve as an "essential lubricant" to much business.[135]

In addition to the more customary forms of *guanxi*, which are based on family, friendship, geographical, co-worker, or schoolmate ties, connections crop up in ironic ways in the course of commercial work itself. One informant described a special hotel in Loyang where procurement personnel from across the country stay when they come to purchase that city's famous tractor parts. Since these personnel are likely to be carrying some cash, they are placed together in this sequestered inn to keep them safe from thieves. The hotel, meant as a haven from illegal activities, has become a hotbed for fostering personal ties, and for swapping and gathering information as to what products can best be obtained where in the country, and from what individuals. Similarly, political meetings for finance and trade cadres at the commune level in the countryside, planned to inspire purity and to propagate official procedures, are also the breeding grounds for relationships that eventually hatch much under-the-counter barter. In these two examples, *guanxi* acts as an aid to the informal collection of market intelligence, and eventually to control over goods.[136]

Guanxi also serves sometimes as a supplement, but more often as a substitute, to gift-giving in the barter and bribery that attend the exchange of scarce goods. In the absence of *guanxi*, exchange is far less likely to take place if one side lacks nothing the other can offer. Connections also make it possible to get access to specialty items in luxury-goods shops for army personnel, overseas Chinese, and cadres.[137]

135. Schwartz, p. 437. Also see Smith, *The Russians*, chap. 3, especially p. 115. Grossman, "'Second Economy,'" on p. 32, also refers to a Russian custom of bringing gifts to one's superior, as "a general and regular way of ingratiating oneself with authority . . . expected by both parties."

136. The material here is drawn from interviews in Hong Kong on October 19, November 27, November 29, and December 11, 1979.

137. The version of the shops that serves cadres contains luxury items in short supply — clothes of fine fabric, delicacies to eat, jewelry—and is popularly termed *gui bin shi* (distinguished-guest lounges). According to various accounts, in these places high-level cadres need merely sign their names; they are then permitted purchases worth up to forty thousand yuan, technically on credit, but often actually gratis. (A yuan is worth about $0.50 US.) See *Jingji pipan* (Red Guard newspaper, copies of which are collected in *Red Guard Publications, Part I: Newspapers*, reprinted by Center for Chinese Research Materials, Association of Research Libraries, Washington, D. C., 1975), February 8, 1967; *Qing bao* [Intelligence] (Hong Kong), no. 2 (1979), p. 20; and Frolic, p. 131. For information on similar shops in the Soviet Union, see Grossman, p. 25; Smith, p. 113.

In the free markets, personal ties have a role to play as well. At these local fairs, where most sellers have similar wares, one's placement is crucial if one is to beat out competitors. Position depends, however, not just on one's time of arrival at the meet, but on presenting gifts or having friends among the control personnel. "But you can't offer money," an interviewee explained. "This could cause problems, if someone were to report you. In such a case, you would immediately be sent to a most unfavorable location."

Connections, whether cemented by gifts or by interpersonal ties, facilitate China's socialist commercial exchange. As distinct from capitalist business, though, these links are generally formed without the aid of money, and they function as its replacement.

Planned business in China, in dictating that the interchange of goods be guided largely by nonmarket factors, when coupled with an anti-market ideology and economic scarcity, has turned commodities into a kind of currency. Furthermore, the targets for profits and sales that the plan imposes on state trading organs pit one type of commercial unit against the next, and a given locality against its supplying superior or its retailing receiver, in contests over the control of this currency. And, finally, on the personal level as well, gifts in goods are the medium by means of which informal deals make up for deficiencies in the distribution network. Thus the plan and its procedures by no means eliminate but simply restructure commercial competition, focusing it more on goods than on money. In the process, battles over the possession and allocation of goods often skew the implementation of planners' designs.

2

Policy Conflict
In Chinese Commerce,
1949–1979

Three great forces are at work in the conflict over Chinese commercial policy, each with its own vision and prescriptions about the proper procedures for marketing and distributing consumer goods. These three policy positions, or in the terms of a scholar of Soviet politics, "tendencies of articulation," can be characterized as stances stressing respectively class conflict, state control, and maximum productivity, and will be referred to here as radical, bureaucrat, and marketeer. These are ideal types, providing a framework for analysis; but at the same time they inform the platforms that individual politicians draw on and support. In the complicated arena of Chinese politics, one politician may align himself with different tendencies at different junctures, depending on his official position, the prevailing political climate, and changing economic circumstances.

Most previous scholars writing on politics in the People's Republic—as well as the bulk of journalistic comment—have cast their interpretations of political conflict in the format offered by the Chinese themselves.[1] This format, one of a battle between "two roads"—one "left" and one "right," one ideological and one pragmatic, or one radical and one moderate— misses many of the finer issues over which arguments have raged, even as it fails to account for alliances sometimes struck among proponents of opposing lines. Perhaps above all, that approach oversimplifies the most basic options among which Chinese politicians choose by presenting only two. For instance, as the story below will make clear (in this chapter and in those that follow), the substantial weakening of the "left" that came with the death of Mao Zedong in 1976 by no means spelled a clear victory for a united market-prone "right."

Moreover, what is most interesting in Chinese politics is not just the existence of alternative approaches to policy formation. A three-line analysis does a better job of uncovering the roots of the conflict, controls, and restriction that have always attended, undermined, and eventually terminated periods of liberalization in the PRC. Also, there is often a middle ground between permissiveness and prohibition that is lost in two-line models. The three-line approach here, by analyzing more closely the social bases, ideological foundations, and power considerations that are attached to each line, illuminates the causes and forms of opposition that limit liberal options over time.

Policies toward the commercial sector are made in China in conjunction with policies toward every other element of economic and social life. Thus the outcome of policy formation at any point is a package of congruent policies, all of which represent the same general orientation, characterized by most scholars in the past as either leftist or rightist. It

---

1. Prominent among the scholars of Chinese politics who have written in terms of a two-line model is Parris Chang, in his *Power and Policy in China*, in which he notes on p. 2 that "the major shifts in policy followed an oscillating pattern between the conservative and radical orientation, as a result of shifting coalitions and balance of power in the decision-making councils." Franz Schurmann also uses this paradigm in *Ideology and Organization in Communist China* when, on p. 354, he refers to a conflict between "reds" and "experts," and speaks on pp. 196, 198, and 202 of a clash between those around Mao favoring a social mobilization approach and those around Chen Yun who preferred to rely on material incentives. Also on this theme, see Byung-joon Ahn, in *Chinese Politics and the Cultural Revolution*. Ahn says on p. 7, "I will pay special attention to what [the Chinese] call the 'struggle between the two roads' not necessarily to agree with their interpretation but to understand the meaning they give to it." On p. 9 he notes that polarization within the Party began after 1955, but on that page and on pp. 11–12 he traces this conflict to "two broad policy orientations" within the Chinese revolutionary experience dating to the 1930s and 1940s. This view of communist politics receives general theoretical treatment in Richard Lowenthal, "Development vs. Utopia in Communist Policy." On pp. 51–54, he lays out his model, which he claims fits all communist states. It is a model of policy conflicts between two kinds of elites over two types of social changes, one revolutionary and one of economic progress.

may be that the three perspectives outlined in this chapter—radical, bureaucrat, and marketeer—do not exist in identical forms vis-à-vis the Party's treatment of other parts of society or even of other branches of the economy. For the "marketeer" tendency must be most prominent toward trade. To give just one example, permitting "free" markets to exist, in which supply and demand and not state planning are the principal determinants of price, is a market-type strategy without an exact analogue in other areas of the economy. Therefore, it may be that in some other realms of policy, conflict is more often bifurcated than it is in this field.

Nevertheless, the trichotomy on which this analysis rests corresponds to universal typologies set out in several influential studies. Three works in particular in recent years have cast their inquiry in terms of tripartite understandings of human experience.[2] The first of these is Amitai Etzioni's comparative investigation of complex organizations, in which he identified three "power-means" by which organizations strive to achieve compliance. He explained that these means include physical, material, and symbolic rewards and deprivations, and he labeled them, respectively, coercive, remunerative, and normative. Each of these, he showed, is best suited to meet a different sort of goal and to handle a separate kind of response (order, economic, and culture goals; and alienative, calculative, and moral involvement, respectively).

Drawing on this model, G. William Skinner and Edwin A. Winckler elaborated a theory to account for the relationship between the Chinese Communist Party and the peasantry over nearly two decades. Although their terminology varies somewhat from Etzioni's, as they speak of order, economic and ideological goals and of alienation, indifference, and commitment forms of involvement, the relationships they outline be-

2. Amitai Etzioni, *A Comparative Analysis of Complex Organizations*, pp. 3–22; G. William Skinner and Edwin A. Winckler, "Compliance Succession in Rural Communist China: A Cyclical Theory"; and Charles E. Lindblom, *Politics and Markets*, pp. 4 and 11–13.

Scholars of the People's Republic in recent years have also written in terms of three-line struggles. For example, see Franz Schurmann, *The Logic of World Power*, pp. 277–83, where he speaks of three "currents," a Liuist one stressing organization, one associated with Chen Yun, stressing a pragmatic approach, and one around Mao, which is experimental, utopian, and spontaneous. Victor C. Falkenheim, in "Political Reform in China," pp. 259–63, 280–81, finds three sets of views on issues of Party-state reform. Also see Edward Friedman, "Maoism, Titoism, Stalinism: Some Origins and Consequences of the Maoist Theory of the Socialist Transition," which focuses on "three broad notions which have legitimated the policies of the socialist transition in the People's Republic of China." In addition, a forthcoming volume to be published by Westview Press (1984) uses this three-line framework to analyze four different policy sectors. Contributors to that volume are, on cultural affairs, Richard C. Kraus; on political organization, Edward Friedman; on foreign policy, Peter Van Ness; and Dorothy J. Solinger on commerce.

tween these categories and the content of their categories are essentially the same as Etzioni's.

The third piece of work presenting a threefold pattern for ordering behavior is Charles E. Lindblom's *Politics and Markets*. This book posits three "fundamental politico-economic alternatives" or "elemental mechanisms for social control that all politico-economic systems employ," namely, persuasion, authority, and exchange. Lindblom points to exchange as being the basic relationship structuring market systems; authority as the "bedrock on which government is erected"; and persuasion as another "major method of elite control of masses, especially in communist systems."

As ideal types, the three stances of the present study draw roughly upon the same dimensions as those used by these earlier authors. That is, radical strategies tend to be rooted in ideological symbolic approaches, and ideally use normative modes in attempting to obtain obedience. They also form the basis for the distinctive "preceptoral" model that Lindblom uses as his reference point for regimes relying on his "persuasive" alternative. The bureaucratic tendency, again in its ideal form, depends on more coercive tactics, as it utilizes authority to overcome alienation and achieve order. And marketeers employ remunerative methods of control, which are most effective in reaching economic goals, and which appeal most to respondents operating from a calculative motivation, within the exchange relationships of the marketplace.

Nevertheless, despite these parallels, the terms here refer to a different aspect of reality and serve a different function from those used by previous scholars. The designations radical, bureaucrat, and marketeer represent competing designs for managing the work of domestic commerce in the People's Republic and, in a larger sense, aim to realize coexisting but often incompatible values in one crucial branch of economic work in a socialist state. Thus, they are more than abstract principles for understanding disparate forms of social organization; they are shorthand allusions to visions in conflict, adhered to and alluded to by policy makers in the heat of factional battle.

Because of the intimate connection between the categories here and actual politics, this study borrows the concept of "tendency" noted above to describe them. For the work on tendencies in the Soviet Union postulates that policies are made through tendency conflicts. This notion is also valuable for the purposes at hand in its delineation of three elements in the content of information conveyed by a given tendency: a value or goal; an analysis of the situation in which the individual or organization is to pursue the given value; and a recommendation or demand stating how the given value should be allocated in a given situation.[3] Thus, at any time, the proponents of each tendency have their own aims, along with specific prescriptions for achieving those aims, and they bring these plans to bear as they engage in policy making.

Notwithstanding their differences, it is important to remember that the adherents to these three lines or tendencies are all socialists. With this in mind, the dynamics between them can best be understood as an internal tension within socialism, as each stresses most heavily one strain in Marxism. Thus, it is as if each were insistently and recurrently posing one key question: Radicals ask, "Which *class* gets the goods?" Bureaucrats inquire, "Does the *state control* the goods?" And the marketeers simply demand, "How can we *produce* and distribute the *optimum* amount of goods?"

This chapter first lays out the three tendencies as they exist as ideal types. It begins by exploring the values associated with each tendency in this ideal sense, and the related assessment each makes of commercial activity. Employing tendency analysis, it then traces the recommendations for action that each poses, in light of these values and assessments, and indicates the potential for alliance among the three. The argument goes on to suggest the likely social bases on which each tendency rests and is followed by sketches of a few important commercial bureaucrats.

The major body of the chapter recounts six controversial episodes in the making of commercial policy and highlights which tendencies were in conflict and over what issues in each instance. Finally, drawing on the evidence from these cases, the conclusion makes some statements about broad trends in policy making toward the commercial sector in the PRC.

Three Tendencies

Each tendency appreciates and to some extent shares concern over the key values the other two hold. But each group is intent on pursuing its principal vision. Thus, class-conscious radicals in trying to ensure that poor peasants and workers are protected, "served," or otherwise benefited by commercial policy, worry that policies that aim only at increasing economic growth or at more control over planning will conflict with a "proletarian" purpose.

3. Franklyn Griffiths, "A Tendency Analysis of Soviet Policy-Making," pp. 337 and 363–64. On p. 360, Griffiths defines a "tendency of articulation" as "a mass of common articulations which persists over time."

Bureaucrats, in their efforts to arrange purchases and supplies in a planned way, through vertically arranged state organs, seem at times to value controls for their own sake and to forget that these controls were instituted in the first place to serve goals of economic development and social redistribution. And marketeers, who want to stimulate growth through a rather free exchange and fluctuating prices, do not ignore class issues and plans altogether, but show most solicitude for those in middling class levels, and advocate a plan that is moderated by the law of value.[4]

Perhaps this quality of fixation on one value is the ultimate weakness of each position: the values which each group treats as secondary and which it thus tends to neglect while in power have always come back to haunt it, once difficulties set in. For its opponents inevitably call for policy changes in the name of the overlooked goals. An analysis of the values of the three groups, respectively, will at the same time illuminate the three central issues around which all controversy in the Chinese commercial sector has centered: class, state control, and productivity.

CLASS AND RADICALS

Besides Marx's more general distaste for market society, with its classes, as one that exploits its laborers, he also made special reference to what he believed to be a distorting effect of class society on "social demand." This factor, he noted, "which regulates the principle of demand, is subject to the mutual relationship of different classes and their respective economic position ... nothing can be explained by the relation of supply to demand before ascertaining the basis on which this relation rests."[5] More simply, Marx believed, and later studies have shown, that markets tend to serve better and to give more clout to those economically better endowed.[6] One economist suggested that in pre-

4. The law of value states that the value of a commodity is established by the amount of labor that is necessary to produce it on the average (among enterprises manufacturing that commodity) in a given society at a certain point in time. Since price is the monetary expression of value, most simply, marketeers want an object's price to be set, not according to political decision, but on the basis of its economically determined worth. Also, the law indicates that allocatory decisions ought to be based on profit considerations, according to which enterprises and sectors are best able to use labor and capital inputs efficiently.

5. Karl Marx, *Capital*, vol. 3, book 3, p. 178. His concern here is echoed in different words by Oskar Lange in *On the Economic Theory of Socialism*, p. 20.

6. Uma J. Lele, in *Food Grain Marketing in India: Private Performance and Public Policy*, explains on pp. 44 and 79 why having more capital gives one a headstart in the marketplace: those with more wealth can hold stocks in anticipation of higher prices at times

1949 China peasants at the upper end of the scale would have been more inclined than poorer ones to rely on the market.[7]

An essay on rural corruption written in 1965 by radicals expressed this tendency's concern for class. It illustrates how radicals, along with Marx, view markets as dominated by the rich and injurious to the indigent:

> Commercial speculation and usurious activities form a bridge that leads the peasant individual economy to capitalism. A peasant must become a merchant and amass a small amount of wealth before he can be a rich peasant and capitalist. On the other hand, the activities of business speculation and usury are bound to cause some of the peasants to become impoverished and bankrupt.[8]

To guard against these eventualities, radicals in power set up these standards for commercial staff and workers, in the hope that if they followed them, lower-class people would benefit:

> (1) Is their feeling for the workers, peasants, and soldiers deep? (2) Are the varieties and items they handle welcomed by the workers, peasants, and soldiers? (3) Is their form of service convenient for the workers, peasants, and soldiers? And (4) does their service quality and attitude satisfy the workers, peasants, and soldiers?[9]

Inspired by a morality of class struggle and power for the poorer, then, the radical assessment of commerce is that it is basically evil. This is so because, dealing in money and profits, it both is based on and, radicals claim, leads to further inequitable distribution. Not only should it be run by and for the least advantaged, they hold, but it should be kept to a minimum. To achieve this, radicals urge commercial workers to engage in productive as well as exchange activities: "Cloth dealers

---

when prices are low; they have the wherewithal to take risks and to acquire more information; they may spread their investments and provide their own transportation; and they may work safely on much smaller profit margins. On this point, also see Introduction to this study, at nn. 7–11.

7. Dwight H. Perkins, *Market Control and Planning in Communist China*, pp. 25–26. Another point of view, however, is offered by the Chinese marketeers of 1980, in whose mouthpiece, *Shichang* [Market] (Beijing), no. 12 (March 25, 1980), p. 6, there appeared a short tale of a poor, many-mouthed peasant family that benefited from the recent opening of free markets, where it was able to earn a bit of cash from its surplus vegetables. Also, old indigent people in China in particular gain from marketing the products of sideline enterprises. See William L. Parish and Martin King Whyte, *Village and Family in Contemporary China*, p. 76.

8. In Gordon Bennett, *China's Finance and Trade: A Policy Reader*, p. 99.

9. *Xuexi yu pipan* [Study and Criticism] (Shanghai) (*XXYPP*), no. 10 (1974), p. 96.

should learn to weave cloth, vegetable-mongers should learn to grow vegetables," in the words of one radically inspired editorial.[10] Whether or not radical policies have had or could have their desired effects of limiting polarization and protecting the needy, they make use of Etzioni's normative means more than do the policies of the other two groups. For they draw more heavily on persuasive, ideologically rooted appeals than do the others.

STATE CONTROL AND BUREAUCRATS

A key issue for bureaucrats in market management is how to deal with the frequently surfacing problem in China (as in all socialist countries) of supply's not meeting demand. There have been numerous bureaucratic answers to this question, all of which circumvent the straightforward approach of the marketeer, who uses prices that move with supply and demand as an incentive to stimulate economic growth.

Bureaucrats believe in increasing production as a way to meet demand, but they prefer not to do so by allowing prices to rise on their own.[11] Instead, they speak of "expanding production in proportion as planned"; and "using the plan to adjust [individual] prices," while keeping the overall price structure intact.[12]

Another alternative they favor is to regulate distribution and guide consumption on the basis of constant supply, rather than to induce more output. This approach includes rationing schemes and "planned supply."[13] Since they control the channels of bureaucratically run supply, such officials no doubt value the opportunity that rationing and planned supply afford them to extract side payments.[14]

Besides shifting planning targets in production and reorganizing allocation, bureaucrats also strive to ensure that the state procures as large a proportion of productive output as possible through its own purchasing organs (again, in line with the analysis in chapter one that points to the importance in socialist societies of control over the flow of goods):

10. *Survey of the China Mainland Press (SCMP)*, no. 4286 (1968), pp. 6–12.
11. See article by Zhang Yifei discussed in chapter 1 above (cited in chap. 1, n. 52).
12. *Da Gong Bao* [Impartial Daily] (*DGB*), April 13, 1959; and *Hong Qi* [Red Flag] (*HQ*), nos. 7, 8 (1963), p. 9.
13. *HQ*, nos. 7, 8 (1963), pp. 7, 9; Bennett, *Finance and Trade*, p. 88; *SCMP*, no. 894 (1954), p. 8. *Extracts from China Mainland Magazines (ECMM)*, no. 31 (1956), p. 12; Yao Yilin, "Shi nian lai de shangye" [Ten years of commerce], in *Jian guo shi nian 1949–1959* [Ten years of national construction] (Hong Kong: Jiwen chubanshe, 1959), vol. 1, p. 269; *Xinhua banyuekan* [New China Semimonthly] (*XHBYK*), no. 10 (1959), p. 167.
14. For an excellent discussion of the operation of this phenomenon in Africa, see Robert Bates, *Markets and States in Tropical Africa*.

The major means [of increasing agricultural produce] is to start from the strengthening of collection and purchasing work for the expansion of the sources of supply. . . . We must strengthen measures for the purchase of those agricultural products included under the scheme of unified purchases, and strictly prohibit them from entering the free market.[15]

And, finally, a last and related option has been the institution, at times, of markets managed by state organs, a form of exchange that, it is hoped, will spur production but direct its issue into the net of the state.[16]

The bureaucrats' assessment of commercial work draws on the strain in Marxism that accepts this activity as a necessary link in the chain of expanded reproduction:

Production determines the market, as well as the market determining production.[17]

And:

Production, distribution, exchange and consumption are all members of one entity, different sides of one unit. Production predominates over all the other elements. . . . Production is also influenced by the other elements—e.g., with the expansion of the market, i.e., of the sphere of exchange, production grows in volume.[18]

Although commerce may, in their view, be necessary, bureaucrats seek to use state organs, fixed prices, hierarchical supervision, and centrally set plans to channel it and limit its spontaneity. Thus, their chief tool is Lindblom's authority, as they focus on order goals. Their recognition of the importance of production gives them grounds for some sympathy with marketeers, except that the ideal-typical representative of each group aims to achieve growth in a different way.

PRODUCTIVITY (THROUGH MARKET FORCES) AND MARKETEERS

Marketeers in socialist China have never gone so far as to advocate a total abandonment of all plans and rations. Rather, the thrust of their initiatives has been to justify methods that permit some combination of

15. *ECMM*, no. 119 (1957), pp. 33–34.
16. Examples are the state grain markets of 1954 (*SCMP*, no. 822 [1954], pp. 20–21) and the goods exchange meets for third-category produce of 1959 (Yao Yilin, p. 269).
17. Marx, *Capital*, p. 187.
18. Karl Marx, *A Contribution to the Critique of Political Economy*, p. 291.

market freedoms at the micro level with nationally guided "balances," in the belief that this is the best way to enhance productivity. Most obviously, with their assessment of commerce as an essentially positive force in stimulating increased growth, they have favored free markets where prices fluctuate with the forces of supply and demand, increased state purchase prices to stimulate output of key crops, indirect planning, enterprise autonomy and profit retention, industrial responsiveness to consumer desires, and a reduction in commercial bureaucracy, with direct exchanges between buyer and seller as the consequence. Thus, their policies evince a faith in material or remunerative incentives to achieve an economic goal through exchange.

The periods when marketeer influence was strong and explicit in China have been relatively brief, normally nipped in the bud in the past by radicals (the 1956–1957 episode ended as the Great Leap got under way; the policies of the early 1960s fell victim to the gathering storms of the Cultural Revolution). Still, at several junctures over the thirty-year period under review the Chinese elite, like economic leaders in other Soviet-type systems, have seriously debated the question of how much market exchange can in fact coexist within a planned, command economy.[19]

Debates on this theme are abstruse and arcane to the uninitiated, and are always fashioned in the purest Marxist jargon as they challenge what the radicals hold to be the most basic presumptions of Marx himself. At issue is the central problem of the extent to which purely economic factors, rather than politicians' perceptions of social need, may govern economic activity in the period termed socialist, after private ownership has been largely eliminated and capitalism pronounced dead.[20]

19. For discussions of debates elsewhere in the Soviet world, see Jere L. Felker, *Soviet Economic Controversies*, esp. chap. 2, "Value and Trade Theories in Evolution"; Hans-Hermann Höhmann et al., *The New Economic Systems of Eastern Europe*, in which chapter 10, on pricing, refers to law-of-value debates of the 1950s which were joined by experts from all countries that had adopted the Soviet economic system (p. 281); Alfred Zauberman, "The Soviet Debate on the Law of Value and Price Formation"; and Deborah D. Milenkovitch, *Plan and Market in Yugoslav Economic Thought*, pp. 24, 33, 38 for Soviet debates, and pp. 123–26 for Yugoslav debates.

20. E. L. Wheelwright and Bruce McFarlane, *The Chinese Road to Socialism*, pp. 82–86, discusses the 1959 debate on the law of value, on the basis of several articles in *Guangming ribao* [Bright Daily] (*GMRB*) from that period. Other representative articles that deal with this issue are Gu Zhun, "Shi lun shehui zhuyi zhidu xia de shangpin shengchan he jiazhi guilu" [A preliminary discussion of commodity production and the law of value in a socialist system], *Jingji yanjiu* [Economic Studies] (Beijing) (*JJYJ*), June 1957; Zhang Chunyin et al., "Bochi Gu Zhun guanyu jiazhi guilu de xiuzheng zhuyi guandian" [Refuting Gu Zhun's revisionist viewpoint on the law of value], *JJYJ*, no. 6 (1957), pp. 27–38; Yuan Lian and Di Wen, "Wo guo jingji xuejie guanyu shangpin shengchan he jiazhi guilu wenti de taolun" [The discussion in my country's economic circles on problems of commodity production and the law of value], *JJYJ*, no. 12 (1958), pp. 12, 77–80, 76 (re-

The terms in which the debate is couched are these: Is commodity production (i.e., the creation of products for the purpose of sale) still necessary or desirable under socialism? If so, what is the appropriate scope of commodity exchange in a socialist society? Can the means of production, such as raw materials for industry and machines (which have traditionally been taken over by the state and then allocated by plan in Soviet systems), be viewed as commodities (and thus be the objects of sales and purchases)? What is the role of the law of value (which rules that a product's value is set by economic criteria, and thus that its price should be, too) in production and in circulation—in the collective sector (which refers to commune organization in the countryside and to small cooperative ventures in cities) and in the state-owned sector?

In essence, controversy around these topics has always amounted in China to arguments over whether it is possible to legitimize ideologically any free exchange after a socialist revolution. The periodic reappearance of identical debates stands as evidence that they have never resulted in a conclusive settlement.

RECOMMENDATIONS AND ALLIANCES

A comparison of the various recommendations that the proponents of each tendency make for commercial work will complete this ideal-typical tendency analysis, as it indicates possible grounds for temporary, if at times uneasy, alliances on some issues between various pairs of the three.[21]

---

views debates over the years 1953–1957); "Beijing bufen jingji lilun gongzuozhe zuotan guanyu shehui zhuyi zhidu xia shangpin shengchan yu jiazhi guilu de taolun qingkuang" [Discussions at the forum held by some economic theoretical workers in Beijing on commodity production and the law of value in a socialist system], *JJYJ*, no. 2 (1959), pp. 31–33; Xue Muqiao, "Shehui zhuyi zhidu xia de shangpin shengchan he jiazhi guilu" [Commodity production and the law of value in the socialist system], *XHBYK*, no. 10 (1959), pp. 165–70 (refers to the 1956 debate); "What Is the Law of Value?" *JJYJ*, no. 2 (1963), pp. 17–23, translated in *Translations from Ching-chi Yen-chiu, Joint Publications Research Service*, no. 18,684 (1964); *HQ*, nos. 7, 8 (1963), pp. 1–9; and "On Commodity Exchange, Commodity Circulation, and the Uniformity and Divergence of Commerce," *JJYJ*, no. 8 (1964), pp. 44–51, translated in *Translations from Ching-chi Yen-chiu, Joint Publications Research Service*, no. 26,800 (1964). See also Cyril Chihren Lin, "The Reinstatement of Economics in China Today."

21. The following analysis is based principally on a reading of articles in *XXYPP* (1973–1976) on marketing, commerce, and planning, for the radical view; and on all articles in *JJYJ* (1978–1979) and U.S. *Foreign Broadcast Information Service* (*FBIS*) (1978–1979) on commerce, the law of value, and planning for the bureaucrat and marketeer views. A few old speeches of Chen Yun from the 1950s also helped in constructing the marketeer view.

TABLE 2 Three Tendencies and Commercial Policy: Selected Issues

Issues/Three Tendencies	Bureaucrat	Marketeer	Radical
Normative assessment of commercial activity; scope for state organs, prices (Assessment/Recommendation)	State control necessary through use of state organs, with bureaucracy, hierarchy.* Use central plans for purchase and sales. Use state prices.* Commerce necessary and potentially either good or bad.	Commerce essentially positive —let everyone do it freely. Eliminate or reduce commercial bureaucracy in favor of direct exchange between buyer and seller.	Commerce basically evil because it involves money and profits and widens income differentials. Should be cut back. Use state organs and prices.* Commercial workers engage in production.
Rural fairs (Recommendation)	Only to be used if planned and only when required to stimulate production.*	Favors fairs and favors maximum freedom in them.	Against them because they lead to class polarization. Use state organs to handle fairs.*
Geographical organization of exchange and distribution (Recommendation)	Take an overall, national view. Use centralized distribution system.	For a national free market, with commodity circulation guided only by the law of comparative advantage.	Prefers local self-reliance.
Proper focus for decision making, proper organization of planning; degree of centralization.	Plan in central ministries downwards. Use detailed targets. Unification through centralization.	Base decisions on law of value, supply and demand, economic accounting and efficiency. Use plan for reference only. Plan from bottom up.	Plan at local levels through ad hoc "socialist cooperation" among work units in consultation with the masses. Plan from the bottom up; decentralize.*
Coordination strategy (Recommendation)	Coordination by plan and vertical hierarchies, using administrative orders, discipline.	Decentralize and coordinate through the market.*	Coordinate through "socialist cooperation".
Views on competition (Value)	It's bad; let the state and its bureaucrats decide who wins and survives according to political criteria.*	It's good because it promotes economic efficiency, weeds out the inefficient.	It's bad: "socialist emulation" is preferred (according to political choice, not market rationality).*

* Indicates alliance between two of the three tendencies on a particular point within a specific issue.

First of all, each takes a position on the role for state organs (state trading companies and their retail shops in the cities and the supply and marketing cooperatives in the countryside) and state-set prices in commercial work. Here bureaucrats and radicals agree that both should be used—bureaucrats in the interests of maintaining price stability and ensuring a balance between social purchasing power and the supply of goods; radicals to guarantee that state-run units crowd "class enemies" out of the marketplace, and to reduce price differentials (regional, seasonal, wholesale-retail), in order to close loopholes for speculation.

Marketeers, however, believe that the state bureaucracy creates too many links in the chain of exchange, thereby unduly prolonging and so stifling the liveliness of the trade, as well as wasting resources and adding to the depletion of the goods. Following upon this, both bureaucrat (perhaps with a bit more tolerance than the radical) and radical sponsor state-managed rural fairs rather than allowing freely conducted ones. This view is countered by the marketeer who values the free markets for the stimulus they give to production. A radical would be more satisfied if fairs of all sorts were abolished.

Deeply distrustful of money and its tendency to promote a class polarization that would especially benefit the economically better-off, the radical hopes that local self-sufficiency can obviate a need for much marketing. While checking the growth of income disparities, central-level bureaucrats, however, planning from Beijing, take centralized distribution as their preferred, organizing principle for exchange and distribution. The marketeer, on the other hand, believes in a mode of distribution that partakes a bit of each view, and thus has sympathized at times with each of the other two: the decentralized exchange of the radicals is good, but not if it means self-sufficiency. For the marketeer, such exchange must revolve around investigation of the genuine conditions of supply and attempts to satisfy market demand in each separate area. The purpose of attention to the locality for the marketeer is to learn its strengths and needs, so as to draw up a nationally coordinated flow of commodities, a "balance." This "balance," however, is dictated, not by the bureaucrat's hierarchical plan, but by the law of comparative advantage. Marketeers also promote enterprise autonomy, a form of decentralization, for its incentive effects.

The bureaucrat synchronizes exchange among parties through the plan, with its detailed targets, vertically drawn lines of command, and administrative orders; and this plan is drawn up in Beijing, working downward. Radical and marketeer challenge this, both beginning their plans from the base. But the marketeer will adjust these plans through the law of value, supply and demand, and economic accounting—in short, through the market; whereas the radical's ideal is mass participation in planning by local-level work units in an ad hoc fashion, with synthesis done purely by "socialist cooperation."

When inflation threatens (because of shortages of supplies), the bureaucrat controls prices and rations supply; the radical urges everyone to engage in production, practice thrift, and use scraps and waste products, all in fine guerrilla style. Meanwhile, the marketeer, accepting a measure of price movement, advises that once the higher prices have incited more production, prices will eventually come down. China's recent history (in the 1940s) of rampant inflation, which ultimately did much to discredit Nationalist Party rule, has made concern over this issue central to commercial policy in the PRC. Leadership fears of "anarchy" or "chaos" in the market no doubt have that experience as a referent.

Radicals and marketeers agree in seeing state monopoly as undesirable, but for different reasons. Radicals view monopolies such as the state companies as adding to the stifling domination of society by bureaucrats, a group they disparage for thwarting mass activism and for enjoying excessive privilege. Marketeers' distaste here centers on the negative effect monopoly has upon competition, which they value for its ability to weed out inefficient enterprises as it promotes the successful ones. It is only the bureaucrat who has no harsh words for the system of total control by the state organs atop which he or she sits.

A last kind of recommendation concerns forms of market control and clearly distinguishes the three positions. For each group relies on a style of market inspection that matches its interests when it goes about checking on the implementation of state commercial policy. In periods of marketeer power, insofar as supervision is used, it includes former businessmen in efforts to oversee the market.[22] Radicals have taken another extreme, relying during and after the Cultural Revolution on investigations by the poor and lower-middle peasants and in the early and mid-1970s on fearsome worker militia teams, whose members enforced price controls and confiscated from marketers any goods that were not permitted to be exchanged freely.[23]

---

22. As an example, *Guangzhou ribao* [Guangzhou Daily] (Canton), November 2, 1979, has an article on enforcing price discipline, in which a municipal price inspection group was formed to check on stores' implementation of state price changes. The group included members of the Municipal Political Consultative Committee, whose participants are drawn from former capitalists.

23. Described in Hong Kong interviews on September 7, October 23, November 29, and December 11, 1979.

Bureaucrats, in their way, have designed "market control committees," composed of representatives of bureaucratic organs.[24] Bureaucrats also depend on the Bureaus for Administrative Management of Industry and Commerce at each administrative level. These organs superintend price control and pass sentence on speculators, as well as manage store and factory registration and examine the quality of industrial output.[25]

Despite the distinctiveness of each tendency in its approach to commercial policy, there are certain grounds for limited alliances between them, as well as points of clash. The fact that no socialist would totally reject goals of social equity, state control, or increased productivity has made it possible on occasion for some two of the three to join for temporary purposes. As was noted above, bureaucrats and radicals both favor the use of state organs and fixed prices. Marketeers and radicals agree on the value of decentralization and some local autonomy (if for very different reasons); both begin planning at the bottom; and both have criticized the monopoly of state organs in trading. And probably both bureaucrats and marketeers place more value on economic growth than radicals do.

But the different motives behind these choices for each group, and the different goals which dispose each to opt for the various tactics listed here, help to account for the short-term nature of joint political platforms, and for the frequent periodic shifts in line that have marked commercial as other work in the PRC.

Social Bases and Politicians

SOCIAL BASES

As was noted above, radical, marketeer, and bureaucratic tendencies or models are the one-dimensional ideal types of social analysis. These tendencies filter through the population, and also have official spokesmen at different times at the leadership echelon. People with opinions on the issues addressed above range from central decision makers and official economic theorists, to management personnel in factories, cadres

24. Gordon Bennett, "Activists and Professionals," lists on p. 307 the members of the committee set up in 1954 in Guangdong.
25. Interview with city commercial official in Guilin, November 1979. A Hong Kong informant told me on November 12, 1979, that these organs have lost prestige in the recent tumultuous years, and so can no longer fulfill their responsibility.

responsible for rural commercial work, provincial leaders, and ordinary workers and peasants.

Sectoral, generational, regional, and occupational divisions within the population are the most relevant factors accounting for the position an individual or a group takes in this conflict.[26] People associated with heavy industry (where state controls are both more possible and necessary) and with the planning apparatus defend the use of the state plan. Cadres from light industrial plants find it more profitable in their work to respond to the incentives of the market; those affiliated with successful enterprises in any sector are more apt to advocate market organization.[27] People working in state-managed commercial organs, attempting to fulfill a sales quota, have fought with industrial units over their being saddled with products to sell that do not meet consumer demand, and so must welcome guidance from market principles. On the other hand, such individuals, as employees of the state, feel endangered by signs that a free market could cut into their own business.

Middle-aged bureaucrats trained and educated in the 1950s, when the Soviet planning model dominated Chinese economic organization, remain a principal power base for plan advocacy. Some older cadres, particularly among the military, recall the pre-1949 days of revolutionary mobilization and guerrilla-style warfare, and still harbor nostalgia for radical approaches.[28] And, again in generational terms, marketeers include among their numbers those educated in the West before 1949, as

26. Griffiths, "Tendency Analysis," on p. 369, suggests that the following variables may account for the propensity of diverse actors to articulate a similar approach to a given policy: organizational affiliation, occupation, role, age, career, ideological orientation, self-interest, and responsiveness to authority. In the following remarks I hazard educated guesses for the Chinese case on the basis of scattered bits of information.

27. This is based on an interview at Stanford University, November 1979, with officials from the Anshan Steel Works. Impressions were supplied by C. Thomas Fingar. Also Yu Qiuli, longtime Head of the State Planning Commission, put heavy emphasis on planning in an article in *Renmin ribao* [People's Daily] (*RMRB*), September 12, 1977, and in his speech at the National Conference on Learning from Daqing and Dazhai in Finance and Trade, in *RMRB*, July 3, 1978, pp. 1, 3. When Yu presented the 1979 economic plans, he barely mentioned the program of economic reform then well under way, and noted that "we must carry out this work energetically and systematically, *under the unified plan* of the State Council" (emphasis added), in *RMRB*, June 29, 1979. See *China News Analysis* (*CNA*), no. 1165 (1979). Also, in 1981 Yu reportedly called price readjustment "rubbish" (*Zheng Ming* [Contend] [*ZM*], no. 43 [May 1981], p. 48). Peter Van Ness reported in a private communication that both workers and economists in China have told him that most managers, not trained in modern management practices, fear and so resist the new reforms because they feel unequipped to reverse old practices and compete on the market.

28. Michael Yahuda, "Political Generations in China," *CQ*, no. 80 (1979), pp. 800–2, on the middle-aged; *ZM*, no. 48 (October 1981), p. 10, on the army's opposition to market reforms.

well as some of the youth of the late 1970s, exposed by the press for the first time to the positive side of capitalism and entranced a bit by it.[29]

Regionally, according to economist Xue Muqiao, "the industrially advanced areas generally advocate more power of self-management, while the less advanced or backward areas press the central government for the unified management and allocation of products."[30] Those in poorer areas, beneficiaries of any nationwide redistribution of key resources,[31] must feel more comfortable as part of a plan, more threatened by the imperatives of market-based exchange.

Among occupational groups, three in particular whose work is expressly economic contain members who relish the market: peasants, especially those living on fertile land near markets, who have a surplus, and whose families have sufficient labor power so that they reap the greatest gains in transactions; the theoretical economists, who all generally champion the observance of economic laws over radically inspired political movements; and managers in factories whose output is thriving and who thus can compete well on the market. Groups, whether rural or industrial, at the lower end of the economic scale, feel insecure without their safe niche within the plan, and also have welcomed the upheaving redistributive bursts and collective forms of social organization that are part of the radical approach.[32]

THREE POLITICIANS

These generalities suggest broad cuts within the population in the conflict over economic organization. When the arena for analysis is reduced

29. Problems of youthful cynicism in the wake of the Cultural Revolution were the subject for much official concern and propaganda, as the regime tried at once in the late 1970s and early 1980s to inspire better productivity through visions of the developed Western economies and at the same time promoted the notion of the "superiority of socialism." See *RMRB*, March 25, 1980. Also, the new urban collective enterprises, promoted by the government beginning in 1979, are essentially a form of private enterprise, and are largely staffed by the unemployed young people who have returned to the cities after their Cultural Revolutionary stint in the countryside. Experience working in these small firms (insofar as they succeed financially) may build up cohorts for market-style management among the young.

30. In *HQ*, no. 8 (1979), p. 21.

31. See Nicholas R. Lardy, "Centralization and Decentralization in China's Fiscal Management," for a description of how this system worked. His book *Economic Growth and Distribution in China* elaborates the argument.

32. *RMRB*, December 18, 1979, p. 1, has an article claiming that "industries feel that if their products have a plan, they have a right to exist." While in China Arthur Wolf found that old people in the countryside who have no offspring and who cannot provide for themselves are fearful of having to depend on the market, rather than being able to rely on the collective. More analysis of the interests of other social and occupational groups and their stance toward markets appears in chapters 4, 5, and 6.

to the level of individuals, however, complexities crop up. An official's organizational affiliation alone provides no easy prediction of viewpoint—leading commercial officials come in various stripes. Moreover, the same individual may subscribe to different tendencies over time, or even to facets of more than one tendency at a given juncture, in accord with the state of the economy or the mix of political forces contending at any point. The efforts of most Chinese politicians to bow in several directions at once, to ensure that no presently (or possibly future) powerful faction is offended, certainly complicates the job of the observer.

Brief sketches follow of Chen Yun (a long-term vice-premier and chief among economic leaders, who served as minister of commerce from 1956 to 1958), Li Xiannian (in charge of the finance and trade bureaucracy for most of the period of the People's Republic), and Yao Yilin (vice-minister of commerce from 1949 to 1959 and minister from 1960 until into the Cultural Revolution, and again for six months beginning in 1978). From between the lines of their important addresses and articles over the years, it is possible to distill a general thrust in the prescriptions of each. The somewhat static pictures in the sketches will come a bit more alive as the case studies that follow portray these men in action over the years.

Of the three, it is Chen who has been the principal architect of schemes using marketeer tactics; Li is an administrator with a penchant for a tempered radicalism; while Yao is a bureaucrat with an openness to marketeer approaches and a skill in radical sloganeering. Since survivors in Chinese politics, which all three are, need a knack for flexibility, it is rare to find complete purity of outlook or total consistency in their presentations, especially in the midst of shifting state policy. Thus, one must bear in mind that the ideal-typical trichotomy is but a tool of analysis when real people become the subject for study.

As a sense of mounting urgency about China's need for a drastic economic renovation rose to the surface in the wake of Mao's death and the arrest of his radical followers in late 1976, Chen Yun's star, fallen from the public limelight since the late 1950s, rose along with this concern, perhaps as early as mid-1977.[33] Reportedly once dubbed "China's number one economist" by Mao Zedong himself,[34] and fifth in line among the very highest ranking of the Party elite in the 1950s,[35] Chen is a man

33. The Hong Kong journal *Guang jiaojing* [Wide Angle] (*GJJ*), no. 59 (1977), notes on p. 19 that a photograph of Chen received special prominence at this time.

34. *ZM*, no. 15 (1979), p. 22.

35. The others, all dead by the late 1970s, were Mao, Liu Shaoqi, Zhu De, and Zhou Enlai.

whose reputation has been renewed and even bolstered after his many years of silence. In 1979 he was billed as one who has always been able to turn economic crises around in China, under whose direction growth has always occurred, and in whose periods of eclipse China has suffered economic setback.[36]

His first significant public showing since 1958–1959, when he met a severe political defeat for opposing the Great Leap Forward, was at the Third Plenum of the Eleventh Party Central Committee, in December 1978.[37] Here, it seems, he nearly led the show despite doctor's orders to speak only one half hour. It is he who called on the Party and the nation to "shift the focus of work to economic modernization." Then, at a crucial Party Work Conference three months later, decisions were made to carry out "economic readjustment." This was to entail reducing the scale of capital construction and shifting the emphasis in development away from steel and heavy industry and toward more investment in agriculture and light industry, stressing consumption proportionately more and accumulation relatively less. These policies too are said to have been proposed by Chen, and indeed are much the same as ones used to good effect in the wake of the Great Leap Forward in the early 1960s, also at his suggestion.[38]

Apparently, though, despite these victories, Chen Yun experienced frustration in his push for a total overhaul of the economy. This quotation, from a July 1979 meeting of the then newly formed State Council Finance and Economic Commission, which he headed, shows the mix of pique and outspokenness that has historically been his style:

> Now China's economic system must definitely be reformed. In the past we studied the Soviet model, but even the Soviet Union itself doesn't use those methods anymore, while we continue to copy them as always. If we want to realize China's socialist modernization, we absolutely must

36. *ZM*, no. 20 (1979), pp. 14, 15.
37. Chen had an important role in the rehabilitation of the national economy after the Leap in the early 1960s, but this was not publicly known at the time. According to *Jing bao* [Mirror] (*JB*), no. 2 (1981), p. 33, he lost standing at the Eleventh Plenum of the Eighth Central Committee in 1966, dropping in the Politburo ranking from fifth to eleventh place. According to CIA directories of public appearances and activities of leading Chinese officials for the years 1972–1978, Chen Yun was referred to as vice-premier through 1973, and thereafter as vice-chairman of the Standing Committee of the National People's Congress, among other positions through 1978, when he was given additional posts. He made 5 appearances in 1972, 10 in 1973, and 5 in 1974, but as many as 17 in 1975, 27 in 1976, 17 in 1977, and 44 in 1978. However, he made no public statements in these years.
38. *Issues & Studies* (Taipei) (*I & S*), 15, no. 9 (1979): 2–3; *ZM*, no. 20 (1979), p. 16; *GJJ*, no. 80 (1979), pp. 4–8, 19; *ZM*, no. 31 (1980), p. 12.

carry out a thorough reform. But a lot of people don't approve of me, so I'll just shut up.[39]

Chen, one of the few proletarians among the Party leadership, having begun his career as a typesetter, has been described variously by his admirers and detractors. The former laud him as "having Deng Xiaoping's competence and Zhou Enlai's character," as "being upright, and never stooping to flattery," one who "works behind the scenes without concern for individual ambition"; the latter, however, take him for a "cunning fox." Those who praise him describe how "he has kept quiet in periods of ultra-leftism when nothing can be done—he does not curry favor with the powerful or drift with the tide. But once something can be done again, he steps forward boldly and upholds justice." Critics, unimpressed, point out that he rarely speaks or writes and only seems overcautious and very honest, "like a great gentleman," but that in fact he follows a most devious course.[40]

Chen's role in politics has been a curious one, befriending Mao at key points,[41] but probably more often acting as gadfly. This latter role got him into political trouble with leftists on several occasions, as he advocated a moderate line in economic policy.[42] Perhaps his early displays of

39. *ZM*, no. 24 (1979), p. 18. It seems that this commission ceased to exist about a year after its creation, though no reason has been given for the disappearance of references to it.

40. *ZM*, no. 20 (1979), p. 16; *ZM*, no. 31 (1980), pp. 11–12; and *JB*, no. 2 (1981), p. 33, all praise him; *Beijing Gongshe* [Beijing Commune] (Beijing) (*BJGS*), March 14, 1967 (a Red Guard tabloid reproduced in *Red Guard Publications* [*RGP*]) criticizes him.

41. Chen was head of the Party's Organization Department in the late 1930s, and wrote on party organization and cadre policy in that period. *I & S*, 15, no. 2 (1979): 90, says that he supported Mao's rectification drive in 1942; Roderick MacFarquhar, *The Origins of the Cultural Revolution*, notes on p. 109 that of the twelve Politburo members and alternate members elected at the Eighth Party Congress in 1956 who addressed that Congress and were still surviving by the time of the Cultural Revolution, Chen was one of the four who expressed agreement with Mao's speech at the Congress. On p. 248 MacFarquhar surmises that Chen was probably for Mao's 1957 rectification campaign. Two Hong Kong journals claim that Mao called on Chen for help in the economic crisis of the Great Leap, according to one in 1959 (*ZM*, no. 20 [1979], p. 14); one in 1960 (*GJJ*, no. 80 [1979], p. 19).

42. MacFarquhar, p. 406, says that during the winter of 1956–1957, Chen insisted on the principle of "three balances" (finance, credit, and materials). Balance, however, MacFarquhar notes, was "the very antithesis of the spirit of the Great Leap Forward," which was soon to loom on the horizon. Cultural Revolution documents state that Chen was criticized by Mao for opposing what Chen called a "rash advance" in agricultural cooperativization, for being too kind to capitalists in the early 1950s, for preventing mergers during socialist transformation; for accumulating ammunition to attack the Great Leap Forward; and for favoring dismantling the collective economy in the early 1960s (see Ding Wang, ed., *Zhonggong wenhua da geming zeliao huibian* [Compilation of materials from China's Great Cultural Revolution] [Hong Kong: Ming Bao Yuekan, 1967], vol. 1, pp. 611–20). He was also attacked for publicizing "the three balances" in 1957 (*Survey of the China Mainland Press-Supplement* [*SCMPS*], no. 232 [1968], p. 29).

loyalty to Mao—and some points of agreement between the two, as on rectification policy and local initiative—along with Mao's appreciation for Chen's character and expertise, were responsible for his escaping the purge suffered by many who had been attacked as he was in the Cultural Revolution.

Chen's economic philosophy contains a variety of concerns, many of which center on the macroeconomics of centralized socialist planning. These involve preferences for satisfying consumption needs before undertaking capital construction; for fitting the scale of construction to the state's financial and material resource levels; for achieving a "synthesized balance" between financial receipts and expenditures, between bank loans and repayments, and between the supply and demand for materials; for setting appropriate ratios between national income and accumulation, national income and state budgetary revenue, and state budgetary expenditure and capital construction investments; and for fixing planning targets that are both feasible and flexible.[43] But the part of his thinking on the economy that pertains specifically to commercial activity focuses on using the market, and is best expressed in two speeches, both of which deal more with incentives at the micro level.

The first of these Chen delivered at the Eighth Party Congress in 1956; the other one he read at the Third Session of the First National People's Congress three months earlier. The position Chen stakes out in the two talks forms the core of what has been described above as the pure marketeer's position: criticism of bureaucratic allocation of commercial (light industrial) goods from higher-level wholesale units to retail shops; a plea for increasing competitiveness in the Chinese economy, in order to break the monopoly of state companies and supply and marketing cooperatives, especially in the procurement of agricultural products; a call for a national flow of commodities among regions, rather than local exclusiveness in exchange; a recommendation for prices for some agricultural products which fluctuate in response to supply and demand in a free market under state leadership; and a suggestion that for most products planned quotas be used for reference only. All of these ideas came back into prominence with Chen himself after 1978.[44]

43. Speeches of Chen's with these emphases are in *ECMM*, no. 166 (1959), pp. 2, 3, 6, and in *Chen Yun tongzhi wengao xuanbian* [Selected Documents of Comrade Chen Yun] (1956–1962) (hereafter *Comrade Chen Yun*), especially the speeches from 1957 and 1962, on pp. 20–26, 27–33, 58–59, 157–72, and 173–80. This volume was generously shared with me by David Bachman. Discussions of Chen's philosophy along these lines can be found in *ZM*, no. 43 (May 1981), pp. 43–45, and in *Beijing Review* (*BR*), no. 12 (1981), pp. 27–28.

44. The first of these speeches is translated in *Eighth National Congress of the Communist Party of China, Volume II: Speeches* (hereafter *Eighth Congress*) (Peking: Foreign Languages

This set of Chen Yun's ideas forms a convenient reference point for the marketeer model; perhaps of no other Chinese politician is it truly possible to say: "Work according to objective laws has been Chen Yun's consistent work style from start to finish."[45]

Li Xiannian's posture as a politician is best described in his own words of advice to others: "While opposing conservatism, one must at the same time oppose the tendency towards impetuosity and adventurism," Li told the 1956 (third) session of the National People's Congress, in reference to what he saw as an overheated production drive then in progress.[46] On another occasion in a similar vein, he recommended that workers in the commercial sector "combine a high degree of revolutionary enthusiasm with a strict scientific spirit."[47]

Li Xiannian's science is the discipline of the plan. Born a poor peasant, he "did not study in a university or receive any kind of higher education." To judge from his career, his expertise in financial and economic work must have all been obtained after 1949.[48] Evidently his personal experience convinced this man that a socialist economy can best be realized by a strict planning system hedged in by central controls. His speeches in periods of radicalism, however, have on occasion evinced an excitement that went beyond mere kowtowing to the leadership then in command.

Mao too of course combined these strains—faith in plans, penchant for mobilization—in his own philosophy, and though Li has been more consistently loyal to planning, perhaps the sympathy between the two lay at least in part in the realm of ideas.[49] In support of Mao, Li, like

---

Press, 1956), pp. 157–76; the other appeared in *GMRB*, July 1, 1956. Besides having to repeat himself twice in one season, Chen had already brought some of these ideas up earlier: "These principles I already spoke about on November 1, 1955, at the forum of the Executive Committee of the All-China Federation of Industry and Commerce," he told his listeners, a bit impatiently, it seems, at the June meeting. When these ideas resurfaced in 1979, they were promoted largely through the writings of Xue Muqiao, as in *RMRB*, June 15, 1979. See Dorothy J. Solinger, "Economic Reform via Reformulation in China: Where Do Rightist Ideas Come From?" Similarities between Chen's ideas here and those of the Soviet politician Bukharin in the 1920s appear in Moshe Lewin, *Political Undercurrents of Soviet Economic Debates*, and in Stephen F. Cohen, *Bukharin and the Bolshevik Revolution: A Political Biography*.

45. *ZM*, no. 20 (1979), p. 14.

46. Quoted in MacFarquhar, *Cultural Revolution*, pp. 86–87.

47. *RMRB*, February 16, 1965.

48. Donald W. Klein and Anne B. Clark, *Biographic Dictionary of Chinese Communism, 1921–1965*, pp. 499–500.

49. Christopher Howe and Kenneth Walker, in "The Economist," refer on p. 190 to an "inconsistency . . . between Mao's advocacy of imbalance and decentralization and his belief in the virtues of 'overall' planning with strong central direction."

Chen Yun, agreed with Mao's report to the Eighth Party Congress; and went along with Mao's 1957 rectification movement, though perhaps with reservations.[50]

The Red Guards of the Cultural Revolution had a hard time deciding where Li stood. The great bulk of the articles attacking him then criticized only his activities during that revolution itself, which mainly centered on shielding others.[51] Li received few slanders for years of "rightist" intrigues, unlike so many other high-level cadres. Only a few Red Guard tabloids cited evidence that Li had had reservations about the Great Leap, or noted that he saw only the value of profits, and opposed the use of political departments in financial offices.[52] And some must have been at least a bit nonplussed when Li joined with Premier Zhou Enlai to request that members of the revolutionary rebel committee for central finance and trade systems not disband their group, despite the order of the Party Central Committee to dissolve all nationwide rebel organizations.[53] The function of this committee, though, was to be confined to transmitting instructions and reporting the situation in the localities.

For Mao's part, he hoped to see Li safely through the Cultural Revolution. At a meeting several months after its inception, Mao showed his solicitude by advising Li to make a self-examination before his accusers.[54] One rumor had it that Li Xiannian was a part of Mao's headquarters.[55]

Li's enthusiasm for revolutionary causes came across quite clearly in an article written on an inspection tour of the communes in September 1958, just as they were first appearing at the start of the Great Leap Forward.[56] Along with making some efforts to retain a measure of central control over finance, Li termed the establishment of communes "a great event without parallel in history," "an event of world significance," which saw the people becoming "more industrious, working with greater vigor." Moreover, through this new organizational form, Li be-

---

50. MacFarquhar, pp. 109, 244, 245, 248.

51. *BJGS*, March 22, 1967, in *RGP*, and *SCMPS*, nos. 181 (1967), pp. 2–5; 183 (1967), pp. 25–26; and 238 (1968), pp. 22–26, all only criticize Li's behavior in the Cultural Revolution, but do not mention any previous "errors."

52. *BJGS*, May 27, 1967, in *RGP*, attacks these economic views of Li's.

53. *SCMP*, no. 3899 (1967), pp. 1–3.

54. See "Talk at a Report Meeting" (24 October 1966) in Stuart Schram, ed., *Chairman Mao Talks to the People*, pp. 265–66.

55. *BJGS*, April 27, 1967.

56. Li Xiannian, "A Glance at the People's Communes," in *ECMM*, no. 149 (1958), pp. 34–39. See also Chang, *Power and Policy*, which indicates on pp. 78 and 118 that Li supported Mao on the Great Leap.

lieved that "many communes can employ their manpower, material, and financial resources still more rationally."

Several months later, discussing the theme of combining centralization with decentralization in rural finance and trade work, Li walked a thin line between too much of either as he argued mainly for strengthened state leadership under a socialist planned economy, so that revenue might be collected. Even here, he praised communism as "our great ideal," and viewed the communes as a force which would "give a further push to the rapid development of the productive power." This in turn, according to Li, would boost the circulation of commodities, a new task not initially entrusted to the communes.[57]

In that 1959 speech, even in the midst of the Leap, however, Li clung to a pet love of his—stable prices fixed by the state in a unified manner, rather than ones that "rise and drop at random." In an earlier era, at the Eighth Party Congress when Chen Yun chose to champion free sales and purchases and competition among marketing organs, there too Li had taken the bureaucrat's approach to price control: adjust individual prices to stimulate production, he said, but stability is our basic policy. All changes require careful planning and cannot be a response to market forces, was the gist of his remarks:

> It will be some time before we can carefully work out and submit to the Central Government for approval detailed plans regarding the range of price readjustments contemplated and the measures for carrying them through.[58]

Red Guards found Li to be a man who "goes back on his word":

> Li Xiannian said at one time that the leftist contingents must be thrown into a general disorder. At the other, he said: "Revolutionary rebel groups may not be disbanded but should be consolidated and expanded."[59]

Rather than being the utterances of a man of deceit, these contradictory instructions may in fact reflect two coexisting strands in Li's politics.

Another type of bureaucrat, less a revolutionary, is Yao Yilin, born of a prominent and well-to-do family.[60] Characteristic of Yao's approach to politics is what radicals termed his "shameless boast" uttered during

---

57. *HQ*, no. 2 (1959), translated in *ECMM*, no. 158 (1959), pp. 27–36.
58. Translated in *Eighth Congress*, p. 219.
59. *SCMPS*, no. 183 (1967), p. 30.
60. Klein and Clark, *Biographic Dictionary*, p. 999.

the Cultural Revolution: "We've been following the Chairman all the time, only not so closely."[61] Unlike Li, whose speeches and writings evince a genuine sense of spirit, Yao's talks in radical periods are far more stereotyped, and his stock radical phrases are always mixed with a more serious message about how to do the actual work of marketing. Another difference between the two is the fact that where Yao deviates from a pure bureaucratic stance, it is in the direction of greater marketing flexibility, and not more mass upheaval. This mix in his approach appears in this comment about him from mid-1981: "Yao Yilin rather agrees about the need to readjust some prices, but he still stresses at the same time that we must 'stabilize prices.'"[62]

During the Leap, even before the first major official reassessment was published in mid-December 1958, Yao defended planned commerce against opponents on the left (radicals who wanted to do away with profits and economic accounting) and on the right (marketeers who favored fluctuating prices).[63] So, in a time of debate and thus one of choice, Yao picked the planner's policy of unified allocation and stable prices.

Yao's openness to some market approaches appeared the next year, when he remarked that "we have used the law of value and adjusted individual prices."[64] Also, in late 1962, just after the Tenth Plenum of the Eighth Party Central Committee, Yao paid proper obeisance to Mao's concern at that time over speculation, spontaneous capitalism, and socialist education.[65] But in the same piece, he also instructed the commercial departments to "understand the market conditions and demands," and recommended that the relationship between wholesale and retail organs be "both planned and flexible." And he even went so far in the marketeer direction as to suggest the use of "handy business patterns," such as peddling in the streets, a practice difficult to divorce altogether from the "spontaneous capitalism" he attacked by rote.

Yao Yilin worked under both Chen Yun and Li Xiannian in the 1950s,[66] and is variously said to have been protected by Zhou Enlai and

61. *BJGS*, April 27, 1967.
62. See *DGB*, January 3, 1966, in *SCMP*, no. 3619 (1966), pp. 1–5, and *HQ*, no. 21 (1962), pp. 4–11, for his articles written in radical periods; *ZM*, no. 43 (May 1981), p. 48, on his more recent remark.
63. Yao Yilin, "Shangye gongzuo fangzhen de yichang bianlun" [A debate on the direction of commercial work], *HQ*, no. 13 (1958). For a closer look at this period, see the following section.
64. *RMRB*, September 28, 1959. Li Xiannian did not choose to refer to the law of value in his early 1959 article (n. 57).
65. *HQ*, no. 21 (1962), pp. 4–11.
66. Yao was vice-minister of commerce when Chen was minister in the mid-1950s; in 1959, he was made deputy director of Li's Finance and Trade Staff Office under the State

by Li Xiannian in the Cultural Revolution, apparently to no avail, as he was purged in 1967.[67] Yao returned to work first in foreign trade in 1973, earlier than many who lost their jobs in that period.

When the Second Session of the Fifth National People's Congress met in July 1979, Chen, Li, and Yao were recognized as China's three leading economic politicians, when that session created an overseer for economic affairs, the State Council's Finance and Economic Commission. Chen was made chairman, Li its vice-chairman, and Yao the secretary-general.[68] And so were joined in one organ commercial marketeer, tempered on the one side by the bureaucrat who got excited about the Great Leap Forward, and by the bureaucrat who also likes the law of value, on the other.

The brief allusion to social bases above does not necessarily help to explain why three particular individuals all affiliated with the same sector should each approach work in this area in rather different fashions. All three were born within about one decade of each other, and all joined the Party between 1924 and 1934.[69] All have served in the same general line of work since 1949, and all have been more closely tied to central-level politics than to any region. It is tempting to speculate that Li's poor peasant background and largely military pre-1949 activities inclined him to favor a plan, mitigated at moments by bouts of mobilization of the underdogs; and that Yao's upper-class origins may tilt him more toward market principles. Why Chen, the old labor organizer, should have chosen to opt for free market forces is a question that class analysis may not be able to answer.

Not only is it difficult to account for a given individual's philosophy; it is also true that most Chinese politicians are not purists, but have shown proclivities toward more than one tendency over a lifetime, or even at one time. As the discussion below unravels the course of commercial policy and the debates that formed it, it will be best not to try to

---

Council. See *I & S*, 15, no. 10 (1979): 88. Yao himself was director of the Party Central Committee's Finance and Trade Political Work Department, as well as being minister of commerce after 1960, as noted above in the text.

67. *I & S*, 15, no. 10 (1979): 89; *BJGS*, April 27, 1967.

68. *I & S*, 15, no. 10 (1979): 87–88. See n. 39 above.

69. According to Klein and Clark, Li was born in 1907, Chen in 1900, and Yao around 1915. *I & S*, 15, no. 10 (1979): 88, says that Yao was born in 1911, as does Union Research Institute, *Hierarchies of the People's Republic of China, March 1975*, p. 252. Klein and Clark say that Yao joined the Party by 1934, Li by 1927, and Chen in 1924.

assign each participant exactly or permanently to any one tendency on all issues. Rather, it will be most important to remember that three sometimes opposed, sometimes overlapping and allied tendencies have addressed most issues, and that these tendencies do find roots in society at large, if not always in the changing stances of central-level elites.

Six Episodes of Commercial Policy Making, 1949–1979

Policies in the commercial sector, and the interplay among politicians in forming them, come sharply into focus when analyzed in terms of conflicts and alliances among the three tendencies. The discussion that follows traces six important periods for commercial work, stressing the principal issue under dispute at each point—whether class, state control, or productivity—and the tendencies that were at war or in alliance over that issue at that time.[70]

For the 1950s, the conflicts behind three policies will be examined: control over the grain supply (1955); the November 1957 decentralization in commerce; and the Great Leap debates over decentralization and market forces in 1959. Later chapters will deal in depth with the other major episodes of that decade—socialist transformation (1956–1957), and the experiment in "selective purchase" of industrial products by commercial departments (1956–1957). Therefore, this chapter will not consider these themes.

For the two decades from 1960 to 1979, these three policies were chosen: the high-price policy in 1962, in the midst of the supply crisis following the Great Leap; the radical stance toward planning during the Cultural Revolution decade; and the triumph of marketeer methods in 1978.

This final section of the chapter has two aims: to outline the shape of commercial-sector politics over these thirty years; and to provide a skeletal history as a context for the material in later chapters. In sketching the interaction among the three lines, the discussion will demonstrate their existence at key historical junctures and indicate the type of issues that have engaged their proponents. This analysis will thereby create the framework for interpretation used in later chapters.

---

70. Tendency analysis posits that specific policies are made through tendency conflicts. See Griffiths, "Tendency Analysis," pp. 337, 361, 362.

TABLE 3 Highlights in the History of Commerce
in the PRC, 1949–1980

Period	Event	
1976–1980 Post-Mao Era	1980	(Dec.) Party Central Work Conference (chap. 5)
	1978	(Dec.) Third Plenum of the Eleventh Central Committee (chaps. 2, 4, 5, 6)
	1978	(June) National Conference of Departments of Finance and Trade on Learning from Daqing and Dazhai (chap. 2)
1966–1976 Cultural Revolution		(chaps. 2, 4, 5, 6)
1961–1965 Readjustment		Second experiment with free marketing (chap. 6)
	1962	(Feb.) Xilou meeting on finance and trade of Politburo Standing Committee (chap. 2)
1958–1960 Great Leap Forward	1959	(July) Lushan Plenum of Eighth Central Committee (chap. 2)
	1958	(Dec.) Wuhan Plenum of Eighth Central Committee (chap. 2)
	1957	Decentralization of commercial management (chap. 2)
1952–1957 First Five Year Plan	1956–57	First use of selective purchasing (chap. 5)
	1956–57	First experiment with free markets (chap. 6)
	1955–56	Socialist Transformation (chap. 4)
	1955	Grain supply crisis and the 3 fixes (chap. 2)
1949–1952 Period of Recovery		State battles with the still-present private sector (chaps. 3, 4)

GRAIN SUPPLY: PLANNED PURCHASE AND PLANNED SUPPLY
AND THE THREE FIXES, 1953–1955

Until the autumn of 1953, the Chinese government permitted—indeed even encouraged—the existence of a generally free market in the countryside. At that time, however, the leadership as a whole recognized that the state's purchases of grain from the peasantry had fallen far short of its needs. For, just as in the Soviet Union in the late 1920s, the large-scale industrialization program then getting under way required the state to obtain increased grain at this time. In particular, with the ambitious industrialization targets set by the First Five Year Plan, it was more important than ever to ensure food for urban and economic-crop-growing populations within China, as well as to trade grain externally to finance imports of machinery.[71] From the start, then, there was no ques-

71. Dwight H. Perkins, *Market Control and Planning in Communist China*, pp. 41 and 184. Also see Pan Ching-yuan, "Two Years of Planned Purchase and Planned Supply of

tion among the elite that state control over grain must be stepped up.

Moreover, by the time that the order for compulsory delivery was promulgated in November 1953,[72] voices raised only a few months earlier in favor of a market-style approach—using an "accurate price policy"—to get more grain for the state had been silenced.[73] Agreement had been reached that

> the method of making purchases from the market could not fit in with the new set of economic conditions ruling, and the situation became increasingly clear that fulfillment of the grain purchasing plan of the state could not be definitely ensured. . . . The quantity of grain sold by the peasants of their own accord failed to meet the purchase plans of the state.[74]

More than two decades later, one source credited Mao Zedong with having "personally taken charge of and formulated" the policy of compulsory delivery, entitled "unified purchase and unified marketing."[75]

Subsequently, over the two years following the institution of planned purchase, the debate over how to handle the state's relationship to this very central commodity turned neither on whether there ought to be state control nor on whether the market mechanism ought to be the means for obtaining this control. Instead, dispute revolved around issues of class and the nature of the rural populace. At stake were varying analyses of the class composition of the countryside, along with differing views about the flaws in existing policy, and how to rectify these flaws, which flowed from those competing class analyses.[76] The main protago-

Grain," *Xin Jianshe* [New Construction], in *ECMM*, no. 9 (1955), pp. 14–33. The same factors motivated the beginning of forcible grain procurement in the Soviet Union. See Alec Nove, *An Economic History of the U.S.S.R.*, pp. 149–50.

72. "Government Administrative Council Order on Implementing Planned Purchase and Planned Supply of Grain," in *Xinhua yuebao* [New China Monthly] (*XHYB*), no. 4 (1954), pp. 158–59, translated in *SCMP*, no. 759 (1954).

73. See editorials in *RMRB* for June 28 and September 12, 1953, advocating use of prices to procure grain.

74. *ECMM*, no. 9 (1955), p. 20. Even Chen Yun attacked the "freedom" of the free market at this time as being "only the 'freedom' to develop capitalism," in *Current Background (CB)*, no. 339, (1955), p. 13.

75. According to an article in *RMRB*, October 20, 1977, this policy was "Mao zhuxi chinzi zhuchi zhiding de."

76. Other analysts of this policy have written as if there were elite consensus on all the measures taken, altered, and taken anew on grain in this period. Thus Perkins, *Market Control*, speaks of a dilemma with respect to grain procurement faced by "the regime," and what "it" chose to do about it, on p. 42; Vivienne Shue, "Reorganizing Rural Trade," says on p. 117 that "the state" revised the purchase procedure; and Thomas P. Bernstein, "Cadre and Peasant Behavior Under Conditions of Insecurity and Deprivation," p. 368, talks of "the Party," and on p. 371 refers to "the nation's leadership."

nists were, on the one side, marketeers, and on the other, radicals.

The initial measure taken in late 1953 to deal with the problem of grain supply required that peasants sell their "excess grain" (a concept undefined in the regulations) to the state at state-set prices, beyond what they had already handed over in the form of taxes.[77] Quotas were fixed by region, and at the lowest or village level the peasants themselves were to apportion the quota by a method of "democratic assessment." Any grain that might be left in a peasant's hands when this process was completed could be sold in state-supervised grain markets, set up in force in spring 1954.[78]

By early 1955, however, it became clear that several elements had combined to produce a situation of real chaos in grain procurement. Chief among these elements were higher-level pressures on cadres to collect more grain, combined with peasant insecurities caused by vaguely specified and so seemingly limitless state purchases. Excessive purchases victimized some peasants; other peasants, anxious about whether they could really depend on the state, cried out for more supply than they genuinely needed.[79] The result was a serious grain-supply crisis acknowledged in print by all shades of opinion.

Over the months March through August 1955, a leadership debate ensued,[80] during which two interim documents emerged, one marketeer-inspired in early March, and one from a radical perspective in late April.[81] Discussion continued throughout the summer, and at last, in late August, the full-blown and final version of the "three fixes" policy (fixed production, purchases, and sales) appeared.[82]

The March measure showed concern over "unfavorable effects on production," and "market stagnancy and the slow interflow of goods." It called both for a reduction in the degree and pace of agricultural cooperativization, and for the distribution of grain quotas to the township level at the time of spring plowing in targets that would not change in a normal year. The stated goal was to improve peasant morale

---

77. Bernstein offers a fascinating and thorough account of the changes in policy and rural reactions to them at peasant and cadre level. See also *ECMM*, no. 9 (1955), pp. 14–33.

78. See n. 72 above.

79. Bernstein, pp. 370–80.

80. The debate is referred to in *Xuexi* [Study] (*XX*), no. 9 (1955), p. 29.

81. The March document is "State Council Decision on Spring Plowing and Production" (March 3, 1955), in *CB*, no. 318 (1955), pp. 1–7; the April document is "State Council and CCP Central Committee Directive on Intensified Reorganization of Planned Marketing of Grain" (April 28, 1955), in *SCMP*, no. 1041 (1955), pp. 24–26.

82. "State Council Provisional Measures for Unified Purchase and Unified Supply of Grain in Rural Districts" and "Provisional Measures for Fixed Supply of Grain in Towns" (August 25, 1955), in *CB*, no. 354 (1955).

through providing some sense of certainty about the amount of state purchase, and so to stimulate enthusiasm for production. The April decree, however, changed the focus, emphasizing that excessive grain sales by state cadres to some peasants, and not insufficient supplies, lay at the heart of the problem. This notice called for mobilization and political work, geared to "compressing unjustified sales." The final "three fix" directive in August, a victory for market proponents, provided instead for incentives aimed at encouraging more output.

Fueling the debate on how to obtain more grain for the state were two radically opposed visions of the class situation in the countryside. Available documents offer no evidence that Mao Zedong was involved specifically in the grain procurement aspect of this controversy; however, it is significant that he made his provocative speech on the closely linked issue of agricultural cooperativization, with its recurrent theme of class polarization, just at this time.

Mao's deep concern for the poor and lower-middle peasantry in that address was tied to his perception that these groups constituted "the great majority" in the countryside. To Mao, the poor were pitted against the well-to-do or fairly well-to-do who, Mao calculated, amounted to a mere 20 or 30 percent of the rural population. For him, capitalist ownership by the rich and poverty for the poor characterized the rural landscape then. Moreover, Mao saw the enthusiasm of the poor for socialist cooperativization as being boundless.[83] In striking contrast, a speech by Chen Yun inspired this analysis:

> After land reform in the older liberated areas, new and old middle peasants account for 70 to 80 percent of the population; in the later liberated areas, these groups account for 60 percent. . . . This group is capable of tipping the scale because of its sensitive position in the rural areas.[84]

The positions taken by the two sides amounted to an eerie replay of differences on the same theme between Stalin and Bukharin in the late

---

83. Mao Zedong, "On the Cooperative Transformation of Agriculture," *Selected Works,* vol. 5, pp. 188, 195, 201, 202. For an effort to assess the accuracy of Mao's views on polarization, see Mark Selden, "Cooperation and Conflict: Cooperative and Collective Formation in China's Countryside," especially pp. 58–67.

84. *XX,* no. 9 (1955), p. 26. The article, by Li Siheng and Wu Shuo, on the three fixes, is subtitled, "Some Understanding on Studying Vice Premier Chen Yun's speech 'On questions of the Unified Purchase and Distribution of Grain.'" Chen himself did not offer this breakdown of the population in the speech these authors were studying.

1920s.[85] Based on their class analysis, radicals consistently accounted for the grain supply crisis in terms of sabotage by "class enemies"—landlords, rich peasants, and hidden counterrevolutionaries. Radicals, noting that these groups were the ones most disadvantaged by state control over the grain market, believed they were trying to subvert this policy. Class enemies caused the crisis, radicals thought, through spreading rumors, making rush purchases, buying at low prices and selling at high ones, and hoarding.[86]

Marketeers, in striking contrast, had something, but much less, to say about such troublemakers. When they spoke of class, it was principally to stress the importance of a firm union with the middle peasantry; or to excuse the masses of peasants, whom they saw as being mainly small producers in mentality, accustomed to disposing of their grain on the open market, even if that meant at times suffering at the hands of the more well-to-do merchants.[87]

Radicals saw the problem as one of a "two-line struggle" between conflicting classes. For them, then, the issue was to bring to a halt the phenomenon they perceived—of nondeficit peasants purchasing from the state grain that they did not need; and to cut back basic-level cadre "collusion" with such sales.[88] Their effort at reorganization in April retained the leftist thrust of the original 1953 policy. That is, township-level congresses and mass meetings were to be used to present supply figures to the masses of peasantry, who were then to deliberate over their distribution. Propaganda to raise political awareness would inform these mass assessments. The main goals in the April document seem difficult, if not impossible, to accomplish simultaneously: to reduce

85. Stalin held that the better-off peasants were able to maneuver more effectively than their poorer neighbors to take advantage of any possibility of obtaining better terms, and so saw them as responsible for hoarding and thereby creating grain shortages (Nove, *Economic History*, p. 149); Bukharin pointed instead to the disincentive effect of state price policies and the primitive state of peasant agriculture (Cohen, *Bukharin*, p. 317).

86. See *SCMP*, nos. 1041, pp. 24–26; 1043, pp. 8–11; 1056, pp. 15–17; and 1083, pp. 13–17 (all are 1955); *ECMM*, no. 31 (1956), pp. 11–18; and *XX*, no. 14 (1957), pp. 14–16. Also, Bernstein, pp. 382–85.

87. See *RMRB*, May 18, 1954, which says that planned purchase cannot eliminate commodity exchange entirely because of the large number of small peasant owners in China; also, *XX*, no. 9 (1955), pp. 25–28; and *ECMM*, no. 9 (1955), pp. 2, 17, 22. Chen Yun in *CB*, no. 339 (1955), pp. 3–14, in his speech on grain supply at the Second Session of the First National People's Congress, described the "more general, more important cause of the tense [grain] situation" in this way: "The peasants are not yet accustomed to government measures of unified purchase and distribution of grain. The peasants are individual small producers, and for thousands of years have cultivated the habit of at least formally disposing of their surplus grain freely."

88. *SCMP*, no. 1056 (1955), pp. 15–17.

state grain sales to the peasantry drastically—by up to 50 percent—and at the same time to ensure that peasants actually in need be given adequate supplies.[89] It is hard to imagine that large-scale starvation would not have been the outcome had their views prevailed.

Marketeers, on the other hand, saw the chief difficulty as one not of class sabotage but of insufficient incentives. Chen Yun, for one, speaking on grain supply in July at the Second Session of the First National People's Congress, concentrated on the need, in "bringing about a fundamental improvement" of the crisis, to increase the output of grain, a solution not mentioned by the radicals. In his view, "the government should adopt necessary measures to reach agreement with the peasants." Chen went on to propose a set of steps that involved allowing the peasantry to retain some of their surplus (defined according to the normal harvest) and setting output norms that remained constant for three years, pegged to the household level. This approach was to reassure the peasants that more production would not mean more state purchases; it would "set the peasants at ease . . . promote their active zeal for production."[90]

The final resolution of this round of debate, which came in late August, followed exactly these measures put forward by Chen Yun in July. The finesse with which the victorious marketeers managed to save face for the losers in the editorials accompanying their August directive could easily convince observers that a unanimous officialdom had steered through this crisis in unison. Thus, the crisis was blamed, not on past wrong policy, but on the fact that "small peasant farming . . . made it difficult to ascertain fully the production, requirements, surplus, and shortage of grain" and that, when the grain policy was first instituted in 1953, "tasks were so heavy, time so pressing, and experience so lacking that it was impossible to ascertain grain output and the position as regards surplus and shortage of grain in the hands of the peasants." Practice had proven, one editorial explained, that the main defect had been a lack of "necessary concrete systems and measures." To remedy this deficiency, the three fixes were offered as a means of "persisting in policy," better to realize the spirit of the initial planned purchase of 1953.[91]

In this particular battle, then, two groups of opponents, each seeing a different class as the majority force in the countryside, and each assess-

89. *SCMP*, nos. 1041, (1955), pp. 24–26, and 1043 (1955), pp. 8–11.
90. *CB*, no. 339 (1955), pp. 9–10.
91. *RMRB* editorials on August 25 and 29, 1955, in *CB*, no. 354 (1955). See especially pp. 15, 21, 22; *XX*, no. 9 (1955), p. 25. Much of the language here, such as that on the effect of small peasant farming on making administration of the policy difficult, also appears in Chen's July address.

ing peasant proclivities for socialism quite differently, agreed on the goal of channeling more goods—in this case, grain—to the state. Radicals thought this could best be accomplished by divesting "class enemies" of their excesses, rather than by encouraging more production, and emphasized that the needy must be involved in the process of quota setting. They based this prescription on a belief that any enhanced output, if not surrendered to the state, would be (as it was then being, they thought) hoarded by the better-off. Trusting the state more than the monied, they expected that only this method could assure the indigent of their basic supplies.

In fact, however, the radicals' defeat in this round may have meant more food for everyone, since Chen Yun's measures enabled all peasants to retain a portion of their grain. For marketeers, believing as always that through increased output lay the solution to supply shortage, wrote their policy platform in the hope that proper incentives would reassure and spur on the small producers to grow and then to give over more grain.

DECENTRALIZATION OF
COMMERCIAL MANAGEMENT, 1957

In October 1957, the Third Plenum of the Party's Eighth Central Committee passed three sets of regulations on the economy. These were directed, respectively, at improving the management systems in industry, commerce, and finance. The three documents were approved in November by the Standing Committee of the National People's Congress and were issued as State Council directives.[92] Previous analysts of the political climate surrounding this meeting connect the decisions with what they consider to have been a power struggle over the issue of decentralization.[93] It is probably true that some conflict existed in higher Party echelons in late 1957.[94] However, insofar as serious debate surrounded the decision on commercial management, it was definitely not over issues of state control—not, that is, related to the subject of central versus local power.[95]

92. These are translated in *SCMP*, no. 1665 (1959). The regulations for commerce are on pp. 6–8.

93. Franz Schurmann, *Ideology and Organization in Communist China*, pp. 86, 195, 198, 208, 354, and Chang, *Power and Policy*, pp. 37–40, 53–57. Schurmann saw it as a "disagreement on how to modify centralism" (p. 86); Chang found the crux of the matter to be "whether central or local authorities would exercise ultimate power over many matters" (p. 53).

94. In particular, as Chang points out, there may have been disagreement over the Twelve-Year Agricultural Program. See Chang, chap. 1.

95. Here my views are closer to Schurmann's as cited in n. 93, except when he states that "the Ministry of Commerce was the great loser," on p. 298. Audrey Donnithorne, in *China's*

As the *People's Daily* editorial accompanying the publication of the regulations points out, the leadership had been agreed on the working out of some program of decentralization of power from at least as early as Mao's April 1956 speech on "The Ten Great Relations."[96] In the course of the year and a half following Mao's speech, a series of conferences and many discussion meetings, including the Eighth Party Congress in September 1956,[97] worked out the arrangements to be used to realize the transfer of powers.[98]

Of the remaining two topics which draw debate in commercial policy circles, class was not an issue at this time. The remaining issue, whether market forces should be allowed to guide a socialist economy, was the one that came into play. Whereas radicals and marketeers had battled over class issues in 1955, this time they were united on the need to devolve authority, but disagreed as to the reasons for doing so. Radicals favored decentralizing to give local administrative and Party units more initiative and input into policy making, in accord with Mao's mass-line approach; marketeers thought in terms of bolstering the autonomous activity of enterprises in the market. The regulations that issued from the Third Plenum and the editorial explaining them represented a fine blend of the two approaches, as the discussion below reveals.

The decision itself had seven major sections, declaring, respectively, that (1) local commercial organs should be established by local governments in accord with local conditions, and administrative and operational units should be merged; (2) wholesaling stations should be placed under dual central and local leadership, where they had been under only one higher-level unit before; (3) most processing enterprises be handed over to local governments; (4) centrally dictated targets in commercial work be reduced to four, of which the profit target be kept secret from the subprovincial units; (5) enterprise profits be divided in an 80–20 ratio between center and locality; (6) localities be granted some authority in price control; and (7) foreign exchange be shared between center and locality.

Because on the surface it appears that the document decrees that much power shall devolve to the lowest administrative levels, observers

---

Economic System, p. 288, with whom I also disagree, says the same thing Schurmann does on this last point.

96. *RMRB*, November 18, 1957, in *SCMP*, no. 1665 (1957), pp. 10–14. See p. 13, where Mao's speech is referred to as Mao's "Mobilizing All Forces to Serve Socialism."

97. The speeches of Chen Yun, Li Fuchun, and Liu Shaoqi at the Eighth Party Congress bear this theme, to name a few.

98. *SCMP*, no. 1665, pp. 10–14.

(Schurmann and Donnithorne, to name two) have concluded that the central-level Ministry of Commerce, and, by implication, its minister, then Chen Yun, lost a great deal of authority. In fact, however, this conclusion is in error, for three reasons.

Most important, Chen himself was behind this decision, and if his ministry was weakened, it was an outcome he chose to produce. Indirect evidence for this conclusion abounds. For the spirit of the November decision is clearly foreshadowed in remarks by Chen himself in late 1956 and at the Third Plenum; in decisions made at a meeting of the Ministry of Commerce itself earlier in the year; and also in an article in the journal *Planned Economy*, written by Xue Muqiao and quoting Chen Yun, which appeared in September 1957, just before the Third Plenum met.[99] These various clues show that Chen and his ministry authored the decision, and were not its victim.

The second error is a notion that the powers of the Ministry of Commerce were significantly undercut by the new regulations. In fact, although the rigid hierarchical control previously entrusted to that office may have been loosened, the document speaks for giving the ministry a different kind of power. This new power left more scope for the market, as it involved only central "guidance," "management," and the authority to bestow "approval" on the activities of lower-level units. And the third error in earlier analyses lies in assuming that Chen Yun would have opposed the decentralization measures in the provisions. This conclusion is probably wrong, because there was little here about which a good marketeer could disagree.

The proposals of the commercial conference held in February and March 1957 were undoubtedly approved if not initiated by Chen, then just recently (in October 1956) made minister of commerce; and indeed,

---

99. Chen Yun's remarks at a Ministry of Commerce meeting held in November 1956 and at the Third Plenum can be found in *Comrade Chen Yun*, pp. 20–33 and 58–59, respectively. The 1957 meeting, the Seventh Conference of the Directors of City Commercial Departments and Bureaus, was held February 16–March 5, to set the direction for commercial work for 1957. Its deliberations are reported in *SCMP*, nos. 1485 (1957), p. 6, and 1492 (1957), pp. 7–9. The article by Xue is "Dui xianxing jihua guanli zhidu de zhubu yijian" [Preliminary opinions on implementing the planned management system], *Jihua jingji* [Planned Economy] (*JHJJ*), no. 9 (1957), pp. 20–24. Both Schurmann, *Ideology and Organization*, p. 197, and Chang, pp. 54–55, interpreted this article in a manner which led them to think that Chen's plan, described therein, was shelved at the Third Plenum. In fact, the November decisions bear much of the imprint of this article, as far as commercial work is concerned. For one thing, Xue proposes (on p. 24) that "state commercial *departments*" (emphasis added) (*guojia shangye bumen*) use processing and ordering, sales and purchases, rather than plans, to deal with less important products. He nowhere refers to the Ministry of Commerce (*shangyebu*) as Schurmann claims. Schurmann's error lies in translating this passage as "The Ministry of Commerce would exercise regulatory control

they repeat themes in his own speeches of late 1956.[100] The great irony of Chen's ministership, which emerges sharply from the recommendations made at that meeting, has escaped most scholars: Chen, wearing his marketeer hat, did not seek greater power for his ministry. Rather, he tried to use his stewardship as minister as a means of realizing his ideas for the organization of the national economy: injecting more market principles, and less bureaucracy, into the commercial sector.

Thus, this March meeting called for less centralization and more powers for local authorities. Local enterprises, it held, should come under the control of provincial and county governments. While the Ministry of Commerce was to retain "overall national leadership," it was to "concentrate only on guiding the big trading enterprises which were under direct central control." Also, commercial departments were to be merged with enterprises, in the interests of reducing administrative staff. Big trading companies under central control were to be limited in their work to placing orders and ensuring wholesale distribution.

In fact, the first three articles in the November decision followed these guidelines rather closely. Only the principles of dual leadership over wholesaling stations, and the handing over of the smaller-scale, centrally run processing enterprises to the localities, increased the degree of decentralization over what had been planned in March. These points, however, jibe well with Xue's article of September, which recommended "management by levels" and giving "local Party and government powers of supervision over centrally managed enterprises and facilities." The Third Plenum decision also retained the March meeting's principles of placing local control over local enterprises and of merging administrative with operational work.

One difference between the March deliberations and the November regulations lies in the fact that only the November meeting prescribed that local branches of the state companies be merged with local com-

---

through the medium of interenterprise contracts." Since Xue (read Chen) never granted powers to the ministry in the *JHJJ* article, the November decision, in also not referring to the ministry, did not contravene his ideas. The thrust of that article is a proposal to have less planning and control from above and more initiative taken by departments, localities, and enterprises directly in charge of economic work at lower levels. That also is the spirit of the November decision. One interesting point both share is the introduction of "flexible" and "nonflexible" targets in industry (*JHJJ*, no. 9 [1957], p. 23, and *SCMP*, no. 1665 [1957], p. 4), an idea that came into vogue again in the late 1970s and early 1980s.

100. *Comrade Chen Yun*, pp. 20–33. In two speeches, both delivered in November 1956, Chen calls for simplifying the work system in the commercial sector; complains that there are too many links in commercial operations; and says that, though concentration is necessary, there has been too much of it in commerce lately (see pp. 23, 29, 30, and 31).

mercial administrative organs or else abolished.[101] But, in mid-September, just before the Third Plenum was held, the journal *Commercial Work*, the organ of the Ministry of Commerce, announced that beginning from 1958,

> a considerable part of the commodities required for supply to the market and subject to unified distribution and control by the ministry ... are to be incorporated into the commodity supply plans of the provinces, autonomous regions, and municipalities directly under the Central Government ... so that plans can be brought into conformity with the actual conditions.[102]

Since the state companies and their branches are in charge of supplying commodities to the market, implementing this recommendation would have amounted to the elimination of the companies. Thus, again, a decrease in the power of central-level commercial organs was called for by the commercial sector itself, under Chen Yun's command, and was not a result of a leftist victory at the Third Plenum in October, as earlier analysts claimed.

A second distinction between the November regulations and the decision of the commercial conference in March was that the March conference explicitly commanded that "the unified leadership of the state" be exercised even while power was delegated to the lower levels, whereas the November document makes no mention of this principle. This difference, more apparent than real, is the source of the second error previous analysts have made (i.e., the incorrect belief that the ministry lost clout in November). For the March meeting, the September *Commercial Work* essay, the third article of the November regulations, and the *People's Daily* editorial publicizing the November regulations all refer to Chen Yun's particular brand of centralism.[103] This is a system in which

101. Donnithorne, *China's Economic System*, p. 288, n. 4, points out that in the wake of this decision the companies were altogether abolished until 1962, at the national level as well. Probably this occurred during the Great Leap Forward. See chap. 1, n. 78.

102. "Why Are Supply Plans for Certain Commodities Under Unified Distribution and Ministry Control To Be Placed in the Hands of Provincial and Municipal Governments?" *Shangye gongzuo* [Commercial Work], no. 37 (September 12, 1957), in *ECMM*, no. 151 (1958), pp. 38–42. Chang, pp. 38–39, and Schurmann, *Ideology*, p. 197, both say that "conservatives" or the "material incentives" group were still in command through September, and if they are correct, this first article, which matches the Third Plenum decision, presumably was not written under "leftist" pressure. *SCMP*, no. 1226 (1956), p. 16, states that *Commercial Work* is the organ of the Ministry of Commerce.

103. This view appears in Chen's article in *HQ*, no. 5 (1959), on "Some Immediate Problems Concerning Capital Construction," in *ECMM*, no. 166 (1959), pp. 1–15, and in *Comrade Chen Yun*, pp. 58–59 and 166. On p. 58, from his speech at the Third Plenum,

national priorities determine how material supplies ought to be "balanced" in the various localities on a national scale. Such "balancing" does not necessarily entail planning through strict vertical hierarchies of allocation. It is best described in the editorial:

> Together with the decentralization of authority it is necessary to further strengthen our work in comprehensive balancing ... enable the local authorities to decide questions according to local circumstances and within certain scope, and not to upset the comprehensive balance;

and in Xue's piece in *Planned Economy*:

> Overall management does not mean the center directly managing all economic activity, or that we need more planning charts and norms, so that we should enter all economic life wholly onto planning tables.

Moreover, every one of the seven sections of the November State Council directive refers to central oversight powers: in the first, "regarding administrative principles and policies [local commercial organs] must still accept guidance from commercial departments to which they were former subordinates." The dual leadership of the second article sees central departments as the principal authority, and since it is barely different from Xue's September essay, it must have had Chen Yun's endorsement.

In the third section, "production tasks, specifications and standards, adjustments of the capacity of production installations, and processing expenses are still to be managed in a unified manner by various central commercial departments." And in the fourth and sixth, respectively, central approval is required for any changes in targets; and local-level price setting must be based on price levels or price-fixing principles set in Beijing. It is clear that the Ministry of Commerce held on to a far larger share of power than it may seem at first glance, and that this retained power was of a sort that Chen Yun saw as proper for a bureaucracy that managed trade.

The third error of earlier observers concerns the last three articles of the November decision, which give explicit powers to echelons below

---

for example, there are these words: "Expanding local authority is completely necessary. ... But we must also strengthen national balance work.... On the one hand, appropriately divide power, but at the same time also strengthen synthesis. We think, after dividing power, balance work oughtn't to be weakened, but should be greatly strengthened." Also see n. 42.

the center. Those observers assume that Chen Yun, in his role as central bureaucrat, would have tried to counter these designs; and that their inclusion is proof of Chen's loss of authority. Indeed, perhaps the greatest differences between decisions reached by the ministry before the Third Plenum and those made during the Plenum are those having to do with the material incentives offered to lower-level units—the profit sharing, the price-setting power, and the foreign exchange allotment given to localities in November in articles five, six, and seven.

But here as well, the conveners of the March conference of the Ministry of Commerce, if not themselves the authors of the articles, would have found nothing to argue about. For the marketeer mood of that March meeting called for a delegation of power expressly "to bring the establishment of commercial enterprises into conformity with local expediency to facilitate purchase and business accounting." And that forum also advised "organizing the sources of goods in accord with market demand." Both these recommendations contain the concern for enlivening the commercial spirit of local-level administrative units and enterprises which is the hallmark of the marketeer approach, and which fits perfectly with the November proposals to increase the material incentives given to the localities.

In fact, probably the only purely radical element in the November decision is the fourth article's order that

> profit norms be transmitted downward only to the level of the province . . . and will not be transmitted to the basic-level enterprises, in order to prevent basic-level shops from engaging in activities in violation of commercial policies while trying to fulfill the targets of profits.

This rule, inspired by a fear of profit seeking, was later attacked by Yao Yilin in late 1958 as one of a batch of apparently radical suggestions that he said had been put forward on the pretext of "representing the masses' interests."[104]

No cutback in strength was suffered by Chen Yun and his ministry at the Third Plenum; instead, through the course of 1957, Chen himself had laid the foundation for much of the material that issued in the November decisions. He thereby managed to fashion a formula that, he hoped, would lay a basis for a loosening up in the top-heavy, vertically ordered hierarchy that had done business in the PRC up to that time.

104. Yao Yilin, *HQ*, no. 13 (1958).

The principal difference between Chen and the radicals[105] comes across in a careful reading of the *People's Daily* editorial on the Plenary directives. There two quite different views on the meaning behind and the value of decentralization are set forth. The piece begins with an appeal to radical values of mass spontaneity: decentralization is to "enhance the initiative and positiveness of local government." And, in its second paragraph, it discusses in typically Maoist form the pros and cons of centralization (too much will "divorce us from the masses, isolate us from reality, and give birth to bureaucratism") and of decentralization (an excess here will produce "extreme democratization, departmentalism and bias, disunity and disorder").

The document goes on, however, to allude to a marketeer's more economics-oriented understanding of the need for delegation: "The plan cannot be fixed rigidly . . . we can only fix the general outline and major items, and let local authorities determine the details according to local circumstances"; and

> as a result of the economic development of various regions, and particularly owing to the appearance of a number of new industrial areas, local governments need comparatively more authority to arrange the economic life of their respective districts and regulate the mutual relations between various enterprises in their districts.[106]

It is in these varying justifications for deputation that two lines, not necessarily always hostile to each other, emerge, one focused on mass participation, the other on comparative advantage. But their agreement here led to the introduction of less centralization into the management of the economy at that time.

The first section of this chapter indicated that there are grounds for alliance between radical and marketeer: they agree on the value of de-

---

105. Chang, p. 39, speaks of a victory by Mao and his radical faction. But even the Red Guards during the Cultural Revolution grasped the superficial similarity of radical and marketeer on the issue of decentralization, as the following attack on Chen Yun evidences: "Dwelling on the ten major relationships in 1956 Chairman Mao proposed that power be given to the localities so as to facilitate production and construction. In view of Chairman Mao's directive and the demand of the masses, Chen Yun was obliged to release power. He sponsored revision of the financial system and maliciously took a measure for releasing power extensively to undermine the state plan. This was actually a line 'Left' in form but Right in substance." In *SCMPS*, no. 232 (1968), p. 29.

106. *RMRB*, November 18, 1957. Chen Yun's Eighth Party Congress address contained the first marketeer-type point here; the article in *Commercial Work* cited in n. 102 above advocates the second.

centralization and some local autonomy, for instance. The 1957 commercial management decision represents their temporary union, even if each side joined the other for reasons of its own. Its significance lies also in the evidence it offers that Chen Yun, who places faith in market strategies, did not as a central bureaucrat, ipso facto, fight for more powers for central organs.

THE GREAT LEAP FORWARD, 1958–1959

The popular mode of analyzing Chinese policy conflicts in terms of a duality—radicals versus moderates, ideologues versus pragmatists—proves especially inadequate in any attempt to understand the leadership line-up in the course of the Great Leap Forward. On the eve of the Leap and in its earlier months, the bureaucrat Li Xiannian supported this radical scheme of Mao's.[107] By late 1958, however, as problems and difficulties mounted, and especially in the months that followed December's Sixth Plenum of the Eighth Party Central Committee (the Wuhan Plenum), a distinct bureaucrat line emerged in clear opposition to marketeers on its right and to radicals on the left.[108]

Class issues did not enter the debate at this time. And though the topic of market exchange filtered through the various formulations, state control was the focus of contention. In terms of the battle for goods, the crux of the issue may be framed in this way: should the larger

107. Chang, pp. 78, 118. See also discussion above of Li's autumn 1958 article on the Leap, written after his inspection tour of the communes (n. 56).

108. Mao's essay on Stalin's economic theories, *A Critique of Soviet Economics*, written sometime in 1959, takes a stance on commerce closer to bureaucrat Li's than to the extreme radicalism criticized below by Li and Yao Yilin and by the theoretical articles of the period. Critiques of the Leap that surfaced in the late 1970s attack Chen Boda for authoring the most radical theories and policies of that time. Radicals and marketeers were clearly distinct on the eve of the Leap. MacFarquhar, *Origins of Cultural Revolution*, p. 61, refers to an April 1956 quarrel between Mao and Chen Yun over the need for financial stringency in an economic drive. In this argument, according to a Red Guard document, Chen said, "To only emphasize *the small things* and not to emphasize the *big things* is wrong, but only to emphasize the big things and not to emphasize the small things is also wrong. Both should be emphasized." I take this to reflect a radical-marketeer debate between the two that ultimately led to Chen's setback as the Leap began. Nearly two years after the conflict on which MacFarquhar reports, *RMRB*, on March 12, 1958, printed an article which read, "If the commercial departments set out from narrow economic accounting and, each time they do something, consider whether it will lose money, only calculating *small accounts*; if they don't consider how to serve production and consumption better and don't calculate *larger accounts* from a political standpoint, they won't be able to develop production actively and so will harm the consumers' interests." (Emphasis added.) It will be recalled that Chen was minister of commerce at this time, so that this article could well be indicative of a long-standing quarrel between Chen and Mao that continued up to the eve of the Leap.

state with its plans and hierarchies regulate the flow of goods, or should the commune, through a free supply system based on self-sufficiency, manage its own goods. A subissue concerned the role of the law of value in drawing up the plan. Virtually all the published documents from the period press for planned control and argue against both direct distribution (desired by radicals) and against more market-based exchange (advocated by marketeers).

Even before the stock-taking Wuhan Plenum thrashed out a planner's reassessment of the direction in which the Great Leap and its commune movement had been going, Yao Yilin, then vice-minister of commerce, published an article in *Red Flag* journal defending China's socialist planned economy against critics from both the left and the right.[109] "Some comrades" (obviously radicals), Yao charged, claiming to "represent the masses' interests," used the occasion of the Leap to clamor against commercial departments calculating profits, or indeed doing economic accounting of any kind. Their complaint, echoed years later in the Cultural Revolution, was that "all the eight hundred thousand commercial personnel work only for profits." This radical group, associated with Mao's confidant Chen Boda, viewed the Leap as a bound into communist society and hoped that financial calculations could immediately be abolished. For them, Yao explained that "commercial, like other economic departments, ought to have responsibility for raising capital accumulation for the state in order to make possible expanded reproduction."[110]

Marketeers too had to be silenced by Yao. It was undoubtedly a set of individuals with a marketeer bias whom Yao described as opposing the Party's stable-price system for its harmful effect on production, and slandering its policy of unified allocation of key commodities. Against these arguments Yao defended price stability and unified purchasing and marketing as the socialist system's special points of superiority, necessary for the present and also into the future. His support for the planned economy was absolute and unflinching.

Within a month of the appearance of Yao's article, at the conclusion of the Wuhan Plenum, the Party Central Committee and the State Coun-

109. See n. 63 above. The Wuhan Plenum ended on December 10, and its resolution on the finance and trade system was released on December 22 (in *RMRB*, December 23, 1958). The Wuhan Plenum was the Party's first effort to deal with the management difficulties arising in the communes. See Chang, pp. 101–5.

110. Radicals apparently even believed that plans should be dispensed with: "After the formation of communes, some comrades think commodity circulation will increasingly decrease in scale . . . that there will be no need to draw up commodity circulation plans." See *ECMM*, no. 192 (1959), pp. 38–42. On this theme, see section below on radicals and the Cultural Revolution.

cil issued a decision on improving financial and trade administration in the communes,[111] which was composed in light of the Wuhan Resolution's reevaluation of the Leap.[112] This document's emphasis on the reassertion of upper-level controls over all aspects of commune management comes across in several ways, all of which involve steering a definite path between radical and marketeer.

In the first place, the decision reaffirms the Wuhan Resolution's proclamation that both self-sufficient and exchange-oriented (commodity) production must occur in the communes. Radicals favored self-sufficiency (and therefore banned markets), as they had hoped to "enter communism" prematurely, the Wuhan meeting concluded. They consequently "tried to abolish the production and exchange of commodities too early and to negate at too soon a stage the possible roles of commodities, value, money, and prices [Marx's 'economic categories']."[113] Thus, even as early as December 1958, only a few months after the Leap began, policies were already being recast in an attempt to counter the massive dislocations and insufficient supplies that were already the effect of these radical initiatives.

But this reference to economic categories did not mean that the time had come for marketeers to get their satisfaction, either. A new system—the "two transfers, three unifications, and one guarantee"—was instituted to ensure that the communes would have no opportunity to strike out on business ventures independently of the overarching state plan.[114] Through the two transfers, experienced county-level financial and trade personnel were sent to the countryside to administer commune budgetary work. They were charged with seeing that communes did not use the new license to engage in commodity exchange as a way to derive income from commercial profits. They were also to oversee enforcement of state-fixed prices in commune transactions: "The transfer of commercial organizations to the lower level should serve to strengthen state market control and planned control instead of weaken-

111. "Decision of the CCP Central Committee and the State Council on Improvement of Financial and Trade Administration in Rural Areas so as to Meet the Situation Arising from Establishment of People's Communes" (hereafter, "Improvement of Finance and Trade"), translated in Union Research Institute, *Documents of the Chinese Communist Party Central Committee 1956–1969* (hereafter, *CCP Documents*), vol. 1, pp. 619–27.

112. The Wuhan Resolution is translated in Robert R. Bowie and John K. Fairbank, *Communist China 1955–1959: Policy Documents with Analysis,* pp. 488–503. Its full title is "Resolution on Some Questions Concerning the People's Communes."

113. Ibid., p. 497.

114. Two transfers were personnel and assets; three unifications meant unified policy and plan, and unified control of working funds; and one guarantee was the guarantee of financial obligations to the state.

ing them."[115] Moreover, the establishment of the communes had brought in its wake the "basic nonexistence of the free market," and the Wuhan Resolution reaffirmed and did not challenge this.[116]

Since there were to be no free exchanges between communes, then, the Wuhan meeting (and the press in subsequent months) decreed that a kind of state-directed contract be used extensively instead—between communes, between the state commercial organs and the communes, and between state-owned factories and the communes. According to an essay by Li Xiannian,

> if a commune has to sell some secondary miscellaneous products or buy some special articles, which the commercial organ at the superior level cannot purchase or supply, it may, under the guidance of the commercial organ at the superior level, enter into contract with some other commune for such an interflow.[117]

Rather than contracts representing market freedoms for lower levels, however, their advocates presumed that under state guidance the contracts could actually extend the scope of what higher-level units could plan in rural production and exchange—they would make communes "aware beforehand of what and how much the state would require of them to produce and sell . . . and what means of production, what means of subsistence and how much the state can supply." Moreover, contracts were eventually to be extended to cover even minor products not included in the state plan. Besides facilitating and extending planning, the contract system was to substitute for the market as well: it would ensure an outlet for goods and so stimulate production. The contract was also to serve as a "reliable guarantee for the supply of goods" and a means of preventing disequilibrium between supply and demand.[118]

As these decisions of the bureaucrats settled, the press told of three sorts of repercussions among officials: one in Beijing, one at the basic levels, and one in the realm of theoretical discussion. First of all, in his January *Hong Qi* article, Li Xiannian pointed to remaining doubters among the central leadership whom he hoped to silence.[119] Some, he claimed, were conservative (more bureaucratic and supportive of verti-

---

115. "Improvement of Finance and Trade," p. 623.
116. Ibid., p. 620.
117. Li Xiannian, *HQ*, no. 2 (1959), in *ECMM*, no. 158 (1959), p. 30.
118. See *SCMP*, nos. 1980, pp. 8–29, and 2009, pp. 14–15 (1959).
119. Li, *HQ*, no. 2 (1959). The wording of this article is so nearly the same as that in the "Improvement" decision that one must conclude that one hand (or group of hands?) composed both.

cal command than he, for our purposes), and, "their thinking lagging behind reality," wondered whether decentralization was advisable.

A second group of skeptics, who could have been either radical or market-prone, whom Li called "departmental," were dubious about the necessity of unification; and a third group, clearly radicals, "think too naively, believing that since the commune is to bear the entire profit or loss it is doubtful whether the commune needs economic calculation within itself." To all of these Li extolled his vision of a properly working bureaucracy: decentralization to stimulate activism in the communes; unification to ensure that the state's unified leadership will "meet the demands of the socialist planned economy."

At levels below that of the central decision-making echelon, another group of cadres, those in the field, had their own reactions. From Li's words it appears that the state-sector cadres transferred to work in the communes became a force fighting for more hierarchy than Li himself favored.[120] For these people felt they were being demoted, that the state-run bureaucracy was suffering a retreat as its workers joined the organs of the collectively run rural sector. Some sensed chaos in the offing; others feared that the denuded county-level organs would have nothing to do.

Li had to reassure these workers that, regardless of the physical reassignment of personnel, this was a step forward from collective to whole-people's ownership, increasing the element of whole-people's ownership within the communes by strengthening state leadership there. Moreover, these cadres were promised, the financial and trade departments at various levels would have more responsibilities than before, as they offered assistance to the commune workers in business leadership, technical matters, cadre training, and supervision.

The third after-effect of the Wuhan meeting was a kind of free-for-all debate on the role of the law of value (thus, of allowing profit criteria to guide production and allocation decisions) and the permissible scope for commodity-exchange (of exchange through market/monetary transactions)[121] within a socialist society. As chapter one indicated, a certain ambiguity on these issues in the works of Marx and Engels left open an

120. Ibid., p. 28. Also see "Improvement of Finance and Trade," pp. 625–26, and *RMRB* editorial, December 23, 1958.

121. This debate is recounted in Wheelwright and McFarlane, *Chinese Road to Socialism*, pp. 81–86. Articles on this debate may be found in *SCMP*, nos. 1939 (1959), pp. 13–17; 1995 (1959), pp. 2–6; 2007 (1959), pp. 25–31; 2014 (1959), pp. 15–21; and 2029 (1959), pp. 9–18. The views presented here are as expressed in these articles. Interestingly, the much maligned Gang of Four radicals of the 1970s saw more of a scope for both the law of value and for commodities than the Leap-era radicals did, as the articles in their journal *XXYPP* (1973–1976) attest.

area of controversy for later socialist theoreticians and politicians. In China in the wake of the Great Leap Forward, although a range of opinions was set out on these questions, the newspapers reveal a clear preference for a middling, bureaucrat's position.

Each issue in this debate had practical implications for questions concerning the extent to which the economy ought to be run according to market criteria; and each group involved in the controversy had pragmatic as well as ideological grounds for taking the positions it took.

On the question of the law of value under socialism, three broad answers are possible, with many shades of variation. Marketeers argue, in essence, that profit criteria ought to be relevant in the allocation of capital among productive enterprises. Also, exchange throughout the system, even among factories all owned by the state, should be governed by the law of value and not by criteria subjectively set by planners. This is so because state enterprises are in fact independent economic units engaged in buying and selling, even if they are all in the possession of a common owner, the state. Managers in successful factories would support such a notion.

Bureaucrats, hoping to shore up the plan they manage, typically assert that the law of value may regulate circulation, but it cannot be the directive force in production, for it is up to the plan (and the planners) and not to profit indicators to make production decisions. A variant bureaucrat position is that the law of value should not even govern circulation within the state-owned sector (i.e., between state-owned factories), for this too is the role of the plan. The only function for the law, according to this view, is to rule exchanges among communes or firms within the collective sector; or those between the collective (rural) economy and the state enterprises, where two different ownership systems come into contact, and thus where economic calculations must be taken into account.[122] Bureaucrats favor using the law of value "consciously" to expand production and to facilitate commodity circulation in a planned way, but abhor the idea of allowing it to operate freely, without state controls.

Radicals, with their distaste for profit seeking and monetary measurement, see the law of value as a product of capitalism, leading to anarchy in production. For them, the law of value cannot influence production decisions in a socialist economy, and may play a role only in regard to the circulation of minor goods not included in the state plan. Also, they think that exchange among state-owned enterprises ought to

---

122. This is Stalin's position in *Economic Problems of Socialism in the U.S.S.R.*.

be organized only by plan, as a kind of transfer akin to the direct distribution that will obtain under communism.

Both marketeers and bureaucrats value commodity production and commodity exchange as positive, insofar as they help to build up the socialist economy, which will lay the groundwork for an eventual transition to communism. Radicals, however, find commodity production and exchange repugnant to communism, and therefore hope to limit their scope, even in advance of the advent of communism. In their stead, radicals advocate self-sufficiency and the free supply system of allocation according to need.

The 1959 press coverage of this three-way debate made it evident that a wide range of opinions was allowed to surface. A close reading, however, reveals the unmistakable dominance of the bureaucrat line. Most typically, bureaucrat views in various shades were presented as the majority, marketeers as the minority, and radicals as objects of criticism.

In late 1957, central leaders argued over whether to mobilize a Great Leap Forward or to manage the economy through a balanced program of stable growth.[123] By late 1958 and early 1959, however, serious economic upheaval had led to a shift in issue, in a conflict over just how to pull the reins on the Leap once it had begun. Along with this shift, the alliances and opposition among the three tendencies changed as well. From late 1957 to mid-1958 a coalition of radicals with some bureaucrats began the Leap in opposition to marketeers; by early 1959 bureaucrats in ascendance battled against both the others, in an effort to stabilize the economy by enforcing central controls once again. In the early 1960s, however, a new alliance came into being in commercial politics, bent on overseeing an economic recovery. It is to an episode from that era that we turn next.

THE "HIGH-PRICE POLICY," 1962

In July 1959, top Party, state, and military leaders met at Lushan, Jiangxi, to review the progress of the Great Leap Forward and attempt to deal with the economic and administrative problems that had emerged in the course of this massive and in many ways disastrous campaign. Chen Yun, in secluded retreat at Dairen, chose not to attend, preferring instead to bide his time before speaking out. "Why did Peng Dehuai criticize Mao at this time?" he asked, when told of the famous "letter of opinion" that

123. Chang, chap. 3.

led to that general's purge at the Lushan meeting.[124]

Thus, Chen perceived that the political climate of 1959 would be one inhospitable to his market-style remedies for an ailing economy. This view was no doubt based in part on Chen's sense of Mao's likely wrathful reaction to criticism. But besides this, as the last section explained, the bureaucrat tendency dominated in the early phase of rectifying Leap excesses—in the line at Wuhan, in theoretical discussions, and in price policy. Both Yao Yilin in December 1958, and Li Xiannian in January 1959, speaking for the majority, had argued for retaining the regime's past policy of basically stabilized prices, making only minor adjustments where necessary. In fact, probably under the influence of chaos caused by the Leap, when Chen did speak out in this period, it was in line with his macro-level concerns. In an article on capital construction in *Hong Qi* journal, he argued that national integration was primary, and thus that a national standpoint and national plans must govern the allotment of all equipment and materials (at least for this sector of the economy).[125]

While Chen waited for a more opportune moment to reorient policy, his strategy was to watch the economic forces unleashed by the Leap play themselves out, while he garnered data and gathered allies. Through the years 1960–1962, as Chen worked quietly, the balance of political forces shifted once again in the wake of the economic disaster, this time toward a joining of marketeer and bureaucrat, in the interest of enhancing productivity and eliminating inflation, with both pitted against the radicals.[126]

The best-documented instance of this alliance at work is the Western Chamber [Xilou] conference held in Beijing in February 1962, an enlarged meeting of the Politburo Standing Committee, attended as well by the regime's top economic officials.[127] According to Red Guard ac-

124. The "showdown at Lushan" is the title of a section in Chang, pp. 110–19, which traces these events. Chen's remark is in *BJGS*, in *RGP*, February 23, 1967; the incident is also described in another Red Guard publication and translated in *SCMPS*, no. 177 (1967), p. 9.

125. For Yao's and Li's position on prices in 1958–1959, see notes 57, 58, and 109 above. Chen's article, on capital construction, was in the March 1959 issue of *HQ* (translated in *ECMM*, no. 166 [1959], pp. 1–15).

126. One reference to radical opposition at this time is in *RMRB*, April 4, 1961, in *SCMP*, no. 2479 (1961), pp. 5–6, which says that some people "try to abolish prematurely commodity production and exchange and deny the positive role of commodities, value, currency and price." Apparently even after the height of the Leap had passed, some radicals continued to argue for their communistic ideals.

127. See *BJGS* in *RGP*, February 23, 1967, and March 14, 1967; *SCMPS*, nos. 170 (1967), pp. 10–11; 172 (1967), p. 10; 177 (1967), p. 9; 232 (1968), pp. 28–29. Also, Chang, pp. 138–39. The account that follows draws on these sources, as well as on Chen's speech at the meeting, in *Comrade Chen Yun*, pp. 157–72.

counts, Liu Shaoqi and Deng Xiaoping, then both Party vice-chairmen concerned with the economy, and Peng Zhen, Politburo member and mayor of Beijing, collaborated with Chen at this meeting to pass the "high-price policy" that was certainly the invention of Chen Yun.[128]

Chen's assessment by early 1962 that the time was ripe for his regimen rested first of all on his view that a great decrease in agricultural production in the aftermath of the Leap meant that the crucial commodities— grain, oil, and clothing—were all in drastically short supply. Moreover, despite the report of the Ministry of Finance that the budget for 1962 would be balanced, Chen was convinced that the regime was in the red. On top of this, rampant inflation, an overall decline in the commercial stock under central government control, and an alarming flow of currency notes from urban to rural areas all combined to feed speculation.[129]

Chen, genuinely concerned that under such circumstances the peasantry would withhold their goods from the state in the hopes of getting better prices on the black market, concluded at the conference: "It is necessary to fight for a high-price policy in the next few years." A few years later, Red Guards, in defense of the previously planned prices that were discarded for some items for the duration of the supply crisis, listed what they viewed to be Chen's crimes at this time: "readjusting commodity prices, raising commodity prices, . . . and devaluing the currency."

To judge from the course of events as retold by Red Guards, this carefully orchestrated convention at the Western Chamber may well have turned the tide in Chen's direction. At the meeting of 7,000 cadres only the month before, Chen reportedly had refused to brief Mao on the nation's financial and economic situation.[130] Instead, he chose a forum

128. Chen's speech bears out his authorship of the policy. This policy is also discussed in Bennett, "Activists and Professionals," for grain, on pp. 181–83. *CNA*, no. 435 (1962), p. 6, noted that the section of Chen Yun's Eighth Party Congress speech advocating higher prices for better quality goods was quoted in a *DGB* article of July 16, 1962. Such a reemergence of a six-year-old speech indicates that its views were again seen as relevant. Evidence that the policy was in effect is in a Red Guard paper, *Caimao zhanshi* [Finance and Trade Warrior], February 18, 1967, in *RGP*. This article says that shops in Shanghai freely set their own prices in this period, especially offering sweets and needlework for capitalists and other goods for intellectuals at higher rates than those that had been set by the state earlier.

129. In *Comrade Chen Yun*, p. 162, Chen notes (in February 1962) that in the past year or so the peasants had sold crops on the free market equal to one billion yuan in normal prices, but that they had received three times that amount of cash in return.

130. *BJGS*, in *RGP*, March 14, 1967. Mao's displeasure with events in the commercial sector surfaced in August 1962 at a meeting in Beidaiho (in *U.S. Joint Publications Research Service*, no. 52029, 21 December 1970, *Translations on Communist China*, no. 128, pp. 26–27). Here he repeated a suggestion he said he had already made in November 1958 to change the name of the Ministry of Commerce to the "Ministry of Destruction." (Also in *BJGS* in *RGP*, April 27, 1967).

where perhaps Mao was not present (no account mentions his name among the participants) to marshal support for his diagnosis and prescription. Then, in May, Chen formed a small group on finance and economic work under the Central Committee, which published his writings and issued them to the whole Party.[131]

One aspect of Chen's policy was to increase the state's procurement prices for some agricultural products, to entice the peasantry to sell more of their produce to the state, less on the free market (as in 1955, using material incentives to direct more goods to the state). For example, both procurement and retail prices for grain were raised for the first time in over a decade, and consumers were permitted to purchase all they could afford, thereby temporarily annulling the regular ration system.[132] By such measures, Chen hoped to bring about the restoration of the shattered agrarian economy and thereby to improve the livelihood of the peasantry after the disasters of the Leap.

A second component of this policy permitted higher-quality goods to take higher prices. It also allowed the expansion of fancy restaurants in the cities, along with the sale of a small number of high-priced, high-class, nonstaple food products, such as pastries and candies. Here the idea was to enable the state to retrieve a portion of the excess currency notes then flowing to rural black markets in search of food, and at the same time to improve the lives of that tiny segment of the population who could afford such items. "As long as prices of the basic means of livelihood don't inflate," Chen opined, "there won't be a big problem."

A look at the past work of Chen's chief cohorts at Xilou—Liu, Deng, and Peng—suggests that each probably had at least some ambivalence about departing from the Party's policy of stable prices. Apparently the range of economic ills illuminated by Chen's investigations, along with the framework of interpretation he placed on his findings, helped to convince a group of bureaucratically inclined officials to support his ideas.

Liu, more open to altering the price structure than either Li Xiannian

131. Chang, p. 139; *BJGS* in *RGP*, March 14, 1967. Chen's influence was felt before this in post-Leap economic policy. For example, Xue Muqiao had quoted Chen as arguing for "large plan, small freedoms" in *JHJJ*, no. 9 (1957), p. 22. Nearly four years later, *DGB*, on April 24, 1961, published an article entitled "big collective, small freedoms" (discussing sideline farming, fairs, and household enterprises), which phrase may well have been coined by or borrowed from Chen. Also, various accounts in Hong Kong journals claim that Chen was responsible for economic policy in the early 1960s (see n. 38 above). But the Xilou meeting, perhaps because it received such publicity in the Cultural Revolution, seems to be a special milestone in the victory of Chen's marketeer strategy.

132. Bennett, "Activists," pp. 181–83. Bennett bases his account on information supplied by a cadre who was working in the Guangdong provincial commercial bureau at the time.

or Zhou Enlai at the Eighth Party Congress, still stood to the left of Chen Yun in 1956 (that is, was less a marketeer, more a bureaucrat).[133] Thus, Li termed stabilization the fundamental policy, spoke of the need for detailed plans in making any changes, and predicated all shifts on a careful balancing of purchasing power and goods supply. Zhou similarly cautioned against "rashness" in readjustment, advocating retention of stable prices with only minor "suitable adjustments." Chen, at the other extreme, criticized "unified" or "frozen" prices and advised high prices for high-quality goods (as did Liu; this was low on Li's list of priorities and ignored altogether by Zhou). Also, Chen even called for "free pricing" for minor local products. "Price stability comes only as a result of a considerable increase in production," Chen lectured, implying that he disagreed with enforcing price stability for all goods through administrative controls, the Party's former approach.

Liu, then, perched in the middle, did speak out in 1956 for correcting shortcomings in price work. His general recommendation, however, was to overhaul irrationalities, but to do so strictly within the confines of a state-fixed system. Thus, where Chen called for "free production carried on within the scope prescribed by the state plan and *in accord with market fluctuations*" (emphasis added), Liu wanted commercial departments to "sum up past experience and, acting under the principle of continuing to stabilize commodity prices, work out a more comprehensive policy and price structure suited to present concrete conditions and beneficial to production."

Deng, after a career in financial work in the early 1950s, was concerned more often with Party life than with economic matters in the mid- and late 1950s. He did, however, turn his hand again to economic affairs in the wake of the Leap. One Red Guard source claims that Deng worked with Bo Yibo and Peng Zhen on the "70 Articles" for industry of December 1961.[134] Although this document did say that industry should "take the market as primary" (article 2), perhaps more important, its concrete instruction (article 54) was to leave industry-commerce relations unchanged, which meant that commercial units would continue to guarantee to purchase whatever industry produced, regardless of market considerations.[135] And Peng Zhen, as mayor of Beijing in 1956, must have

133. See *Eighth Congress*, vol. 1, pp. 62–63, for Liu; vol. 1, pp. 268, 305, and 306, for Zhou; vol. 2, pp. 170–72 and 176, for Chen; and vol. 2, pp. 215, 217, 219 and 221–22, for Li, on price policy.

134. *SCMPS*, July 8, 1968, p. 37. Deng is also credited with sponsorship of the 1975 "20 points," alternatively entitled "Some Problems in Speeding Up Industrial Development," *I&S*, 13, no. 7 (1977): 90–113, a very bureaucratically oriented document.

135. *CCP Documents*, pp. 689–93.

been responsible for the early shutting down of the urban free market there, three months before such markets were closed throughout the country.[136]

Each of the three, then, in the interest of procuring more commodities for the state and stabilizing the economy, modified his former stance. As each did so, he moved toward more management by means of a market mechanism than he had sanctioned heretofore, in lining up with Chen Yun to let some prices rise. Interpretations of the Leap and its aftermath which focus only on "radicals" and "pragmatists" or "left" and "right" factions miss the fine shades of distinction that truly clarify the political process of the early 1960s in the commercial realm. Whereas in 1959 bureaucrats in command had battled marketeers, as the overall economic situation in the country continued to deteriorate, the two joined forces by 1961–1962.

By 1963 radicals were largely isolated, confronted by a coalition composed of marketeers and some bureaucrats who seemed to have forsaken a few key elements of the planned economy. Although radicals themselves sometimes chafed under the restrictiveness of the plan's regulations, during the decade of the Cultural Revolution they often chose to praise the planned economy, as they juxtaposed it in their rhetoric to the use of market strategies.

RADICALS AND THE CULTURAL REVOLUTION:
THE PLANNED ECONOMY, 1966–1976

In commercial as in all other lines of work, the period of the Great Proletarian Cultural Revolution saw much critical rhetoric coined by the radicals. New practices appeared as well, but these programs—a stress on producing and supplying only commodities that radicals viewed as useful and suitable to workers, peasants, and soldiers;[137] poor and lower-middle peasant management of rural commerce (its administrative and personnel matters only, but not its financial, price, sales, marketing, or delivery affairs, which remained the purview of commercial cadres);[138] curbs on rural free markets[139]—are all straightforward and less entangled with the three-way debates under analysis here.

136. *DGB*, May 20, 1956. See chapter 6. It was Chen Yun's suggestion that these fairs be opened, in 1956.
137. For example, see *SCMP*, no. 4767 (1970), p. 97.
138. *CB*, no. 875 (1969); *SCMP*, nos. 4379 (1969), pp. 8–9, 4400 (1969), pp. 7–9, and 4489 (1969), pp. 9–11, to list only a very few articles on this scheme.
139. See chapter 6 below.

All three issues on which commercial controversies have repeatedly turned in China rose to the surface during this era of conflict: the use of market forces to stimulate productivity, the class basis on which to organize exchange, and the proper degree and type of state controls. Radicals' opposition to the profits and prices of the market, and their preference for a trade that helps proletarian and peasant, are well known. This discussion, then, will shed some light on the third central question that engaged the radicals, revolving around their stance toward the plan: who may plan the disposition of goods and in what manner?

On first glance, the radicals' abhorrence of the free market and material incentives would lead one to surmise that they would be adherents of a planned approach to economic organization. And in fact their critiques are filled with defenses of the planned economy.[140] But the picture is complicated by the fact that in some diatribes they attack targets, a key component of socialist planning, along with their criticism of market paraphernalia, as in this quotation maligning Liu Shaoqi:

> For a long time China's Khrushchev and his agents have frenziedly pushed the counter-revolutionary revisionist line for commerce and followed the capitalist way of doing business, promoting such feudal capitalist and revisionist practices as putting profits in command, putting targets in command, giving first place to business, high prices.[141]

The anger directed against both profits and targets in this assault is puzzling, and coaxes us to explore radicals' perceptions of the plan and their notion of how it ought to operate.

A fascinating account from 1962 of conflict over planning between a radical politician, Mao's confidant Chen Boda, and the bureaucrat Li Xiannian has been noted (but not analyzed in terms of radical versus bureaucrat) in another work.[142] Reportedly, Chen pressed for a fixed (*ding gou*) system of procurement in the countryside, which was to give a greater role to quota setting by the masses through consultation with the peasant producers. Li, however, faithful to his bureaucrat position, insisted on the administratively assigned target system for purchases (*pai gou*), claiming a need for compulsory orders. This tale reveals a great deal about radical feelings toward bureaucrats' plans: apparently

---

140. *CB*, no. 836 (1967), pp. 20–24, and *SCMP*, no. 4363 (1969), pp. 5–6, to cite just two examples among hundreds.

141. *SCMP*, no. 4341 (1969), p. 12.

142. Bennett, "Activists," pp. 150–51.

the rural populace in each locality would compose its own requisition schedules in the radicals' ideal set-up.

This clue on radical approaches to planning from the eve of the Cultural Revolution is bolstered by two other sorts of data. One is the body of censures of the radical Gang of Four after its arrest in September 1976; the other consists of articles in the radical-managed journal, *Study and Criticism*, printed in Shanghai over the years 1973–1976. These articles contained model stories of how radicals thought society ought to work.

According to the post-Gang pictures of this faction, they "opposed allocation and distribution of commodities in accord with the unified state plan, and sabotaged socialist unified markets." Further, "they described the commodity control system which calls for unified leadership and decentralization of power over management as a dictatorship of the bourgeoisie. . . . They vilified our commercial sector as a 'bourgeois monopoly.'"[143] These statements would be hard to reconcile with oft-proclaimed radical proclivities for planning over markets, were it not for the essays in *Study and Criticism* which show that in fact radicals really thought plans were fine, so long as they were compiled according to radicals' criteria.

The articles on markets and plans in this journal illustrate radical efforts to avoid use of the market mechanism. In one piece a "vegetable investigation team" solves problems of supply, seasonal differentials in output, and range of varieties simply by adjusting production conditions, in defiance of Liu Shaoqi's principle of "looking at the price and then planting and marketing vegetables."[144] Another article tells how the Cultural Revolution swept from a certain market superstitious and luxury items used by the "exploiting classes" to earn exorbitant profits, and replaced them with the simple, wholesome products that radicals held were truly needed by workers and peasants.[145]

Thus, for these writers "the plan is number one, price number two"; rather than "banknotes in command," they exhort, "think of a way to plant more according to the state's unified plan."[146] But when it actually comes to planning, it is not the state's unified plan that forms the measure. For "planning should be done by the masses, not by a minority behind closed doors"; "we must get the masses' opinions in planning,

143. Wuhan Radio, May 12, 1977; New China News Agency (Beijing), December 15, 1977.
144. *XXYPP*, no. 1, (1973), pp. 77–81.
145. *XXYPP*, no. 10, (1974), pp. 92–96.
146. *XXYPP*, no. 6 (1976), pp. 61–63; no. 1 (1973), pp. 77–81.

because they must agree on the plans or they cannot be implemented."[147] And when a certain brigade in Jiading county set its own six-year plan (a long-term one, a distant objective to strive for, the better to "concentrate the masses' scattered enthusiasm"), it was in no way linked with the larger schemes of the state, but relied instead on mobilization of the local people.[148] It is in light of this framework for planning that radicals in their own words resisted Deng Xiaoping's "strict systems." The radicals, here perceiving Deng as a bureaucrat, not a marketeer (as he has been viewed since 1978), predicted that such systems not only would thwart mass activism but would harm the productive forces as well.[149]

Thus, radicals were torn between the antipathy they felt on the one hand for the class-polarizing and money-centered nature of the market, and their rebellion against the restraints of the central plan, on the other. Advocacy for an active role for the masses in economic decisions, for which they stood, faded steadily with the death of Mao, and was seldom heard by 1979.

FROM PLAN TO MARKET, MID-1978

In the immediate aftermath of Mao's passing and the Gang's arrest, the remaining Chinese leadership roundly proclaimed the economy to be in a state of near collapse. Initially the remedy chosen, just as in late 1958 when bureaucrats stepped in first to handle Leap excesses, was to strengthen the planning system and to enforce discipline through administrative rules and regulations. This was no doubt a decision reached (or reinforced) at the Eleventh Party Congress in late summer 1977, which coincided with the reemergence of Deng Xiaoping after his disgrace at the hands of the radicals in April 1976.[150] An authoritative article praising planning appeared in the *People's Daily* shortly thereafter.[151]

The first few years after Mao had gone were complex ones in which bureaucrat and surviving radical groups sometimes cooperated and sometimes competed for the mantle of the dead leader and the legitimacy that close association with his ideas seemed then to lend. An overly ambitious ten-year plan produced in this period was delivered by the then Party chairman and premier, Hua Guofeng, in February 1978 at

147. *XXYPP*, no. 9 (1974), pp. 60–61.

148. *XXYPP*, no. 7 (1974), pp. 37–40, and no. 9 (1974), pp. 53–59.

149. *XXYPP*, no. 6 (1976), pp. 61–63.

150. For an analysis of this period, and the effort to rectify chaos through plans that marked it, see Dorothy J. Solinger, "Some Speculations on the Return of the Regions: Parallels With the Past."

151. *RMRB*, September 12, 1977, authored by the State Planning Commission.

the opening session of the Fifth National People's Congress, in which Deng, then managing the economy, could not have failed to have had a hand.[152] Its evocation of "the socialist initiative of the peasant masses," and its call to "serve the people," both radical slogans, were coupled with good bureaucratic commands to "bring all economic undertakings into the orbit of planned, proportionate development," to "strengthen the leadership of the central authorities," "and to tighten price and market controls."

For commercial work, the June–July 1978 National Conference on Learning from Daqing and Dazhai in Finance and Trade was a quiet turning point in the larger evolution from plan to market that went on between the Fifth NPC and the momentous Third Plenum of the Eleventh Party Central Committee in December 1978. Trickles of the coming stress on market management of the economy had appeared in Hua's February talk: he did mention that agricultural purchase prices should be raised to promote production, which the Third Plenum realized as policy; and he called for fully utilizing finance, banking, and credit to supervise economic undertakings. But, on balance this was a speech fashioned by bureaucrats and delivered by a radical sympathizer.

The summer Finance-Trade Conference represented a last-ditch effort for both radicals and bureaucrats to advance their views on the proper business of commercial work and how it ought to be run. It was also a battleground on which the two sets of losers—radicals in the person of Hua Guofeng and bureaucrats represented by Li Xiannian and Yu Qiuli (head of the State Planning Commission for many years)—soon sensed the shift of the wind and properly peppered their convention addresses to accommodate it.

On the eve of the conference, three telltale documents went to print: a *People's Daily* editorial heralding the convocation of the meeting; a *Hong Qi* article in its honor by the theoretical group of the Ministry of Commerce; and a collection of essays praising model units in the commercial sector in the then year-old nationwide campaign for finance and trade to study Daqing, the exemplar oil field, and Dazhai, the famous rural production brigade.[153] The themes of the first two pieces are nearly

152. *Peking Review*, no. 10 (1978). On p. 19 Hua notes that this plan was first drawn up in autumn 1975, but was attacked and blocked at that time by the Gang of Four. He goes on to say that the plan being presented in 1978 was merely a revision of that earlier one. In 1975, Deng was in charge of the work of the Party Central Committee, according to *BR*, no. 44 (1981), p. 25.

153. *RMRB*, June 21, 1978; *HQ*, no. 7 (1978), pp. 74–78; *Quanguo caimao xue daqing xue dazhai huiyi dianxing cailiao xuanbian* [Selected model materials from the National Conference to Study Daqing and Dazhai in Finance and Trade]. The campaign was

identical, and as they echo as well throughout the speeches of Li and Yu, no doubt contain the mainly bureaucratic message that the conference was prepared to deliver.

Some of the motifs in these two writings also recall the spirit of Hua's February address to the National People's Congress, in their exhortation to let socialist commerce serve as a promoter of a great leap forward in the national economy. They emphasize too Hua's inscription for the meeting, which drew on a 1942 quotation of Mao's to "develop the economy and ensure supplies." In referring to the market, it is the "unified socialist market" they evoke; and, thinking as bureaucrats always have in socialist China, they prescribe that finance and trade should achieve a balance between commodity supply and social purchasing power. Political and ideological work get a plug, as does Party leadership and commercial workers' participation in production. Li Xiannian's opening speech, defending the planned socialist economy, systems, and discipline, followed this same line closely.[154] Either Li knew what was coming and still stuck by his guns; or else, speaking first, he was unaware of the changes in store for the agenda.

The pamphlet containing tales of models veered off in another direction. It is almost completely filled with pure radical approaches to commercial activity, as stories from every province attest to the need to attack capitalism while consolidating and expanding socialism, to manage rural commerce through poor and lower-middle peasant management committees, to put politics in command, to carry out a continuous revolution under the dictatorship of the proletariat, and to wage class struggle in the market. It is this line that creeps at times into the speech of Hua Guofeng.[155]

But Hua, closing the meeting, injected much marketeer jargon into his words as well: he spoke of "economic levers" (prices, taxes, loans); "objective economic laws" (in contradistinction to a subjectively designed plan); problems of management; social economic accounting; strict financial supervision. Hua also managed to take his stand for radi-

---

launched at a May 1977 conference to study Daqing and Dazhai in industry, where Hua was the keynote speaker. Against the bureaucratic thrust of the editorial and the article, the initial State Council circular calling for the convocation of the meeting, written at the end of 1977, had envisioned the meeting as one that would be more geared to delivering radical messages, as it had urged a vigorous support of production, working "wholeheartedly for the people's livelihood," becoming "one at heart with the people," and "resolutely attack[ing] capitalist forces and develop[ing] the socialist economy." In *FBIS*, December 16, 1977, pp. E6–E11.

154. *RMRB*, June 27, 1978, in *FBIS*, June 28, E1-E13.

155. *RMRB*, July 8, 1978, in *FBIS*, July 11, 1978, pp. E1-E12.

cal values in economic work, perhaps for the last time. For he often quoted Mao here, asked his listeners to keep to the socialist orientation in their work, to put proletarian politics in command of all work, to follow the mass line, and to accept mass supervision. Finally, aligning himself with the bureaucrats, he reminded the audience that Mao advised reading Stalin on the law of value, for his position was that of a bureaucrat on this issue.[156]

Yu Qiuli's speech, delivered five days before Hua's and twelve after Li's, takes from the premeeting *People's Daily* editorial as does Li's, but also, like Hua's, bows toward the ascendant marketeers.[157] Whereas Hua's talk stands out for its frequent references to Mao, Yu's conceptions constantly touch on the ways that planning can influence marketeer methods: special factories and areas are to be set up *according to plan* for export goods; advanced technology is to be introduced *in a planned way*; foreign trade should be carried out in accordance *with unified state policy and plan*; funds are to be allocated *in accord with overall planning* (emphasis added). The head of state planning was not in a hurry to see the plan superseded!

Just after the conference ended, the *People's Daily* carried a report on applying the law of value.[158] The reporter claimed that the piece was based on notes from the conference, much to the surprise of any outside reader who had been following the proceedings as published in the press. A comparison of this article with the one that had appeared on the eve of the meeting shows clearly that the agenda had shifted, that a whole new line of discussion had entered the debate after the meeting began.

Moreover, the addresses of the delegates from the provinces and localities as carried in the newspaper during the days of the deliberations had had nothing to say of the law of value. They had spoken instead in inspirational tones, about reaching world progressive levels in commercial work and of speedy economic development; had given accounts of their units' successes, as in plan completion, milk supply, and scientific grain-storage; or had used the meeting as a forum to complain about poor past treatment of the commercial sector.[159] But, according to this postconvention *People's Daily* report, aimed at legitimizing a new line, talk of the law of value had dominated the forum: its role in socialist commodity production, its ability to enhance fulfillment of state plans, and its function as the basis for setting prices.

156. See n. 122 above.
157. *RMRB*, July 3, 1978, in *FBIS*, July 6, 1978, pp. E1-E13.
158. *RMRB*, July 5, 1978.
159. See articles on the meeting in *RMRB* on June 24, 28, 30 (two articles), and July 9, 1978.

Although the three principal speakers had each made mention of this law, none had done so in the manner of a marketeer: for Yu it was to be "consciously utilized under the direction of the state's unified plans"; for Li it was to "serve planned production"; and for Hua it was to "promote the development of socialist production under the conditions of the socialist planned economy." None of these men had bothered to mention it more than once, and each had showed his commitment to the subordination of its role to something they each took to be larger concerns— plans and socialist production. The dominant figure at the meeting, who gave no published address there, must have been Hu Qiaomu, named in March 1978 as president of the Chinese Academy of Social Sciences.[160] His remarks on economic laws at a July State Council meeting, not printed until October, carry the self-same message as the post-conference *People's Daily* article.[161]

The victory of the marketeer line was not sealed for some months, however. One piece of evidence is the Thirty-Point Decision on Industry, published on July 3, which puts far more emphasis on strengthening unified state planning than it does on market principles and economic levers. One analyst has surmised that this document, like the Twenty Points of 1975 on which it builds, was drafted under Deng Xiaoping's instruction.[162] Furthermore, just following the meeting Beijing Radio complained that one group of comrades "aims mechanically to copy, reproduce, and transmit the conference documents, but their implementation comes to naught."[163]

Perhaps the most illuminating, if somewhat whimsical, bit of evidence that market considerations had finally overcome those connected with planning, at least at the level of rhetoric, comes from a comparison

---

160. *I&S*, 14, no. 7 (1978): 75–80.

161. *RMRB*, October 6, 1978, in *FBIS*, October 11, 1978, pp. E1-E22. That Hu did attend the Finance and Trade meeting is confirmed in *FBIS*, July 10, 1978, p. E1. An article on controversy between the "Economic Faction" (my marketeers) and the "Petroleum Faction" (my bureaucrats) in *Dongxiang* [Trend], no. 24 (September 1980), on p. 10, confirms that conflict "began to brew" after May 1978, and that Hu Qiaomu "sounded the bugle call" with his July speech. This article also documents opposition to Hu and points to this as the reason that the speech was not published until October.

162. See *I&S*, 15, no. 1 (1979): 48–63; and 14, no. 11 (1978): 90. Articles 9, 11, 12, 20, and 28 heavily stress the plan. Note 134 above refers to Deng's 20 Points, and to the 70 articles in 1961 from which both derive.

163. Beijing Radio, July 9, in *FBIS*, July 14, 1978, p. E2. Also in July some articles in the *People's Daily* show that the radicals had not yet given up. A tribute to an old-model rural commercial worker from Hunan on July 11 and a poem on July 16 both heralded the well-rounded salesman, who not only sells but also helps peasants and workers with technical problems, undertakes repairs, washes their clothes, and carries goods to their homes, taking their worries away so that they can fully serve production.

of two similar diatribes against back-door dealings featured in the press.[164] The interdicted behavior is nearly the same in both: in one, a mill sold high-quality cloth cheaply to its workers and other units for "trial use"; in the second, some enterprises were giving away commodities to their staff and workers "under all sorts of names—year-end bonuses, labor safety devices."

But the moral drawn in each case was quite different. In July the journalist queried: "If all enterprises operate like that, how can there be any unified policy and planning?" In January 1979, however, concerns had shifted, as the commentator revealed: "Not everyone should receive goods in kind ... it increases pressure on the market and creates an imbalance in the supply of certain commodities." It was the pivotal Third Plenum in December that changed the official perspective on the proper channels for the distribution of goods.[165]

An overview of six different episodes has illustrated the dynamics of arguments and policy shifts in the commercial sector over three decades. To summarize briefly, the grain supply crisis of 1955 saw marketeer pitted against radical, with class the main issue in contention. In late 1957, these two tendency groups disagreed over why (but not whether) to decentralize power to lower levels, with radicals thinking in terms of eliciting the participation of local governmental and Party bodies, and marketeers in favor of arousing the initiative of enterprises by allowing them to respond to market forces operating in their regions.

By early 1959, both these forces had been bested by the bureaucrats, who now found it both necessary and possible to fight for the state planning system. All groups had once taken that system's discipline for granted, but its hierarchies of control had come unstuck in the chaos of the early Leap period. Three years beyond that time, however, some politicians who usually took a bureaucratic outlook accepted a marketeer diagnosis of the malfunctioning of the state economic mechanism and agreed to a marketeer remedy for its rehabilitation, in the arena of commercial goods circulation.

164. *RMRB*, July 27, 1978, in *FBIS*, August 1, 1978, pp. K1–K3 (see also *FBIS*, August 4, 1978, E13–E15 on this case); and *RMRB*, January 25, 1979, in *FBIS*, January 26, 1979, pp. E22–E23.

165. *RMRB*, April 3, 1980, p. 5, says that the spirit of the Third Plenum called for "combining regulation by the plan with regulation by the market, using the plan as primary, but still paying full attention to the role of the market." Of course, planned distribution still remained by far the predominant mode of goods distribution after the Third Plenum. But experiments with use of the market did begin then, and a market consciousness began to pervade the official press. See chapters 4, 5, and 6 for the impact of decisions here on commercial policy.

TABLE 4 Six Episodes of Conflict over Commercial Policy, 1955–1978

Conflict, Date	Tendencies in Conflict	Key Issues	Victor
Grain supply crisis March–August 1955	Marketeer vs. Radical	Class	Marketeer
Decentralization March–November 1957	Marketeer with Radical	Market forces	Marketeer and Radical
Tidying up the communes, December 1958–April 1959	Bureaucrat vs. Marketeer and vs. Radical	State control	Bureaucrat
High-price policy February 1962	Bureaucrat with Marketeer vs. Radical	Productivity	Marketeer and Bureaucrat
The Cultural Revolution 1966–1976	Radical vs. Marketeer and Bureaucrat	State control	Radical
Daqing-Dazhai Conference on Finance and Trade June–July 1978	Bureaucrat and Radical vs. Marketeer	Productivity	Marketeer

The Cultural Revolution amounted to a radical reaction against that productivity-prone alliance of bureaucrat and marketeer, as radicals mounted attacks on that alliance's class, planning, and profits policies. During their decade, economic activity was disturbed, if not deflected, in part as a result of the relatively lower priority that radicals placed on economic development in the abstract (relative to bureaucrats or marketeers, and relative to its own emphasis on class issues and mass initiative); and in part because of continuing factional battles encouraged by the general political upheaval. By 1978, after a short-lived bureaucrat initiative, marketeer strategies came into dominance in full force.

The three issues that divide the three tendencies are intertwined, so that most of the episodes analyzed contain shades of each, and several involve alliances between tendencies. Thus, though radicals argued most pointedly against profits or plans, their purpose in doing so was to keep the poorer sections of the populace from suffering disadvantage or exploitation. Where this was not an issue (as in 1957), they could cooperate with marketeers. Bureaucrats at times were as concerned about productivity gains as were marketeers, and indeed allied with them (in 1962) when this was most the case. But often their stance was to worry more about the possibility that free market forces would throw state control and prices into chaos. And marketeers, while putting most stress on creating plenty through the use of material incentives, could come together with radicals on behalf of decentralization, and with those bureaucrats who were willing to foresake some controls for the benefit of economic recovery. On the other hand, marketeer advocacy of using central organs to balance overall national supply in periods of decentralization has at times made possible their joining with the bureaucrats on behalf of the central plan.

This historical survey raises crucial questions that go to the heart of the political process in China: What accounts for the victory of a given tendency at any particular time? And how can one explain the repeated rise and fall of political factions associated with the different tendencies?

Two broad findings emerge from the narrative here and address these queries. Most basically, leadership perception of the state of the economy at any specific juncture—of grain shortage in 1955, bureaucratic chaos in 1959, near-starvation in 1962, lax discipline and low productivity in 1978—is the most significant determinant of the tendency that dominates at that time, and thus of the policy chosen. Sometimes this perception must be created: sometimes, as in 1962, it has been necessary for one leader to wait until the political climate is hospitable to the formation of a winning coalition that will support his view of the situation and his prescription for dealing with it. But at other times, as in 1959, the magnitude of economic ills facing the country has been so compelling as to cause politicians who at other times favor market strategies to line up with those adhering to the bureaucrat tendency, in the hope that enhanced state control can begin to tackle the difficulty.

The second general finding is of one of a set of patterns that have characterized shifting policies and the varying political fortunes of groups advocating these policies over time. Bureaucrats, because they represent economic stability, have come into ascendance at each point when the policies of either of the other tendencies are viewed as having upset the planned socialist economy, either through the efforts of radicals to abolish markets, or because of marketeers' excessive encouragement of decentralized profit maximization. This recurrent return to bureaucratic solutions is a theme that will structure later chapters of this book.

But interestingly, in this socialist system, though the first response to trouble has always been a bureaucratic one, to tighten planning controls (in April 1955, in December 1958, and in 1977), much of the leadership of the People's Republic, when truly gripped by a sense of real economic crisis—over grain supply in 1955; over inflation, deficit, and a declining stock of food and consumer goods in 1962; and over politically induced disorder in 1978—has been willing to turn, at least temporarily, to the doctoring administered by marketeers.

3

Technological Underdevelopment:

A Case Study of Corruption in the Southwest Countryside, 1949–1952

In addition to the framework that the planned economy (with its competition) and the conflict within the elite concerning policy have imposed upon marketing behavior in the People's Republic, a third element, the economic environment in which commerce occurs, creates constraints as well. This chapter focuses on the cast that the low level of economic development in much of China, and the attendant inadequacy of technological supports for commerce, lends to this activity.

Primitive conditions for trading have a number of effects, many of which are addressed in later chapters. The discussion here will tell a story that illustrates just one of these, with the intent of sharply delineating the nature of these conditions. In particular, it will elucidate one key proposition: that the type of corruption that characterizes commerce in the PRC is intimately tied to the country's level of development. That is, the insufficiencies in the technological infrastructure within which trade must operate here make necessary certain forms of middleman (or-woman) conduct, and at the same time facilitate accompanying excesses.

Setting the tale in a locale where circumstances render marketing especially cumbersome will make this point in graphic terms. Hence, this tale of small-scale corruption and its repression draws on documents from the Southwest China countryside in the early years just after takeover. This case is an apt one, since it exemplifies—if in an extreme form—the essence of the issues at stake. For in this mountainous region of the country, transportation difficulties are unusually severe, so that the technological backwardness that marks other places is compounded by geography to produce a milieu for marketing similar to that in many less developed economies.[1]

There are temporal factors that dictated this choice of data base as well. For these pre-1953 sources are especially rich in episodes of localized corruption, as the malpractices they describe were widespread in that era. The national economy, backward to begin with, was damaged and still just reviving then, after many years of warfare; and the political leadership turned its energies to fostering this recovery at first, rather than to undertaking strict control of economic activity. Those restrictions and punishments that did exist were fewer then than later, and also easier to skirt, since the state itself was still too weak to act as a forceful adversary. The Party had not yet begun its "socialist transformation" of the petty traders in the countryside, and so the ranks of these merchants were far fuller than they would be in the future. Thus, the relationship between underdeveloped technology and market corruption which this chapter will illuminate was especially clear in that region and at that time.

Following the general use of the term "corrupt" in China (according to both traditional morality and socialist ideology), the discussion here will consider commercial behavior to be corrupt when it creates what the Chinese view as excessively large profits for dealers or when it diverts needed goods to them, and in the process either raises costs to consumers or deprives them of essential supplies. The several components of this formulation differentiate practices falling under this category from the semilegal barter and gift giving addressed in chapter one.

---

1. Commerce in the Southwest nicely illustrates G. William Skinner's model of trade in the peripheral (as opposed to core) areas of a regional economic system. In such places a rugged topography, low population density, and high transport costs limit commercialization and thereby reduce or eliminate competition between markets and firms. See G. William Skinner, "Cities and the Hierarchy of Local System," pp. 277–85. See also Albert Feuerwerker, *The Chinese Economy, ca. 1870–1911*, pp. 44–50, passim., which notes the constraints on the marketing structure and size of China's domestic commerce in the late nineteenth and early twentieth centuries posed by its premodern transport and communications.

Urban markets in late-nineteenth-century China.

Though the latter activities are officially criticized under the label "back-doorism," they do not generally receive the same serious censure and penalties as acts in the corrupt category.

Commercial practices that are viewed as corrupt in China are essentially forms of market manipulation: speculation, profiteering, adulteration, dealing in futures, giving short weight, and otherwise colluding to undermine the state's commercial system and its price structure. This behavior is distinct from the competition for goods that marks regular, legal commercial dealings in socialist China, dealings, that is, that operate within the constraints of the planning system and so at least implicitly accept its strictures. For the accumulation of wealth, and not just the hoarding of choice goods, is the goal of corruption.[2] Its focus on profit has led radical critics to label this behavior "capitalist."

Besides sketching out relevant features of the technological environment in backward parts of China and the types of merchant tactics that thrive in such places, this chapter will also analyze the response of the state to this corruption. A central dimension of the state's strategy in combatting corruption, beginning just after takeover and carrying on with more energy at some times than at others, has been the attempt to undermine the environmental supports for these malpractices. This long-term project to upgrade the technology of trade has been fraught with obstacles, however, all of which surfaced immediately.

Thus, despite periodic campaigns by the leadership to stamp out market corruption, and despite some efforts at modernization of the infrastructure, crucial elements of the economic environment have remained essentially unchanged in much of China, and these have provided a continuing context for illegalities. As a result, corruption has persisted in China over the years, under cover in black markets in times of stringent state control, more openly in periods of lax supervision or of permissiveness.

To generalize, corruption in the marketplace attracts the most official attention when radicals are in ascendance. Frequently, following on pe-

2. A similar distinction is drawn in Gregory Grossman, "The 'Shadow Economy' in the Socialist Sector of the USSR and Eastern Europe." There, on p. 2, Grossman labels as the "shadow economy" "activities involving (substantial) 'violations of plan, financial, and other norms' . . . [a concept that] pertains to the socialist sector alone." The "second economy," then, he understands as the "aggregate of economic activities meeting at least one of the following two tests: a given activity is on private account (for direct private gain), whether it is legal or illegal, and the activity in some substantial respect [is] knowingly illegal, whether it be conducted on private or socialist account." His "shadow economy" corresponds to the behavior described in chapter 1 of the present study; the "second economy" describes the activities in the present chapter.

riods of marketeer dominance, when liberal economic policies have allowed a relative lack of restraint in buying and selling, radicals have repeatedly been able to gain a hearing on what is for them a source of constant concern: their repugnance toward the injustices the poor may suffer in market exchanges where the wilier and wealthier win out. At such junctures radicals, sometimes linked to bureaucrats, have often managed to create a consensus opposing "capitalism" and on behalf of tighter administrative controls over markets.

Examples of this are the period of the five-anti (*wu fan*) campaign that began in late 1951;[3] the eve of the installation of the policy of unified state purchase of grain in late 1953 and during the supply crisis of early and mid-1955;[4] the time of the closing of free markets in late summer 1957;[5] during the "Four Cleans" movement of 1963–1965;[6] through the Cultural Revolution and its immediate aftermath;[7] and the 1975 campaign against bourgeois rights that aimed to extend and even perpetuate the concerns of the Cultural Revolution.[8] As the account below only recounts events in the rural pre-1953 Southwest, footnotes will alert the reader to parallel material in the press from these subsequent periods.

3. This movement, which lasted about six months, was directed against urban businessmen. Its aim, besides the appropriation of a portion of the bourgeoisie's wealth, was to eliminate bribery, tax evasion, stealing state property, cheating on government contracts, and stealing secret government economic data. For an excellent treatment of that campaign, see Kenneth G. Lieberthal, *Revolution and Tradition in Tientsin, 1949 to 1959*.

4. Examples from late 1953 and early 1954 are in *Survey of the China Mainland Press* (*SCMP*), no. 701 (1953), pp. 30–36; no. 774 (1954), pp. 19–22; for summer 1955, see chap. 2, no. 86.

5. There were numerous articles complaining about corruption in the free markets in 1957, including cases of agricultural production cooperatives engaging in speculative business activity. A few are: *SCMP*, nos. 1592 (1957), pp. 13–15; 1608 (1957), pp. 19–20; 1612 (1957), pp. 26–27; 1649 (1957), pp. 10–12; and 1661 (1957), pp. 17–23. See chap. 6. Lynn T. White III, in "Low Power: Small Enterprises in Shanghai, 1949–1967," *CQ*, no. 73 (March 1978), p. 61, discusses forms of illegal small economic crimes in the urban areas attacked in 1957. Chapter 6 discusses this 1957 closing of free markets.

6. See Richard Baum, *Prelude to Revolution: Mao, the Party, and the Peasant Question, 1962–66*, for a thorough treatment of rural corruption in this period, the ideological climate of the time, and attendant leadership conflicts over corrupt practices then. See also C. S. Chen, ed., *Rural People's Communes in Lien-chiang*, for a cataloguing of rural corruption in one county, 1962–1963.

7. The Cultural Revolutionary Red Guard press is filled with attacks on the corruption that markets, deemed capitalistic by these rebel groups, breed. Also, during that revolution itself, political upheaval permitted irregularities to mushroom in the market. For example, see *U.S. Joint Publications Research Service*, no. 45,417 (May 17, 1968), *Translations from Communist China*, no. 15, which reports on black markets, and *SCMP*, no. 4129 (1968), pp. 1–3, which calls for strengthening market control.

8. Examples of articles published in the immediate aftermath of the Cultural Revolution and during the 1975 campaign to limit bourgeois rights (prices, wage differentials, profits) can be found in Gordon Bennett, ed., *China's Finance and Trade: A Policy Reader*, pp. 82 ff.

The Technological Environment
of Premodern Commerce and Its
Behavioral Correlates

TECHNOLOGICAL FACTORS

The influence of technology on marketing behavior becomes apparent in an analysis of traditional merchant style in China, and also in the finding that this style has been common in many countries at similar levels of economic development. Marketing studies across a large number of premodern economies reveal over and over again the presence of the same or analogous procedures of doing business in them all. Thus, a wide range of "corrupt" practices that marked Chinese commerce at the local levels historically—manipulation of measures, adulteration of goods, regrating (profiting from price differentials in neighboring markets), hoarding and gaining monopolies in local areas, speculating and creating artificial shortages, haggling, and forestalling (buying goods outside the marketplace)—were also present in such culturally diverse societies as the Low Countries, Italy, France, and England, in medieval times; and in Uganda, Nigeria, the Caribbean, Indonesia, the Philippines, Colombia, and Mexico, in the twentieth century, to name just a few. And besides the data from numerous empirical examinations of individual market systems, two more theory-oriented volumes specifically note the technological facilitating factors behind these common phenomena.[9]

Probably the two most central features of premodern technology that have affected marketing throughout the world are the level of transport development and the sophistication of storage facilities. This is so because transport and stockpiling constitute the most essential supports for trading activity. In a premodern economy, inadequate, expensive, or

9. On this point, see Henri Pirenne, *Early Democracies in the Low Countries;* N.S.B. Gras, *The Evolution of the English Corn Market from the 12th to the 18th Century;* Robert S. Lopez and Irving N. Raymond, eds., *Medieval Trade in the Mediterranean World;* W. Cunningham, D.D., *The Growth of English Industry and Commerce During the Early and Middle Ages;* Charles Tilly, "Food Supply and Public Order in Modern Europe"; Abott Payson Usher, *The History of the Grain Trade in France, 1400–1710;* Charles M. Good, *Rural Markets and Trade in East Africa: Study of the Functions and Development of Exchange Institution in Ankole, Uganda;* B. W. Hodder and U. I. Ukwu, *Markets in West Africa;* Sidney W. Mintz, "The Role of the Middleman in the Internal Distribution System of a Caribbean Peasant Economy"; Alice G. Dewey, *Peasant Marketing in Java;* William G. Davis, *Social Relations in a Philippine Market;* Clifford Geertz, *Peddlers and Princes;* Sutti Ortiz, "Columbia Rural Market Organization: An Exploratory Model"; and Ralph L. Beals, *The Peasant Marketing System of Oaxaca, Mexico.* The two theoretical accounts are Cyril S. Belshaw, *Traditional Exchange and Modern Markets;* and Gideon Sjoberg, *The Preindustrial City: Past and Present.*

an insufficient quantity of transport facilities, and numerically limited, rudimentary depositories for accumulating goods, force trading to occur within geographically small-scale, localized areas, put a premium on the possession of knowledge about larger, more distant trading areas, and give power to those who have the capital and time to travel and store.[10]

This regionalization of commerce that is attendant on poor transport and storage technology, then, is a third feature of the premodern marketing environment, and it in turn sets the conditions for three other aspects of premodern trade. Specifically, great variability and unpredictability of supply flows, especially among seasons, is common: people in each area are either forced to rely on the weather conditions there or they must wait upon uncertain and often untimely imports;[11] large price differentials exist between areas, also resulting from subjection to nature and inadequacies in transport and storage capacity;[12] and in the absence of governmental attention and control, standardization of all types—in weights and measures, currency, prices, and quality of goods—is absent across and sometimes even within local areas.[13]

BEHAVIORAL CORRELATES

Each of these six features of the preindustrial economy have tended to foster, or at least facilitate, particular forms of merchant behavior across the world. The distance between localized market areas and the need to dispose of perishables quickly (because of inadequate storage) create a role for various types of middlemen.[14] Moreover, since these middlemen are people who use their time and capital for trading, they are able to take advantage of and especially to manipulate price differentials between areas, as they transfer supplies from places of plenty to areas of dearth (regrating). They also typically corner the market and store up

10. On the importance of transportation and storage to marketing, see Belshaw, p. 57; Sjoberg, pp. 103, 207–8; Davis, pp. 74, 137; Beals, p. 57; Good, p. 81; Hodder and Ukwu, p. 74; and Mintz, p. 21. The focus in this chapter is on the trade of everyday life for the majority of the Chinese people. Thus, it ignores the long-distance commerce between markets hundreds and thousands of miles apart, a trade termed "small and confined to a few key commodities" in Dwight Perkins, *Agricultural Development in China 1368–1968*, p. 112. Perkins estimates that, prior to 1900, only about 6 to 8 percent of farm output entered into long-distance trade (p. 115), and states that it dealt mainly in luxury products consumed by the official and landlord classes, or in grain managed by the state (p. 113).

11. See, for example, Sjoberg, pp. 206–7, and Belshaw, p. 70.

12. Gras, p. 55; Davis, p. 79; Beals, pp. 202, 211; and Hodder and Ukwu, pp. 90–91.

13. See, for example, Usher, p. 355; Sjoberg, pp. 206, 209, 211–12, 214; Lopez and Raymond, p. 152.

14. See Gras, p. 208; Beals, p. 210; Belshaw, p. 73.

goods, even badly needed essentials, until it is profitable to sell them dearly (hoarding and speculating).

The wealthy merchant, because of his or her greater holdings and margin for risk, is also in a position to benefit from bargaining where there are no fixed prices, and to forestall goods on the way to market, often by buying in bulk at lower prices. Irregularity in supply flows is also to the advantage of those who can afford to travel and stockpile. Finally, lack of standardization makes it possible to manipulate weights and measures and encourages adulteration of goods. Thus, merchant activity in less developed economies is closely linked to structural weaknesses in marketing technology. While the inadequacies in technology mean that the merchant courts great risks in the performance of a useful function, they also offer him or her a chance to earn high profits. Much illicit merchant activity, in fact, can be seen as attempts to reduce such risks.

These market conditions that derive from transport and storage insufficiencies help to account for other traits, besides a tendency toward "corrupt" practices, that characterize marketing culture in many "developing" countries. For example, merchant partnerships and combinations, often in the form of guilds, are common in such societies, for the purpose of pooling resources where an individual's capital is often localized and limited; controlling output where supply is variable; fixing prices where prices are negotiable; and gaining protection against the bureaucracy. The independence of local-level markets from governmental control which such guilds both thrive under and increase is typical, particularly where transport and communications are problematic.[15]

Ambivalence toward traders is also the rule in such societies: merchants are viewed as nonproductive self-seekers; however, since governmental officials are anxious to see the state profit from investment and taxes on trade, and are unable themselves to undertake all the work of local-level exchange that dealers do, the officials may allow more marketing to occur than their orthodox ideology supports. Too, bureaucrats across the world have put limits on merchant activity at the same time that they have secretly engaged in it themselves.[16]

These features of merchant behavior have all characterized Chinese commerce throughout history, particularly among the larger merchants. First of all, as chapter one has noted, for more than two millennia, governmental dependence on the functions that merchants perform was recognized. Then as later, however, a certain ambiguity existed in the official view of traders: they were considered parasitic, but at the same

15. Sjoberg, pp. 187–96, 207.
16. Sjoberg, p. 140; Good, pp. v, 119; Usher, p. 125; and Tilly, p. 437.

time, officials knew that they carried out crucial exchange operations.[17] This ambivalence was never fully resolved in pre-PRC times—merchants might have been used and at times exploited to serve official ends, and attempts were sometimes made to limit and control their activities, but there was never an effort to abolish them as a class.

Along with this ambiguity toward merchants went a second aspect of traditional merchant culture in China—elaborate systems of alliance and cooperation between officials and businessmen.[18] A typical pattern involved bureaucrats extending monopoly rights to merchants, for which merchants were forced to pay a fee. Merchants took their profits and the court obtained its extra revenue. Also, officially licensed brokers acted as intermediaries between the bureaucracy and marketgoers and got official support and protection as they helped in tax collection and coordinated the work of traveling merchants and retailers. These arrangements were further strengthened as officials invested in commercial undertakings and traders bought their way into government service by late traditional times. These alliances, at times covert and running counter to prescribed ideology, were often welded at the peasantry's expense.

The more elaborate forms of merchant-official partnership occurred at the higher levels of the administrative hierarchy. Although governmental ambiguity toward trade, plus bureaucrat-business combinations, also conditioned local-level rural trade, the crucial connections in marketing at the lower levels in the countryside were those among merchants and those between the merchants, the landed gentry, and the moneylenders.[19] The cooperation that existed among these local power-holders is related to a third aspect of traditional Chinese marketing style: as long ago as the third and fourth centuries A.D., a system of autonomous, unofficial markets existed in the countryside.[20] These markets were outside the system of officially controlled, regulated, and taxed

17. Mark Elvin, *The Pattern of the Chinese Past*, p. 164; and Albert Feuerwerker, "Economic Conditions in the Late Ch'ing Period," p. 118.

18. On this theme, see Denis Twitchett, "The T'ang Market System," p. 217; Shiba Yoshinobu, *Commerce and Society in Sung China*, pp. 74–75, 154–55, 165–68, 171, 203; Elvin, pp. 169, 172; Ho P'ing-ti, *The Ladder of Success in Imperial China*, pp. 77, 81–83; Frederic Wakeman, Jr., *The Fall of Imperial China*, pp. 44–45; Etienne Balazs, *Chinese Civilization and Bureaucracy*, pp. 40–42; G. William Skinner, "Marketing and Social Structure in Rural China, Part I," p. 42; Feuerwerker, "Economic Conditions," p. 119; Ray Huang, *Taxation and Governmental Finance in 16th Century Ming China*, p. 232; and Thomas A. Metzger, "The State and Commerce in Imperial China."

19. Skinner, "Marketing and Social Structure... Part I," p. 37. A study that carefully traces these relationships in a Hebei county fair in the early twentieth century is Susan Mann Jones, "Trade, Transport, and Taxes: The Decline of a National Medicine Fair in Republican China."

20. Elvin, p. 166; see also Twitchett, pp. 205, 240.

markets, and their actors were left largely to their own devices.[21]

Again, these patterns matched those cited above as typical of merchant behavior in other preindustrial environments. For example, various forms of traders' partnerships have marked Chinese commercial activity; and the same array of "corrupt" practices were found here as elsewhere.

Merchant organization existed in Song dynasty times (tenth to thirteenth centuries), when small businessmen banded together in groups of ten and sometimes became linked into networks for longer-range ventures with richer merchants.[22] At a more formalized level of operation, merchant guilds in modern times were able to fix prices and to pressure officials on their own behalf.[23]

"Corrupt" practices among men of commerce were criticized from the dawn of marketplace trading in China. Twitchett has found a derogatory reference to hoarders who focus on profits, push prices up, use unfair weights, swindle, and forestall, as long ago as 808 A.D.[24] A few centuries later, Zhu Xi (Chu Hsi), the twelfth-century scholar, complained about deceitful rice-brokers who engaged in adulteration of goods, sold with irregular measures, stockpiled, and hoarded.[25]

Modern-day social scientists reporting on rural marketing practices in various corners of China in the 1930s and 1940s all noted the same type of tricks that were employed for centuries in the country markets;[26] and many of these observers cited a connection between the technological environment there and commercial activity. Thus, advantages were reaped by holders of capital who could obtain access to superior transport facilities, especially but not only in areas where topography severely limited interdistrict movement.[27] And dealers with storage facilities to hold reserves in stock generally managed to outdo peasants in the marketplace.[28]

These observers found that, as in other places at the same technological level, localization of trade compounded the seasonal variability in sup-

21. Skinner, p. 31; H. B. Morse, *The Trade and Administration of the Chinese Empire*, p. 170.
22. Shiba, pp. 197–98.
23. R. H. Tawney, *Land and Labor in China*, p. 56.
24. Twitchett, pp. 229–30.
25. Shiba, pp. 68–69, 71–72.
26. Morton H. Fried, *The Fabric of Chinese Society*, p. 126; Skinner, p. 30; Ching-kun Yang, *A North China Local Market Economy*, p. 18; Liao T'ai-ch'u, "The Rape Markets on the Chengtu Plain," pp. 1017, 1019; Tawney, p. 57.
27. Yang, pp. 18, 29; Liao, pp. 1016–17; Tawney, p. 55; C. P. Fitzgerald, *The Tower of the Five Glories*, pp. 12, 191; Zhang Xiaomei, *Guizhou jingji* [The Economy of Guizhou], p. K35; Lou Yunlin, ed., *Sichuan fensheng dizhi* [Sichuan's geography], p. 174.
28. Tawney, p. 57.

ply flows and also led to price differentials in neighboring areas.[29] And the lack of standardization in weights and measures and in the quality of goods in mid-twentieth-century China, along with the absence of fixed prices even within one market, permitted the bargaining, price manipulation, and adulteration of commodities noted elsewhere.[30]

That these same procedures prevailed in English and Continental markets in medieval times is evident from the numerous regulations against such customs mentioned in studies of the period. In the various countries laws were on the books against monopolizing wares to the detriment of the general public;[31] forbidding secret agreements among merchants to control prices and supplies, and banning even simple partnerships;[32] against adulterating goods and for instituting standardized uniform weights and measures;[33] against speculation and hoarding goods;[34] and against regrating and forestalling.[35] In these places, too, though the state authorities eventually chose to collaborate with merchants to ensure that key populations were fed, as well as to enrich its own coffers,[36] medieval regulations were often informed by a desire to eliminate the profit-seeking middleman and to create a system of direct, face-to-face exchange.[37] In preindustrial Europe, as in mid-twentieth-century China, then, an early stage of economic development fostered trading practices that ran counter to prevailing morality.

A conclusion that can be drawn from this material is that, despite governmental disapproval of profit-seeking behavior in medieval Western Europe as well as under the PRC, basic commercial habits could not be altered by regulations alone. Rather, the close interconnection between a primitive technology and state-defined market "corruption" meant that the technological supports for such behavior had to be trans-

29. Fitzgerald, p. 55; Yang, p. 21; Skinner, p. 31; and Tawney, p. 56, discuss the localized nature of trade; Tawney, pp. 56–57, and Zhang, p. K35, talk about seasonal fluctuations in supply; and Skinner, p. 30, and Tawney, pp. 56–57, describe the differentials in pricing among markets.

30. See Skinner, pp. 39–40; Yang, pp. 18, 20–21; Liao, pp. 1016–17.

31. Lopez and Raymond, p. 126; and Cunningham, p. 249.

32. Lopez and Raymond, p. 127; Henri Pirenne, *Medieval Cities*, pp. 118, 120; Gras, p. 161; and Usher, pp. 93, 302.

33. Lopez and Raymond, pp. 152, 266; and Gras, pp. 69, 132.

34. Pirenne, *Early Democracies*, p. 81; Cunningham, p. 249; and Usher, p. 141.

35. Gras, pp. 66–67, 131 (he notes that the injunctions against forestalling go back to the Anglo-Saxon period, and that it is the first commercial act to be termed illegal); and Cunningham, pp. 254, 320–21.

36. Tilly, p. 437, and Pirenne, *Medieval Cities*, pp. 127–28.

37. Pirenne, *Early Democracies*, p. 81; and Pirenne, *Medieval Cities*, p. 209.

formed before the merchant's position could be truly undermined. The sections below will trace the PRC's initial efforts along these lines.

The Parties to the Conflict:
State Goals and Merchant Resources

STATE GOALS

The state in China after 1949 hoped to control commerce in order to ensure that consumers were supplied at reasonable prices, and also to shift to its own hands the revenue that commerce yielded. Twelve years of civil and international war had bequeathed to the Communists a severely run-down and chaotic economy. In the field of commercial work, the recovery effort was concentrated on restoring and regularizing disrupted supply flows, reestablishing damaged communications links and creating new transport facilities, pacifying bandits and other rebellious social elements whose sabotage destroyed the basic security required for trade, and working to bring rampant inflation under control.[38]

Once a modicum of order had been introduced into the economy, the leadership's goals in trade work expanded to include a renewed establishment of commercial ties between urban and rural areas and an increase in the economic integration of larger regions across China as a whole.[39] Finally, the regime sought to institute rudimentary controls over prices in this early period and to lessen price differentials between regions and seasons while also cutting down the disparity between wholesale and retail prices.[40]

The eventual success of all these activities would indeed go a long way toward satisfying the population's needs for food and other basic com-

38. For discussion of these points, see Ch'en Yün, [Chen Yun], "The Financial and Economic Situation in the PRC During the Past Year" (October 1, 1950), in *New China's Economic Achievements 1949–1952 (NCEA)*, pp. 96, 100; Ch'en Yün, "The Problem of Commodity Prices and the Issuance of Government Bonds" (December 2, 1949), in *NCEA*, p. 34; Ch'en Yün, "The Economic Situation and Problems in the Readjustment of Industry, Commerce and Taxation" (June 15, 1950), in *NCEA*, p. 64; Hsüeh Mu-ch'iao [Xue Muqiao], "China's Great Victories on the Economic Front in the Past Three Years" (October 1, 1952), in *NCEA*, pp. 270–71; T. J. Hughes and D. E. T. Luard, *The Economic Development of Communist China 1949–1958*, p. 27; and Dwight H. Perkins, *Market Control and Planning in Communist China*, pp. 1–2.

39. Hsüeh Mu-ch'iao, p. 271; Po I-po [Bo Yibo], "Three Years of Achievements in the PRC," in *NCEA*, p. 159; Yao Yi-lin, "The Readjustment and Development of China's Commerce Since 1949" (October 3, 1952), in *NCEA*, p. 223; *Xinhua yuebao* [New China Monthly] (Peking) (*XHYB*), no. 22 (1951), p. 868; and *Renmin ribao* [People's Daily] (Beijing) (*RMRB*), March 13, 1951, p. 2.

40. Ch'en Yün, in *NCEA*, pp. 69–70; and Yao Yi-lin, p. 221. Treatment of price differentials is a political issue. In periods of radicalism some have been eliminated. Thus, Yao

modities. But the PRC government had a larger vision, a longer-range plan in its efforts to control the revenues bound up with trade. Its leaders believed that intensified and state-directed commercial activity could raise the people's purchasing power and thus stimulate an overall recovery and development of production and of the economy generally.[41] Moreover, increased governmental control over commerce would permit the state to divert the profits that private businessmen had gained from their trade for use in state-planned financial endeavors, particularly for savings for capital formation.[42]

In seeking to fulfill these economic goals in the first few years after takeover, the new state set forth a policy that carried on the traditional official ambivalence toward traders. Thus, the state planned to rely at first on the aid of those it viewed as "nonexploitative," "proper" or "legitimate" traders. At the same time, however, its leaders utilized a divide-and-rule strategy in managing merchants. This they did by entitling these "legitimate" or "proper" merchants to a certain "legal" profit, thereby splitting them off from another group of "speculating, illegitimate" businessmen who were to be discriminated against, punished, and ultimately eliminated as a class. Presumably, the distinction between the two groups was a matter of degree, since all merchants were obviously involved to some extent in profit seeking. Also, as scholars of the early 1950s point out, the regime saw the value of managerial and entrepreneurial skills and hoped to retain the services of those members of the capitalist class who seemed likely to serve the ends of the regime.[43]

This divisive approach appeared in a speech on industry and commerce delivered by Mao Zedong in February 1948;[44] in Article 37 of the Common Program of the Chinese People's Political Consultative Confer-

---

Yi-lin, during the Great Leap Forward, stated in *RMRB* (September 28, 1959) that at that time there was no seasonal differential for grain; *RMRB*, March 16, 1980, in a marketeer period, reported on the reinstitution of egg price seasonal differentials, which was to be "beneficial to improving the business management of fresh eggs and market supply and to developing egg production." See also *Jingji yanjiu* [Economic Studies] (Beijing) no. 4 (1958), p. 57, where there is a reference to debates over how much to reduce (and whether to eliminate) seasonal differentials, in the interests of eliminating opportunities for profiteers to carry out exploitation. A reduction of differentials still requires the state to subsidize necessary storage and transport costs, the author points out.

41. Yao Yi-lin, p. 225.

42. Victor D. Lippit, *Land Reform and Economic Development in China*, pp. 113–20 and 139.

43. See, for example, Lippit, pp. 98–99; and John Gardner, "The *Wu-fan* Campaign in Shanghai: A Study in the Consolidation of Urban Control," pp. 479, 485–86. I have been unable to find any clear guidelines or criteria that would specify how to distinguish between these two types of merchants.

44. Mao Tse-tung, "On the Policy Concerning Industry and Commerce."

ence, promulgated in September 1949, which served as a state constitution until 1954;[45] and in speeches delivered by Vice-Premier Chen Yun in 1950. The message in all these statements was basically the same, that, in Chen's words,

> as long as private commerce does not engage in commercial speculation, state-owned trading enterprises should provide an outlet for it by setting goods at fair prices and making room for it in the market, so that it may assist in circulating goods between the city and the countryside, between China and foreign countries.[46]

Thus, the plan was to co-opt compatible businessmen to enlist their aid in economic recovery and development, but to suppress those who were excessive in their profit seeking, and to substitute state organs in their place.

MERCHANT RESOURCES

To understand the position of the rural merchants in China in 1949, it is useful to go back to the structural environment in which they operated. To the extent that "corrupt" merchants had a power base in the countryside, it rested on the fact that this environment offered opportunities that the merchants not only knew how to exploit but held the resources necessary to do so. At the same time power for merchants—not a popular group in themselves—also depended on their building certain alliances and partnerships to enhance their own strength.

Thus, the resources that were crucial to merchant operations in the early PRC (or to merchants in any less-developed economy) were of two kinds. One can be labeled associational/political: these resources were connected with the social aspects of the merchant's milieu as discussed above, that is, the types of alliances traders fashioned. The other type of resource can be termed material/technical: this type relates to the structural features of the environment in which businessmen operated in the countryside in China.

Merchants held two sorts of associational/political resources at the time of takeover (as they did throughout Chinese history): mutually profitable business alliances with officials and local power-holders, and partnerships among themselves. These were the organizational factors that enabled them to take advantage of their economic environment.

45. "Common Program of the CPPCC," translated in Albert P. Blaustein, *Fundamental Legal Documents of Communist China*, p. 48.
46. Ch'en Yün, in *NCEA*, pp. 105–6. See also ibid., pp. 69–70, and *XHYB*, 3, no. 2 (1950), 346.

Material/technical resources relevant to merchant activity and important in accounting for merchant power were capital, information, and skills. Capital was needed first of all to acquire and control storage and transport facilities: stockpiling and hoarding, speculating and regrating all depended on access to storage facilities; transport vehicles were needed to take advantage of pricing differentials between areas and irregularities in supply flows. Capital was essential also in bribery and bargaining.

The type of information that counted concerned supply flows, price differentials between areas, and discrepancies between weights, measures, and grades of goods within a given trading network; and the business skills required involved the ability to manipulate this kind of information. Thus, capital, information, and skills were important resources for merchants insofar as they could be utilized to rig the markets, to take advantage of the structural, technological weaknesses in the commercial system in the countryside. In the early years of the PRC, to the extent that rural merchants could still draw on this traditional set of resources, they were able to retain at least some of their hold on trade. Undermining their power over the local, rural economy would entail stripping them of these various resources.

The Showdown: Merchant and State Strategies in the Battle for Control over the Local Economy, 1949–1952

THE ADMINISTRATIVE CONTEXT

A brief look at some of the administrative difficulties the state encountered in its initial effort to get a foothold in the rural economy will set the scene for evaluating merchant-state interactions in the early PRC. Successes were claimed in many aspects of commercial work on a nationwide scale by the third anniversary of the new state.[47] However, reported cases of lack of vigilance; faulty liaison among units and levels; and laziness, profit seeking, and ignorance on the part of cadres at times must have created just the same kinds of loopholes for resourceful traders as did the structural factors described above.

47. See articles by Hsüeh Mu-ch'iao, Yao Yi-lin, Po I-po, Ch'eng Tse-hua [Cheng Zi-hua], and Teng Tai-yüan [Deng Daiyuan] in NCEA.

Arranging proper storage for goods remained a problem in the early 1950s (and in the decades to follow). The difficulties caused by inadequate technology were very likely compounded by the inexperience of state-run organs in handling trading facilities. In one example, since the Southwest branch of the China grains company lacked "technical facilities," transportation, loading, packaging, and safekeeping costs were high in late 1951.[48] Another article related to this problem of storage tells how a local branch of a state company set up to purchase and resell oxen in South Sichuan was so ill equipped to look after the poor beasts properly that it eventually was forced to slaughter rather than sell the uncared-for, diseased animals. In another case, white ants infested goods stored in an unkempt warehouse.[49]

Besides poor storage, other old problems remained or intensified. Especially in the first year or two after takeover, local-level markets retained a good deal of their historical autonomy, since it took time to set up healthy, functioning, uniform, and coordinated state organs in commerce. Repeatedly, the press complained about how easy it was for private merchants to retain their foothold under these conditions.[50] Later, the localized, uncontrolled nature of local rural markets was perpetuated when state trade organs in some areas preferred to turn their attention to the cities, neglecting even important country market towns.[51]

Irregularities in supply flows constituted another ongoing problem at times: press articles describe situations in which state-run sales-promotion teams did not prepare well, so that there was no grain, production implements, or daily necessities on hand to supply the needs of peasants

48. *Xinhua ribao* [New China Daily] (Chongqing) (*XHRB*), Nov. 29, 1951, p. 1. This was the press organ for the Southwest region from 1949 to 1954. The storage problem has never been thoroughly solved in China. For an analysis several years later, see *China News Analysis (CNA)*, no. 27 (1954). Several articles on inadequacies in storage work appeared during the Great Leap Forward, as in *SCMP*, no. 1996 (1959), pp. 3–16, which urges warehouses to implement the six-no's and one-fast: no fires, no spoilage by damp or mildew, no breakage, no rusting or erosion by worms and vermin, no shortage or pilferage, no injury or accidents; and speedy storage into and removal from warehouses. Obviously all these issues remained problems in 1959. The article termed basic (county)-level warehouses at that time "in a ramshackle condition." For more recent attention to technical problems, see *RMRB*, April 29, 1978, p. 3, which urges an improvement in the quality of packaging and transport work; and *RMRB*, August 6, 1981, p. 2, continues to complain about technical shortcomings in the technology of trade.

49. *XHRB*, January 6, 1952, p. 2; December 22, 1951, p. 1.

50. For example, *XHRB*, Oct. 13, 1951, p. 2; Nov. 2, 1951, p. 2; Nov. 22, 1951, p. 2; March 11, 1952, April 17, 1952, p. 2; *SCMP*, no. 202 (1951), p. 21.

51. *XHRB*, Oct. 13, 1951, p. 2.

who had recently sold their cotton.[52] Other supply problems resulted from rich peasants with grain surpluses who refused to sell their grain,[53] and from cadres who were lazy about purchasing.[54]

Eliminating excessive price differentials between districts was a prime focus of governmental attention. Nevertheless, the behavior of some units made it difficult for the state to monopolize the management of this issue in a coordinated way. In one instance, since glass was cheaper in Hankou than locally, state trade organs from the Southwest area went directly to Hankou to purchase the glass, rather than following regulations by buying from the state trade companies in their own area which were charged with responsibility for procuring the glass.[55] In another case, in two subcounty-level markets about four miles apart prices were so dissimilar that residents of the market town where goods were cheaper had to safeguard their marketplace with arms to prohibit people from taking grain out before the state could intervene![56]

The difficulties associated with lack of standardization were far from resolved immediately either. Some local branches of state native-products companies refused to post prices or lowered them on their own initiative;[57] only markets with taxation offices for important products (grain, cotton, oil, salt) used standard weights and measures for these goods, while for other goods haphazard measures prevailed.[58] A state general-goods company failed to sort goods into classes;[59] and some

52. For example, XHRB, Nov. 14, 1951, p. 2.

53. XHRB, Nov. 28, 1951, p. 2, and Dec. 17, 1951, p. 2.

54. XHRB, Nov. 28, 1951, p. 2, and Dec. 27, 1951, p. 2.

55. XHRB, Dec. 22, 1951, p. 1. SCMP, no. 1592 (1957), pp. 13–15, mentions interdistrict price differentials as a cause of speculation in 1957.

56. XHRB, Jan. 13, 1952, p. 6.

57. XHRB, Oct. 20, 1951, p. 2. See also Dec. 22, 1951, p. 1, on cadres "blindly adjusting prices."

58. XHRB, Nov. 2, 1951, p. 2. CNA, no. 427 (1962), reports on a persistent lack of standardization in weights and measures at the local level, even as of 1962. White, "Small Enterprises in Shanghai," p. 72, mentions meetings on standardizing the steel rod in Shanghai in 1964. And New China News Agency, July 24, 1977, referred to (then) recent great progress in unifying *basically* the system of measurements and the standards of quantities which had brought *nearly* to an end the "chaos left over by old China" in measurements (emphasis added). This was in response to new regulations, commented upon in RMRB, July 20, 1977. Shichang [Market] (Beijing) (SC), no. 15 (May 10, 1980), p. 14, has two articles on cheating fostered by nonstandard measures.

59. XHRB, Nov. 4, 1951, p. 2. The problem of setting quality standards is an ongoing one in China, in part because "the variety of native and special products is complex and the specification of products and the standard of testing is not very scientific" (SCMP, no. 1379 [1956], pp. 4–5). The other problem here is that commercial personnel intentionally

state trade companies were said to sell adulterated rice to state-sponsored supply and marketing cooperatives (SMCs) because the company personnel were interested in seeking profits for the company alone, not for the state sector as a whole.[60]

Other problems—such as tax personnel's encouraging high prices in order to collect extra tax revenue;[61] lower-level governmental units' ignoring instructions from the *xian* (county) business section and purchasing charcoal on their own;[62] and state trade personnel and cooperatives' workers' unfamiliarity with business methods[63]—all retarded the attack on the backward structural factors that complicated commerce. Consequently, a fair portion of the traditional structural edifice was left standing.

MERCHANT STRATEGIES

In the first few years after 1949, regardless of how widespread these problems were, the presence of such difficulties probably gave the small merchants in the countryside the idea that there existed a chance to circumvent, subvert, or even sabotage the regulations and new arrangements of the Communist rulers. There is no way to calculate either the extent of merchant obstruction or its actual effect on the economy. It is clear, however, that loopholes in the system left scope for merchant interference, and that at least some merchants made use of these opportunities. In the political arena their obstructionist behavior consisted of resisting or co-opting any organs or individuals who interfered with their ability to earn a profit.

---

downgrade the quality standards of produce as they procure, in order to siphon off more profit from the transaction. See U.S. *Foreign Broadcast Information Service (FBIS)*, September 27, 1979, pp. S2–S3.

60. *XHRB*, Dec. 3, 1951, p. 2. A corrupt food cooperative team was accused of substituting inferior for superior goods in 1970 (see *Survey of the China Mainland Press-Supplement [SCMPS]*, no. 267 [1967], p. 29); and employees of some state stores were said to "mix bad with good or pass off inferior goods as approved products," in *SCMP*, no. 4341 (1969), p. 11.

61. *XHRB*, Nov. 6, 1951, p. 2.

62. *XHRB*, Dec. 6, 1951, p. 2.

63. *XHRB*, April 16, 1952, p. 1. Another, and probably more serious, sort of problem must have derived from the fact that many of those who were private, noncommunist merchants before 1949 were employed as state trade cadres after takeover. There was a shortage of cadres of all types in the Southwest at that time, and it must have been natural to rely on those who knew the local trade customs and networks.

Soon after takeover the new regime quickly went to work trying to establish some minimal organizational control over marketing activity at the local level. An amazing array of groups, teams, and societies proliferated in the commercial realm, including joint-management societies,[64] sales promotion teams,[65] go-to-the-countryside groups under state trading companies,[66] purchase teams,[67] small-trade teams,[68] and SMCs, to name only a few of the more common types. These ad hoc organs constituted one of the two prime political targets at which rural merchants directed their activities at the local level after 1949.

Besides these organs, merchants had a second target in their efforts to ensure a continuing profit in their trading. This second target was the group of officials charged with executing state commercial policy—with favoring only "legitimate" traders and with eliminating "speculative, illegitimate" trade and the conditions that fostered it. Thus, in their political behavior merchants mobilized themselves to counter the new organizational forms and the cadres that staffed them, since these forms and cadres posed a definite challenge to their own traditional hold over the rural economy as well as to their traditional political resource bases— their own merchant partnerships and their alliances with officials.[69]

Rural merchants employed several types of strategies in seeking to interfere with officials in their implementation of the new PRC commercial policy. In each case, merchants fell back on their habitual ties with officials, but managed to adapt these ties to the new, changed environment and regulations under the PRC. In the simplest strategy, resistant merchants used traditional tricks of bribery, seduction, and giving commissions to officials in order to get control over state funds or to obtain goods at reduced rates.

64. See especially *XHRB*, October 6, 1951, p. 2, which discusses the intended positive functions for this type of organ. All of these bodies (except for the supply and marketing cooperatives) were only creatures of this early period.

65. *XHRB*, October 9, 1951, p. 2.

66. *XHRB*, October 11, 1951, p. 2.

67. *XHRB*, November 12, 1951, p. 2.

68. *XHRB*, December 12, 1951, p. 2.

69. Illicit partnerships (or "connivance with friends and relatives"), collusion between corrupt elements and cadres, and posing as members of state organs, all criticized before 1952, continued to occur throughout subsequent years, according to official media. On partnerships, see *SCMP*, nos. 701 (1953), pp. 30–33, and 4504 (1969), pp. 1–3, and *RMRB*, August 7, 1957. On collusion, see *SCMP*, nos. 775 (1954), pp. 19–22; 1592 (1957), pp. 13–15; and 4341 (1969), p. 12; *SCMPS*, no. 267 (1970), pp. 30, 32; and *Union Research Service*, 30, no. 26 (1963): 434. On posing as state cadres, see *SCMP*, nos. 701 (1953), pp. 30–31, and 1522 (1957), p. 30.

In one such case, profiteers colluded with officials retained from the period of Guomindang rule then working in the Southwest Military Region Logistics Bureau, and with those who had owned factories before 1949, to buy up goods at a cheap price, which could then be sold at higher prices. In another case, the assistant manager of a state native-products company collaborated with his subordinates and, after being bribed, sold cloth to private merchants without paying attention to market supply conditions and without getting approval from higher levels.[70]

A somewhat more complicated form of cooperation involved cases where illegitimate merchants stationed one of their number inside state trade organs. In similar situations officials already working in state trade organs were befriended and bribed in an effort to entice them to join in the merchants' schemes. Generally, such tactics were employed to steal market intelligence pertaining to the changes and adjustments in government price regulations and to government organs' purchase plans in trying to control supply flows.[71]

One article describes the intricate machinations such activities entailed.[72] An individual acting as a spy in a state native-products company discovered that the company would soon be purchasing pitch from the local peasants. The spy then informed his fellow profiteers, who immediately bought up pitch of inferior quality and then bribed some company officials to buy the low-grade pitch from the profiteers.

Once the profiteers had thereby depleted much of the company's capital, they used it to go to the area producing good pitch and purchased this in large batches at low, bulk-rate prices. The profiteers then rushed the pitch to Chongqing and Hankou, where they sold it at a high price. Finally, when the state company actually went to purchase the pitch as scheduled, prices were high, since supplies had been exhausted by the profiteers; meanwhile, the market where the company had intended to sell pitch was glutted, and prices fell there.

In a third form of collusion between officials and merchants, members of the two groups actively cooperated in various plans to manipulate the market. This category of behavior included profiteers' cornering the entire market in one line of products through their connections with

70. *XHRB*, Jan. 13, 1952, p. 1. Also see Jan. 1, 1951, p. 2, Dec. 11, 1951, p. 1, and Feb. 4, 1952. See *SCMP*, no. 4584 (1970), pp. 5–6, for an attack on the "bourgeoisie" for corrupting commercial personnel through bribes and banquets.

71. *XHRB*, Feb. 6, 1952, p. 2; April 13, 1952, p. 1.

72. *XHRB*, March 11, 1952, p. 2.

state-employed accountants, inspectors, weighers, and business cadres. When this occurred, such gangs could monopolize supplies, adulterate goods, tamper with measures, and squeeze out smaller merchants.[73]

Interestingly, each of these three forms of alliance between officials and merchants corresponds to one of the three types of material/technical resources that merchants possessed: capital, information, and skills. They were able to draw on their capital in the first form of alliance — bribing officials — and this bribery helped them to amass more capital. In the second form, merchants used spies or agents to obtain crucial market information, which they were then able to draw upon in manipulating the market. And in the third, more elaborate form of linkage, merchants and "corrupted" officials combined their skills in creating monopolies and adulterating goods. None of this activity would have been possible if structural factors did not facilitate it: prices still varied among districts, supply flows were still largely uncontrolled, and uniformity had not yet been imposed on weights, measures, and the quality of goods.

In trying to attack the new organs set up after 1949 to deal with local-level trade, merchants resorted also to their own typical pattern of forming partnerships among themselves. Thus, as in their dealings with government officials, where they utilized their first historical associational/political resource, alliances with officials, so in this case they drew on their second traditional associational/political resource, internal combinations within the merchant group. Here, as in their collaboration with individual officials, merchants managed not only to rely on simple partnerships very much in a traditional style; they also designed new associational methods of subverting the intruding organs. To the extent that former private merchants were employed as state trade cadres, these two types of behavior shaded one into the next.

Again beginning with the straightforward type of merchant combinations, a number of press accounts relate how small numbers of merchants operated together in some sort of marketing network to the disadvantage of peasant traders. Such combinations included collusion between resident and traveling merchants to sidestep regulations on purchasing and bank loan quotas;[74] deals between vendors operating on a small, local scale and wealthier merchants based in the bigger city of

73. *XHRB*, April 17, 1952, p. 2; Feb. 10, 1952, p. 1.
74. See *XHRB*, Oct. 4, 1951, p. 2; Oct. 9, 1951, p. 2.

Chengdu, whereby the smaller merchants were given "pass-through-the-hands-money" for turning over goods purchased cheaply from peasants in the local markets;[75] agreements between vendors in the same trade to hoard goods and corner the market by pooling capital;[76] ganging up in the marketplace to enforce forestallers' low prices;[77] and joining together to adulterate goods such as salt, sugar, and vegetables, by mixing in "moldy, filthy things" and applying coloring.[78]

A more sophisticated form of combination was frequently inveighed against in the press in the fall of 1951: many merchant groups used the name and trappings of state-sponsored business groups and organs as covers under which to play havoc with state policy. After the land reform, which confiscated the capital of the landlord and capitalist class, which had been the foundation of rural business before liberation, markets were sluggish and inactive. In this situation, private and public businesses were encouraged to join forces to try to reinvigorate commerce. The prescribed organizational form, the "joint enterprise society," was designed and advocated as a way to combine capital for manufacture, buying, transport, and marketing.[79]

This organizational form was the one most often exploited by "illegitimate" merchants. Once created within a trade, these groups engaged in speculation; monopolization of the market; tampering with prices, the grading of goods, and weights and measures; hoarding; and regrating.[80] Landlords also used such groups as "bomb shelters" during land reform for secretly investing their capital to escape peasants' "settling of accounts."[81]

A story of behavior of this kind tells of a group of "illegitimate merchants" who established a partnership and then forged the names of over one hundred salt merchants in order to get a large salt ration from the upper levels. They used this ration to supply their own needs, and forced small merchants to buy from them at a fee.[82] Yet another group of

75. *XHRB*, Oct. 7, 1951, p. 2; Nov. 2, 1951, p. 2, Oct. 28, 1951, p. 2.
76. *XHRB*, Jan. 20, 1951, p. 6; Nov. 6, 1951, p. 2; March 11, 1952, p. 2; April 12, 1952, p. 2.
77. *XHRB*, Oct. 28, 1951, p. 2.
78. *XHRB*, March 1, 1952, p. 2.
79. *XHRB*, Oct. 6, 1951, p. 2. Such prescribed cooperation between public and private operators was also aimed at cutting down on competitive behavior from the private sector.
80. *XHRB*, Oct. 7, 1951, p. 2; Oct. 27, 1951, p. 2; Oct. 28, 1951, p. 2; Nov. 14, 1951, p. 2; Dec. 15, 1951, p. 2; April 17, 1952, p. 2.
81. *XHRB*, Dec. 23, 1951, p. 2.
82. *XHRB*, Feb. 10, 1952, p. 1.

bankrupt landlords ganged up with some illicit businessmen to form a mock "joint sales small team" and pretended to operate under the jurisdiction of a state company. When the state personnel left the countryside temporarily to do business in the city, this group posed as the company, rigging scales and spreading rumors.[83]

Besides straightforward merchant combinations and groups that disguised themselves as state organs, a third type of subversion involved groups that were especially strong. Such groups were in a position to compete actively with state trade organs in the market. At times this involved buying and hoarding a state grain company's grain and then selling it at an increased price.[84] At other times a group would undersell an SMC, destroying the co-ops' prestige.[85] The general rule for such competition seemed to be this: use low prices to buy up goods from the peasants before the company can act, thereby cornering the market; or raise the prices in purchasing to procure goods from small merchants and vendors when it is not possible to beat the company in timing.[86]

The fourth form of behavior concerned with organizing to undermine new state organs entailed penetrating the new organs themselves, either through investing capital or through taking over important leadership positions and placing subordinates in key posts. Organs so affected included "market management committees," which, in Chengdu, were infiltrated by capitalists who manipulated prices and created artificial scarcities;[87] SMCs, when landlords and merchants managed to become managers and chairmen of the board;[88] and a "joint enterprise service team," to which a commercial clique at the *xiang* (township) level— composed of landlords, pre-1949 village officials, Guomindang youth propaganda department personnel, and ex-Guomindang party secretaries—transferred its capital and soon came to dominate.[89]

Also, in a local branch of a state salt company ex-Guomindang officials usurped the leading power and delegated "lackeys" to conspire with profiteers. These people established a group that illegally rationed salt to stores by forging a phony document; and hired a "specialist technical"

83. *XHRB*, Oct. 7, 1951, p. 2.
84. *XHRB*, April 12, 1952, p. 2.
85. *XHRB*, Oct. 17, 1951, p. 2.
86. *XHRB*, Dec. 23, 1951, p. 2; March 11, 1952, p. 2.
87. *XHRB*, April 20, 1952, p. 2.
88. *XHRB*, Oct. 15, 1951, p. 2.
89. *XHRB*, Oct. 20, 1951, p. 2.

weigher whose specialized technique was to use any standard scale to change 100 catties of goods to 95 catties in buying from peasants, and then to weigh out the same 100 catties as 105 catties when selling![90]

Skillful merchants even penetrated governmental administrative bodies with their members. In at least one case profiteers representing various trades first combined and promoted one of their group to serve as a local Business Federation manager and as the standing-committee member of the local all-circles' people's representative conference. Later they bribed the chief of a tax affairs bureau and used his influence to acquire the position of business-section head in the *xian* people's government.[91]

Whether these merchants utilized old-style partnerships, created new organizations that posed as legitimate Communist model groups, competed with proper organs, or penetrated state business and governmental units, they employed the range of "corrupt" practices—monopolizing, manipulating prices, speculating and hoarding, and tampering with weights and quality—that the still unmodernized economic and technological structure in the countryside permitted.

And, in organizational subversion, such as the forming of alliances with officials, merchants were able to continue to act according to their traditional style in the early PRC to the extent that they still retained their traditional material/technical resources: capital to bribe officials, build partnerships, and form new organizations, and information and skills to compete with and penetrate state organs.

STATE STRATEGIES

Thus, in order seriously to undercut private merchant activity that interfered with regime goals, more was required than just regulations. Legal and administrative measures—and even institutional change—had to be supplemented by a program of technological transformation in the countryside if the Communists were to compete with and eventually push aside these old-style men of trade.

The new regime's attack on the merchants can be analyzed by showing that its work involved efforts to strip away the resources on which merchant power had rested. In short, the regime took over merchants' capital and tried to end their monopoly on information. At the same

90. *XHRB*, March 20, 1952, p. 2.
91. *XHRB*, April 17, 1952, p. 2. The Business Federation and the all-circles' people's representative conference were mass organizations instituted by the Communists to give concerned people some chance to participate in politics and to co-opt liberal and middle-class elements who might otherwise oppose the regime.

time, the government began to change the structural and cultural environment that had supported merchant resources. Moreover, it created new state-sponsored organs and trained new state cadres who were to substitute for the disfavored merchants by performing the merchants' jobs. The regime itself offered no sophisticated economic analysis to show the connection between the causes of market manipulation by merchants, on the one hand, and the remedial program it designed and followed, on the other. It is clear, however, that such a program was essential to state success in squeezing out these competitors for commercial control and profit.

Merchant material/technical resources had consisted of capital, information, and skills. As early as 1950, and with greatly stepped-up intensity in 1951 and 1952, punishments for merchants caught speculating, hoarding, manipulating prices, and adulterating goods included such measures to obtain their capital as forcing them to recompense peasants for goods procured but not fully paid for by using a heavier than standard scale; fining them, freezing their capital, and confiscating their goods; and even auctioning off their whole property.[92]

The government also was involved during this period in redistributing the capital traditionally used in rural commerce. Peasants obtained additional income as a result of land reform, which they then invested in marketing.[93] The joint-enterprise society, when it worked as it should have, concentrated small capital holdings among "legitimate" dealers.[94] SMCs drew together peasant investments.[95] These measures filled the gap created when those "illegitimate" merchants whose funds had supported marketing were divested of their wealth.

Efforts were also made to destroy these merchants' monopoly on market information. For one thing, state-run organs labeled and publicized the prices of goods in the marketplace.[96] And private traders who were considered "legitimate" worked with state companies in investigating and researching the situation in local markets. One article called on these two groups to establish a "mutual reporting" intelligence system to keep each other informed of market activity.[97]

---

92. XHYB, 3, no. 2 (1950), 347; XHRB, Oct. 7, 1951, p. 2; Oct. 9, 1951, p. 2; Oct. 13, 1951, p. 2; Oct. 31, 1951, p. 2; Nov. 10, 1951, p. 2.

93. XHRB, Oct. 4, 1951, p. 2.

94. XHRB, Oct. 6, 1951, p. 2. See also Nov. 8, 1951, p. 2, on a public-private jointly operated investment company set up in Guizhou "to guide idle capital and develop production."

95. XHRB, Oct. 10, 1951, p. 1. Peasants supposedly invested shares in these state-run cooperatives.

96. XHRB, Oct. 16, 1951, p. 2.

97. See XHRB, Oct. 13 and Oct. 16, 1951, p. 2 in both issues.

Merchants' third material/technical resource, their skills in manipulating the market, rested upon a certain technological structural environment, as was demonstrated above. Thus, to undermine merchant activity, it was essential to transform the central features of this environment: the primitive transport and storage facilities, the localization of marketing activity, supply fluctuations, pricing differentials, and lack of standardization. As was related above, administrative problems stymied these efforts at times, but the regime's overall work in commerce was clearly geared to the undermining of this environmental context in the long run.

The new regime was particularly energetic in attacking transport difficulties, especially in Southwest China where interdistrict movement was extremely difficult throughout much of the region. Numerous articles detail the measures used: constructing the massive Chongqing-Chengdu Railway;[98] encouraging the masses to "utilize backward facilities," such as horses, oxen, carts, and manpower; repairing and opening roads and horsepaths; dredging waterways and constructing bridges; trying to organize transport facilities in a way that coordinated goods' points of origin, circulation patterns, and destinations; and creating a Southwest Transportation Company to link up new and old transport modes.[99]

The government also showed its concern with transport by regulating freight charges and by requiring state companies to process goods on the spot (grain at the granary, for example) to save shipping fees.[100] In effect, SMCs were a transport-saving device for the peasantry: by going directly to the production site to purchase, and by selling in the villages, they saved peasants from having to travel to market.[101]

In the period before state-operated granaries and warehouses were widespread, state organs united with private merchants in organizing

98. See *XHRB*, Jan. 1, 1952, p. 3, for a map of the railroad.

99. *XHRB*, Oct. 22, 1951, p. 2; Nov. 7, 1951, p. 2; Nov. 8, 1951, p. 2; Oct. 24, 1951, p. 2; Oct. 31, 1951, p. 2. Transportation nationwide and in mountainous regions especially, however, has remained an unsolved problem. The issue has been discussed from several angles: in terms of transportation's receiving little attention and so being the cause of accidents and irrationalities ("blindly shipping" and reshipping the same cargo) in *SCMP*, no. 925 (1954), pp. 17–19; short-distance transport vehicles being insufficient to meet the demands of goods circulation, and continued reliance on traditional facilities such as ox-carts and wheelbarrows in *SCMP*, no. 1996 (1959), pp. 3–16; and lack of organization (*CNA*, no. 417 [1962], states that even at that time there was no organization below the county level for transportation and communication in many areas; that human carriers were indispensable; and that there was no network to link primitive and modern forms of transportation). Even in 1980 human carriers and carts remained important modes of conveying goods, as visitors outside the major cities can quickly discern.

100. *SCMP*, no. 202 (1951), p. 22, and *XHRB*, Jan. 4, 1952, p. 2.

101. *XHRB*, Oct. 11, 1951, p. 2; Nov. 27, 1951, p. 2.

public-private jointly managed warehouses,[102] thus depriving speculators of the power they had held as the only traders with control over
storage facilities.

The state worked to break down the localization of markets in several
ways. Goods-exchange meets, a kind of fair to exchange local products,
were held among units at the same administrative level, beginning at the
xiang level and going all the way up the hierarchy to the Great Administrative Region level, which encompassed several provinces.[103] Also at all
levels, public trade organs and private businessmen organized groups to
visit the larger towns and even neighboring provinces to sign exchange
agreements.[104] Once commercial ties were expanded beyond the more
local boundaries in which, especially where travel was cumbersome,
they had often been concentrated, it was more difficult for the local merchants to dominate trade.

In the regime's battle to bring inflation under control during the first
years after takeover, the leadership was especially concerned with controlling the fourth structural factor listed above, fluctuations in supply
flows. For if supplies could be regularized, stable prices should follow.
Consequently, much of the work in commerce in the early years involved
attempts by state trading companies to ensure a constancy in the availability of goods over time and space.

In order to regularize supply flows over time, companies would buy up
large amounts of grain at harvest time to sell at lowered prices when grain
became scarce in the spring.[105] Over space, the companies combatted regional price differentials, the fifth factor, by transferring goods from areas
where they were available in large quantities to other places where they
were in demand.[106] With the government involved in regulating supplies
and actively trying to coordinate prices in neighboring markets,[107] there
would eventually be less scope for "illegitimate" merchants to draw large
profits from privately organized regrating and stockpiling.

The last of the structural features addressed above—the lack of standardization in grading and sorting goods, in weights and measures, and
in prices within a given market—was also attacked by the new government. Newspaper accounts tell of attempts to eliminate these inconsis-

102. *XHRB*, Oct. 11, 1951, p. 2.
103. *XHRB*, Oct. 16, 1951, p. 2, contains one of the many articles of this period on this
topic.
104. *XHRB*, Nov. 7, 1951, p. 2; Nov. 8, 1951, p. 2.
105. *XHRB*, Oct. 11, 1951, p. 2; Oct. 12, 1951, p. 2.
106. *XHRB*, Dec. 1, 1951, p. 2; Dec. 29, 1951, p. 2; April 8, 1952, p. 2.
107. *XHRB*, Oct. 16, 1951, p. 2; Dec. 14, 1951, p. 2; April 12, 1951, p. 2; April 16,
1951, p. 1.

tencies. The Guizhou provincial native-products company set up grades of tobacco and corresponding prices for each grade;[108] the Xikang provincial branch of the China tea company divided tea into classes and used a standard method to weigh the tea, which was to be wholly dry during weighing;[109] and wheat price differentials were regularized between different markets according to grade.[110] Also, a finance and economics conference held in South Sichuan district "initially unified weights and measures" within the district in August 1951.[111]

Price standardization—both within and across markets for a given line of goods in a given region—was attempted (though it was hardly always successful during this period) through the use of government-designated "list prices" for each line of goods. Apparently, a rather elaborate procedure was involved in determining this set price. Cadres working in such areas as storage, transport, and marketing negotiated with private merchants and, using production and transport costs, taxation rates, variations in seasonal supply, and quality, arrived at a price. Profiteers who did not use this negotiated price were to be strictly punished.[112] Although profiteers seem to have engaged in a significant amount of circumvention of these regulations, the state's intent was clearly to eliminate the profit-seeking businessman, and genuine efforts were certainly made to control the conditions (one was the former lack of fixed prices) that fostered his activities.

Along with these measures aimed at transforming the economic and technological surroundings for commercial activity in the countryside, steps were also taken to alter the alliance patterns and attitudes toward merchants in the countryside. Merchants' traditional associational/political resources centered around cooperative deals with bureaucrats and partnerships among themselves, all of which thrived under an ambivalent official attitude.

The PRC set out to weaken ties between officials and "illegitimate" traders, from the earliest days after the takeover but especially during the three- and five-anti movements of 1952;[113] and to strengthen the bonds between cadres and "proper" merchants.[114] Also, proper mer-

108. *XHRB*, Oct. 19, 1951, p. 2.
109. *XHRB*, April 12, 1952, p. 2.
110. *XHRB*, April 16, 1952, p. 1.
111. *XHRB*, Nov. 22, 1951, p. 2. See notes 58 and 59 above on continuing problems in these matters.
112. See *XHRB*, Dec. 7, 1951, p. 1; Dec. 14, 1951, p. 2; and April 9, 1952, p. 2.
113. The three-anti movement was directed against the bureaucracy and attacked corruption, waste, and bureaucracy. See notes 3 and 43 above on the five-anti movement.
114. See *XHYB*, 3, no. 2 (1950): 346–47; *XHRB*, Jan. 1, 1952, p. 2; Oct. 11, 1951, p. 2; Nov. 28, 1951, p. 2.

chants were rewarded by being allowed to draw a certain "legal" rate of profit, whereas serious speculators were fined and jailed.[115] New commercial organizations were urged to choose as their heads persons with prestige among the masses.[116] Thus, the state exploited cleavages among merchants and undertook to forge new types of alliances.

While relying on these means of splitting the businessmen's ranks, the regime also sought to change the overall attitude toward trade and to ensure that businessmen acted in conformity with Chinese Communist Party values. Articles spoke of "educating" the private merchants, and of training and organizing peddlers to "serve the peasants." Meetings were held where these traders had to carry out self-investigations of their own past speculative and profit-making orientation.[117] At the same time, SMCs educated the peasants to learn to separate legitimate from speculating merchants.[118]

The three-anti movement was especially active in this work of remolding ideology, and the new cadres who emerged in the movement and were trained in its aftermath were also given education in political thought.[119] These assaults on the consciousness of commercial workers were meant to undermine the cultural climate in which merchants had historically prospered in China.

As the resources (capital and monopoly over information) and the structural and cultural underpinnings of "illicit" merchant operations were initially chiseled away, substitutes were found for those the regime felt had exploited the peasantry and tampered with the economy. At first this substitution was done on an individual level: state trade companies advertised for educated youths and unemployed intellectuals and technical personnel to run rural purchase stations in production centers; "legitimate" businessmen were led to get involved in rural and urban township-level purchase and sales work; and active elements in the villages were trained to serve as cadres in basic-level SMCs.[120]

After the three-anti campaign, during which "capitalist agents" and the "blood-sucking officials" that the "capitalist class had inserted into state economic organs" were ferreted out, many active young cadres

115. *XHRB*, Oct. 11, 1951, p. 2; Dec. 7, 1951, p. 1; Nov. 6, 1951, p. 2. Unfortunately, these sources do not indicate what was considered a "legal" rate of profit.

116. *XHRB*, Oct. 15, 1951, p. 2, and Oct. 27, 1951, p. 2.

117. *XHRB*, Oct. 16, 1951, p. 2, Dec. 11, 1951, p. 1; Dec. 29, 1951, p. 2. Of course such activity was greatly intensified during "socialist transformation" a few years later.

118. *XHRB*, Oct. 17, 1951, p. 2.

119. *XHRB*, April 16 and 17, p. 1 of both issues.

120. *XHRB*, Oct. 9, 1951, p. 2; Oct. 14, 1951, p. 2; Oct. 12, 1951, p. 2; Oct. 13, 1951, p. 2; Oct. 17, 1951, p. 1; Dec. 7, 1951, p. 1.

were promoted and trained in technical business skills.[121] At the same time, but increasingly after 1952, state-sponsored organizations, such as the local branches of the state trading companies and the basic-level SMCs, began to take over more and more of the tasks once performed by individual merchants or their partnerships.

As Shue points out, the really concerted attempt to abolish private merchants' speculation and hoarding did not begin until late 1953, when the policy of unified state grain purchase decreed compulsory grain sales to the state at fixed prices,[122] and severe punishments accompanied its enforcement. However, before such sales could take place with any assurance of success, the measures outlined above must have served as essential prerequisites for gnawing away at the foundations of merchant power. Structural and cultural transformation in the countryside had to prepare the groundwork for an assault on the private merchants.

This chapter has delineated the economic and technological context that conditioned commercial activity in China before this sector was socialized or brought under state control in the mid-1950s. It has described one of the effects of this context, by focusing on its manipulation by merchants. Presumably, the private merchant class in the countryside was initially undercut as attempts were made to refashion this environment and as state-operated units increasingly took over work in trading.

As the discussion (and especially the accompanying footnotes) have indicated, however, the structural framework for commerce outlined here has by no means been altered in its most fundamental aspects. Consequently, for years thereafter, when radical politicians have had control of the media, the press has continued to rail against "corruption," and to resonate with charges of "capitalist tendencies" creeping through the loopholes of China's socialist commerce.[123]

121. *XHRB*, April 16, p. 1; April 17, p. 1; April 20, p. 1, 1952.

122. Vivienne Shue, "Reorganizing Rural Trade: Unified Purchase and Socialist Transformation," pp. 105–6. See chapter 4 for a continuation of this story.

123. See, for example, *Peking Review*, no. 39 (1977), pp. 28–29, 32, which, pointing to a "capitalist resurgence," accuses private traders of stockpiling and cornering goods, jacking up prices to exploit consumers, profiteering, and manipulating the market in other ways. Also, issues of *SC* from mid-1980 give reports in a similar vein of excesses accompanying the new economic reforms and liberalization.

PART TWO

The Three Central Issues in Commercial Policy in China

4

The Private Sector:

The Regulation of Small Rural Traders

Under the People's Republic, as in historical times, state policy toward the private sector in Chinese commerce has alternated between harshness and leniency.[1] These two extremes have been most pronounced in the oscillating fate of the smaller merchants and peddlers, who have sometimes been encouraged, other times forbidden, to practice their profession. This chapter analyzes these vacillations in policy—and the difficulties of implementation—by relying on a framework fashioned from the three factors addressed in the preceding chapters. The two chapters that follow will also use this framework as they examine the other two aspects of commercial policy, trade in industrial goods and in farm products.

1. Susan Mann, in an early draft of the second chapter of her book in progress, "The Order of the Marketplace in Agrarian China," states that, historically, "Chinese official commercial policy was a dialectic fluctuating between intervention and laissez-faire." (Permission to quote has been granted by the author.)

157

"Sidewalk capitalist," late 1979, Guilin, Guangxi.

The present chapter begins by identifying the two approaches to the handling of small private business—harshness and leniency—and relating these to the special features of Chinese business under socialism presented in chapters one through three, respectively. These features are competition under conditions of a state-managed economy; three tendencies in political conflict; and the low level of technological support for Chinese commerce.

Two subsequent sections apply this material to several episodes in the history of the state's dealings with small-scale traders.[2] They do so by

2. According to various sources, immediately upon the Communist political takeover in 1949, the new government nationalized some three thousand private enterprises without compensation to their owners, changing them into a part of the socialist sector of the national economy. This confiscation of all "bureaucratic capital," that industrial and commercial capital owned by the Nationalist government and its officials and by foreign concerns, drew approximately 80 percent of the capitalist sector's wealth into state coffers. See Kuan Ta-t'ung, *The Socialist Transformation of Capitalist Industry and Commerce in China*, p. 35; *Beijing Review* (*BR*), no. 17 (1980), p. 18. This transfer aside, about three-quarters of a million "national bourgeoisie," those capitalists (again, both industrial and commercial) with middling and smaller-sized enterprises remained (*BR*, no. 17 [1980], p. 21, says there were 760,000 members of the national bourgeoisie in 1956; *Jingji yanjiu* [Economic Studies] [*JJYJ*], no. 2 [1956], p. 42, says there were about six or seven hundred thousand of them); as did upwards of ten million small merchants and peddlers. For data on the small traders, the subject of this chapter, see *Da Gong Bao* [Impartial Daily] (*DGB*), April 26 and September 27, 1955. *DGB* cites ten million, as did Chen Yun in June 1956, in

linking these approaches and features to the beliefs and interests of central policy makers, local cadres, and small traders. The first does this by looking intensively at the "high tide" period of socialist transformation, a period for which there is especially rich documentation. Here the purpose is to illuminate the play of interests, motivations, fears, and struggle which then marked the reactions of and the interactions between the groups engaged in this process. Considerations that informed the behavior of economic actors then have continued to be relevant, as the concluding section documents. It traces the history of policy toward the small private sector from the years after the "high tide" up to 1980, using the features of commerce pinpointed earlier to account for shifts in policy.

Two Approaches to the Regulation of Small Private Commerce

The Chinese Communist leadership has in its repertoire two approaches to the managing of small merchants, which, to borrow terminology from the literature on economic regulation in the United States, are "managerial" and "policing."[3] At the lenient, or managerial, extreme (defined in the literature on the United States as reliance on self-regulation, with minimal interference by the government in market-induced behavior), the Chinese state has at times permitted peddlers and

---

Current Background (CB), no. 393 (1956), p. 14. *JJYJ*, no. 2 (1956), p. 43, notes three million private shops and stalls, with a total of four and a half million people working in them in 1954. Only 2.02 percent of these hired two or more workers, and 96.03 percent hired none. *DGB*, June 18, 1955, and *Renmin ribao* [People's Daily] (*RMRB*), February 4, 1955, lists three and a half million rural private merchants at the end of 1954, working in 2,410,000 firms, of which over 90 percent were small merchants and peddlers. Other sources cite figures that differ from these, sometimes rather markedly, indicating, no doubt, the difficulty of obtaining exact data in this sector. For example, Kuan, p. 24, says that in 1950 there were 4,020,000 commercial firms, including small merchants and peddlers, containing a total of 6,620,000 persons. And *DGB*, May 28, 1955, states that there were about three million private merchants at that time. Socialist transformation alone could not have accounted for the discrepancy between these last two figures (over six and a half million in 1950; only three million in mid-1955), since, according to *DGB*, September 6 and 27, 1955, only 550,000, or 17.3 percent of the total number of rural private merchants, had gone through any kind of transformation as of June 30, 1955.

3. See Richard A. Posner, "Theories of Economic Regulation," pp. 335–39, for discussion of these terms; also, on dichotomous conceptions of regulation in the U.S., see also James Q. Wilson, "The Politics of Regulation," p. 138; Paul A. Sabatier, "Regulatory Policy-Making: Toward a Framework of Analysis," p. 418. Though these terms take on different meanings in the Chinese context, they serve well to label the two poles of Chinese policy.

the owners of small shops and stalls to retain traditional business forms and practices, with only slight intervention from the state, and has even used economic incentives (such as tax exemption for new firms)[4] to stimulate their activity.

At other points, however, policing policies have restrained or curtailed the activities of these traders, by levying harsh taxes and other fees; by eliminating firms through forcing them to combine; and by driving them out of business by gathering into state hands the stocks in which they deal. How can the analytic features of socialist commerce in China adduced earlier in this volume help to explain this polarity?

Commerce is the only economic sector in which the cadres, staffing their own separate state (or cooperative, in the case of the supply and marketing cooperatives in the countryside) business, have stood in direct competition with the objects of governmental regulation, the private merchants. This rivalry came sharply into play at the time of the initial socialist transformation campaign (as it did at an analogous phase of Soviet economic development),[5] and has remained important in all subsequent interactions between the state commercial bureaucracy and the private sector. Driven by their obligation to fulfill state-designated quotas in business volume, commercial cadres have generally been a potent force dedicated to the policing of private peddlers and other traders. This key element motivating the behavior of cadres toward merchants is illustrated in the following quotation from mid-1956:

> A *xian* supply and marketing cooperative worker said to a rural small merchant, "If you come to buy, this will obstruct my completing the plan."
> ... State-operated commercial departments, calculating the profits of their own units, can't solve the difficulties of the small merchants and peddlers.[6]

The result of this contention has been that the cadres, striving to obtain for their organs (and ultimately for the state) the major share of the goods and of the commercial profits accruing from the circulation of goods, have often tried to eliminate and themselves replace the private sector. This is the prime motive that fuels the policing approach to small traders.

---

4. For example, BR, no. 44 (1981), p. 27, states that all new individually and collectively owned enterprises would be exempted from commercial tax for three years.

5. Trade cadres behaved similarly in the Soviet Union in the late 1920s, as they tried to eliminate the private sector in order to get control of its resources and to ensure that the state trade organs handled the maximum quantity of goods. See Charles Bettelheim, *Class Struggles in the U.S.S.R.: Second Period: 1923–1930*, pp. 203, 205, 206.

6. *RMRB*, June 10, 1956.

*A pet bird, a drink of tea, or a plant, anyone? Wuhan's
merchants don't hawk, but they do sell just about
anything, May 1983.*

A desire to reconcile socialist commerce with the technological backwardness of China's marketing environment has informed the other,
managerial approach to dealing with the marketplace and its participants. As was shown in chapter three, the technological base for commerce in China—whether the practitioners are rural pole-peddlers,
owners of small urban shops, or stall and cart operators—is primitive,
and its placement is widely dispersed and often mobile.[7] Given these
conditions, those arguing against the elimination of enterprises and the
mergers of firms and farms (such as those that occurred in other sectors
in the 1950s) believed that such actions could not contribute in commerce to economies of scale. Moreover, they would in fact have cut off
commerce's customary function of stimulating economic activity. This
view is reflected in the proposal for the Second Five Year Plan, which

7. Most reports on commerce list this set of traits possessed by small-scale trade: it is
without strict division of labor or specialization; has scattered activities; is spread over
extensive areas and points; depends on crude and inadequate communications facilities;
has simple equipment and a small amount of capital; uses mobile, convenient, and flexible
business procedures; makes sales in fragmentary amounts; and is backward in character.
See *RMRB* editorials on June 7, 1955, April 14 and 28, 1956, and July 21, 1956, and an
article in *RMRB* on December 23, 1955; and *DGB*, April 26, 1955, and March 2, 1956.

issued from the Eighth Congress of the Chinese Communist Party in
September 1956:

> Do not amalgamate more than necessary small factories and shops which
> are operationally flexible. In the commercial field, it is *even more neces-*
> *sary* to operate in various ways. . . . Trading establishments must be scat-
> tered and managed separately while being put under the guidance of state
> companies and cooperatives.[8]

Arguments in support of a managerial approach were made with special force and clarity in the mid-1950s, at the time of the transformation
campaign, but their gist has reappeared in later periods whenever private trading was permitted. First of all, such reasoning points to the
dependence of the rural masses on this trade. Thus, "small merchants
and peddlers have close ties to the peasantry, and go down into remote
villages"; they operate "in keeping with the peasants' customs and in
ways suited to their needs . . . by handling fragmentary supplies, stocking great varieties, managing both large and small deals, lacking fixed
business hours and traveling and bartering." Small shops have been
noted for their wide distribution, fixed clientele, familiarity with needs
and tastes that fit the people's lives, and their extension of short-term
credit to regular customers.[9]

Beyond the question of their importance to the customers, the peddlers and shopowners of the countryside have "plenty of connections for
the supply of goods and extensive links for their sales," as they compose
a "historically formed network, which could not be replaced by socialist
commerce."[10] Or, as another account put it, they are "like a spider web
that can't be done without."[11]

8. "Proposals of the Eighth National Congress of the Communist Party of China for the
Second Five Year Plan for the Dèvelopment of the National Economy (1958–1962)," in
Eighth National Congress of the Communist Party of China (hereafter *Eighth National
Congress*), *Volume I: Documents*, p. 247.

9. *RMRB* editorial, February 4, 1955; *DGB*, March 2 and 3, 1956; *RMRB*, April 28,
1956; *JJYJ*, no. 2 (1958), p. 15.

10. Sources from the mid-1950s show the inadequacy of the state commercial bureaucracy
by citing figures. One source from 1955 states that private commercial personnel in the countryside numbered more than three times as many as the employees of state and cooperative
commerce there (*RMRB* editorial, February 4, 1955, in *Survey of China Mainland Press*
[*SCMP*], no. 999 [1955], pp. 5–7). Another article estimated that 3,600,000 commercial
personnel were needed for work in the villages, including SMC wholesale and retail workers,
those engaged in processing work, administrative personnel and workers in county seats
(*RMRB*, editorial, March 10, 1955). This figure corresponds to the three and a half million
rural merchants cited in note 2 above. Later that year, however, the claim was only that "we
have 1,100,000 basic-level SMC cadres with a year of experience in transformation work"
(*DGB*, December 1, 1955). In later years, this same justification for activating the private
sector was used, as in *RMRB*, June 20, 1980, p. 5.

11. These various points are made in an *RMRB* editorial, April 14, 1956, in *SCMP*, no.

Also, they have long since mastered the special skills required in this underdeveloped marketing setting: "They understand safekeeping, packaging, shipping and sales promotion techniques, while socialist commerce lacks this," explained one proponent of managing rural traders in the mid-1950s. Put differently, "no other form of transportation can completely replace them; in addition, they do their own storage."[12]

There is yet another feature of the rural economy that analyses employing the managerial outlook in the mid-1950s point to as requiring the participation of the private sector. This is the dependence of this economy on the presence of large numbers of persons who purchase and sell frequently. For the local subsidiary products of the villages are essential to the state's export and industrialization needs, and squeezing out local merchants could create serious obstacles in their procurement.[13]

This point is related to the habitual tendency toward self-sufficiency of the peasantry. According to the analysis in one article, peasants would rather buy and use less than travel long distances for a small bit of goods. Therefore, if merchants and peddlers became fewer in the rural areas, the peasants would lapse into producing less because, without supplies easy to purchase, they would find no reason to go to market. The net effect, it was feared, would be to increase tension in the supply of agricultural products, which in turn would influence the fulfillment of urban and export needs.[14]

And finally, depriving small traders of their business has been viewed as a waste of social commercial capital. The capital of this sector rests on its quick circulation; if that circulation were stopped up, that is, if this capital were not permitted to be used in exchange ventures, it would quickly be depleted.[15] Thus, besides the fact of their possessing a special expertise, the very numbers of small traders and their incessant activity in the marketplace have been seen as crucial to the enlivening of the national economy. So the dispersion of small commerce, with its independent operations, has been perceived as one of its defining characteristics for those wishing to manage but not police it.

1288 (1956), p. 12, and Zhongguo shehui kexue yuan, jingji yanjiuso [Chinese Academy of Social Sciences, Economic Research Institute], *Zhongguo ziben zhuyi gongshangye de shehui zhuyi gaizao* [The socialist transformation of China's capitalist industry and commerce] (CASS), p. 193; and *RMRB*, June 10, 1956.

12. *DGB*, April 26 and August 4, 1955.

13. *DGB*, May 28, 1955.

14. *DGB*, April 26, 1955. On the peasantry's tendency toward self-sufficiency, see article by G. W. Skinner, cited in chapter 1, n. 16; and Albert Feuerwerker, *The Chinese Economy, ca. 1870–1911*, p. 45 (which speaks of "the relative self-sufficiency in basic grains of much of rural China").

15. *DGB*, June 18, 1955.

*Forms of sidewalk private enterprise: selling ices, fixing
shoes, and transport by pedicab, May 1983, Wuhan.*

These two approaches can also be tied into the three tendencies in
policy conflict. Thus, it is marketeers who are most sensitive to the limitations of the technological environment in which commerce operates,
and so it is they who have favored lenient, managerial treatment for the
small traders, who work best under these conditions. Those supporting
a bureaucratic reliance on the plan prefer to police the peddlers and
merchants. For their dedication to state control inclines them to devise
policies that place productive output and the prices charged for it under
state direction. And since they thus favor a form of state business, they
worry over the competition that merchants pose for state procurement
organs. Adherents to the radical tendency combine with bureaucrats,
less out of institutional concerns than from suspicion of the class background of the traders, and from a fear that their activity will lead China
back toward capitalism.

To radicals, small merchants are the private owners of an individual
economy. Since their labor is done in the sphere of commodity circulation, often in contact with wealthier commercial capitalists, this viewpoint sees them as being susceptible to the influence of capitalism and

prone to participate in its profit seeking, speculation, and "sharp operations style."[16]

Radicalism has been especially popular among local cadres. The press in the "high tide" period of the transformation constantly enjoined cadres to differentiate between three types of private rural merchants: the small traders who made up well over 90 percent of all rural traders, the commercial capitalists, and the rich peasants who did some business on the side.[17] But these efforts often proved to be in vain, for at least a fair portion of basic-level cadres continued to believe that all merchants "reaped without sowing" (*bu lao er huo*), exploiting others but not creating any new value for society.[18]

On the issue of regulation of the private sector, then, those with a marketeer mentality, who because of the state of China's economy prefer a managerial approach, often face an alliance prone to policing and composed of supporters of the other two tendencies.

Clashes among these two approaches were especially clear in the mid-1950s socialist transformation of commerce, although they have continued to reemerge through the years in times of debate over the treatment of the private sector. At the elite level at that time, one group of central-level politicians advocated a managerial approach, whereas another policed. Most important among those leaders on the managerial or marketeer side of this conflict were Chen Yun, his predecessor as minister of commerce, Zeng Shan, and the then Party vice-chairman, Liu Shaoqi.[19] These leaders, accused during the Cultural Revolution of having been co-opted by capitalists, in fact acted mainly from the economist's faith in invigorating the market as a means of generating greater prosperity, if one can judge from their remarks at the time.

Their support for retaining and utilizing these traders and their style appears in the words of Liu Shaoqi at the September 1956 Eighth Party Congress:

> Small merchants and peddlers' cooperative teams should act as agents for state and supply and marketing co-op commerce. . . . This, with their scat-

16. See *DGB*, July 26 and August 4, 1955.

17. *RMRB*, February 4, 1955, and *DGB*, April 26 and May 28, 1955. The first of these articles states that, at the end of 1954, only 1.7 percent of the rural private merchants were either commercial capitalists or rich peasants-cum-merchants.

18. *DGB*, August 4, 1955.

19. Chen's role is described in Roderick MacFarquhar, *The Origins of the Cultural Revolution*, pp. 19 ff. See Zeng Shan's speeches at the Eighth Party Congress in *CB*, no. 423 (1956), p. 3, and on the commercial tasks in the First Five Year Plan in *Extracts from China Mainland Magazines* (*ECMM*), no. 5 (1955), pp. 12–17, which both follow a very moder-

tered, mobile style of operations, will provide convenience for the customers, and will preserve the old business traits that fit social needs.[20]

And, similarly, Chen Yun explained:

The large part of those in small shops and stalls and the pole peddlers are scattered in residential districts. We will need them for a long period in the future. We can't merge them all to form joint enterprises and cooperative shops, because that wouldn't facilitate the people's consumption.[21]

For these officials, socialist transformation of commerce had a particular meaning, a special goal, rather different from the aims of enhanced social justice often claimed for state takeover of property under socialist regimes. In their view, it was to be a process that would issue in an expanded production and circulation of commodities, a bigger volume of business operations, and overall, higher-quality operations.[22]

A second set of officials took a combative stance toward small merchants during transformation. Among this group, Peng Zhen, then mayor and Party first secretary of Beijing, pursued an especially aggressive course. The centrality of Peng's role in hastening the pace of transformation in Beijing, which in turn set off with spiraling momentum a huge nationwide speedup at the end of 1955, has been deftly uncovered by MacFarquhar.[23] This was not the first time that Peng had been associated with aggressive policies toward capitalists. In 1952 it was he who presented the draft regulations for the punishment of corruption as the *wu fan* (five-antis) campaign against the bourgeoisie drew to a close.[24] Those supporting policing hark back to Mao's designation of small merchants as part of the petty bourgeoisie and of small peddlers as being in the semi-[not full] proletariat. Such a view stands in contradistinction to

---

ate line for transformation. The Red Guards attacked Liu's views on socialist transformation, as reprinted in *SCMP*, nos. 4159 (1968), pp. 13–19, and 4347 (1969), pp. 10–11; *Survey of the China Mainland Press-Supplement (SCMPS)*, no. 180 (1967), p. 14; *Selections from China Mainland Magazines (SCMM)*, no. 619 (1968), pp. 1–79; and *CB*, no. 836 (1967), pp. 31–37.

20. Quoted in *JJYJ*, no. 2 (1958), p. 16.

21. Ibid., p. 20. MacFarquhar, p. 22, is confident that "Chen Yun was clearly in charge of the whole [socialist transformation of capitalist industry and commerce] operation."

22. *DGB*, March 2, 1956, pp. 2 and 3, March 7, 1956, and Chen Yun's speech at the Third Session of the First National People's Congress in June 1956 in *CB*, no. 393, p. 21.

23. MacFarquhar, pp. 23–24.

24. See John Gardner, "The Wu-fan Campaign in Shanghai," p. 523.

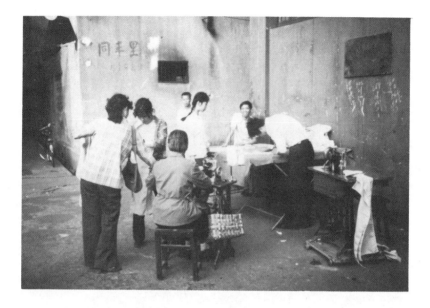

Sewing on the sidewalk, May 1983, Wuhan.

one presented by Liu Shaoqi, which characterized them as simply individual laborers.[25]

For this second group, socialist transformation was to aim at rather different goals from those it was to have for the first group. For them, it would "put the peasantry's buying and selling activity into the state plan ... transform private commerce to change its private ownership and make it become socialist commerce ... [and] make it serve the planned expanded circulation of commodities under the leadership of socialist commerce," a formulation including both bureaucratic (plan-oriented) and radical (anticapitalist) goals. The bias of this approach was toward merging the small commercial units in disregard of market principles, in an effort to obliterate market transactions. "They think that creating large-scale commerce through blind mergers is the only method for transforming individual industrial and commercial firms," according to a criti-

25. *Xuexi* [Study] (Beijing) (*XX*), no. 6 (1955), pp. 11–13, and *JJYJ*, no.2 (1958), pp. 15–16. Liu's words were part of his report on the Draft State Constitution in 1954 and also appeared in his report to the Eighth Party Congress; Mao's statements are found in his "Analysis of Chinese Social Classes" and "The Chinese Revolution and the Chinese Communist Party," written in 1926 and 1936, respectively.

cism of this approach made by a proponent of the managerial strategy.[26]

In sum, then, the two approaches toward small trade in the PRC have their roots in inherited economic conditions as well as in the new socialist bureaucracy imposed on commerce. The belief systems of the leadership and the self-interest of its cadre act to shape and reinforce these influences. The discussion that follows will examine these two approaches in action: first in the midst of the major and first campaign to regulate this trade; second, over some twenty years of policy shifts.

The Socialist Transformation
of Small Rural Trade, 1954–1956:
Methods and Political Forces

Some initial steps were taken to reorient the business of rural traders in the years before 1955, as some few were organized into elementary forms of transformation, which essentially entailed agency and commission-agent relationships with state-owned distributors.[27] But, as of the end of 1954, only two hundred thousand of some three million private rural merchants, or less than 6 percent, were participants in some form of transformation.[28] The heart of the tale of the countryside commercial transition is bracketed by the period from mid-1954 until late summer 1956.

A close analysis of policy shifts over this period clearly indicates the existence of conflicting visions for the transformation in the minds of different central-level decision makers. These shifts divide this two-year period into four distinct phases, in two of which the policy was policing, and in two of which it was managerial. The first, beginning with a mid-1954 central government directive, spurred a belligerent attack on private traders, which the second, the period of "overall consideration and all-around arrangement," which started in early 1955, set out to cancel.

Then, soon after Mao's heavily class-conscious, July 31, 1955, speech on agricultural cooperativization, a sudden concern with the negative traits of the small traders filled the press. In accord with that interpretation, by late fall, as larger-scale trade and industry began its accelerated changeover to socialism, another aggressive drive got under way. By early 1956, however, a second "arrangement" phase commenced with the issuance of the State Council's February 8 directive on the transfor-

26. *DGB*, December 18, 1955, and March 2, 1956, p. 2.
27. See appendix D, on small retail trade.
28. *RMRB* editorial, March 10, 1955.

mation. In the months that followed, Chen Yun was able to impose his concern over the upheaval that precipitous change had wreaked on the economy. In this spirit, the campaign as a whole petered out by August, its goals of institutional change largely served, if somewhat altered in the process.

The narrative below uncovers the ways in which these changes in conception and policy at the top shaped perceptions and elicited responses from those directly affected by the process—the local-level cadres and the merchants, rich and poor. In the Chinese definition current at the time, the wealthier, the "commercial capitalists," were those rural merchants who relied mainly on speculation for their income and who did little or no labor.[29] By contrast, the other major grouping among the merchants, and by far the more numerous, were the smaller, poorer of them, those who hired no workers or only a few, who did not have the financial means for extensive speculation, and who lived off the earnings from their own labor in transporting and exchanging goods.[30] In reporting on the campaign, the press often indicated the separate views and feelings of these two sets of traders. In describing cadre behavior, the media made no class analysis, but depicted an array of motives entertained by them, including a desire to display socialist ardor, assiduousness in tending to their own business plan, fear of association with the bourgeoisie, and simple laziness.

This section aims to delineate how the course of the transformation campaign itself altered the hopes and expectations of these different actors over time and caused them to redefine their interests as events unfolded. This story, which reveals the play of motivations, fears, and struggles that accompanied this one drawn-out movement, is instructive for an understanding of the regulation of the small private commercial sector thereafter. For many of the reactions of the actors here have attended subsequent interactions between the state and the private sector in the decades that followed.

PHASE ONE: MID-1954 TO THE END OF 1954

Opening the period of intensified attention to small retail trade was a central-level policy document, decidedly policing in tone. This "Directive on Strengthening Market Control and the Transformation of Private Merchants," put out in July 1954 by the central government, called for

29. *DGB*, August 4, 1955, p. 2.
30. *RMRB* editorial, February 4, 1955, and *DGB*, April 5, 1955.

Bicycle repairs in the alleyway, May 1983, Wuhan.

the steady and active transformation of private traders into various forms of state capitalism.[31] The enthusiastic compliance that followed was fed by the ever-present urge of the cadres to replace their competitors in business. According to a favorable source writing in 1956, rapid progress was the result.[32] Thus, at this point most cadres were in sympathy with policing policies emanating from the politicians then in charge in Beijing.

Aside from the issuance of this particular document, two other developments at about this time had the same effect of cutting back market activity being performed by members of the private sector. First, the institution of state monopolies over grain (in November 1953) and then over oil and cotton (in September 1954) gave over the trade in these goods to state organs, whose cadres worked with plan quotas and not through the market; and second, as private wholesale firms were forced to close their doors, the retailers were left without their traditional trading links.[33]

31. See appendix C, on wholesale and large retail trade.
32. *ECMM*, no. 52 (1956), pp. 23.
33. Ibid., p. 22; *RMRB*, December 23, 1955. For information on shutting down privately owned wholesaling, see appendix C, on wholesale and large retail trade.

Whether or not the then minister of commerce, Zeng Shan, had initially authored or even agreed with this harsher policy when it was promulgated, one year after the directive was issued, during what was then a moderate period, Zeng took it upon himself to write a recantation. Then he spoke of 1954 as a time when there had been "too rapid growth in the retail sales volume of socialist commerce," and during which "private retail merchants, especially the small merchants and peddlers in the villages, had not been utilized fully enough."[34]

According to condemnatory accounts of this earlier policy which surfaced in the months that followed its rescission, to note that the merchants had not been fully utilized was, to say the least, a euphemism. In fact, the behavior of the local cadres had led directly to this result.[35] For one thing, in some areas SMCs set prices for all commodities, not just for certain ones as directed from Beijing, so that small merchants suffered losses. Once this was the case, the merchants no longer cared to engage in trade.[36] Besides, state wholesale organs in some areas ignored the private traders altogether, allocating their stocks only to state and SMC stores, while the SMCs too refused to sell goods to them in bulk.[37] A third kind of discouragement, besides prices and supplies, revolved around the complicated wholesaling procedures that some SMCs instituted, which made taking in stocks painfully cumbersome for the peddlers.[38]

A report on an SMC near Zhengzhou is replete with cadre practices that, by late 1954, had caused the majority of local merchants to feel there was no way they could continue to operate, such that on their own they ceased doing business.[39] Here in 1952 the SMC had already begun to squeeze out all the merchants, by cornering the market in the area's specialty, straw braid. It went on to delimit the permissible purchasing territory for each of the nearly two hundred local traders, used market day to call meetings of small merchants and peddlers, and controlled by decree the amount a private trader could purchase. After the merchants had been eliminated by these measures, however, the SMC was unable to pick up the business, or to penetrate into the villages. Peasants in the marketplace, dissatisfied, complained that in the past they could stay home and still sell their straw, whereas under the new conditions they

34. *ECMM*, no. 5 (1955), p. 13. Probably his position required that he offer this self-criticism when policy shifted.
35. *RMRB*, March 10, 1955, editorial, June 7, 1955; December 11, 1955; *DGB*, April 3, 8, 15, 1955, and June 4, 1955.
36. *DGB*, April 15, 1955.
37. *DGB*, April 26, 1955.
38. *DGB*, May 20, 1955, p. 3.
39. *DGB*, May 20, 1955, p. 3.

were forced to fritter away their time in queues, waiting for the SMC to buy from them.[40] In other places, the peasantry fretted over having to travel several *li* for such ordinary items as salt or matches.[41]

Besides the inconveniences to peasants, other ill effects of this early period also received censure later on: goods often reached the county and district-level depots and stagnated there, with no local merchants in evidence to market them.[42] In one rural district that included four market towns, over 50 percent of the peddlers closed shop; while in a Zhejiang *xian*, because the SMC had paid for nearly all the local specialty products (hairs and bamboo) in advance of their production, by early February the local free market was almost depleted of goods for sale, and each private merchant was earning only sixteen cents a day on the average.[43]

In interpreting the behavior of the local cadres, the national press found two motives for their harsh, policing treatment of the merchants, one institutional, one ideological. First, they cared only about their own work unit, the SMC, and about expanding its business affairs. Second, they subscribed to a belief that they were "better left than right," and so eschewed any action that might be seen as smacking of sympathy for the bourgeoisie.[44]

This "bourgeoisie," however, clearly was composed of two quite separate groupings, in terms of the effect that the aggressive policies had upon them. In one Shanxi district, for example, once the private wholesalers had been eliminated, the small-time peddlers had to journey more than thirty *li* to a city and then make a detour of another seventy *li* to replenish their stocks from the nearest SMC. And since their capital was quite limited, they could not afford to purchase much at any one time, and so were compelled to make these one-to-two-day trips with some frequency. They were entirely at the mercy of the SMCs as their business ebbed away.[45]

By contrast, richer merchants at this point could still fall back on their larger capital holdings to seek an alternative to the SMC. When the local SMC introduced irrational and complicated wholesaling proce-

40. *RMRB*, March 10, 1955.
41. *RMRB*, December 11, 1955. One *li* is 500 meters or a little less than one-third of a mile.
42. *RMRB*, March 10, 1955; *DGB*, April 8 and 15, 1955, and June 4, 1955.
43. *RMRB*, December 11, 1955, and *DGB*, July 5, 1955, p. 3.
44. *DGB*, April 3 and 29, 1955.
45. *DGB*, April 3, 1955.

dures, the larger merchants (presumably with superior means of transport at their command) were able to travel long distances into a big city to procure their own stocks in bulk.[46] Both groups were much inconvenienced by SMC cadres' behavior, but the poor went under, whereas the rich could cope, if with difficulty.

At this first stage, although merchants with holdings of different sizes were touched differentially by the policy and its probably somewhat excessive implementation, all of them could unite around opposition to it. In this period, then, the battle lines were drawn quite simply: all merchants preferred a situation in which markets still existed, rather than one in which they must try to live entirely without them; radical and bureaucratic politicians designed a policy to phase out the markets, a policy that was supported by the merchants' competitors, the plan-conscious local cadres.

PHASE TWO: EARLY 1955 TO SUMMER 1955

No particular document signaled the shift to the managerial policy of "overall consideration and all-around arrangement" (*tongchou jiangu, quanmian anpai*), which began to receive publicity in the press in early 1955.[47] This "arrangement" program was clearly the creation of central leaders who were aghast at the destructiveness that had been wrought on the rural economy by the vigorous expansion of state-led retail trade in the preceding autumn. It amounted to an attempt to revive the all-but-extinguished commercial activity of private traders, both in the interests of rebuilding a healthy rural market and in the belief that a meaningful transformation could only be made by working with active merchants.

The spirit of this policy is captured in the following two quotations, the first of which appeared in the program for the First Five Year Plan, promulgated in the midst of this phase, the second of which was stated by the then minister of commerce, Zeng Shan:

> Socialist transformation of private commerce should be steadily done while taking account of market conditions. . . . Maintain the livelihood of the people engaged in private commerce while transformation goes ahead.[48]

46. *DGB*, May 20, 1955, p. 3.
47. According to *DGB*, May 28, 1955, in *SCMP*, no. 1070 (1955), pp. 11–13, this policy began in the spring.
48. *First Five Year Plan for the Development of the National Economy of the People's Republic of China in 1953–1957*, p. 167. See also *DGB*, July 1, 1955, p. 1.

Keep [the private retail establishments] in operation and gradually subject them to socialist transformation. . . . They can play a positive
role. . . . Fully utilize their capital, equipment, and business experience.[49]

Policy in this phase dictated that these goals be met through three sorts
of measures: the aspect of gradual transformation entailed rearranging
the commercial network so that a greater balance—of geographical distribution and of income—was achieved within individual trades and
among districts. At the same time, private trade as a whole was to be
resuscitated and preserved through readjusting the total business volume
between publicly and privately conducted operations within trades and
regions, so that the private merchants received an income sufficient at
least to sustain their livelihood.[50] And third, the managerially inclined
leadership who designed this policy shift encouraged the SMC cadres to
engage in wholesaling to the private sector, instead of competing with it in
retailing, as had been the case in the previous period.[51]

Since the leaders authoring this policy hoped to maintain an active if
somewhat reorganized private sector, they planned that merchants of all
sorts should obtain a new lease on life. Even the poorer merchants were
supposed to receive the special consideration that would put them on
their feet again. To facilitate this new relationship in which the merchants became retailers for state organs, SMCs were told to expand the
differentials between wholesale and retail prices from which the small
traders obtained their income; to raise the commission rates for their
private agents; to provide bank loans with more liberal terms (less of a
collateral required, longer repayment periods); and to lower the starting
point permitted for purchasing stocks wholesale.[52] Official intention
thus redefined the role of the cadres and the position of the merchants.

Cadres, by and large, vehemently opposed this turn of strategy, and at
times expressed their opposition in idealistic terms: "Some cadres think
[the arrangement policy] is weakening the socialist camp, developing
capitalism, contravening the working class and the people's interest."[53]
What they stated in these ideological terms, however, was ultimately
tied to their own career considerations. As the press revealed, many

49. *ECMM*, no. 5 (1955), pp. 11–18.
50. *DGB*, July 5, 1955, tells how the ratio should be calculated between public and
private sectors, as it gives the example of this process in a Zhejiang *xian*.
51. *DGB*, November 5, 1955, p. 2. It is surprising to find a clear statement of this policy
printed at so late a date. The main period of the campaign was actually between February
and June.
52. *DGB*, May 28, 1955; *RMRB*, May 17, 1955.
53. *DGB*, May 7, 1955, p. 2.

*With the private sector's comeback, an old cobbler plies
his trade again, May 1983, Wuhan.*

feared that by following the present policy they might later be attacked
for committing a rightist deviation, which could even result in the loss of
their jobs, should the line switch in the future.[54] Some wondered how,
after once coddling capitalists, they could ever go on to transform them
later on.[55]

Looking to their own interests as members of a bureaucracy, cadres
became anxious that their own work unit, the SMC, either would register losses or would fail to fulfill its own retail sales plan if merchants got
a significant share of this trade. They also viewed it as their responsibility to stabilize the market and worried that, should they lose control,
they might be blamed for any price fluctuation that might result. In
larger terms, some thought the policy would "reduce the profits for socialist commerce and influence the state's capital accumulation."[56]

At first cadres manifested these feelings of mistrust, competition, and
apprehension by using their superior political position and their grow-

54. *RMRB*, June 10, 1956, and *DGB*, May 20, 1955.
55. *DGB*, February 4, May 17, May 28, and June 8 and 21, 1955.
56. *DGB*, February 4, May 7, 10, and 28, 1955; and *RMRB*, May 22, 1955, and June
10, 1956.

ing power over goods to continue the harsher policies of the previous phase, thus ignoring and even deliberately flouting orders from above to "arrange." For instance, they continued to try to hoard the better goods for their own work units to handle. In the first four months of 1955, SMCs throughout the nation overfulfilled their retail plan (38 percent of the annual plan was completed in this first third of the year), while they had only wholesaled 7.3 percent of their own retail volume to the private sector.[57] Specifically, they held onto things that were easy to sell and that promised a large monetary turnover (such as woolen yarn) or other fast-selling items (oils, fats, white towels) and namebrands (in toothpaste, galoshes, and dry cells—apparently this mattered to the peasant customers). Sometimes the poor merchants were even handed deteriorated cigarettes, so that they had to lower or subsidize the price themselves.[58]

Other assaults on private business included enforcing low wholesale-retail differentials and commissions, intentionally set below the rates dictated by the Ministry of Commerce; working through overly complicated procedures; and fixing the wholesale starting point at a higher level than that set in Beijing.[59] One hapless soybean-milk peddler, unable to afford the fifty *jin* minimum,[60] stood from morning to night before the food bureau's doors looking for people to join with him in replenishing his stocks, but unable to find a taker, had to depart empty-handed. Another was forced to buy a two-years supply of needles.[61]

As the campaign wore on, however, and the cadres became overtaxed with the conflicting and multifarious demands upon them—at once lending support to the private sector while themselves having to meet quotas in their own work; upholding and stabilizing the market while keeping an eye open for corruption—the initial aggressiveness of some melted into an apathetic laxity, which was picked up by the press.[62] Thus, by late June, cadres were failing to calculate the market's capacity and were blindly yielding goods; "arranging" only in the market towns, toward the main trades or those already organized, but not among the smaller business firms of the villages; simply offering "relief" without activating the merchants' initiative; ignoring scattered, fragmentary rural products and the purchase of scraps; and absently giving over "the wrong types of goods to the wrong parties."

57. *DGB*, May 28, 1955, p. 1.
58. *DGB*, April 8 and May 10 and 22, 1955; *RMRB*, June 10, 1956.
59. *DGB*, April 8 and May 10 and 22, 1955; *RMRB*, June 10, 1956.
60. One *jin* (or catty) is equal to about 1.1 pounds.
61. *RMRB*, June 10, 1956.
62. *DGB*, June 21 and 24, and July 5, 6, 11, and 26, 1955.

In one Henan district, for example, the local SMC wholesaled chemical fertilizer to a number of private merchants who had neither the scales nor the warehouses that this trade required. Some SMCs, throwing in the towel, gave the private merchants whatever they wanted, so that the SMC even ceased to sell agricultural tools, its principal stock-in-trade. As this mood reached its peak in mid-July, in one negative model criticized in the press, cadres, afraid of being chastised for exceeding their sales norm, refused to sell at all, some even "think[ing] it's a mess if customers come to buy goods."[63] In short, whether from careerist concerns or out of confusion, local cadres contravened the Ministry of Commerce's orders to revive the same traders these cadres had once been given leave to repress. How did the merchants adapt to this interlude?

By this time merchants as a whole were growing increasingly nervous about their future, in spite of the efforts of leaders then in charge at the center to improve their lot. Many were anxious that they would lose money and that their lives would become difficult as their incomes dwindled. They were generally uneasy about the advent of socialism and their own place in this new system: Could they become accustomed to organized life? Would they be free to use money? Could they work with a plan?—they wondered.[64]

Despite this generalized reaction, as this period introduced alternative methods of handling merchants, beyond the simple abolition of the market that phase one had entailed, a split in the ranks of the merchants began to become apparent. Among the bigger merchants, the widespread feeling was one of "only want[ing] arrangement and not transformation." Some of them even tended to judge socialist transformation by its ability to develop the activism of the richer merchants.[65] Moreover, those with some ingenuity and means rallied themselves to take advantage of any slack in the system, and maneuvered to benefit from the campaign.

Thus, those clever enough to realize that the arrangement policy called for helping out merchants in difficulty withdrew capital from their firms so that they might be classified as poorer and so receive more care from the state.[66] Others, having been organized, thought their status had been elevated to that of laborers, and so felt free to demand popular goods from the SMC and generous loans from the bank;[67]

63. *DGB*, July 11, 1955.
64. *DGB*, February 4, April 3, May 1 and 10, and July 13, 1955.
65. *DGB*, June 29 and September 5, 1955.
66. *DGB*, May 6 and June 29, 1955.
67. *DGB*, April 15, 1955.

Clothing for sale on the city streets, June 1983, Wuhan.

while yet others threatened to close down their businesses if they were not given loans, and requested credit even if they had savings.[68] Having once obtained the loans, many spent them as they pleased; surpassed the figures for sales turnover specified by the SMCs; refused to deal in the goods allotted to them; raised prices; and tried to edge out competitors, doing their own business, which often involved corruption of various forms, behind the signboard of the cooperative into which they had been merged.[69]

Meanwhile, the less enterprising among the merchants, or perhaps those with less capital to fall back on, became depressed with the low-profit goods dumped on them, and felt disinclined to procure from the SMC. Having no alternative supplier to deal with, these merchants slowly slipped from the scene.

In this second phase, managerially-minded officials in the Ministry of Commerce, concerned over the collapse of the rural market, created a policy that they hoped would revive the failing private merchants. But while the policy they specified did not entail better treatment for the richer among the merchants, several forces worked to produce this ef-

68. *DGB*, July 11, 1955.
69. *DGB*, April 15, May 1, 22, and 27, June 24, and July 11 and 13, 1955.

fect. First of all, local cadres, pitting their own interests against this policy (because it helped their competitors), implemented a harsher line than the one imposed from above. And when this involved such acts as setting the minimum wholesale purchase at a high level, the poor were left stranded.

Then, when the cadres became lazy as the campaign dragged on, they found it easier to give over business to the merchants already more visible—those in the market towns and in the main trades—and supplied goods only to them. Among the merchants themselves, it was the richer who were best able to manipulate the new regulations, taking advantage of the arrangement policy through use of their superior business skills. Thus, arrangement, essentially a managerial strategy geared to a very mild regulation of the market, had the effect of favoring the more affluent among the private commercial firms.

PHASE THREE: SUMMER 1955 TO JANUARY 1956

The third phase of the transformation campaign for commerce in the countryside got under way while arrangement was still the official policy. That the two periods overlapped is evident in the nearly simultaneous announcement of two quite different messages: one by Minister of Commerce Zeng Shan in the July 25, 1955, issue of *Shishi shouce* [Current Events]; the other by the then head of the State Planning Commission, Vice-Premier Li Fuchun, some three weeks earlier. Although Zeng did warn that the ten million employees of private retail establishments should be kept from engaging in illegal activities, his general tone indicated that these commercial personnel should be treated gently. Li Fuchun, on the other hand, told the Second Session of the First National People's Congress on July 5 that socialist transformation was

> a special form of class struggle. . . . Although private retail merchants who do not hire staff and workers are themselves laboring people, and we should unite with them, still, their labor is performed in the sphere of commodity circulation, and at the same time they are private owners, so it is very easy for them to change into speculators. Their socialist transformation must go through a certain degree and form of struggle.[70]

It was Li's tone that foreshadowed the next phase, one oriented toward policing.

70. *DGB*, July 8, 1955, p. 4.

The major impetus behind this shift was Mao Zedong's speech on speeding up agricultural cooperativization at the end of July, in which Mao championed what he saw as an urge for socialism among the poorer peasantry. In the period following that speech, the press switched to presenting an increasingly intolerant perspective on peddlers and merchants. Now these small traders were painted as participants in the bourgeois business world, not so different after all from the richer commercial capitalists from whom they had been differentiated in official accounts only a few weeks earlier. Suddenly, in July, the small-time businessmen were viewed not so much as laboring people but as potential profiteers, as they became objects of class struggle. The papers advised public accusations, trials, and other legal punishments for those caught at cheating.[71]

Despite all the obstructions by local cadres which had attended the implementation of the arrangement policy, an article appeared in the *Da Gong Bao* [Impartial Daily] in early August unexpectedly proclaiming that "by now the majority of districts of private commerce are already arranged," and that all those private commercial firms that had gone through arrangement should begin to carry out transformation.[72] Within another month, the entire process of arrangement was rather arbitrarily pronounced concluded.[73] Pure arranging, claimed one article, would lead to capitalism, so the business volume and profits of the private sector should now be controlled, not guaranteed as they had been before.[74]

The Sixth Plenum of the Seventh Central Committee of the Party met in early October and adopted Mao's July speech. On the heels of this meeting, urban businesses became the focus of socialist transformation.[75] As the capitalist sector in the cities attended meetings in preparation, and the top Party leadership hashed out its program for a big push here over the next several months, the work in rural commercial conversion was pressed to accelerate as well.

Taking its cue from the "more advanced" work in other sectors of the economy, the National Federation of Supply and Marketing Cooperatives held a meeting on the transformation of rural private merchants in

71. Articles in *DGB* on July 26, August 2 and 29, September 8 and 27, October 1 and 28, and November 14, 1955; *RMRB* on August 10 and November 22, 1955, all contain this type of analysis.

72. *DGB*, August 3, 1955, p. 2.

73. *DGB*, September 8, 1955, in *SCMP*, no. 1134 (1955), pp. 32–36, and *SCMP*, no. 1153 (1955), p. 4.

74. *DGB*, October 14 and November 14, 1955.

75. See MacFarquhar, pp. 19 ff.

late November. There it planned this movement "on the basis of new requirements deriving from agricultural cooperativization and the needs of the transformation of urban capitalist industry and commerce." By then, according to the press release from the conference, the work with rural merchants was "far behind the development of rural wholesale business and behind the small merchants' and peddlers' demands."[76] As a contemporary analysis put it, "Agricultural cooperativization on socialist principles can't be combined with a free market. That would be indulgence toward speculation."[77]

Having been restrained by the Ministry of Commerce for some months (on paper, at any rate), here finally, it would seem the cadres had a chance to complete the work they had begun the year before, of eliminating large numbers of private rural merchants and of abolishing the private market in the countryside. This policy of transformation, however, unlike that in the earlier policing phase, dictated not the abolition of private trading but the large-scale merging of private firms. The response of the cadres was mixed. Some did force giant amalgamations in December and January, but there was at least as strong a tendency among other cadres to refrain from taking action.[78]

Activism had several motives. As in agricultural cooperativization, to promote the combination of firms helped prove a cadre's zeal for socialism, and so his political purity.[79] Other factors as well were probably behind the commercial cadres' fervor to join private businesses. For the amalgamation of firms meant moving some and getting rid of others, which in all would make way for state-directed trade organs to take their place.

In some areas of Liaoning and Zhejiang, peddlers of eatables disappeared altogether, both during the day and at night. In Xuxian, Hubei, 96 mobile peddlers, dealing in peanuts, cigarettes, and candy, were transferred into one fixed center to do their business. Cadres in a Jilin *zhen* combined husband-and-wife shops, mobile peddlers, and fixed stallkeepers all together, until 82 of the merchants and peddlers there had been merged into one huge cooperative team. In a Jiangsu *zhen*,

---

76. *DGB*, December 1, 1955.
77. *DGB*, November 13, December 1 and 11, 1955.
78. Those cadres who refrained from action can be contrasted to the situation in the collectivization of agriculture, where, according to Kenneth Walker, "Collectivisation in Retrospect," pp. 36 and 43, collectives were attractive to the cadres, and cadres went further in the direction of socialism than their orders indicated. Although this was true for some commercial-sector cadres, it was by no means the case for them all. Perhaps this was because some commercial cadres viewed the enlarged private firms as yet more competition for their own business, and so hesitated to create them.
79. Walker, p. 34.

another noteworthy case occurred when 134 small traders were joined to organize a synthesized miscellaneous-goods shop and work together in it. The merchants so mated included fixed, stall, and mobile ones, and dealt in the salt, cigarettes, cord, candy, and shoe-repairing trades, to name only a few. These disparate firms briefly became one unwieldy economic accounting unit. In some places, as many as 40 percent of the private merchants were transferred to agricultural production when their firms folded.[80]

The cadres also instituted accounting arrangements in which, as was later charged, they "carried to excess the system of fixed rewards in the form of wages."[81] In extreme forms, some merged units totally abolished distribution on the basis of the shares contributed, paying all the "transformed" capitalists solely in accord with their labor. Such plans facilitated an increased accumulation of wealth for the state, as the state could then draw more taxes from the firms.[82]

But alongside this enthusiastic eradication of a portion of the private sector and of its habitual practices there existed another set of cadre behaviors. This entailed the reluctance of many cadres to get involved in the "high tide."[83] In some instances this hesitation was fueled by pessimism about the campaign: "Some cadres think socialism is more than ten years away." Others preferred to steer clear of too much involvement with the merchants, now seen as persons of suspect class background.

These more passive cadres refused to approve mergers organized spontaneously by the merchants themselves, disbanded unions already in place, and even set such severe limits for entry into unions that some of the merchants in one Henan district demanded permission to switch to agriculture instead (no one who had evaded taxes, who had any business skills, or who had made cynical, complaining remarks could enter; no one over forty-five years of age or whose family owned much land could join). Several of these restrictions suggest that the cadres tried to

80. See *DGB*, March 3, 1956, in *SCMP*, no. 1254 (1956), pp. 11–15; *DGB*, December 28, 1955, p. 2, January 4, February 1, March 9, and April 22, 1956, p. 1, for examples.

81. *RMRB*, April 14, 1956, in *SCMP*, no. 1288 (1956), pp. 12–14.

82. See *DGB*, January 4 and 17, 1956. One less extreme case, described in the press, involved a district in Zhejiang which set out a work plan according to which fluid capital became shares; fixed assets (large equipment) were turned over to the team, and the former owner received periodic compensation; small facilities became shares after conversion to their monetary equivalent; and the enterprise temporarily rented tools it would have no use for in the future. The individual capitalist was permitted to keep any fragmentary items he or she individually used in working.

83. See *DGB*, December 18, 1955. See also December 1, 11, 28, 29, and 30, 1955, and January 3 and 23, 1956, for material from which the following was taken.

prevent the forming of larger enterprises by those with ability or wealth that might help them create competition for the cadres' own work.

Cadres' awareness of their responsibilities as workers for the state bureaucracy was also an important factor in the negligence with which many treated the campaign. Besides being charged with the task of regulating small business, these functionaries still had their own business plans to fulfill at the same time. Others were afraid that they would not be able to consolidate the new collective units properly, and worried that organized merchants would simply become a burden to them.[84] Others wondered how, with an insufficient number of cadres, they would be able to lead the masses, who, they surmised, would become "chaotic" once they were brought together.[85] Often socialist transformation appeared a risky interlude, which could jeopardize other work, in the view of those trained to concentrate on the completion of their ordinarily designated job. In short, the activist as well as the more timid among the cadres kept consideration for their own commercial activities at the forefront of their minds, either in vigorously organizing gigantic mergers or in letting the campaign pass them by.

As for the merchants themselves, it was the smaller merchants and peddlers who were particularly enthusiastic, according to the newspapers. "We're also laboring people," some proclaimed, "and now that the high tide of agricultural cooperation is here, if we don't follow, we'll lose rank." In their ardor, these merchants reproached the cadres: "In the past you urged us to go the socialist road. Now we want to, and you don't take action, worrying that we can't swallow it."[86] These less fortunate merchants, dissatisfied with more elementary agency forms of transformation, hoped for the greater benefits that could come from pooling their capital in cooperative shops, and voluntarily organized themselves. More than one thousand cooperative stores and teams were so created in Henan and Shandong provinces alone; in Shandong, 98 percent of those so combining were the smaller tradesmen.[87]

Not surprisingly, resistance to cooperativization came principally from the better-off among the businessmen, the commercial capitalists and rich peasant-merchants. Many of these, at least at first, preferred to wait and see, worrying rightly that their incomes would drop. Some of those with a larger amount of capital and an active business declined to join, for the

84. *DGB*, December 18, 29, and 30, 1955.
85. *DGB*, December 30, 1955, and January 23, 1956.
86. *DGB*, January 3, 1956.
87. *DGB*, December 4, 18, 28, and 30, 1955.

time being. Others, once having joined, subsequently thought of pulling out their capital and working alone in order to earn more money. And some, when first organizing, tried to set the proportion of profits reserved for dividends too high (at 65 percent of profits), leaving only 15 percent for the joint reserve fund for capital accumulation.

This third, policing phase of the transformation campaign against commercial capitalists, that is, the zenith of the "high tide," was conceived by hard-liners in Beijing as one that would extinguish private trade by forcing its practitioners into amalgamations that the state could far more easily control. At this point, both the poorer merchants and the activist cadres appreciated the policy, on which they pinned high hopes. The former expected that merging their meager funds with others of their kind could bring them more economic power; the latter perhaps presumed that the space cleared by relocated peddlers might provide extra markets for their own state-run business, or at a minimum that combining merchants would facilitate their own command.

On the other side of the issue, many rich merchants continued to put their faith in the quickly dwindling marketplace. These people were probably able to benefit from the fact that a certain segment of the state personnel, concerned about their duty to their own enterprise operations plan and its fulfillment, remained aloof from the campaign. Thus, at this juncture in the effort to achieve a socialist regulation of private trade, the prospects of regulation appealed to the poor, frightened the wealthy, and appeared as either an opportunity or a hindrance to the regulators, who had a business of their own to run.

PHASE FOUR: FEBRUARY TO LATE 1956

Set in motion by Beijing's Mayor Peng Zhen's strike for glory for his city in early December,[88] and gathering nationwide momentum as other localities were determined not to be left behind, the "government plan originally scheduled to be carried out," according to Chen Yun, "by stages and groups and by different trades in two years,"[89] was thus torn to shreds, in an upsurge of mergers in December and January. By early 1956, half the private commercial firms in the country had been made participants in some form of socialist transformation.[90]

88. MacFarquhar, pp. 23–24.
89. Chen Yun, "On the Socialist Transformation of Private Industry and Commerce," June 18, 1956, in CB, no. 393 (1956), p. 19.
90. DGB, March 3, 1956, in SCMP, no. 1254 (1956), pp. 11–15.

Given the nearly total lack of preparation and the insufficient number of cadres to manage it, however, the effect of this rapid changeover, according to a later analysis by Chen Yun, was that

> [in] the days when cymbals and drums were struck to celebrate the transformation, quite a few factories, handicraft shops, stores, and transport establishments in many places were merged one after another. Among these, there were some that should not have merged, and some that could be merged but became too big.

Not only were the amalgamated units too large, Chen went on, but there occurred an "artificial split in the original relationship of supply and sales and coordination in industry and commerce."[91]

In the countryside, the purchasing and marketing activities of the peasantry had been deeply disturbed. As was noted at a meeting on rural transformation held by the National Federation of SMCs, the main causes behind the upheaval there were the creation of too many joint enterprises and cooperative shops, too few simple commission-agency arrangements, and too many mergers; an overreliance on fixed wages; undue decreases in sales differentials and commission rates; and a reduction in the varieties of products.[92]

Ironically, in light of their initial enthusiasm, the small merchants and peddlers bore the brunt more than the others did. For many, the "high tide" had caused their incomes to drop to a serious degree, as their operations atrophied, they were taxed beyond their means, and the rates fixed for the commissions and differentials from which they drew their only income became pitiably inadequate. In Foshan, Guangdong, for example, 764 small-merchant firms that had regularly done business in the countryside were all without a future, having no way to support themselves.[93]

In the process of forming mergers, cadres tended to ignore the smallest traders, as their meager capital was not worth the state's trifling with. Beyond this, the transformation process as a whole acted as a squeeze on these poorer merchants. First of all, the expansion of the operations of the new public-private joint enterprises (which only merged firms of some means) tended to cut into the trade of the remaining individual

91. *CB*, no. 393 (1956), p. 19, and *SCMP*, no. 1226 (1956), pp. 16–18. See also "State Council Decisions on the Socialist Transformation of Private Industry, Commerce and Handicrafts" of February 8, 1956, in *SCMP*, no. 1232 (1956), pp. 16–18.

92. *DGB*, March 6, 1955, and March 23, 1956, in *SCMP*, no. 1262 (1956), pp. 15–16.

93. *RMRB*, June 10, 1956.

merchants. Then, the organizing of handicraft workers and the peasantry, and the elimination of small private wholesalers, meant that the major habitual sources of goods for the petty business sector had dried up, and their old relations of credit with the handicraft workers and wholesalers disappeared. The state and SMC organs were unable—and probably unwilling—to fill the vacuum in supplying goods to these miserable traders.[94]

The initial reaction of the Ministry of Commerce to these disruptions was simply to try to bring a halt to the momentum, which it did first of all in an editorial in its press organ, "Commercial Work," on January 19.[95] Presumably in response to the obvious havoc that had ensued in the wake of Peng Zhen's "high tide," Chen Yun and Zeng Shan were able at this point to snatch control of the campaign back into their own hands. From this time onward, they set managerial criteria for the transformation—orderliness, supplying the needs of the rural population, more varieties, higher quality and better service, expanding the circulation of commodities—which sounded much like those of the earlier arrangement phase.[96] In fact, the thrust of their effort then was indeed to return the course of the campaign to the track it had left gradually in the previous autumn and abruptly in December.

The main message of the directives and press articles in this emergency period of reversal, beginning with the "Commercial Work" editorial was twofold: first, do not lightly change systems. All original systems (for stocking, purchasing, pricing, sales, management, processing, service, business hours, accounting, and wages) were to be maintained intact for at least six months, even if a firm had already been approved for conversion.[97] Firms were merely allowed to change their signboards, as a way of indicating that they had received permission to change, while cadres in charge were to use the extra time to study the possible effects on the market of any merger. Scattered mobile small merchants and peddlers in the villages could only register, as they were to "keep their original business forms permanently"; and even traders with slightly more capital were once again to be confined to the elementary agency forms of transformation.

94. RMRB, July 21, 1956, in SCMP, no. 1343, pp. 8–10; and DGB, April 1, 1956, editorial.

95. Translated in SCMP, no. 1226 (1956), pp. 16–18.

96. DGB editorials, February 4 and April 28, 1956, and DGB, March 6, 1956, p. 2, and April 13, 1956.

97. DGB, February 4, 1956; SCMP, no. 1226, pp. 16–18, and no. 1232, pp. 16–18; and DGB, March 3, 1956.

The second part of the message was to reintroduce the procedures supportive of private trade which had been stressed in the arrangement phase, in a grand effort to undo the damage of "high tide." Thus, SMCs were to use shops, stalls, and mobile peddlers rationally, not to reduce their numbers; they were to make adjustments in the commercial network only with regard to a minority of firms; they were to allot business quotas and distribute sources of supply in a balanced fashion; they were to abolish the newly instituted fixed-wage system for small traders and to reintroduce price flexibility; and, as before, to raise commission and sales differential rates while lowering the minimum quantity that could be taken in as wholesale purchases.[98]

Several months later, beginning with a speech by Chen Yun to the Third Session of the First National People's Congress in June (1956), even more extensive measures were proposed to help the small merchants and peddlers. For 25 percent of them were in difficulty in most places, and as many as 50 percent were suffering in a few areas, according to Chen's figuring.[99] He said that their major demands were for supplies, credit, and tax relief, and that they desired to enter into socialism; and he outlined a package of governmental aid that would ensure their basic income, stir up their business initiative, and restore convenience in marketing for the people. Chen advocated relying for the main organizational form on the cooperative team, the component firms of which would each operate largely independently, as they continued to act as separate accounting units. And he recommended the creation of state wholesale shops to look after these groups, to solve their problems in obtaining goods and loans, collect their taxes for them to simplify procedures, and conduct political education among their workers.

Other measures followed, based on Chen's speech, which were put forward by the press, proposed by Zeng Shan at a State Council forum, and embodied in a new State Council "Directive on the Socialist Transformation of Industry, Commerce, Handicrafts, and Transportation" (on July 28).[100] Among the more lenient departures from past policy were these: certain types of goods were to be left only for the small merchants and peddlers to handle; the security deposits that merchants working on commission for the state had left with the SMCs were to be

98. *DGB*, February 1, March 23 and 29, April 14 and 22, 1956, and *RMRB*, June 10, 1956.
99. *CB*, no. 393 (1956), pp. 13–21.
100. *SCMP*, nos. 1334 (1956), pp. 3–7; 1346 (1956), pp. 5–9; *RMRB*, July 21, 1956, editorial, in *SCMP*, no. 1343 (1956), pp. 8–10; and *DGB*, August 2, 1956.

returned to the merchants, or their owners were to receive interest on
them at the rate a bank would pay on a loan; a welfare reserve fund was
to be created in the cooperative teams once the members had reached a
certain income level; and dividends in cooperative stores (a slightly more
advanced form in which rather better-off shops invested capital shares)
could be as high as 10 percent. But probably most extreme of all, a July
21 *People's Daily* editorial suggested that state and SMC shops merge
some of their own stores and set aside certain markets to make way for
the poverty-stricken merchants.

In early August new tax regulations for private commerce and industry favored the small traders, who did not need to pay any taxes at all if
their profits could not cover their wages. Also, the new policy set a fixed
amount of tax on the basis of the business volume of each separate firm,
which would remain unchanged for one year.[101] This mood of care and
concession toward the petty capitalists lasted as policy through the
Eighth Party Congress held in September that year.[102]

The orchestrators of phase four, then, the phase that wound down the
transformation campaign, authored a policy more managerial in intent
than any oth;r that had been issued over the entire two-year period of
the campaign. If its design had been followed, the effect of the policy
would have been to reverse much of the work of earlier months. To see
whether the policy achieved its goals will require a look at the behavior
of its implementers, the local-level SMC cadres, and at the plight of their
targets, the merchants.

In fact, just as during the arrangement stage of a year before, many
cadres contravened the directions of the Ministry of Commerce in its
effort to preserve unorganized and small-scale trade. Most of them were
not at all inclined to investigate or to prop up the private market. Instead, their most frequent behavior, criticized in the press, involved
"forcibly seeking unity and universally establishing cooperative stores."
Despite its endorsement by Premier Zhou Enlai, some cadres looked
down on the more elementary commission-agency form of transformation and neglected it in their work.[103]

Furthermore, cadres ignored or discriminated against the small merchants and peddlers, those who had not been entered into joint public-
private enterprises or cooperative stores. For example, SMCs supplied

101. *SCMP*, nos. 1361, pp. 2–3, and 1368, pp. 9–11 (both 1956).

102. See the proposals for the Second Five Year Plan in *Eighth National Congress*, vol. I,
pp. 246–47, and Chen Yun's speech in vol. II, pp. 157–76.

103. *DGB*, February 4 and March 3, 1956.

only unpopular goods, if any, to those who had not been organized, preferring to deal only with businessmen whose firms had been merged.[104]

As for their motives, those most often mentioned in the press centered around the cadres' urge to facilitate their control over the private sector. Thus, a desire for ease of management moved them to concentrate the dealers of fragmentary, though often unrelated, commodities into one large shop.[105] And their rejection of those traders still using the commission-agency form of transformation was rooted as much in the difficulty of leading these scattered little independent firms as in an ideologically based choice for socialism.[106]

How did the merchants react? Some small traders, in dire straits, for a time nursed hopes of being taken into the joint enterprises, that they might lose their burdens by becoming submerged in a large accounting unit. Once they realized how unlikely was the realization of this dream—only the larger firms with some means were allowed to pool their holdings in this final phase of transformation—the petty traders felt left out of socialism and grew pessimistic. Unhappy about being forced to remain in their tiny family shops as commission agents for the state, they became anxious as their former competitors merged into joint enterprises, and they felt certain they would be "eaten up" and "squeezed out" by the competition. By June 1956 a number of small merchants in Guangdong were crying, not without justification, that "the government wants only the meat [the larger capitalists], not the bones [us]," and that "no one cares."[107]

Meanwhile, the more fortunate, those with a bit of capital who were therefore included in some kind of combination, were the previously successful merchants who were more accustomed to manipulation and maneuver in the marketplace.[108] According to press accounts, some turned rude, thinking they were now a part of public business, and put on airs, while others felt that their lives now had a guarantee, and so cut back on their working hours. More than a few, deciding to depend on state largesse, refused to deal in the small, miscellaneous commodities they had once handled, deeming them now too troublesome. In one Zhejiang *zhen* a stall peddler who had formerly habitually delivered goods to the countryside demanded to stay in the city after transformation,

---

104. *DGB*, April 1 and August 2, 1956.
105. *DGB*, February 4, March 6, and April 28, 1956.
106. *DGB*, March 3 and April 1 and 10, 1956.
107. *DGB*, February 1 and March 3, 1956, and *RMRB*, June 10, 1956.
108. *DGB*, February 7, March 6, April 1, 10 and 13, 1956.

thinking that there he could draw fixed wages and eat well; in another part of the province, a private merchant, quite active in former days, refused to continue taking in stocks once he became part of the group.

In this fourth and final phase of socialist transformation of the village markets, the managerial policy designed by marketeer officials at the center proved difficult to realize in the localities. With the marketplace now more or less monopolized by state trade cadres and by the mergers of bigger merchants they had formed, the smaller, poorer traders found that earning a bare livelihood was a nearly impossible struggle. Their hopes for improving their position and augmenting their power, which the campaign had kindled in the "high tide," were quelled at the end, as the cadres recognized only the organized, those with some capital to contribute to the state.

This review of the stages through which the campaign of socialist transformation of rural small-scale trade progressed illuminates the links between the social and economic interests of specific groups, on the one hand, and the three tendencies toward economic policy that show up at the central, policy-making level, on the other. It is clear from the documents that emerged from this two-year process that two distinct lines existed at the center. One, for policing, was subscribed to by officials such as Peng Zhen and Li Fuchun who had institutional, bureaucratic concerns at the forefront of their minds, and also by Mao Zedong, who seemed mainly interested in radical, class-based issues. The other, a managerial line, was propounded by Chen Yun and Zeng Shan at the Ministry of Commerce. Their views—for gradual change with a place for some private trade—were informed by the marketeer's belief in the efficacy of the rural market in meeting mass needs.

At the local level, however, it is not so simple to assign each of the relevant parties to one tendency or another. As policy switched with the play of central factions, the alternatives before each group shifted. As a result, the various groups had different reactions over time. In the first phase, in which radical central officials and plan-conscious local cadres agreed on the benefits of shutting down the private marketplace, merchants of all stripes felt threatened, and thus could all have been described as adhering to a marketeer tendency. And again in the second phase, though policy making had fallen to the marketeer politicians in Beijing, cadres nevertheless continued with practices that limited private marketing activity, and so both sets of merchants still supported marketeerism. In both these phases, the richer traders, as ever, bested those with less means.

By the third phase, however, the choice was no longer one between markets or no markets, as central-level hard-liners tried to abolish pri-

TABLE 5 The Situation in the Transformation of Privately Operated Commerce, 1956

	Absolute Numbers			Proportions by Percentage		
	No. of Firms (×1,000)	No. of Personnel (×1,000)	Capital Volume (million yuan)	% of Total Number of Private Firms	% of Total Number of Private Personnel	% of Total Capital Volume of Original Private Commerce
Already transformed as of about August 1956	1,991	2,824	785	82.2	85.1	93.3
Those in state-operated and SMC firms	147	224	—	6.1	6.8	—
Those in public-private jointly-operated firms	401	877	601	16.5	26.4	71.5
Those in jointly-operated firms who were receiving a fixed yearly dividend from the government	281	706	554	11.6	21.3	65.9
Those in cooperativized commerce	1,443	1,723	184	59.6	51.9	21.8
Those in cooperativized commerce who were in cooperative shops	581	722	104	24.0	21.8	12.4
Not yet transformed private trade	432	494	56	17.8	14.9	6.7
Totals	2,423	3,318	841	100.0	100.0	100.0

SOURCE: Zhongguo shehui kexue yuan, jingji yanjiuso (Chinese Academy of Social Science, Economic Research Institute), *Zhongguo zibenzhuyi gongshangye de shehui zhuyi gaizao* (The socialist transformation of China's capitalist industry and commerce) (Beijing: Renmin chubanshe, 1978), p. 229.

vate trade through dictating mergers. At this point, the poorer of the traders placed their faith in this radical, mobilizational strategy, while their wealthier rivals yet held on to the disappearing marketplace. Some cadres, afraid that getting too involved in the campaign would mean that they would fail to fulfill their own business quotas, seemed more interested in participating in marketing than in eliminating it.

Finally, at the close of the campaign, when unmerging and even subsidizing traders in trouble became the official line, amalgamated businesses had already become a significant feature of the rural landscape, and these housed only the better-off among the dealers. By this time, many of the poor, who had been largely passed by, had become disillusioned with a radical strategy that had failed in its promise, but they no longer had any market to turn to. Meanwhile, the richer salesmen, once brought into the state bureaucracy, as it were, made their accommodation with the perquisites that the world of the plan had to offer. Whether a given group embraced one tendency over another, then, could not simply be deduced a priori by its presumed economic interest, since its interests changed necessarily as the organizational alternatives available were altered by central policy makers. The material below, in broad sweeps, follows this tale of regulation over subsequent years and draws upon insights afforded by the foregoing.

The Continuing Process of Socialist Transformation and the Small Merchants, 1957–1980

The "high tide" period of socialist transformation, those months between late autumn 1955 and early spring 1956 when a policing policy forced top-speed joinings and eliminations of firms, is the time best known for governmental interference with private business. But among the small merchants especially, state tampering with trade has in fact been nearly continuous over the years, as politicians have frequently focused their attention on arranging and rearranging their numbers and their affairs. In effect, aggressive and lenient phases continued to come and go for the little trader, whose pole-and-bundle was dusted off for use, but then put back on the shelf again more than once.

As was noted above, the process of transformation left some small merchants behind. According to different sources, those passed over amounted to some five to eight hundred thousand persons.[109] This meant that in the first few years after 1956, there was a ready pool for further state inroads among these elements. In the decades that followed, the firms of these and others of their class were merged into enterprises that were subsequently unmerged on more than one occasion. These fluctuations in policy can be explained by the same factors used in the analysis above.

The technology of their work—the small scope of their operations and the crude state of their facilities—made it a relatively simple matter (compared with agricultural and industrial institutions) to connect and disconnect groups of these traders. Also, the quick stimulation their activity could give to the economy at local levels, both in city and country settings, has induced pro-market politicians when in power to turn to them at times of economic recovery. In such periods their class nature has easily been redefined.

But the ambiguity surrounding the class status of small merchants and peddlers has lingered on, for the decision as to whether they are primarily laboring people close in nature to the peasantry or mainly petty capitalists prone to speculation was not made once and for all. As a result, policy makers in periods of differing political climate have viewed them in disparate ways, and they have been a convenient target during ideologically oriented movements. Local cadres bent on doing away with the competition they pose have consistently drawn on radical class designations of this group in their efforts to squeeze them out of the market.

But still, given their shortage of capital, not only was their presence as free traders more palatable for the ideologically motivated than would have been that of the wealthier capitalists, but the costs of meddling with and rearranging their enterprises were also far lower than would have been the costs in the case of the firms of the former big businessmen.

If the years 1957 to 1980 are broken down into six blocks of years, half of the blocks could be counted as managerial or more lenient toward the small merchants, half as principally policing or aggressive.

109. See *JJYJ*, no. 2 (1958), p. 17, which states that, at the end of 1956, 212,600 small traders had been approved for public-private joint operations, but were not given fixed interest payments by the state, nor did they work with shares; and that another 620,000 traders were continuing to deal completely on their own. Both these groups, then, were left unorganized. CASS, p. 229, says that 14.9 percent of a total original pool of 3,318,000 small merchants was not transformed, which amounts to about 500,000 people. There is also discussion of this issue in *SCMP*, no. 1863 (1958), pp. 9–18. The *JJYJ* article explains that those not cooperativized were the old, the weak, and the sick; those for whom commercial work was not their main line of income; those whose site of operations was very scattered and who were consequently hard to link together with others; criminal elements; and those whose income was high and so refused to join.

TABLE 6 Numbers of Private Individual Laborers and Collective Private Firms, Selected Areas and Years, 1953–1981

Numbers of Laborers, Firms (Terms as Used in Chinese Sources)

Area	Individual Laborers, All Sorts (industrial, commercial)	Self-employed	Small Merchants & Peddlers	Individual Firms, Industrial & Commercial (includes handicraft & service trades)	Individual Firms, Commercial (shops, restaurants, repair)	Collective Firms, Commercial	Date and Source / References
Nationwide: Cities, Towns	9,000,000						1953[a]
Nationwide	2,270,000						1957[b]
Nationwide					3,590,000		1964[l]
Nationwide					610,000		1978[b]
Nationwide: Cities, Towns				100,000 new ones approved			1979[c]
Nationwide: Cities, Towns				250,000			12/31/79[c]
Nationwide: Cities, Towns				400,000			7/80[c]
Nationwide					nearly 1,000,000		
Nationwide				100,000+		1,300,000+	12/31/80[d] 12/31/80[d]
Shanghai	200,000						early 1950s[e]
Shanghai	100,000						1955[e]
Shanghai	8,000						1957[k]
Shanghai							1976[k]
Shanghai				10,000*			7/24/80[e]
Canton		50,000					mid-1962[f]

City				Date
Canton			6,159	10/80g
Canton	14,000			11/81h
Beijing	56,769			1956i
Beijing			42,080	1956i
Beijing		33,000		10/80g
Nanjing			1,298	mid-1962j
Nanjing			1,000	10/80g
Tianjin			4,365	10/80g
Shenyang			7,203	10/80g
Changchun			3,600	10/80g
Harbin			7,600	10/80g
Wuhan			3,250	10/80g
Chengdu			2,800	10/80g
Sian			1,792	10/80g
Lanzhou			1,200	10/80g
Shijiazhuang			358	10/80g
Huhoerto			1,756	10/80g

* *Beijing Review*, no. 3 (1982), p. 24, states that Shanghai had 11,000 private enterprises at the end of 1980, and that their volume of business was less than one-thousandth of the city's total turnover from retail trade.

a *Beijing Review*, no. 45 (November 10, 1980), p. 20.

b *Jingji yanjiu* (Economic Studies), no. 6 (1980), p. 58.

c *Renmin ribao* (People's Daily), August 21, 1980, p. 2.

d *Renmin ribao*, April 1, 1981, p. 2.

e *Renmin ribao*, July 24, 1980, p. 2.

f *Yangcheng wanbao* (Yangcheng Evening News), August 10, 1962.

g *Shichang* (Market), no. 26 (October 25, 1980), p. 6.

h *New York Times*, November 24, 1981.

i *Renmin ribao*, June 22, 1980, p. 2.

j *Da Gong Bao* (Impartial Daily), June 16, 1962.

k *Renmin ribao*, October 19, 1981, p. 2.

l *Hong Qi* (Red Flag), no. 24 (1981), p. 14.

These six are the 1957–1958 period of the Hundred Flowers, anti-rightist movement, and rectification; the Great Leap Forward (1958–1959); the post-Leap recovery of 1961–1962; the socialist education movement of 1964–1965; the Cultural Revolution (1966–1976); and the early post-Mao era (1978–1980). Treatment of small traders was mainly managerial overall in 1957–1958, more so in 1961–1962, and most so in 1978–1980; and it took a policing form in 1958–1959 and from 1963 to 1976.

During the Hundred Flowers movement, the larger ex-capitalists dared to bring forward such demanding proposals as the extension of the period during which the state would "buy out" their firms (i.e., pay them interest annually). They suggested lengthening this period from the planned seven years to twenty, and removing the representatives of the public side from their firms.[110] At this time, the poor peddlers' only requests were such meager ones as for more jars of liquor to sell or to receive their egg deliveries on time.[111]

In the antirightist/rectification movement that counterattacked the spokespersons of the Hundred Flowers, "unlawful capitalists and other speculators" were to be "stamped out" and given "complete exposure and resolute criticism"; and they were forced to donate their remaining financial holdings, their technical knowledge, and their expertise to the now state-owned firms, and to identify completely with the workers. Simultaneously, the Ministry of Commerce more or less excused the small traders from the heat of the battle, at least through 1957, claiming that socialist education, report meetings, and debates would do for them.[112] In general, these smaller business-people were less of a threat— and also had less to offer—than the big capitalists, and so were easier to exempt or ignore.

In early 1958 a harsher tone set in, a prelude to the Great Leap, as Tianjin began a rectification campaign against "capitalist spontaneity," a campaign that involved organizing small traders. Also, the state began to reduce bank favors to the traders, and extra state retail shops appeared. The explanation for these moves came in the form of charges that some traders were amassing overlarge incomes.[113] As radical politi-

110. *SCMP*, nos. 1536 (1957), pp. 4–12, and 1574 (1957), p. 14.
111. Lynn T. White III, "Low Power: Small Enterprises in Shanghai, 1949–1967," p. 60.
112. *SCMP*, nos. 1603, pp. 9–14, 1615, pp. 9–13, 1618, pp. 7–19 (all 1957) and 1852 (1958), pp. 8–15. Also, *ECMM*, no. 115 (1957), p. 29; George Ecklund, "Protracted Expropriation of Private Business in Communist China," p. 245.
113. *SCMP*, no. 1863 (1958), pp. 33–34; *DGB*, January 7, 1958; *ECMM*, no. 140 (1958), pp. 42–46. Why Tianjin was a pace setter at the time is not mentioned in the sources. However, its mayor, Huang Huoqing, may have been especially interested in capi-

cians gained power at the center, the little merchant found that he or she could no longer be an exception.

The Great Leap Forward was a movement that enveloped the whole of society. The remnant private sector, now considered a suspect seedbed for "spontaneous capitalism," attracted attention quickly, again in Tianjin, where 27,000 (over 73 percent) of the remaining small traders were drawn into cooperative shops and another 5,000 into cooperative teams, while 3,000 were transferred to industrial, agricultural, and transport enterprises.[114] In this period, then, the small merchants were lumped into the capitalist category with their bigger cousins, and the media highlighted their tendency to engage in exploitation.[115] This stance served to justify an aggressive treatment of them, as the state gathered in all possible resources.

In Tianjin the new policing policy entailed the reorganization of all lower cooperative stores and groups and all remaining individual peddlers into higher (larger) cooperatives, each of which was to act as an accounting unit that offered no dividends to its members. The goal here was to overcome the past imbalances between the wretched and the fortunate.[116] In Guangdong province, merchants and peddlers not only had to perform agricultural labor, but had to invest in it funds from their shops as well.[117] Elsewhere, small capitalists were now included in the supply and marketing departments in the communes, and received critical comment for expecting an "iron rice bowl" or steady wages for doing less labor than usual.[118] In Guizhou's Guiding county, excess commercial personnel of small-merchant origin were sent off to the mountains and wastelands, to clear terrain and build up farms, and they had to donate capital to these projects from their shop's public accumulation funds.[119] Vice-Premier Li Xiannian was surprised (and pleased, it seems) to note in his travels that "in many places, there's not a single

---

talists. Klein and Clark note that he delivered a report to the Eighth Party Congress on the reform of the Tianjin capitalists in September 1956. See Donald W. Klein and Anne B. Clark, *Biographic Dictionary of Chinese Communism, 1921–1965*, p. 397.

114. *SCMP*, nos. 1859 (1958), p. 30, and 1863 (1958), pp. 33–34. *DGB*, July 7, 1958, notes that there are three ways of getting rid of individual operations: cooperativization, absorption into state and SMC enterprises; and transferral to other economic sectors to work.

115. *Xin Gong Shang* [New Industry and Commerce] (*XGS*), May 9, 1959, and *DGB*, June 15, 1959.

116. *SCMP*, no. 1876 (1958), pp. 4–9; also see *DGB*, September 17, 1958.

117. *Nanfang ribao* [Southern Daily] (Canton), April 2, 1958.

118. *XGS*, March 9, 1959.

119. *DGB*, September 25, 1958.

small merchant or peddler. Such is the case for Xushui county, Hebei as a whole."[120]

In light of recent charges that collective enterprises (essentially private firms responsible for their own profits and losses) were abolished in 1958,[121] it is instructive to note that several sources from the Leap period itself do speak of "the 1958 overall liquidation, tidying up, and reform through education" of remnant private enterprise and its owners, who were "incorporated into the socialist economy"; and of public-private joint enterprises being "transformed along the lines of state commercial enterprises."[122] In the Leap, then, all private enterprise was eliminated, new mergers occurred, and the petty holdings of the smallest traders were confiscated, as policing policies capitalized on the fact that all merchants could be categorized as members of the bourgeoisie.

One aspect of the undoing of Leap strategies in the years 1961–1962 was a rebirth of a lenient, managerial approach to the little business-men. No longer was there talk of mergers, labor reform, or the contribu-tion of funds. Instead, beginning in June 1961 a new policy urged state trade organs, companies, and retail shops to aid, supervise, and guide cooperative shops in the cities in political study as in 1957; and autho-rized market-control personnel merely to set quality norms and to deter-mine price and gross profit rates, by way of dealing with these traders. In Hangzhou, commercial departments also led the merchants to engage in some self-regulation in the form of "mutual cooperation and supervi-sion." At the same time, the state concerns were urged to encourage the cooperatives to develop their "traditional operations characteristics" — those same traits praised during managerial phases of the transforma-tion "high tide" era for enlivening the market and facilitating marketing for the masses.[123]

Besides reinstalling this mild form of economic regulation of cooper-ative groups, the early 1960s also saw a revival of the very smallest types of firms, those whose operators had been eliminated as independent traders in the few previous years. In Xi'an stalls and pole-peddlers re-appeared; and in Nanjing the "cooperative commerce" network was "everywhere in the whole city," as over 4,000 "operations points" reap-peared, including mobile carts and service traders, much in the style, no

120. *ECMM*, no. 149 (1958), p. 36.
121. See *RMRB*, August 4, 1979; *JJYJ* no. 3 (1980), p. 74.
122. *ECMM*, no. 140 (1958), p. 45; *SCMP*, no. 2015 (1959), pp. 16–20.
123. *DGB*, July 20 and 27, 1961; *Yangcheng wanbao* [Yangcheng Evening News] (Can-ton) (*YCWB*), July 21, 1961; *RMRB*, July 27, August 5, September 21, and October 14, 1961.

doubt, of the "sidewalk capitalists" made much of in the Western press in 1979–1980.[124] By mid-1962 Nanjing reported having over 33,000 small merchants and peddlers; Canton had more than 50,000. Each city organized these individuals into a union, presumably as a loose form of regulation, "to strengthen leadership, develop market supply work, and improve operations management."[125]

Perhaps of greatest interest is the case of Tahe City, Henan, reported no doubt as just one example of a process in motion throughout the country.[126] Here the city's 34 original cooperative shops were once joined (the article does not tell whether the merger occurred in 1956 or 1958) into one huge accounting unit, under a fixed-wage egalitarian allocation system. In mid-1961 the city government broke down the big unit and, using its component cooperative-retail-shop outlets as a foundation, set up 41 small cooperative shops (even more than the original number), each an independent accounting unit responsible for its own gains and losses, paying workers now by "piece-rate wages." Many of these newly constituted shops sent out peddlers, and 149 stalls emerged from the conversion. The flexible technological base of small trade, and the quick fix its rapid turnover could give to the ailing urban economy, made its restoration both possible and attractive in the early post-Leap recovery period.

However, as the socialist education movement got under way and developed in the next few years, with its critique of rural corruption,[127] the official appraisal of all merchants and their operations again underwent a change. Increasingly, after the September 1962 Tenth Plenum of the Eighth Party Central Committee (where Mao stressed class struggle), the press printed stories of trader speculation and cheating in the markets. A graphic example comes from a description of a marketplace in Canton, where over 90 percent of the dealers were small merchants and peddlers who were members of cooperative groups:

> Some salesmen may put salt on stale fish to make it look fresh or give a customer one more piece of meat to please. In fact the meat weighs less

124. *Gongren ribao* [Worker's Daily] (Beijing) (*GRRB*), September 5, 1961; *GRRB*, May 26, 1962.

125. *DGB*, June 16, 1962; *YCWB*, August 10, 1962.

126. *RMRB*, November 11, 1961.

127. On the socialist education movement, see Richard Baum, *Prelude to Revolution.* According to Xiao Xiangzi, "Obstacles to the Development of the Chinese Individual Economy," *Zheng Ming* [Contend], no. 48 (October 1981), p. 73, individual enterprises were wiped out in the Four Cleans movement of 1964.

than what the customer has paid for. . . . On the wall of the market there hung two public steelyards without weights. A woman named Wu . . . once bought one catty of fish. . . . When she weighed her fish by the public steelyard, she found the weight fell short by 1.8 *liang* [one-tenth of a catty, or about 1 ¾ ounces]. She then went back to the stall and urged the salesman to make it good, but was refused. A few days later, she bought some vegetables and again she wanted to use the public steelyard. However, the weights on the steelyards had disappeared. Ever since, the weight shortages in the market have become even more serious.[128]

In this mood of critical reassessment, small merchants were attacked as being members of the exploiting bourgeoisie, who had to be annihilated along with all other capitalists.[129]

In the countryside in those years, SMCs were no longer to aid but to "outwit speculative merchants and peddlers" and to be certain to procure even minor commodities so that the bourgeoisie could not "take the opportunity to buy and sell [these items] for speculative purposes." The SMCs were also instructed to organize any unorganized traders, in order to strengthen control, and to "intensify transformation and education" yet one more time over those who were organized.[130] In Shanghai, itinerant vendors had disappeared once again by the mid-1960s, so that the only private shops were family businesses selling hot water and tea.[131] Apparently, the unmerging of the first few years of the decade was short-lived, as cadres began to bask in a heyday for state-run business that was to last over a decade.

Further and more intensive policing was the policy during the Cultural Revolutionary years, 1966–1976. Several documents from that ideologically charged epoch counsel "repression" for unlicensed traders and dictate that "cooperative stores and teams and individual traders and vendors must accept the leadership of the state economy . . . and accept socialist transformation." Other directives call on the cadres to "hit hard at speculation and manipulation and take a firm hand to deal with unlicensed peddlers."[132] One Red Guard tabloid called for "a serious struggle to strengthen the socialist transformation of cooperative

128. *YCWB*, December 10, 1962, in *SCMPS*, no. 105 (1963), p. 11.

129. *DGB*, May 29, 1965. This analysis appeared in a critique of Mao Dun's short story "The Lin's Store," made into a movie by Xia Yan in 1958 and reshown in the mid-1960s. See *Union Research Service*, 39, no. 23 (1965): 333, 336.

130. *SCMP*, no. 2861 (1962), pp. 8–10, and no. 3367 (1964), pp. 6–8; and *SCMM*, no. 421 (1964), pp. 1–5.

131. White, p. 73.

132. As in White, p. 75; *SCMP*, no. 4129 (1968), p. 3; *RMRB*, February 6, 1967, in *CB*, no. 818 (1967), pp. 27–29.

shops and groups," as some merchants in them took advantage of up-heaval to misappropriate the shops' public welfare and accumulation funds.[133] And though Shanghai private peddlers organized a rebel group that "poured out bitterness" and cried for better treatment in goods al-location and in taxation rates,[134] the Cultural Revolution was by all later accounts a time when individual operators "were all swept away."[135]

That era of policing came to a close most decisively with the Third Plenum of the Eleventh Central Committee in December 1978,[136] which uncritically redefined a large majority of the entire bourgeoisie, large and small, as having been transformed into people who live by their own labor. It accepted the small traders as socialist, once again laboring peo-ple, an unambiguous title they had not enjoyed since the mid-1950s. As the big ex-capitalists received the fixed interest on their assets and the bank deposits that had been confiscated during the Cultural Revolution, and had their full wages restored and any deductions refunded retroac-tively,[137] the small shops of the little merchants were (as in 1961) once again unattached from larger mergers. At the same time, official policy dictated that discrimination against them as "the tail of capitalism" be terminated.

This 1979–1980 rehabilitation of the private sector was clearly a new managerial effort to reinvigorate the economy by enlivening its market, and to solve problems of massive unemployment in the cities. Official justification for this drew in part on the old arguments: the paucity of state commercial personnel and China's low technology ("our produc-tive forces are low, transportation is inconvenient, and our production tools and transport facilities are backward").[138] As was explained by Wang Wenke, then deputy director of the National Administration of Industry and Commerce, privately owned and operated firms increase

133. *Caimao hongqi* [Trade and Finance Red Flag], February 15, 1967 (a Red Guard tabloid reproduced in *Red Guard Publications, Part I: Newspapers*, reprinted by Center for Chinese Research Materials, Association of Research Libraries, Washington, D.C., 1975).

134. Hong Yung Lee, *The Politics of the Chinese Cultural Revolution*, pp. 133–34.

135. See, for example, *Shichang* [Market] (Beijing) (*SC*), no. 5 (1979). This article tells of Canton's experience, which was no doubt typical. Also, *BR*, no. 33 (1980), pp. 3–4, speaks of individually owned shops having been branded as "capitalist tails" and closed down.

136. *RMRB*, August 21, 1980, p. 2, and March 28, 1981, p. 2, trace the change to the Third Plenum; *BR*, no. 45 (1980), p. 20, notes that at the First Session of the Fifth National People's Congress in March 1978 "permission to develop individually operated industrial and commercial establishments as laid down in the Chinese Constitution was reiterated."

137. *BR*, no. 11 (1980), pp. 5–6, and no. 17 (1980), p. 21. Also see U.S. *Foreign Broad-cast Information Service (FBIS)*, January 24, 1979, pp. G5–6, and August 14, 1979, pp. L1–3.

138. *RMRB*, June 20, 1980, p. 5.

social wealth, activate markets, create job opportunities, help accumulate funds for the state through the taxes they pay, enrich people's lives by promoting the revival of traditional skills, fill the vacuum left by state and cooperative industry and trade, and stimulate state business through competition.[139]

To effect this turn in policy, various cities passed measures to facilitate the rebirth of small-scale trading.[140] Shanghai issued licenses to anyone who possessed a certain business skill so long as he or she had formal registration in the city and was without other work, increased the goods that would be made available to them, and gave them tax benefits. In Wenzhou, Zhejiang, privately run shops were permitted to deal in more items and a larger number of varieties than before. Local government offices were to arrange space in the cities for them, help them raise capital and receive bank loans, treat them politically and socially in the same manner as state and cooperative firms were treated, and not fine them arbitrarily.[141]

However, as in 1955–1956, despite vigorous central-level advocacy of this policy, these new enterprises came under pressure from local cadres. According to some accounts, this pressure was rooted in ideological "leftism," but according to others, it occurred because the state workers envied the bigger profits some of the small firms were able to amass.[142] "Some think individual commerce is a retreat," one article combining these interpretations reported; "worrying it will steal business from the state, compete for profits, and, if individual firms struggle for money, will lead to capitalism." The national media conveyed the sentiment in a Henan district, where within the state-operated commercial departments some comrades were saying, "That the market is too lively, that the market is chaotic, that prices are chaotic, that the scope of operations is chaotic is all the result of allowing too much individual commerce." No doubt the case was typical.

Some such state commercial offices, continued the Henan story, then used the pretexts of "rectifying the market" and "attacking speculation" to adopt "so-called measures to control the chaos." This stance enabled bureaucrats in charge of state business to discriminate against the pri-

139. *BR*, no. 45 (1980), p. 22.
140. *RMRB*, July 24, 1980, p. 2, July 25, 1980, p. 3, and August 5, 1980, p. 2.
141. These directions were formalized in a State Council "Regulations on the Urban Nonagricultural Individual Economy" of July 15, 1981 (in *RMRB*, July 16, 1981, p. 2).
142. Xiao Xiangzi (n. 127 above), p. 73; *RMRB*, July 5, 1980, p. 1; *SC*, no. 22 (August 25, 1980), p. 2; *RMRB*, August 21, 1981, p. 3, are only examples of many, many such accounts.

vate concerns, even at times to deal with them more harshly than capitalists of the 1950s had been handled.[143]

As a consequence, according to numerous statements in the papers, in many instances these private enterprises had to struggle to exist. For example, local state offices set exorbitant tax rates, as much as 86 percent of their business volume in some cases.[144] Though some firms run collectively by a group of individuals were able to use funds accumulated by their neighborhood residents' committees, scarcity of capital was a pervasive problem for many of those attempting to go into business.[145] While the state-run banks were urged by central authorities to issue loans to them, the loans had to be paid back in only six months' time; and in some places banks would not allow the small operators even to open an account.[146] Seeing an opportunity to collect extra income, various city government departments, including those for sanitation, urban construction, transport, and weights and measures, charged the firms different sorts of fees, which sometimes amounted to nearly the total of the net profits the firms had taken in.[147]

Getting goods in stock was a particularly outstanding issue for these commercial enterprises.[148] It was sometimes possible for them to obtain their wares directly from the producer, or by working through connections and giving gifts to workers in state organs. But a report from Wenzhou City claimed that only half the total sales volume of the collective shops there came from goods that the shops had procured through their own devices. For the rest, they were dependent on state wholesale distributors, which sometimes refused to sell to them at all, or which often offered only spoiled or unpopular items. Also, the state companies sold to them at retail prices, not at wholesale as they did for the state-owned firms, so that the private shops had trouble earning any profit.

Besides placing all these obstacles in the path of the small firms' business, some urban cadres engaged in simple harassment as well.[149] Cadres

143. *RMRB*, August 21, 1981, p. 3, and Xiao, p. 73.

144. *RMRB*, July 10, 1980, p. 5; Xiao, p. 73. This same story says that in Harbin the tax department set a monthly maximum business volume of 170 yuan, for which the tax was 27.30 yuan. If the volume of business surpassed that limit, taxes were increased. Shanghai changed the nationally set fourteen-level progressive tax to a two-level tax (*RMRB*, August 5, 1980, p. 2).

145. *SC*, no. 11 (March 10, 1980), p. 7; Xiao, p. 74.

146. *SC*, no. 20 (July 25, 1980), p. 1, and *RMRB*, July 10, 1980, p. 5.

147. Xiao, p. 74; *SC*, no. 20 (July 25, 1980), p. 1.

148. On stocking goods and problems with this, see *SC*, no. 19 (July 10, 1980), p. 7, and no. 21 (August 10, 1980), p. 1; Xiao, p. 74, and *RMRB*, August 5 and 10, 1980 (p. 2 for both), April 12, 1981, p. 3, and July 5, 1981, p. 5.

149. Xiao, p. 73.

would come to investigate their work, or summon their staff to city offices. At the extreme, official workers were reported to have stolen their tools of trade, threatened their customers, ransacked their premises, and ruined their materials. Although cadres so inclined capriciously confiscated the licenses of these merchants, several reports admit that some of the entrepreneurs themselves, unable to sustain a livelihood, voluntarily abandoned their enterprises and relinquished their licenses. In Tianjin, there were 50 percent fewer small individual firms in early 1981 than at the same time in 1980.[150] In sum, read one critique, "In general, the local cadres have this kind of viewpoint: 'Only permit the individual firms to open a business, but don't let them earn any money.'"[151]

Because of key features of China's retail trade, especially its small-scale rural component (which accounts for the bulk of China's business class), this type of trade was not fully transformed in the "high tide" period, and was by turns further infringed upon and let go nearly free in subsequent years. Its simple technological foundation, its close ties to clients, its ability, once set in motion, to invigorate the local economy, its meager capital, and its dubious but not altogether damnable class status have made its practitioners the brunt of state and SMC cadres' competition. But these same traits have at times earned them a respite from the more aggressive policies of attack and reorganization visited upon firms in other sectors. The outcome has been to leave the small traders less assaulted but at the same time more neglected than any of the other major economic groups.

Within this class, a rough breakdown in this chapter (following the PRC sources) has divided these traders into two broad groupings. Whenever a policing policy (supported by radicals and bureaucrats) has specified that the marketplace and its activities may not be used to organize economic life, the largest of the firms have been brought into the confines of state management, which, happily for their personnel, involves benefits and supports.

Ironically, in a society built to benefit the poorer groups, it has been the underdog, the petty capitalist, who has been shunted aside and often left to fend for himself or herself. For, at times of aggressive regulation, the poor peddler has been castigated for his bad class background and his cheating; also, in these phases the state merges and

150. See *SC*, no. 20 (July 25, 1980), p. 1; Xiao, p. 74; and *RMRB*, March 28, 1981, p. 2.
151. Xiao, p. 74.

eliminates even the firms of the little fellows and appropriates their tiny holdings in the process.

On the other hand, in more lenient, managerial periods (designed by marketeers), the small merchant has been ignored and left out of the system, since his or her scant wealth does not qualify for admission into cooperatives, for bank loans, or for saleable supplies. Lacking personal resources to fall back on, the small merchant has suffered the most from the onslaughts of the competitive state and SMC business cadres. In 1956 and at several junctures thereafter, the petty traders begged for admission into the ranks of the joint enterprises, to no avail.[152] Thus, though the policy toward the small businessmen at times seems indulgent, in that they may continue to work on their own, the deprivations associated with this privilege have often been severe.

This story shows that in Chinese socialist society, extremely lenient treatment and only intermittent attention toward a group is often the result of its being accorded a low priority, and neglect and discrimination often follow as concomitants.[153] Just as in a capitalist economy, forces of competition, along with the superior clout of the economically better endowed in handling regulation, work to the detriment of the small entrepreneur. Not surprisingly, the victims themselves have not failed to take note, as is expressed in this plaint of Shanghai private peddlers during the Cultural Revolution: "The individual peddler is the worst off in the new society."[154]

152. Ezra Vogel, *Canton Under Communism*, pp. 171–73.
153. See Dorothy J. Solinger, "Minority Nationalities in China's Yunnan Province: Assimilation, Power, and Policy in a Socialist State," for a discussion of small minority groups which have also been relatively ignored.
154. Lee, pp. 133–34. Original in *Jiefang ribao* [Liberation Daily], March 7, 1967.

5

Commerce and Industry:

Strains and Models

A central theme of chapter four, that the private sector finds trading tense and uncertain in this socialist, economically underdeveloped society, must have come as no surprise. But within the Chinese state bureaucracy as well, commercial actors are often crossed. For the branch responsible for the exchange of goods often experiences strains in its relations with units managing state-run industrial production, as each sector strives for dominance in the disposal and control of goods. This chapter looks at those strains, most of which occur also in the interaction between sales and production departments within capitalist firms. It gives special consideration to the ways in which China's planned economy and its low technology aggravate and add to these tensions.

After setting out the nature of the troubled tie between trade and industry, the body of the discussion focuses on the political and organizational dimensions of this relationship in China. It does so through presenting three models that have been designed to order the dealings between these two sectors. Each model is associated with one of the three tendencies in political conflict; each entails a widely divergent view of the role commercial work plays in the increase of productive activity and thereby in the enhancement of the wealth of the state. And each, in championing one sector over the other, calls forth support and opposition from different quarters.

Structural Bases for Antagonism between Industry and Commerce

Relations between state-owned commercial firms and factories (or, respectively, departments of trade and industry) were already hostile enough in the 1950s to be described as a "mutual tearing to shreds." Another source from the same time noted that the two types of agencies were frequently involved in disputes at all stages during their interactions—when drawing up production and marketing plans and signing contracts, to inspecting commodities at the time of delivery.[1]

Two decades later, in the early 1970s, proponents of industry attacked Liu Shaoqi, number one "capitalist-roader" scapegoat of the Cultural Revolution, for what they called his "fallacy" that circulation determines production. These critics labeled this view "a vain attempt to apply the law of value and the relationship between supply and demand in regulating and manipulating production." They also castigated what they termed Liu's effort to "use the commercial department to rule the production department."[2]

Staff in commercial organs, however, have also resented being placed in the subservient role, having "to sell what[ever] is produced and palm off garlic as spring onion."[3] These controversies have their origins in the disparate missions of the two functions under any economic system. But they are compounded by the existence of the plan and the backwardness of China's technological infrastructure for both production and exchange.

Despite the overarching goal in capitalist firms of obtaining maximum profits for the enterprise as a whole, clashes between those managing output and sales take place within that type of firm as well. Students of capitalist business concerns point to a set of uncertainties and pressures under which each of these separate departments must operate, un-

1. *Da Gong Bao* [Impartial Daily] (Beijing) (*DGB*), October 1, 1958, p. 5; *Extracts from China Mainland Magazines* (*ECMM*), no. 136 (1958), p. 39.
2. *Renmin ribao* [People's Daily] (Beijing) (*RMRB*), October 19, 1970.
3. *RMRB*, February 5, 1971.

certainties caused in part by demands from the other.[4] That is, sections in charge of production face variability in deliveries from suppliers and unevenness in the behavior of the market for the final product. But sales departments must adjust to the scheduling and growth needs of the productive process and must respond to requests from the inventory division to maintain a certain level and range of goods in stock.

In the case of capitalist managers, however, internal struggles over supplies, the market, production scheduling, and inventories are softened to an extent. For in their firms the rewards for employees in all divisions are enhanced when smooth cooperation among sections leads to large sales.[5] In socialist China's planned economy, by contrast, industrial and commercial organs each submit to the control of separate hierarchies. Each of these, in turn, must individually account for its successes and failures to distinct ministries in Beijing and, ultimately, to the State Council. Also, in China, only the commercial bureaucracy, not the industrial one, had responsibility for sales in the period under review.

Moreover, in the socialist economy each of these two bureaucracies is the executor of a very different sort of plan; and the directives that order the work of the two sectors are actually mutually incompatible. Industrial workers have generally been charged with striving for the maximum attainable quantity of output, often in disregard of the quality of the product; commerce, on the other hand, aims to meet sales targets, a feat difficult to accomplish when the commodities turned out by the factories are shoddy. Each side has the best chance to fulfill its target quotas, then, if it manages to outdo its rival by realizing its own approach to the handling of goods. Thus, the most clear-cut manifestation of tension between trade and industry in this type of economy appears as a form of contention over commodities—in this case, over their quantity versus their quality.[6]

4. Richard M. Cyert and James G. March, *A Behavioral Theory of the Firm*, pp. 41, 119, 153.
5. Despite tensions, according to Oliver Williamson, *Markets and Hierarchies: Analysis and Antitrust Implications*, pp. 9–10 and 29, the internal divisions in a capitalist firm are likely to cooperate, for these reasons: separate divisions in the firm (unlike separate sectors in the Chinese economy) "do not have preemptive claims on their respective profit streams"; "the aggressive pursuit of individual interests redounds to the disadvantage of the system"; "present and prospective compensation (including promotions) can be easily varied by the general office to reflect noncooperation"; and "internal incentive and control machinery is much more extensive and refined [in one firm] than that which obtains in market exchanges, [between firms]" (or between sectors in the Chinese economy). "Altogether," he concludes, "a more nearly joint profit maximizing attitude and result is to be expected" within one large capitalist firm than among autonomous contractors in a market exchange (or among sectors in a planned economy).
6. That similar antagonisms exist in other socialist planned economies is evident from Alec Nove's chapter 10 on trade in *The Soviet Economic System*. Nove states, on p. 258, for

Yet one more form of discord introduced by the plan grows out of the fact that one sector's profits are partially the result of its outwitting the other. Although the prices for major, important commodities are set by the Ministry of Commerce at the central government level, municipal commercial departments have jurisdiction over adjustments for other products within specified ranges. In many instances, the marketing agent can determine to a certain degree the cost at which it offers supplies and the price of a manufactured item as it leaves the factory. The price level will then determine the relative profit each sector receives. One press analysis seeking to create harmony between departments advised, "If both sides benefit from the price, they won't compete for profits."[7]

The procurement agencies have two principal methods of preventing a factory from receiving an anticipated rate of return. One common practice, a particular irritant to the industrial departments, is to classify products at a lower grade than the producer believes is accurate, permitting the trade units to purchase them from the factory more cheaply. The wholesale company can then go on to earn extra profits by selling the goods to the retailing units at the price for the higher grade of the item. Commercial organs use this strategy especially at times of excess supply.[8]

Another area affected by commerce's control over pricing is that of new products. To cite just one illustrative incident, in 1957 Shanghai's industrial departments designed over forty new products, but since commerce and industry failed to agree on their prices, only one was ever put on the market.[9]

Units under the Ministry of Commerce provide some of the raw materials for the factories and also purchase their end products.[10] This gives them a chance to dictate prices at this link in the production cycle

---

instance, that the common practice has been for the factories in effect to dump goods of questionable marketability onto the procurement agencies.

7. *Jingji yanjiu* [Economic Studies] *(JJYJ)*, no. 5 (1956), p. 15. On procedures used in price setting, see chapter 1, above, and Kenneth Lieberthal, "Beijing's Consumer Market," pp. 37–38.

8. *Sichuan ribao* [Sichuan Daily] *(SCRB)*, October 15, 1956; *Hong Qi* [Red Flag] *(HQ)*, no. 10 (May 16, 1960), p. 40.

9. *DGB*, March 31, 1958.

10. Commercial departments are more apt to supply, through sales, raw materials in the forms of agricultural cash crops, the wherewithal for light industry, small tools, and minor chemicals than they are to deal in the metallurgical materials and machinery used in heavy industry. The latter are distributed by Materials Supplies departments under the Ministry for the Supply of Materials, as a part of the industrial state plan, according to Barry M. Richman, *Industrial Society in Communist China*, pp. 704–6.

as well. Their range of leeway is evident in the following criticism by a clothing factory: it charged that the commercial organs, instead of supplying raw cloth to the factory at the state-designated wholesale price, chose instead to supply it at a price 6 percent higher than the legal wholesale price. In this way the commercial bureaucracy earned the 6 percent profit that properly belonged to the factory.[11]

Thus, the plan subordinates industrial and commercial organs to separate hierarchies that issue incongruous instructions, and creates a contest between them, as if between rival firms, for a larger share of profits. As a result, the planned economy only intensifies the strains that characterize industrial and marketing activities even in its absence.

In addition, the backward condition of much of the storage equipment in China, unevenness in the quality of raw materials used in production, and the primitive state of transport facilities and of the tools and machinery used in production are among the technological factors that aggravate the four basic tensions identified above—in regard to supplies, the market, production scheduling, and inventories.

In the area of supplies, Chinese factory managers raise a variety of complaints against marketing units. One important root of the problems here, industrial workers charge, is that the personnel in sales organs are preoccupied with trying to avoid excessive accumulation of stocks and spoilage in their warehouses, and are worried about fulfilling their own turnover quotas; therefore, the factories cannot count on getting the raw materials they need, according to this analysis.[12] This critique suggests that storage facilities are inadequate; thus, commercial units hesitate to overstock supplies that may well rot or deteriorate before they can be delivered to the factories. In that eventuality, the commercial system would both lose income and fail to meet its own targets.

Yet another area of dissatisfaction for the factories is that they find it difficult to acquire the proper grade and quality of raw materials for the job at hand. In one case, the factories wanted second- or third-grade rubber, but, perhaps because of poor coordination in the planning bureaucracy, received first-grade supplies instead, which affected their chemical formula and their costs. At other times, despite having placed a request for high-grade materials, they have had to make do with more ordinary types, which influenced the quality of their products.[13]

When commercial departments are unable to satisfy the raw-material needs of the factories, either in amount or in terms of specifications,

11. *RMRB*, December 2, 1979.
12. *DGB*, August 2, 1958, p. 3.
13. *DGB*, March 31, 1958.

they "match up" the supplies the factories require with other, unwanted items to make a full package, thereby meeting their own sales targets, but forcing factories to waste their capital. Production departments, in defense, typically order more supplies of scarce raw materials than they really need, and pile up hoards.[14] But though these problems of supplies cause antagonisms between industry and commerce, the shortages that plague the Chinese production system are in fact ultimately beyond the control of the commercial units, as this quotation illustrates: "Some commercial cadres feel we cannot help industry if we have nothing—'a clever housewife cannot cook without rice.'"

In sum, industrial units feel insecure about whether they will obtain the supplies they need, find that the quality of what they do receive is often low and its grade inappropriate, and are dissatisfied because specifications are frequently improper and amounts inadequate. Although receipt of just the right supplies is never wholly certain in any economy, in an underdeveloped one like China's, where the plan pits the supplier's interest against the producer's, tension in this area is common for the average factory.

A second kind of uncertainty that affects any industrial producer comes from the variability of the market. Personnel in productive enterprises in China have often viewed the changeableness of the market as a threat to their ability to have some control over the flow of output, and so this concern also involves the third intersectoral strain identified above, the one related to production scheduling and growth. Clashes occur when marketers grow impatient with the frequent mismatch between what they are given to dispose of and what consumers wish to buy. In part this is a question of identifying and satisfying the current tastes of the customers; it is also a matter of adjusting to unforeseen as well as to normal seasonal changes in purchasing by the populace.

The existence of the plan is the cause of many of these problems. For the plan has generally bound industry to fulfill rigid output targets drawn up with little reference to the market. The plan has also limited the commercial organs' freedom to act upon consumers' preferences, as their own orders dictate the procurement of whatever the planners have told the factories to produce.

But this problem has technological bases as well. For example, the relatively primitive state of much of the productive machinery in China, plus a lack of sophistication in management techniques, has made it all the more difficult for factories to produce goods of a quality the market

14. *Changjiang ribao* [Yangtze River Daily] (*CJRB*), May 31, 1957.

demands, to present a reasonably varied product mix in response to taste, to be versatile in anticipation of shifting demand, and to adapt flexibly once the need for modifications has arisen. With their crude equipment, factories often prefer to produce in batches, which is simpler, but which often results in output unsuited to mass tastes.[15] On the commercial side, offices suffer from the lack of computers that might permit them to do relatively accurate market research, or of other techniques for conducting sophisticated survey research.

That the issue of the market is an explicit source of strain between the sectors is apparent in the industrial departments' repeated accusations in the press that commerce cares too much about tastes, and that trading units overemphasize imports and other popular, famous-brand, large-batch, and high-class goods, and slight the ordinary products of domestic firms. Since popular items sell faster, dealing in these enables commercial organs to enjoy a speedy circulation of their capital, and so helps them avoid tying up this capital on unsaleable products.[16]

Not surprising for a marketing agency, China's state commercial sector's concern over quality varies with market conditions: when business is slow and stocks are in excess, sales organs become more quality conscious, as a representative of state-run industry laments here:

> Commercial departments don't care about quality when sales are brisk; then [commerce's] inspection personnel become "counting personnel." In the slow season, though, they nitpick to excess, using the pretext of low quality to refuse to purchase.[17]

Commercial units' attempts to adjust to change in the market have also drawn fire from members of the industrial bureaucracy, as in these remarks, expressed as complaints: "Commerce seeks that varieties, specifications, and amounts change following market changes"; and commerce "lacks foresight."[18] This problem finds concrete expression in the commercial departments' tendency to order goods in the brisk season which they later refuse to buy (perhaps because delivery of the finished product was too slow) when sales become slack. One press story told of a commercial unit that ordered 50,000 bottles of "ten drops," a popular medicine for summer ailments, in April, and 250,000 in June. This left

15. *RMRB*, January 23, 1979, p. 2.
16. *DGB*, April 23, 1958, August 2, 1958, and February 12, 1963; *Jiangxi ribao* [Jiangxi Daily] (*JXRB*), December 9, 1956; and *Guangming ribao* [Bright Daily] (*GMRB*), May 17, 1965.
17. *CJRB*, May 31, 1957.
18. *DGB*, June 14, 1963.

the factory with too little work in the spring and too great a burden in June.[19] Another tale of tensions caused by the market is of an industrial firm responsible for producing general goods, which once expressed the hope that it could receive a production and purchase plan, concretely specifying the colors and varieties needed, at least sixty days before the season began. But the commercial wholesale depot, because of changes in the market, found it hard even thirty-five days prior to the season to present a plan to which it could adhere.[20]

Thus, the relatively primitive factories of China's industrial system have found it cumbersome, annoying, and even impossible to have to cope with the requests of the marketing organs for quality, for marketable goods, and for alterations to meet the requirements of season and taste.

Control over goods in stock—over inventories—is the fourth issue causing clashes between the two departments in any economy. In China it is a source of conflict when the factories dump unmarketable goods onto the procurement agencies. For then the problem of accumulated stocks, tying up capital, becomes one for commerce to handle. In this case, the commercial units would prefer to stock only those goods in seasonal demand, to avoid paying interest on capital outlays for the goods and to avoid storage costs and rental fees.

Commercial personnel have also tried to take in stocks in accord with what they already have in store, and have badgered industry managers to gear output to this consideration, as this speaker for industry complains: "When certain goods are in abundance for a time, commercial units refuse to purchase, and limit production. But when the supply of commodities does not meet demand, commerce tries to stimulate production blindly." Representatives of industry similarly castigate the habit of "some commercial cadres" who "unscrupulously make the production departments work extra time and use shock tactics at one moment, but reduce or suspend production at another moment": they "'lash the whip' when products are short and 'slash with a knife' when products are a glut." Thus, in the biased vision of industry's spokespersons, commerce selfishly exhibits "hot and cold treatment toward production's development," making it difficult for industry to improve its own management level and its overall technical performance.[21]

19. *CJRB*, May 31, 1957; *Chengdu ribao* [Chengdu Daily], May 24, 1957.
20. *DGB*, March 31, 1958.
21. Chen Xing, "Zhengque jiejue youguan shangye gongzuo de gexiang maodun" [Accurately solve various contradictions concerned with commercial work], *Xuexi* [Study] (*XX*), no. 12 (1958), pp. 30–31; and *Survey of the China Mainland Press (SCMP)*, no. 4767 (1970), p. 92, and *RMRB*, July 6, 1971, in *SCMP*, no. 4943 (1970), p. 19.

The commercial side has legitimate grievances as well. In one extreme case, a county commercial bureau in Shandong paid out twenty thousand yuan in interest to the bank while it held goods it was unable to sell. Often in such a situation the products in question deteriorate over time in rudimentary storage facilities, with the result that eventually they must be sold out as *chuli shangpin* (goods for disposal) at a price below production costs.[22] The effect on the commercial units' plan fulfillment is noted here:

> If the quality of commodities is raised and they fit the people's needs, their market outlet will expand and [commerce's] financial plan can be completed. If quality falls, and products are not welcomed by the masses, [commerce] cannot complete its financial plan.[23]

Though the commercial sector has usually been placed by the plan in the more passive role, its workers have at their command strategies for circumventing normal procedures. Out of fear of piling up inventories, commercial organs have reduced their purchases even of goods needed on the market,[24] and have sometimes refused altogether to accept goods that might not sell. One report tells of several hundred tons of laundry soap piling up in a Loyang factory for this reason.[25] A curious incident of this sort involved a group of commercial workers who, "fearing that having too many goods on hand would be a nuisance, and thinking that having marketable goods to sell would influence the sales of unmarketable goods, put the marketable goods into the warehouse so they could not be sold."[26]

Thus, conflicts over the management of inventories, sharpened by backward facilities, threaten each sector's ability to meet its commitments to the state economy. To the extent that each party to the problem tries to look out for its own separate interests, the outcome becomes dysfunctional for the distribution of goods.

22. *DGB*, June 8, 1964, and *RMRB*, December 2, 1979, both speak of the interest problem; *DGB*, August 2, 1958, p. 3, mentions commerce's fear of spoilage. An interview in Hong Kong on October 25 discussed the institution of *chuli shangpin*. According to Lin Wenyi and Jia Lurang, "On the Law of Supply and Demand and Its Role in the Socialist Economy," *JJYJ*, no. 9 (1981), p. 33, in 1978 the commercial system lost more than a half billion yuan as a result of having to use this method to dispose of low-quality industrial products.

23. *JXRB*, December 9, 1956.

24. *Beijing Review*, no. 14 (1980), p. 23.

25. *RMRB*, December 2, 1979.

26. *RMRB*, March 29, 1956.

Conflicting plan targets, coupled with the concern of each side for its own separate financial success, plus the low technological level of productive and marketing infrastructures in China, compound the tensions usually found in the interchange between factories and the marketers of their output. The following section will sketch out three models that have been repeatedly experimented with in China to handle this relationship and alleviate these strains. The first of these is the classic model of planned exchange; the other two, "selective purchase" and "buy whatever," are efforts to cope with the plan's shortcomings, as these shortcomings have been variously defined from the right and the left.

Three Models for Connecting
Industry and Commerce

Put simply, it is as if the proponents of each model had devised a system that especially emphasized the features of one of the three phases of Marx's picture of the transition from capitalism to communism. Marketeers, writing as if China were still in the presocialist stage, continue to draw on a philosophy embodied in this quotation from 1950, as they advocate using the market to stimulate economic growth:

> Flowing urban-rural trade promotes industrial and agricultural production.... A broad agricultural market where purchasing power is continuously raised is also the basic condition for the development of industrial production.[27]

In this phase, it is commercial activity that enhances productivity, and so the market has an active role.

Bureaucrats, then, in propounding the plan as the guide for growth, draw upon a vision of China as being in the transitional, socialist phase. During this period, Marx, Engels, and Lenin expected the state, through the dictatorship of the proletariat, to control all economic activity as the best means to achieve a rapid increase in social wealth. Thus, in one bureaucrat's words, "only by completing the plan can we continuously promote production's speedy development."[28] Here the market is absent, and bureaucratic dominance is the prerequisite to productivity.

---

27. *Dongbei ribao* [Northeast Daily], September 9, 1950.
28. *DGB*, April 1, 1959, p. 3.

But commercial activity, if under strict state control and management, still exists in the bureaucrats' world.

Third, radicals dream of a communist future, but at the same time yearn to hasten its course by implementing its ideals in the present. They hope better to unleash the productive forces by encouraging maximum participation in the process of creative labor by the workers of all sectors, the commercial one included. For them, total concentration on production alone is the primary consideration, which activity in itself will advance exchange: "Only by developing production and increasing products can we make the markets flow . . . all our work must proceed from an angle favorable for developing production."[29] Here it is commerce that is in the passive position, relative to the act of production.

Of these three visions, the one that has most often informed reality in China is fitted into the planned economy, and gives industry the superior position in the wrangling between sectors. This is the design of the bureaucrats. According to this system, state commercial agencies purchase the output of the factories in disregard of market demand. The other two models, one from the left and one from the right, have appeared at several junctures as experimental critiques of the planned economy. The leftist or radical model, predominant during the Great Leap Forward and to a certain extent during the Cultural Revolution, accords industry even more dominance and nearly obliterates the role of commercial work altogether. Then, the marketeer model, in effect in the mid-1950s and again in 1979–1980, favors giving the initiative to the commercial sector as it allows sales to determine production. Each model deals with the strains between sectors in rather different ways, in each case relieving one or two of the strains, but in the process intensifying others.

Historically, there has been a cycling of the three models, within a long-term secular trend of increased learning. The 1950s saw experimentation with each model in its most extreme variant; in the 1960s, less than total versions came into use; and by the late 1970s, though there was a return to the marketeer methods of the mid-1950s, the earlier model was rationalized and moderated that time around.

In general, although China's economy has been more or less consistently directed by plan from the early postliberation days, the bureaucratic model, *tonggou baoxiao* (unified purchase and guaranteed sales) has received special emphasis in policy making under particular economic and political conditions. That is, it was stressed whenever the goals of a dominant group among the leadership were to maximize production quickly

29. U.S. *Foreign Broadcast Information Service* (*FBIS*), June 27, 1977, p. L4 (Harbin Radio, June 23).

and to undo what it saw as excessive local autonomy and relative chaos in the economy resulting from civil war or mass movements. Thus, planning (throughout the economy as a whole and, as a corollary, in the spheres of commodity procurement and circulation) was especially championed following takeover in the initial years of the First Five Year Plan (before mid-1956); in the wake of the Sixth Plenum of the Eighth Party Central Committee (1959–1960), as a means of restoring order to economic activity after the early heady months of the Great Leap;[30] and after the death of Mao and the purge of the Gang of Four had brought to a close the era of the Cultural Revolution (from 1976 to 1978).[31]

Such periods of excessive concentration upon the planned routing of commodities have several times been succeeded by liberal interludes. In these eras marketeers criticized the rigidities and red tape of exchange which is organized by dictate from the top down through a bureaucracy; and put forward in its stead their *xuangou*, or selective purchase model. This model permits commercial units some freedom to follow market trends in their procurements of goods from industry. But the marketeer tendency to celebrate what amounts to more profitable dealings has met attack from the left, as radicals demanded on two prominent occasions that productive, not moneymaking, activity be pushed to the limit, and that trade organs buy in infinite quantities whatever the factories turn out, without any concern for the salability of the output.

The cycle has come full circle more than once when the bureaucratic tendency emerged to rectify what its proponents perceived as disorder caused by radical schemes. This repetitious rotation of stratagems for directing industrial output to its buyers must derive from a continual jockeying among departments and among the politicians who represent them in advocating these different models.

TONGGOU BAOXIAO AND PLANNED LINKAGES

The dominant model that has structured the interaction between state trade and industrial firms over thirty years has been that of the bureaucrats, *tonggou baoxiao* (unified purchase and guaranteed sales).

30. See *DGB*, January 21, 1959, p. 2, which says, "The Sixth Plenum called for planning in production, exchange, consumption and accumulation"; also *DGB*, April 1, 1959, p. 3, which says that, as the whole country is a chessboard, "both production and circulation must have a unified plan"; and *DGB*, April 4, 1959, p. 3, which dictates: "as much as possible put all scattered economic activity onto the path of planning."
31. For example, *FBIS*, September 23, 1977, p. J2, carries a broadcast from Guizhou province, which calls for "protect[ing] the planned economy and mak[ing] socialism firmly occupy the position of third-category materials." Third-category goods are small sundry items which in times of economic liberalization may be traded outside the plan.

This model, borrowed wholesale from the Soviet economic system, was initially instituted in the early 1950s in China. Its purpose at first was to draw the products of then private industry into the state's hands, in the process emasculating the economic power of the private capitalists in both industry and commerce.[32]

Under this system, industrial units produce in accord with the plan's dictates and leave all marketing operations to the state trade companies, which supply some raw materials to the factories and purchase all finished goods. This arrangement entails the use of a long series of commercial links between the producer and the ultimate consumer.[33] As the previous section has indicated, disjunction between social need (as defined by the market) and industrial output has often been the result, in terms of amounts, quality, varieties, and distribution. Despite its potential for error, of the three, this model is the one most geared to, as well as most capable of, giving state planners maximum guidance over what goods are produced and what their destination will be. This is one of two models that favor industry and it consequently treats commerce as of secondary importance.

In line with its goal of achieving utmost state control over commodities, the *tonggou* model specifies three prescriptions for state-run trade in its dealings with factories. Trading units are to serve as logistical back-up for industrial activity, through providing factories with necessary supplies; they must stimulate productivity through ensuring a purchasing outlet; and they are to help draft and then realize the plans of the producers by placing detailed procurement orders. Unlike the marketeers' selective purchase model, according to this design state commerce is not to concern itself with the suitability of output for the market at a given time.

In periods of emergency, commercial units have had to improvise in order to fulfill this supportive mission. In the immediate aftermath of the Great Leap Forward, when statistical confusion and local autonomy had played havoc with the supply system, it would have been far more difficult to restore orderly production without the work of the commercial sector. In Jilin province, for example, the commercial sector had to borrow from other units tools and equipment needed by factories but

32. Marshall I. Goldman, *Soviet Marketing: Distribution in a Controlled Economy*, pp. 56–57; and Jere L. Felker, *Soviet Economic Controversies*, p. 146; Nove, *Soviet Economic System*, pp. 259–61. See *RMRB*, January 23, 1979, p. 2, on the origin of the system in China. This article gives an analysis of the flaws of the system.

33. Audrey Donnithorne, *China's Economic System*, p. 283; and *DGB*, October 20, 1956. See chapter 1 above.

beyond their budgets, help industrial departments utilize substitute raw materials, and search for old scraps that might be of use in production.[34]

In times when supply conditions have been less tense, the job of commercial departments was still an auxiliary one as long as the *tonggou* model held sway. Thus, in early 1961 in Shenyang, a general-goods company collected samples of new varieties and new production materials for the factories' reference, and organized the exchange of technical experience among factories.[35]

The second aspect of the marketing agents' servitorial position under this model lies in their responsibility, in the absence of a true market, to guarantee a sales outlet for the products of the factories. As one article put it:

> Since the free market has basically been abolished, communes, factories, mines, and the masses must completely rely on commercial departments to arrange the market . . . and organize commodity exchange, so that procurement and supply work can be more concentrated and unified.

This planned market, according to its advocates, can have the same properties as a spontaneous one, as it "activat[es] commodity circulation and encourag[es] agricultural and industrial development."[36]

Anecdotal accounts in the press have sought to bolster the claim that state trade organs could supplant a free market. In one such story, a paper factory in Henan lacked raw materials. Meanwhile, a potential supplier, unaware of the need for paper and without a buyer, prepared to use its wood as fire fuel, until the state commercial units provided the market linkage.[37]

The third facet of commerce's work in shoring up industry's efforts, as outlined by promoters of *tonggou*, entails involvement in drawing up the production plan for factories. Commercial units do this either by placing orders and signing contracts or by giving advice on the basis of rudimentary market research (by "reflecting consumers' opinions"). The production-sales contract constitutes an important means by which commercial organs guide the content and scope of industrial output. Contracts in China (and in the Soviet Union as well)[38] have been used in direct dealings between productive and marketing firms, often for com-

34. *DGB*, May 16, 1959, p. 2.
35. *DGB*, February 18, 1961.
36. *DGB*, March 24, 1959, p. 2, and July 30, 1959, in *SCMP*, no. 2083 (1959), p. 7.
37. Ibid.
38. Goldman, p. 59.

modities of low priority and so not listed in state plans. This does not necessarily mean, however, that state encouragement of contract-writing is a step in the direction away from state planning.

For contracts have served as one method of "strengthening the planning of production," as they "divert the production of nonstaple commodities gradually to state control." And the contract has been hailed as "the best form for promoting the combination of production plans and purchasing plans."[39] In specifying varieties, amounts, time and place of purchase, price, and the two sides' powers and duties, the contract can promote production and at the same time guarantee the realization of the state plan, as the products ordered in the contract become incorporated into the state's plan and are then purchased by state trade units.[40] The writing of such contracts, far from representing a kind of free dealing between firms, is often closely guided at state-run commodity-circulation conferences. These meets, held for goods not written into state plans, have had as their purpose the "avoid[ing of] blind transactions on the market."[41]

The planners' *tonggou baoxiao* model, then, aims to afford the state bureaucracy the greatest possible domination over the design and the destination of industrial output; and commerce's role in this scheme is to provide supplies, to ensure an outlet, and through its purchase orders, to guide the direction production takes. With regard to the strains between sectors identified above, this scheme mainly strives to ease industry's scheduling and growth needs. Meanwhile, it largely ignores the strains on the commercial sector to fit market demands or keep stocks from becoming excessive. Most plant managers in ordinary factories have been comfortable with and prefer this system.[42] But because of rigidities resulting from this method, critics have proposed and experimented with alternative models over the years, one from the right and one from the left.

SELECTIVE PURCHASE (XUANGOU)

Three times since Communist takeover (1956–1957, 1961–1963, and 1979 and thereafter), when marketeer proposals for liberalizing the

39. *DGB*, October 10, 1959, in *SCMP*, no. 2083 (1959), p. 11, and August 21, 1959, in *SCMP*, no. 2093 (1959), p. 28.
40. *DGB*, February 15 and 23, 1959 (pp. 3 and 2, respectively), and January 27, 1959, p. 2.
41. Guan Datong, "Our Country's United Socialist Domestic Market," *HQ*, no. 6 (April 1, 1963), pp. 28–35.
42. Private communication from Peter Van Ness on the basis of his conversations in China.

economy triumphed in policy councils, variants of a scheme called selective purchase (*xuangou*) were implemented in China. This model, first introduced by Chen Yun in mid-1956, constitutes the rightist corrective to the inflexibilities of planned allocation.

In inspiration it resembles ideas that Liberman and his colleagues advocated in the Soviet Union beginning in 1955 and that were first publicized openly in *Pravda* in September 1962. These Soviet proposals argued for a widespread use of the profit motive throughout the economy, and suggested that plans for factory output be based on direct connections between the producer and the consumer.[43] Despite the affinities with the Liberman precedent, however, a scholar of Soviet and Eastern European economies termed selective purchase "an invention of Chinese right-wing communism."[44] Its essence is that procuring agents may refuse to purchase low-quality products they deem unsaleable, and so it alone among the three models bolsters the position of the commercial sector against the industrial one.

This model loosens up the rigidly demarcated procedures for exchange usually dictated by the state plan. Thus, it allows factories to obtain on the free market (and not just through planned allocation) any raw materials that are both relatively abundant and not considered critical to the national economy. In the commercial sector, it permits retail shops to replenish their stocks by establishing their own supply connections in the case of fragmentary industrial products whose specifications are complicated and whose varieties are many (such as towels, socks, and soap). Shops may base their selection on the quality of the products and on the demands of the market, as they procure from any wholesale organ in the country (not simply from the local branch of the state company dealing in their line of goods, as under *tonggou*), and directly from factories (thus, not necessarily going through the state wholesale organs).

Any unselected products are left in the hands of the factory officials (not in the warehouses of the commercial organs, as under *tonggou*). These officials can choose to sell them by setting up factory retail out-

43. Alec Nove, "The Liberman Proposals." Various reforms in the Soviet Union have aimed at liberalizing the Soviet economy along lines similar to the spirit of the Liberman proposals and to "selective purchase," but in general their implementation has been frustrated. See Goldman, p. 70; Felker, pp. 8, 36, 55; Nove, *Soviet Economic System*, pp. 260, 311–12; and Egon Neuberger and William Duffy, *Comparative Economic Systems*, p. 189. Such reforms included counting only goods sold in calculating whether production plans had been fulfilled; instructing factories to manufacture only items that retail outlets can actually sell; injecting consumers' wants into planners' preference lists; and increasing the number of goods distributed through direct contracts for transactions that are not specified in the plan.

44. P. J. D. Wiles, *The Political Economy of Communism*, pp. 168, 175, 182.

lets; or they may entrust them to the commercial departments to sell on a commission basis. Under this system, the state commercial organs, not the individual factory, continue to fix the ex-factory prices of all commodities involved (the prices at which the products are purchased by commercial organs from the factory); or, in some cases, the state industrial and commercial departments may negotiate these prices, but they must still set the price within a range specified by the state. The principles of selective purchase, as proposed by Chen, were to apply in relations between upper-level wholesale organs and their retail recipients, as well as between state industrial and commercial firms.

The goal of the scheme is to avoid the waste issuing from the "blind production" of goods that, not meeting market needs, pile up unsold in commercial warehouses. It aims to achieve this end by making the factory management concerned about improving the quality of products, in order to ensure a sales outlet for its products. Since the factories would have to divert time and funds from their productive work to dispose of the unchosen products (whether by setting up retail outlets or by paying a commission to commercial departments to take on the job for them), this model contains an incentive intended to prod industry to perform better.[45]

This plan is based on a view of the job of commercial work quite different from the vision that informs the *tonggou* model. In this setup, commerce's principal function does not lie in facilitating the productive process or in expediting maximum state control over the specifications and routing of output, as it does in the *tonggou* model. Rather, commerce's role resides in

> keep[ing]track of changes in supply and demand and changes in consumption ... decid[ing] what should be produced more, what should be produced less, what should be readjusted and what should be developed further.[46]

45. See Chen Yun's speech at the Third Session of the First National People's Congress in *GMRB*, July 1, 1956; Zeng Shan's speech at the Eighth Party Congress in *DGB*, September 28, 1956, and one by Chen Yun at the Eighth Party Congress in *Renmin shouce* [People's Handbook], *1957*, pp. 85–88. *Tonggou baoxiao* was to continue in use for large-batch commodities such as cotton cloth, oils and fats, sugar, paper, coal, tobacco, and matches, whose varieties were few and specifications simple. Such goods accounted for some 70 to 80 percent of the total value of retail sales. Also, any other commodities in short supply were to be bought up by state commercial departments to make possible a rational interdistrict distribution.

46. Kuan Ta-t'ung [Guan Datong], "Commerce to Serve the Countryside," *JJYJ*, no. 12 (December 20, 1965), in *Selections from China Mainland Magazines* (*SCMM*), no. 536 (1966), pp. 23–24.

Furthermore, in this conception:

> Commerce must fully understand seasonal market conditions and consumer demands and inform the industrial departments about them; and it must assist the latter to arrange production plans, elevate quality, and increase varieties, according to consumer demands and objective conditions.[47]

This arrangement has also been expected to accelerate the flow of commodities and reduce expenditures in the circulation of goods (by eliminating some of the wholesaling bureaucracy). And its proponents predict that its institution will lead to improvement in the quality of goods and to an increase in the designs and varieties of products, as factories make an effort to satisfy the market. Some hoped too that its lenient procedures would eliminate the practice among districts of putting up barriers against products made elsewhere in the country.[48] Despite the apparent liberalization in the design of this model, however, it has been billed as having a potential payoff for the socialist state if the scheme succeeds: "If sales are better, remittance to the state [in the form of enterprise profits sent to the central government] will be better."[49]

This model, then, forces the industrial sector to deal with the tensions that are shifted to commerce by the *tonggou* model—in regard to supplies, the fickleness of the market, and excess stocks. It also frees commercial personnel from the responsibility, imposed on them by the *tonggou* plan, of accommodating to the factories' needs in scheduling and growth. Therefore, while selective purchase is addressed to the relief of the strains in supplies, marketing, and inventories that issue from the use of *tonggou*'s planning, it has aroused opposition from supporters of the industrial sector. Such people maintain that its attention to the market neglects the concerns of industrial management.

Central features of the Chinese economic system have prevented this model from developing its full potential. On the commercial side, China's serious deficiencies in marketing research, consumer-demand analysis, product planning, and the gathering and processing of statistics and other information have stymied the effort. And the continued weighting of the plan's success indicators in favor of physical output, along with the absence of opportunity cost-efficiency pricing (so that

47. Yao Yilin, "Raise High the Banner of Mao Zedong's Ideology for Better Socialist Commerce," *HQ*, no. 21 (1962), pp. 4–11.

48. *SCMP*, no. 1497 (1957), pp. 5–6; *SCMP*, no. 2809 (1962), pp. 4–5; *Guangxi ribao* [Guangxi Daily] (*GXRB*), November 17, 1956; *DGB*, January 18, 1963; *DGB*, February 16, 1963.

49. *RMRB*, April 3, 1980, p. 5.

prices and thus profits in China do not respond to changes in consumer preferences), has meant that those in charge of industry have had little incentive to comply.[50] The review below of the history of experimentation with the selective purchase scheme will illuminate the nature of the opposition it has met and the bases for it.

Of the three periods in which variants of selective purchase were put into effect, the first one, from mid-1956 until early 1957, was both the most unrestrained and the most short-lived. Marketeers in ascendance in the early 1960s revived the term "selective purchase," but its content involved a far more circumscribed arrangement than the earlier episode did. In 1979, marketeers again dusted off this element of their reform package, but this time they imposed more explicit guidelines from the start and built into its implementation more incentives for the factories. The first experiment led to a heyday for the retailing organs, and as confusion ensued and resistance mounted, it was gradually cut back and ultimately rescinded. Although each of the later experiences met opposition, the tentativeness of the early 1960s version and the more careful recent conceptualization both offer evidence of learning over time.

The Mid-1950s

The 1956 experiment began in July, soon after Chen Yun's presentation of his model at the Third Session of the First National People's Congress.[51] By mid-October, however, the press was already full of ideological opposition and practical objections to the scheme, behind both of which lay fears of the "chaos" that this system was introducing into the economy. The ideologically based dissatisfaction echoed radical values, while worries over the mechanics of operating the scheme centered on the harm done to the planning system, and so reflect bureaucrats' concerns.

From an ideological standpoint, leftist laments came from those who "feared capitalist chaos and inflation." Some worried that selective purchase would cause enterprises in the interior regions of the country to suffer from competition with the coastal factories, as their level of technology was lower, their equipment inferior, and their costs higher.[52] Obviously, a program that encouraged this type of departure from a planned distribution of commodities would benefit superior firms, a genuine issue

50. Richman, *Industrial Society*, p. 882; Jan S. Prybyla, *The Political Economy of Communist China*, pp. 238, 395.

51. Examples of early implementation are in *DGB*, July 8, 1956, which reports on experiments in the All-China General Goods Company, and *RMRB*, July 23, 1956, in the cotton knitwear company.

52. *DGB*, October 20, 1956; *RMRB* editorial, July 15, 1956, in *SCMP*, no. 1342 (1956), p. 8; *DGB*, September 28, 1956.

for those dedicated to the norm of equity. Other objections focused on the problem of scarcity. Thus, some people thought that "only when goods are plentiful can we speak of selecting; now that supply still does not meet demand, there is no way" to implement this policy.[53] In their view, shortages required a central system of allocation, in order that certain groups and areas would not benefit at the expense of others.

Those upset because of havoc caused in the planning system pointed to a reckless scrambling for "hot items" by retail units, in their excitement over being able to place their own orders. Some such purchasing departments, afraid that getting goods would be difficult in the future, took to hoarding. Bureaucrats objected too to local procurement agents that "did a niggling business"—in one instance, for example, ordering only one pair of rubbers and just thirty toothbrushes from their local wholesaler, as their cadres took a "wait-and-see attitude" in the hope of finding more attractive goods later on in another district.

The outcome of such behavior caused real problems for factories and planners, given the unchanged planned framework of the total economy. For retailers tended to engage in "crash ordering" late in the season in a tense market, which by then was understocked because of the small orders they had placed earlier. The planners also could not deal with demands from supply and marketing cooperatives for nothing but the name-brand goods their consumers requested. When the state companies were unable to supply these items in large amounts, and when the cooperatives then refused to accept substitute products, *tonggou*'s planned allocation appeared to some to be a far more workable alternative.[54]

Thus, selective purchase drew its principal support from the basic-level retailers, pleased for once to have a chance to satisfy customers' preferences. Meanwhile, wholesaling units charged with organizing supplies grumbled that selective purchase's "freedom [was] a freedom only for the ordering units, but that there [was] no freedom for the suppliers in allocating goods."[55] And the producing and planning departments found the system inimical to their interests.

Chen Yun had been quite clear in presenting his plan, by specifying the sorts of goods that would come within the scope of his new system and those that would not, and in indicating that the state plan would

53. *Gongren ribao* [Workers' Daily] (Beijing) (*GRRB*), editorial, October 16, 1956. See also Audrey Donnithorne, "Organizational Aspects of the Internal Trade of the Chinese People's Republic With Special Reference to 1958–1960," p. 64, where the same point is made.
54. *GRRB*, editorial, October 16, 1956; *GXRB*, November 17, 1956; *GXRB*, December 26, 1956; *DGB*, October 23, 1956.
55. *GXRB*, November 18, 1956; *DGB*, April 23, 1958.

apply only to the latter category. Further, he had expressly directed that "lower-level shops can freely purchase selectively from any wholesale organ in the whole country, and directly from factories." As the resistance grew, however, opponents redefined the system, as a prelude to abandoning it. Although this redefinition permitted the experiment to be eased out gradually, in effect it amounted to an undermining of the basic concept of the reform itself, while the label was retained for another few months.

One part of the reinterpretation stipulated, as if such an idea had been a part of the system from the start, that selection was to be made "according to plan" after the supply and marketing cooperatives had carefully investigated mass needs and made out reliable order plans, which had to be prepared in advance of the season. As one article put it, "only with a perfect plan is it possible rationally to organize goods to supply selective purchase,"[56] a somewhat incongruous prescription to impose on an arrangement meant to loosen up the rigidities of planning.

The other reformulation was, like the first one, injected into later discussions of the new system as if it had been an original provision that was now being transgressed. It maintained that the idea of selective purchase was not to involve "flying all over the sky," but rather was to allow the retailers to go outside their own districts in search of supplies only when their district lacked certain specific items.[57] Both these rewritings of the scheme amounted to efforts to reimpose the strictly planned and geographically delimited allocation system upon the circulation of all commodities, in order to avoid chaos and deal with scarcity.

The 1956 episode of selective purchase came to a halt in January 1957, with a State Council directive that the relations between industry and commerce were to remain as usual in 1957. The reason given was that the selective purchase system would have required changes in the taxation system too cumbersome to undertake quickly. That is, part of the profits that had been remitted to the state by the commercial departments' wholesale organs according to the *tonggou* model would under selective purchase have been passed to the industrial departments. The state financial bureaucracy would then have had to collect these funds from the factories in the form of taxes. The State Council decision indicated a fear that some state income might be lost, should industrial units fail to hand over the requisite taxes in sufficient quantity. Thus, the bureaucratic impulse toward maximum state control triumphed over a carelessly implemented design of the marketeers.

But the scheme did not die an easy death. Apparently, Chen contin-

56. *DGB*, October 23, 1956; *GXRB*, November 17, 1956 and December 26, 1956.
57. *GXRB*, October 31, 1956, and November 17, 1956.

ued for a time to hold on to his hopes for its realization. This is indicated in the State Council decision terminating the experiment, as well as in a press release from a conference for heads of commercial departments held in February 1957. Both documents continued to list the benefits of the reform and to permit local peoples' councils to carry on with trials of it where experiments were already under way.[58] But although one article from 1958 spoke of selective purchase, the reference there was to retail units choosing goods from their wholesalers, not to industry-commerce relations.[59] As the following section will show, the Great Leap Forward brought with it a whole new model for these relations, and the term selective purchase disappeared from the press until early 1961.

The Early 1960s

For all the abuse that radicals in the Cultural Revolution heaped upon the economic policies of the early 1960s, only the mildest of innovations were ever actually implemented in the sphere of industrial-commercial interchange in that era. For one thing, policy makers were no doubt cautious after retailers' zeal in overstepping fixed procedures for distribution in 1956 had seriously disrupted planning. Besides that, radical critiques that began to dominate the media by late 1962 discouraged any business undertakings that in any way smacked of capitalism. These two influences combined to dispose economic politicians to refrain from designing any schemes that represented a significant departure from planning.

Two new programs did appear in the early 1960s; both were inspired by a vision of the role of commerce under socialism similar to that of selective purchase; and both had some of the same objectives as the original selective-purchase model. These two designs, though, involved less freedom for marketing organs than the earlier setup had, and each involved from its inception an approach that was more tightly controlled and more carefully planned. There was little indication in the papers of that period that either met much opposition, no doubt in part at least because little was ventured.

In the early 1960s, as in 1956, the publicized view was that the proper function of commerce was to provide market intelligence to the factories, as this remark illustrates:

> Commercial departments should, taking advantage of [commerce's] favorable conditions like knowledge of the market and consumption, help

58. *DGB*, January 28, 1957, in *SCMP*, no. 1473 (1957), pp. 10–11; *SCMP*, nos. 1492 (1957), pp. 7–9; and 1497 (1957), pp. 5–6.

59. Hsiao Lin, "The Leap Forward in Commercial Work," *Financial Research*, no. 3, 1958, in *ECMM*, no. 140 (1958), pp. 42–46.

the industrial enterprises at the link of supply and marketing to turn out more saleable commodities to meet the rural market demands.[60]

Also, as in the 1956 selective purchase experiment, at least some writers suggested that commerce could best serve industry by returning bad items, by strengthening quality inspection even as the production process was going on, by not permitting those commodities that did not meet specifications to enter the market, and by using the price tool.[61] What distinguished the early 1960s from the mid-1950s, however, was that from the start there was a far greater emphasis on planning than there had been in the 1956 experiment. As one article put it, "Under the socialist system, the planned character of production and that of the market are components of a complete set."[62] This emphasis on planning is not surprising, in light of the gist of the key document for industrial policy promulgated in this era, the December 1961 "Seventy Articles of Industrial Policy." Two of its clauses affirm the basic planned model for dealings between producers and procurers.[63] Thus, in this period the marketeer tendency was compromised by, or allied with, the bureaucratic one.

Liberalization was also limited by a dictum that each sector was to serve the other so that neither would be especially favored over the other. The essence of policy during this period was captured in a line from a mid-1963 article: "Rely on linking up the two sides' plans to solve [their mutual problems], which requires attention to the market, using market research as the basis for the plan."[64] In 1956, on the other hand, Chen Yun had given priority to both the commercial sector and the market, with industry and planning clearly taken as secondary, even though others later modified his intent.

One of the programs of the early 1960s that was akin to the 1956 selective purchase scheme received that same label. In practice, however,

60. Chiang Huai, "On the Channels of Socialist Circulation of Commodities," *JJYJ*, no. 5 (1963), in *SCMM*, no. 372 (1963), p. 9.

61. *DGB*, February 1, 1963.

62. *DGB*, October 5, 1962, in *SCMP*, no. 2851 (1962), p. 6. See also Guan (n. 46 above), and *DGB*, February 1, 1963, and June 14, 1963.

63. Translated in Union Research Institute, *Documents of the Chinese Communist Party Central Committee September 1956–April 1969*, vol. 1, pp. 689–93. Article 50 reads: "*Having fulfilled the state quotas*, factories may procure and process raw materials by way of solving their present shortage of raw materials." Article 54, which is even more restrictive, states: "All products turned out by state-owned factories shall be marketed by the state commercial departments and may not be marketed by the factories themselves or handled as products turned out for other factories." (Emphasis added.)

64. *DGB*, June 14, 1963. Also see *Nanfang ribao* [Southern Daily] (*NFRB*), November 2, 1961.

the two had little in common. This 1961 version merely represented an effort to invigorate the retail market by urging wholesale depots to clean out their warehouses and let workers in basic-level shops pick out what they thought they could sell.[65]

The other market-style arrangement from this period, generally referred to as the cooperation or link-up of shop and factory, took its inspiration from a view current in 1962 and 1963. This view, as expressed by the then minister of commerce, Yao Yilin, was that "retail units, within a specific sphere, should be permitted to deal directly with production units, to reduce the links in the circulation of commodities."[66]

The concrete linkage between store and workshop took several forms.[67] These included combining the two into one accounting unit, shop in front, workshop behind, as well as planned, direct procurement from the factory by the store, eliminating the wholesale middleman. Other variants were a system of "fixed links" for small commodities sold by given factories to certain stores, and contracts between shops and factories for goods not in the plan. Only one of these forms (mentioned only once, and then as the fourth in a group of five alternatives), involved truly "free linkages" outside the plan, enabling shops to carry out selective purchase from factories. But even this was to apply only for small goods within a very limited scope.

The aims of this system were much like those in 1956: to speed up capital circulation, avoid circuitous transportation of goods and so reduce loss, and to meet consumers' needs better. But restrictions were clearly spelled out in this episode, and explicit formulas were provided, so that the earlier havoc was avoided.

Radical criticisms of direct links between factory and shop began to emerge by the eve of the Cultural Revolution. As one example, factories were denounced for giving gifts to retailers to win their goodwill,[68] a gesture that should have been unnecessary were all allocation dictated by the plan. Then, beginning with the start of the Cultural Revolution in 1966, for over a decade there were of course no ventures into liberalization in the business sector. But the marketeer victory at the Third Plenum of the Eleventh Central Committee again ushered in a period of experimentation with extra-plan exchange. Taking a lesson from the past, marketeers this time, as in the 1960s, laid down precise limits.

65. *DGB*, July 30, 1961, and August 15, 1961, and *NFRB*, September 7, 1961.
66. Yao (no. 47, above).
67. *DGB*, January 18, February 12, February 16, February 19, 1963.
68. *DGB*, January 14, 1966, mentioned in Donnithorne, *China's Economic System*, p. 283.

Mao's death and the discrediting of radicalism that followed on the arrest of the Gang of Four enabled reformers to return to the wider-ranging proposals Chen Yun had put forward over twenty years before.

1979 and After

Thus, twenty-three years after Chen delivered his Eighth Party Congress address outlining selective purchase, State Planning Commission adviser Xue Muqiao published exactly the same plan in mid-1979 as he and other marketeer economic politicians and theoreticians came to the fore.[69] The guiding principle of Xue's article unmistakably harks back to 1956:

> Henceforth, the purchasing plan should be drawn up on the basis of market needs, and production plans drawn up on the basis of purchasing plans. Sales on the market must not be determined by production plans but the other way around.[70]

Despite Xue's advocacy of a fair degree of autonomy for factories in raw material procurement and in sales, and for shops in replenishing their stocks, various contemporaneous statements specifying how to carry out the reform contained restrictions. One broadcast in March 1979 from Sichuan, the province most heralded for its advances in market liberalization at that time, forbade enterprises from selling on their own commodities covered by contract plans—such commodities had to be purchased, as ever, by the state commercial departments. Furthermore, factories had to obtain approval from higher levels even for selling whatever nonessential commodities had not been procured by state marketing organs.[71]

Then, from Canton, a city also noted in that period for its marketing freedoms, a broadcast half a year thereafter decreed that state commercial departments must monopolize the buying and selling of all products covered by state plans. Commercial selective purchase and industrial self-sales, both of which had to be done in strict accord with state price

69. It is unclear whether Xue, Chen, or a group of people including both of them originally authored this policy in 1956. In the Cultural Revolution, Xue was castigated as a "villainous adviser" of Liu Shaoqi, Deng Xiaoping, Chen Yun, and others, and as the "henchman" of Chen, in a diatribe that described Chen himself as the "founder of the counterrevolutionary revisionist line in economic circles." See the Red Guard tabloid *Beijing gongshe* [Peking Commune], March 22, 1967, p. 2.

70. See the article by Xue in *RMRB*, June 15, 1979, translated in *BR*, no. 43 (1979), pp. 14–20.

71. Chengdu Radio, March 11, 1979, in *FBIS*, March 13, p. J1.

policy, were possible only for items not covered by the plan, or that had been produced in excess of planned quotas.[72]

Even as late as August 1980, nearly two years after the marketeer victory, restrictions were still in force. Yao Yilin, then the newly-named head of the State Planning Commission, explained at the Third Session of the Fifth National People's Congress that an industrial enterprise could fix its production plans according to market demand only on condition that it had first ensured the supply of goods to the state as specified in its plan. He also decreed that such an enterprise could market only those goods that it had produced over and above its planned quota. Yao did permit commercial units to exercise free choice in their purchases of certain consumer goods from industrial firms. But he referred to "exercising choice" in this regard, along with the less free forms of "planned purchase" and "placing orders," as being number three in this list of possible alternatives that state trade organs might use in procuring nonessential consumer goods.[73]

Throughout late 1979 and 1980 the press heralded the execution of the scheme, with tales of machinery factories trial-producing new products and marketing them themselves, outside the plan and on the basis of market research; of light industrial enterprises organizing the items in their production plans in the order of their marketability; of clothing shops procuring directly from factories, after investigating consumer demand; of stores ordering from wholesale depots, industrial companies, and factories in various places, rather than passively accepting stocks from their regional wholesaler, as was once specified in the plan.[74]

In spite of the superficial promise of great change in these stories, however, a closer look confirms the clear limitations specified in the policy statements noted above. For one thing, virtually all reported activity of this sort pertained to goods not covered in the state plans. It is true that the incentive effects could be significant: industrial firms and shops were motivated to reach their planned targets all the sooner and the more efficiently (sometimes made possible by bargains struck with planners for lower targets), in order to take advantage of any excess productive or sales capacity to make more profits (although the amount of these that could be retained by the firm was not, through this period, either

72. Guangzhou Radio, October 27, 1979, in *FBIS*, October 31, p. P2.
73. *BR*, no. 38 (1980), pp. 41–42; see also *BR*, no. 33 (1980), p. 3.
74. See, for example, articles in *Guangzhou ribao* [Canton Daily], November 9, *RMRB*, November 12, December 11 and 18, 1979; *RMRB*, March 20 and April 4, 1980 and *Shichang* [Market] (*SC*), no. 9 (1980), p. 1.

particularly large or definitively specified).[75] But it is important to point out that the plan itself stood in place, and its demands continued to dominate the major part of each firm's behavior. Furthermore, anomalies in the price system meant that efficiency was not necessarily rewarded by higher profits.[76]

Another kind of qualification that gives one pause as one evaluates these innovations is the fact of the opposition they encountered. Some of this came from the producers of low-quality, rudely produced, or otherwise unpopular goods; of goods whose supply temporarily exceeded demand; and of products whose low prices had led to losses. Managers in such firms found the new market-oriented policies to be contrary to their interests and worried that their plants might be forced to cease production.[77]

Also, disapproval of the reforms came from defenders of the plan in mid-1980. In their critiques they insisted that attention to the market was producing a "chaotic readjustment" whenever the market temporarily lacked something; that overconcern for consumer needs had resulted in excess production of fans, sewing machines, and bicycles, with every place competing to produce these popular items, to the point that the raw materials required for them could not fill the demand; that factories had taken to selling on their own products that were properly a part of their plan; and, as in 1966, that "bad practices" were cropping up, such as firms' holding banquets to encourage customers to buy their goods.[78] One article went so far as to speak of the "bad results" of the 1979 experiment in letting sales determine production. Its author claimed that the market initiative was restraining

75. For example, *BR*, no. 12 (1980), p. 25, has this characterization of the reforms: "Enterprises involved were all given extended powers to handle their own finances, materials and personnel and were allowed to carry out some business activities on their own. For instance, an enterprise, on condition that it fulfills the targets set in the state plan, *may use its own judgment* to produce merchandise in response to the demand and sell it on the market; it *may draw* a certain percentage of its profits to build up the enterprise fund which will be used at its own discretion." (Emphasis added.) Robert F. Dernberger, in "P.R.C. Industrial Policies . . . Goals and Results" (Paper for presentation at the 10th Sino-American Conference on Mainland China, Berkeley, California, June 16–18, 1981), on p. 34 notes that "the reforms still limit the total share of retainable profits to below 20 percent." But according to Lin Zili, in "Initial Reform in China's Economic Structure," p. 180, eighty-four enterprises under experiment in Sichuan province (the birthplace of the reforms) retained only 8 percent of their profits in 1979. *BR*, no. 1 (1982), p. 23, states, too, that of the profits obtained by 1,284 major industrial enterprises in Shanghai which had been designated experimental units, 92 percent was handed over to the state, and only 8 percent was retained for reinvestment and bonuses for workers and staff members.

76. Lin, p. 185–86.

77. *RMRB*, January 23, 1979, p. 2, and April 3, 1980, p. 5.

78. See *RMRB*, May 3, p. 2, May 12, p. 3, and June 22, p. 3, 1980.

the speed of industrial production, limiting the activity of firms producing unpopular goods, neglecting consumers' real interests as factories became involved in a heady pursuit of profits and commissions, and upsetting the state production plan.[79]

Though some successful factories welcomed the reform as an opportunity to sell more goods on their own, sometimes they found their chances to apply it obstructed by the wholesale departments in the commercial sector. Personnel in these departments fought to maintain their status as the sole purchasers and distributors of manufactured goods. Some issued warnings to factories trying to sell any of their products on their own, and even threatened to stop handling their output altogether.

One egregious case involved a cigarette factory in Anhui province. After it sold some cigarettes independently, the prefectural state wholesale company for sugar, tobacco, and liquor in its region stopped purchasing its output for a month. As a result, the factory had to shut down for the entire following month because its warehouses were packed with unsold cigarettes, and so cigarettes that would have been worth over eleven million yuan were not produced that month. This meant a loss of seven million yuan to the state in revenue and industrial profit.

In another case, a certain well-priced television brand disappeared from the market. The reason for this was that commercial departments demanded a 9 percent profit and a 2 percent warranty fee on sales from the factory. To ensure that they obtained these earnings, the personnel in the commercial units refused to permit the factory to deal directly with the retail shop, as this would have enabled the factory to bypass the wholesale company (and thereby avoid paying the commercial unit's fees in the process). As the factory lost money because of having to pay these fees, and the television sets' semiconductors became depleted from going through the extra circulation links, the factory finally found itself no longer able to produce this popular brand.[80]

Thus, in the third effort to realize the selective purchase reform, limitations were written into the policy from the beginning, in order to avoid chaos; profit retention guidelines were unclear, and the unchanged price structure continued to give ambiguous signals; and opposition thwarted implementation at times, especially from some state wholesaling organs, whose personnel were determined to retain control themselves over the commodities involved.

In sum, variants of selective purchase—a scheme that allows retailers

79. Tao Sheng, "Is [the Policy of] Sales Setting Production Accurate?" *JJYJ*, no. 6 (1980), p. 63.

80. Lin, pp. 183–84, and *SC*, no. 25 (October 10, 1980), p. 4.

to participate in a kind of market activity in their relation to producers—
have been proposed and tested three times in China since 1949. The dis-
ruption of the state plan which this arrangement caused led to opposition
the first time through, on grounds of ideology, as well as because of vested
institutional interests. Even though the later episodes entailed deliberate
attempts to cope with these problems, resistance still checked the operation of market principles in this socialist society.

PARTICIPATE IN PRODUCTION; "BUY WHATEVER"

Radicals as well as marketeers have at times been able to promote a
corrective to what they perceive to be flaws in the planned approach to
production-exchange relations. A radical critique of bureaucratically
organized output and procurement has it that the plan places fetters on
production's potential; and that the activity of commercial intermediaries wastes social energy that could better be put to the service of creating material wealth.

The purest and most enthusiastic promotion of the radical alternative—participate in production and "buy whatever"—issued from the
Great Leap Forward of 1958. The model reappeared in somewhat wa-
tered-down versions in 1965–1966, and throughout the 1970s intermit-
tently to 1978.

The Great Leap Forward

During the Leap, the principle guiding commercial work was that,
since the revolution's purpose was to "change the relations of production and to liberate the productive forces," the sole task of commercial
work was to encourage and support the development of production.[81]
Also, commercial units were enjoined from concentrating on "only buying and selling," as this was considered a purely professional viewpoint
that showed a lack of concern for production, and thus a neglect of politics and the masses.[82] This linking together of politics and production
characterized the Leap, in contradistinction to later periods when the
two were viewed by radicals as being antithetical.

Based on this notion of the primacy of production, the commercial
departments received several prescriptions for their activity: first and
most centrally, they were to purchase as much as industrial units could
produce, indiscriminately buying up whatever issued from farm and

81. *DGB*, April 23, 1958 (speech by Yao Yilin).
82. *DGB*, October 23, 1958, p. 3.

factory.[83] Such guaranteed procurement was to keep the producers from worrying about having an outlet for their output, which was to motivate them to produce in ever greater quantities.

In this spirit, Yao Yilin, at that time serving as vice-minister of the First Ministry of Commerce,[84] encouraged "great procurement" (*da shou*), as he claimed that things that could not be sold next year could perhaps be sold later on. As for the argument posed by doubters that things might spoil or deteriorate in the interim, Yao professed skepticism, pronouncing that those who believed that steel could rust were wrong, and that the future need for items such as staplers, which had only a limited market at present, might well increase. As under the *tonggou* system, it would be up to the commercial agents simply to store any excess commodities which they temporarily could not dispose of. Commercial personnel have generally abhorred such "high tides" in industrial production (a hallmark of radical phases) when they are compelled to purchase the excessive quantities of low-grade commodities spewed out by the factories.[85]

Another major component of commerce's work in this period, one that differentiates this model from *tonggou*, was its workers' direct participation in the productive process. For a time in 1958, units in the commercial sector were directed not only to aid local authorities and communes in running factories and other forms of industrial enterprise; not just to go to the workshops for the purpose of better understanding the difficulties and needs of productive enterprises; and not merely to invest their own capital in factories so that the factories could purchase new machinery. Besides these support activities, commercial personnel were now themselves to engage in productive labor as "an ordinary thing," joining and even leading work on the shop floor when the market was not busy.[86]

83. Chen Xing, "Accurately Solve Some Contradictions in Commercial Work," *XX*, no. 12, 1958, pp. 30–31; *DGB*, December 5, 1958, p. 2, and October 29, 1959; *ECMM*, no. 136 (1958), p. 39; *ECMM*, no. 140 (1958), p. 45; and Minister of Commerce Cheng Zihua's speech to the First Session of the Second National People's Congress (April 25, 1959), translated in *Current Background*, no. 580 (1959), p. 2.

84. In February 1958 the former Ministry of Urban Services was merged with the All-China Federation of Supply and Marketing Cooperatives, and the two offices were placed under a newly created Second Ministry of Commerce. The original Ministry of Commerce was then renamed the First Ministry of Commerce. In September of that year, the two ministries were merged. See Donnithorne, *China's Economic System*, p. 274. Yao's speech is in *DGB*, April 23, 1958.

85. *DGB*, April 6, 1965.

86. *XX*, no. 12, 1958, pp. 30–31; *RMRB*, June 23, 1958, in *SCMP*, no. 1806, pp. 17–18; *DGB*, August 2, 1958, p. 3, and October 19, 1958, p. 2.

And beyond that, following upon the decentralization measures of 1957,[87] commercial organs began to control some industrial concerns on their own. Such undertakings were aimed at filling in gaps in productive work left undone by industrial departments, and at expanding the sources of goods. The types of enterprises they ran included processing plants for agricultural by-products; workshops for assembling and repairing farm tools; and minor operations that utilized wastes, scraps, and wild plants, did small-scale smelting or made crude kinds of fertilizer, pesticides, or cement; or were outlets that designed accessories for industrial departments.[88] In short, commerce was considered a less valuable activity than production in the Leap's heyday. Therefore, the demand that marketing organs give up their regular jobs was seen by those dictating economic policy as causing no significant loss.

In this same spirit of opposition to commercialism, there were also moves during the Leap to cut back the commercial bureaucracy that had joined producer to end-user, which meant reducing the role of the wholesale middleman.[89] Under the label of direct-line transport, commodities were allocated to shops "on the spot." This was a measure that shared the marketeer's distaste for bureaucracy in its preference for "self-sales" by the producers. In Shanghai, commercial organs adopted a purchasing procedure that greatly simplified past practices (under the *tonggou* model), which had involved twenty-eight steps from the time of ordering goods until the factory finally turned over the end-product and collected its payment. The radicals, in promoting these retrenchments, hoped that such changes would free labor power for more productive work.

Besides the shift of the commercial sector's focus from activities in the sphere of circulation to various efforts to increase output, the Leap ushered in another temporary modification in the conception of socialist commerce. This new notion derived from the institution of communes in the countryside from mid- to late 1958. Since the theoretical underpinning of the communes included the value of local self-reliance, their creation spelled a reduction in commodity exchange in the rural areas.

The idea here was that each commune should become capable of fulfilling its own needs, so that commercial units would be responsible only for directly allocating the commune's output among its members, dispensing with the procedures once used for sales and purchases. Along

87. See chapter 2 above, and Donnithorne, *China's Economic System*, p. 283.

88. *SCMP*, no. 1806 (1958), pp. 17–18; *DGB*, August 16, 1958, p. 2, and October 23, p. 3; and *ECMM*, no. 140, p. 46.

89. See *DGB*, September 16, 1958, p. 3, and *RMRB*, March 18, 1958. The state-owned wholesale companies were abolished in late 1957 and not restored until 1962. See chapter 1, note 76, and Donnithorne, *China's Economic System*, p. 288.

with this went the introduction of a contract system that reduced the scope of monetary exchange. The very institution of this system convinced radicals that the transition to communism was at hand.[90] Unfortunately, the larger effort that characterized Leap policies as a whole to eschew any material incentives stymied both self-reliance and exchange of any sort as production faltered and distribution became chaotic.

In practice, this attempt to heighten local self-sufficiency had several effects. Since the communes made their own small and middle-sized tools, their members no longer needed to purchase implements from commercial units. Instead, they required the raw materials, power, and fuel needed for manufacturing these items. Also, with the establishment of commune mess halls, such foodstuffs as oil, salt, sauce, vinegar, and noodles had to be procured in large quantities, while the vegetables and meats that supply and marketing cooperatives had supplied were now produced within the commune and directly distributed there, without the aid of the market.[91] Thus the items in which trade units trafficked were altered as their rural buyers turned to being producers of the items they once had purchased.

The extremes of this experiment reached their limits by December 1958, when the Sixth (Wuhan) Plenum of the Eighth Central Committee, its members already aware of massive disorders resulting from the Leap, issued a formal retrenchment.[92] Beginning at that time and continuing over the next two years, criticism of early Leap measures surfaced in the press. This opposition took several forms: some commentators complained that Leap practices had damaged commercial work, whereas others charged that production itself had suffered as a result.

While the Leap was still gathering momentum in September 1958, scorn had been heaped on the idea that the simplification of procedures and the elimination of some marketing might lead to severe disruptions. In fact, one article even claimed that belief in "superstition" was responsible for some cadres' thinking that it was necessary to use commercial organs for distribution. "Some people" were ridiculed then for supposing that things might get lost if they did not go through the wholesale station, or that articles might be shipped to the wrong place.

Just over a half year later, however, the same paper insisted that "if commercial departments neglect their own work [meaning market-

90. *DGB*, November 5, 1958, p. 1, January 23, 1959, p. 2; and *Caijing yanjiu* [Financial Research] (*CJYJ*), no. 2 (1959), pp. 14–17, 35.
91. *SCMP*, nos. 1886 (1958), pp. 15–16; and 1910 (1958), pp. 14–17; and Yan Kelun, "New Changes in the Present Management System in Rural Finance and Trade," *Xinhua banyuekan* [New China Semimonthly] (*XHBYK*), no. 22 (1958), pp. 111–12.
92. See chapter 2.

ing] . . . this will lead to chaos in the social division of labor and obstruct the basic role of commercial work."[93] Other articles spoke of the "mistake" of allowing a number of personnel in the commercial field "whom we thought to be superfluous" to be transferred to posts of ordinary labor. Furthermore, the closing down of shops for days in the busy farm season while commercial personnel went to the fields to sow and reap was now seen as ill-advised neglect of trade; and the fact that some commercial staff and workers had worked in the factories, disregarding their own duties, now became a matter for correction.[94]

In early December 1958, Yao Yilin published an article in that month's *Red Flag* journal maintaining that only a minority of commercial cadres then thought that the main task of commerce ought to be the managing of production in a big way.[95] By mid-1960, as if the exhortations to give top priority to productive activity and to engage in it had never existed, another article in *Red Flag* informed finance and trade workers that if they were really determined to serve production, there were many things that they could do.

None of these jobs, however, involved the labor on the workshop floor that had marked the early Leap days. Rather, they consisted of doing business that was properly commercial, such as helping to organize the technology for production and accumulating capital through exchange, which could then be applied to the reproductive process. "Of course, when we talk about participation in production," the article explained, as it sought to correct what its author pretended had been a "misunderstanding," "it does not imply neglecting our own duties, but instead means matching our work of circulation and distribution with productive work."[96] Clearly, the Leap view that commerce was insignificant no longer held sway, as spokespersons for its interests could once again present their views openly in writing.

Not only was there concern that commerce had suffered during the heyday of the Leap. As reappraisal became the order of the day, some held that production itself could be set back through cutting off commercial activity. At the simplest level, this view held that during the period that trade organs were still participating in productive labor, some commercial units had been "too interested" in factory work, and so had competed for

93. *DGB*, September 16, 1958, p. 3, and April 6, 1959, p. 2.
94. *DGB*, October 10,1959, in *SCMP*, no. 2083 (1959), pp. 7–13; *DGB*, April 6, 1959, p. 2.
95. Yao Yilin, "A Debate on the Direction of Commercial Work," *HQ*, no. 13 (1958), in *XHBYK*, no. 23 (1958), pp. 94–96.
96. Mo Mingfang, "Several Problems in Trade and Financial Work Under the New Trends," *HQ*, no. 10 (1960), pp. 23–30.

facilities and raw materials with the production departments.[97]

Besides, as commercial units stopped handling the process of exchange, industrial units found it hard to acquire the means for their productive activity as supply work became sloppy, causing production to suffer in yet another way. As for procurement, as one piece put it: "If everyone does production, who will purchase the goods produced and organize their exchange? Without that, production will be obstructed."[98]

Just as the question of whether trade-unit cadres ought to become involved in production was reassessed after December's Wuhan Plenum, so was the issue of whether commodity production (that is, production for the market) should continue under the commune system. By January discussions of this subject uniformly maintained that the barter of products that went with the use of contracts was not at all a higher level of exchange; nor was it a sign of having already made a speedy transition to communism.[99] Any such interpretation was now branded a "misunderstanding."

Apparently, some of the ideas spawned by the Leap did not disappear readily. As late as mid-1962, the notion of purchasing in disregard of need through buying whatever was produced was still alive, as continuing attacks on it evinced. Opponents of this practice pointed to its tendencies to encourage "blind production" and to lower the quality of service. And criticism continued against commercial units for "getting out of the circle of purchase, marketing, transportation, storage, and profit making, and ignoring the special function of commerce itself." According to the legitimate view then current, such behavior would "result in commerce becoming a production enterprise instead of playing the role of bridge in the national economy."[100]

As the philosophy of the Leap gradually fell from favor, commercial units once again could purchase with some selectivity, withdraw their workers from the shop floor and the field, restore the wholesale agencies to their place in the commercial process, and engage in exchange through purchases and sales. In the early 1960s industry no longer monopolized the superior position, and this meant gains for commerce in their ongoing competition. But that victory was a temporary one—in 1965 and 1966 radicals once again trumpeted the transcendence of producer over trader.

97. *DGB*, October 23, 1958, p. 3.
98. *DGB*, October 10, 1959; May 17, 1959, p. 3.
99. *DGB*, January 23, 1959, p. 2, and *CJYJ*, no. 2 (1959), pp. 14–17, 35.
100. *DGB*, July 13, 1962, in *SCMP*, no. 2792 (1962), p. 12; and *SCMM*, no. 348 (1962), p. 28. Also see *China News Analysis*, no. 435 (1962), p. 5.

The Cultural Revolution Era

The early 1960s market initiative had amounted to a far milder version of the more extreme 1956 selective purchase plan. So also this second radical thrust, during the Cultural Revolution, was much less bold than the Leap had been. A few articles from that period, however, do mark the return of some of the themes of 1958.

Again, radicals championed what they saw as the innate superiority of productive labor over exchange: "Oppose the unilateral demand for subjecting production units to the irrational domination of the commercial departments," cried one article. Once more, too, high productivity was in itself a goal: "A greater quantity is better than a smaller . . . an abundance of commodities will only have advantages, no disadvantages." Furthermore, to accommodate and encourage productive units in their effort to attain unlimited output, commercial agents were to revise (by expanding) their purchase plans whenever there was a bumper harvest, and then to exert themselves somehow to find a market.[101]

Yet another Leap feature reintroduced in the mid-1960s was the participation of commercial workers in productive activity. In one journalist's account of that period, many contracts between supply and marketing cooperatives and production teams in a Guizhou county were not being fulfilled. The reason for this, he maintained, was that the SMCs had not joined in the labor of the teams. Another article told of a vegetable sales station whose workers realized that only when the supply of vegetables was ample could the market be well stocked. This finding led the business personnel to journey to the fields, where they helped to grow more.[102]

Rhetoricians during the Cultural Revolution, unlike those in the Leap period, visited much abuse upon those who ignored political matters while emphasizing production. Still, throughout the 1970s, labor in the service of increasing the productive forces was once again (as in Leap days) praised as a form of behavior superior to dealing in money or seeking profits.

Another key difference between this period and 1958 was the more rational approach to procurement this time, as if policy makers had absorbed a lesson from that earlier chaotic episode: "Prompt purchase does not mean the purchase of the whole lot which has been produced, irrespective of the quality or the varieties of the products."[103] Never

101. *DGB*, April 5, 1966, p. 1; *SCMM*, no. 491 (1965), pp. 9–10; *RMRB*, June 6, 1965, in *SCMP*, no. 3485 (1965), p. 11.
102. *Union Research Service* 43, no. 12 (1966), pp. 178 and 182.
103. *SCMM*, no. 491 (1965), p. 10.

again, in fact, were commercial agencies directed to buy up any sort of output that issued from the factories.

During most of the decade from 1966 to 1976, propaganda for commercial workers stressed the importance of supporting maximum output, urged them to participate in labor, ordered them to set up factories and production bases, and, in one instance, even asked them to donate 70 to 80 percent of their units' financial resources to the development of agriculture and industries that aid agriculture.[104] Typical of the spirit of this period was a series of articles written in the late 1960s on the subject "Cloth dealers should learn to weave cloth, vegetable-mongers should learn to grow vegetables."[105] A bureaucratic interlude from 1976 to 1978 was capped by the December 1978 Third Plenum of the Eleventh Central Committee, which quashed the radical approach, as marketeers, back in power, began once again to set up the machinery of selective purchase.

The "buy whatever" model, partial to industry, tries to solve all the strains between trade and industry in industry's favor. Though its decimation of the commercial bureaucracy aggravates the problem of getting adequate supplies to the factories, it forces the personnel from the commercial departments to do everything they can to ease the growth needs of production. And under it, the factories are absolved altogether of having to concern themselves with the market's demands or even with the salability of what their workers turn out, while the commercial units have to buy any junk produced, and manage single-handedly the headaches of surplus stocks.

It is this model's disregard for consumers and its wasteful inventories that have eventually paved the way on two occasions for a return of selective purchase, the only model that seriously addresses commercial issues.

Three models exist in socialist China for delivering industrial products from the factories to consumers. Each strives for a socialist solution to the same strains that beset relations between production and sales

---

104. *RMRB*, October 19, 1970, in *SCMP*, no. 4767 (1970), p. 93; *RMRB*, July 6, 1971, in *SCMP*, no. 4943 (1971),p. 18; *RMRB*, January 26, 1972, in *SCMP*, no. 5073 (1972),p. 157; *SCMP* no. 5118 (1972), pp. 29–30; *RMRB*, October 6, 1972, in *SCMP*, no. 5238 (1972), p. 131; *SCMM*, no. 755 (1973), pp. 78–80; *Shangye zhanxian qixiang xin* [A new atmosphere on the commercial front], pp. 10, 85; *China Pictorial*, no. 3 (1978), p. 38; and *FBIS*, June 30, 1978, p. E18 (a broadcast from Changsha, capital of Hunan, a province that, as birthplace of Mao Zedong and workplace of Hua Guofeng, hung onto radical approaches in trade work much later than most).

105. The articles appeared in Shanghai's *Wenhui bao*, and are translated in *SCMP*, nos. 4276, p. 4, and 4286 (both 1968), pp. 6–12.

divisions in a capitalist setting. Two of the three models, *tonggou* and "buy whatever," honor productive over commercial labor. These two are alike in that they both prescribe means of dealing with the issues of supplies, the market, scheduling, and inventories that lift the burden from the factory managers and place it squarely on the shoulders of the commercial personnel. Both models slight the market (though "buy whatever" does so far more definitively), in an attempt to further industrial growth while eschewing the profit motive, which, in the view of their advocates, drives capitalist firms to concentrate more on returns to capital than on meeting people's needs.

But the choice that one of these models makes to play down profit by planning all production and exchange through quotas only creates new and different forms of competition, growing out of incompatible targets—a competition waged between state-run economic departments instead of among capitalism's private firms. When marketeers attain clout and advance their own model, one which transfers the four strains to the factories to handle, they allow market considerations to break through the tensions between incongruous plans. But they have never managed or even wished to dispose altogether of the planned economy. Thus their scheme, selective purchase, is simply laid over the plan without altering its foundations. This model too, then, itself intensifies rivalries, as it shifts factory managers' attention to questions of price and profit, again in an intersectoral rather than an interfirm arena.

Radicals have hoped to dispense not just with the pursuit of profit but with planning as well. Their model so decisively glorifies industrial production over commercial activity that any similarity with capitalist business, which sets production goals in response to sales, is wiped away altogether. But the technological weaknesses of the Chinese economy place a limit on the designs of the radicals. For most localities do not have the wherewithal for the self-sufficiency in production that radicals yearn for; and inadequate storage facilities make it impossible for commercial units to buy up and lay away whatever amounts of goods are produced.

The Chinese leadership has collectively made repeated attempts to rearrange the relations between state-run industry and commerce. But it has done so always in the context of maintaining the primacy of the plan, in the hopes of finding a solution that is at once equitable and under control. However, the state plan and the underdeveloped technologies that characterize Chinese industry and commerce not only aggravate strains between departments. Being part and parcel of the entire economic system, they have also hampered the realization of a solution.

6

Commerce
and Agriculture:

Fights over "Free" Markets

Unlike the less obtrusive liberalizing experiments in the circulation of industrial products addressed in chapter five, "free" markets have been the focus of much open controversy over three decades of Communist rule in China. By comparison, reforms of exchange in the industrial sector have been brief in duration, have involved enterprises more than individuals, and directly touch the lives of far fewer people. Produce markets, on the other hand, have usually been available in some form over three decades of Communist rule, if under widely varying degrees of state control. Their patrons are the 80 percent of the Chinese population who dwell in the countryside, and at times the city folk as well.

In addition to their greater social impact, rural fairs have aroused a much livelier debate in doctrinal circles. For they reveal a central difficulty in China's effort to practice socialism, and so they raise troubling questions. Marx had predicted that the socialist revolution, emerging in an era of plenty, would render markets obsolete as it replaced them, first

*Urban free market, not yet officially sanctioned, late
1978, Changsha, Hunan.*

with a plan, and ultimately with free supply according to need. The Chinese, however, precisely because their economy remains so impoverished even after their revolution, have been unable to do without this small-scale, localized, and somewhat ungoverned form of trade. Indeed, theoretical arguments that justify the continuation of this business do so in terms of the low level of China's technological infrastructure for marketing. Those in opposition, though, have censured this relatively untrammeled use of a market that responds to supply and demand, and not to a plan, in a socialist state. Thus, in this realm as well, political debate, economic scarcity, and the presence of the plan all structure the treatment of yet another form of trade.

Free markets have also been an issue for those concerned about the growth of the economy and the state's control over the economy. Some maintain that fairs have caused inflation, diverted energy from purely productive activity, and drawn produce away from state purchasing agents. Heated discussion has flared up over such social questions as the fairs' effect on income distribution and class polarization. And fairs are the source of conflict between disparate state organs, politicians at different government levels, social classes, geographical regions, and occupational groups. Indeed, state bureaucrats and various segments of the population all turn against each other because of this institution.

This chapter, then, analyzes the rural fair in the same terms that have organized the study to this point. That is, it considers the effects on the marketing of rural produce which economic underdevelopment, state ownership and planning of much of the economy, and leadership conflict have had. Also, it emphasizes the competition over the control of goods highlighted in earlier chapters. Its aim is to determine the social and structural roots of controversy over free marketing in socialist China.

The first section describes the nature of these fairs, sketches their purposes, and presents the arguments offered by their supporters to justify them. A second section will set these markets in the historical and political contexts of the periods in which they were sanctioned. It traces their cyclical appearance and temporary elimination over three decades, and points to secular trends in this development.

The third section focuses on the several sorts of struggles that attend rural markets. The approach of radical, marketeer, and bureaucrat each has its own stance on a range of issues about the social and economic effects of fairs, and this part of the chapter lays out these lines of controversy. Next, the discussion will delineate divisions within society and between state and private actors at local levels which issue from or are accentuated by the open marketplace in the People's Republic. Then, three cases of clashes between provincial and national elites, one in each of the three periods when fairs were approved in central policy councils, provide an insight into the political dimensions of control over fairs.

In all, this chapter will examine the tensions between an economically based need for free marketing in China at this stage, on the one hand, and the social and political forces that resist this need, on the other. This tension has caused much ambivalence, which has been manifested in the comings and goings of fairs over time, obstructions placed on their workings, and conflict over their legitimacy. The pages below tell this story.

Fairs and Their Justification

The institution of compulsory state purchase of grain, oil, and cotton after 1953 eliminated the free exchange of these products in rural markets; and with the socialist transformation of commerce in 1955–1956, state-managed units replaced private merchants. However, while there has been some difference in the sorts of goods involved, in the types of people participating, and in the level of state supervision over them, the sites and schedules for holding fairs seem to be the same as those used in standard markets in China before 1949. In periods when the leadership encouraged the activation of these marts, there have been from thirty to forty thousand of them across the country.[1]

Self-sufficiency within localized marketing regions was greater in the days before the creation of state trading companies and supply and marketing cooperatives, which by 1956 already monopolized trade in some 70 percent of the nation's commodities.[2] Still, the proportion of output exchanged by peasants at regionalized, periodic markets has been remarkably constant over time at 20–40 percent, and at about one-fourth to one-third the total value of agricultural products and by-products.[3]

Whenever the fairs have been permitted, this principle, no doubt difficult to put into practice, is to guide them: "under control but without being suffocated, alive but without chaos" (*guan er bu si, huo er bu luan*). To fulfill this formula, all fairs since the rampantly unrestricted ones of late 1956 have been officially hemmed in by a set of regulations.[4] These make mandatory, among other things, "leadership" by state organs, which are to purchase and release goods in a manner that will control supply and demand and so restrain price movements; the guarantee of state procurement targets for goods that are part of the compulsory purchase system, before putting such goods on the market; limitation of participation to producers, both collective and individual, and usually just to small traders who travel only short distances, and a ban

1. This argument is elaborated in G. William Skinner, "Marketing and Social Structure in Rural China, Part III," pp. 379–80. Skinner defines the standard market in Part I of this essay as "that type of rural market which met all the normal trade needs of the peasant household." *Survey of the China Mainland Press (SCMP)*, no. 2614 (1961), p. 17, lists more than forty thousand as of 1961; *Renmin ribao* [People's Daily] (*RMRB*), March 10, 1980, p. 2, cites a figure of "more than 36,000." Skinner (Part III) estimates on p. 386 that there were about 65,000 markets in China during the period 1900–1948. Perhaps transport modernization accounts for there being only one-half to two-thirds as many sites today as in the past.

2. *Extracts from China Mainland Magazines (ECMM)*, no. 64 (1956), p. 28.

3. Dwight H. Perkins, *Agricultural Development in China, 1368–1968*, pp. 114–15, cites 30 to 40 percent for the period 1920–1950, and 20 to 30 percent before 1900. *Da Gong Bao* [Impartial Daily](*DGB*), June 3, 1955, notes that what then went by the name of "peasant trade," trade of products produced and sold by the peasants themselves, reached more than 20 percent of the retail amount of social commodities in some districts. *DGB*, April 29, 1955, says that peasant trade accounts for the trade of 35.5 percent of the vegetables and 30.33 percent of the hogs traded in a Hubei *zhen*; and *Hong Qi* [Red Flag] (*HQ*), no. 18, 1961, in *Selections from China Mainland Magazines (SCMM)*, no. 282 (1961), p. 9, says that, of the aggregate amount of commodities circulated in the rural areas, about 25 percent is transacted through rural fairs. *ECMM*, no. 66 (1957), p. 24, says that 20–30 percent of all commodities are handled on the free market; and *RMRB*, January 27, 1957, says that one-third the total value of the country's agricultural products and by-products are traded on the free market. Apparently, whether the discussion is cast in terms of percentage of output or percentage of marketed output, the figures cited are in the same general range. At the individual fair, the volume of trade can be singularly unimpressive. See *DGB*, April 25, 1962, which tells of an annual fair held in Jiangyin county of

on capitalists and long-distance merchants; and prohibition of and punishment for abandoning agriculture for peddling, and for activities considered "speculative," such as resale for profit, long-distance trading, and adulteration of goods. Many of these same restrictions were also applied to rural markets in China historically,[5] whereas those that deal with first meeting state-set purchase targets in the planned economy must have been learned from the Russians, as the rules governing their kolkhoz or collective-farm markets are identical.[6]

The forces of supply and demand govern prices to a greater extent in these markets than in any other arena of exchange in China. Nevertheless, market control committees operate in each marketplace to supervise pricing under Party leadership. Members of these committees include representatives from the local government's financial and trade, tax and food grains departments, from the local branch of the supply and marketing cooperative, from state companies, and from the local industry and commerce administrative management organs. Their function, among other things, is to ensure that the prices negotiated between buyer and seller do not exceed the maxima nor fall below the minima of state-set list prices (set at different levels of government for different types of produce). The government taxes sales at the fairs, although a recent source claims that it does so only for exchanges of over one hun-

---

Jiangsu province's Sunan district. There the business volume of 62,000 yuan included 17,000 yuan in trading among 50,000 participants at the fair, or an average of about 30 cents per person! *Beijing Review* (*BR*), 24, no. 36 (1981):28, told of a three-day fair which drew 100,000 customers, where the total volume of sales was 654,700 yuan, or 6 yuan per person, on the average. Also, Tong-eng Wang, in *Economic Policies and Price Stability in China*, notes on p. 4 that "as much as 25–30% of total retail sales were conducted in the nonsocialist market in 1956–57, and 10–20% in early 1962." Nai-ruenn Chen, in an unpublished paper, "China's Inflation, 1979–82: A Quantitative Assessment" (Draft, February 15, 1983), states on p. 21 that in 1977 there were virtually no free markets in urban areas, and that rural free markets then accounted for only 4.4% of total retail sales. By 1978, urban markets began to appear and, with rural ones, accounted for 6.6% of total retail sales. In 1979, the figure rose to 9.5%, and in 1980, to 10.2%.

4. Kevin Bucknall, "Capitalism and Chinese Agriculture, 1960–66," pp. 70 ff., gives a thorough analysis of the regulations in effect in the early 1960s, whose stipulations generally obtained in later years as well. The second section of this chapter will discuss variations among the regulations in different periods.

5. Susan Mann discusses historical Chinese laws for the marketplace in her manuscript, "The Order of the Marketplace in Agrarian China"; as does Sybille van der Sprenkel, in "Urban Social Control," pp. 612–14. See also chapter 3 above.

6. See Gregory Grossman, "The 'Second Economy' of the U.S.S.R.," pp. 26, 27; Naum Jasny, *The Socialized Agriculture of the U.S.S.R.: Plans and Performance*, pp. 384–86; Alec Nove, *The Soviet Economic System*, p. 265; and Karl-Eugen Wädekin, *The Private Sector in Soviet Agriculture*, pp. 133, 141, 171.

dred yuan.[7] Fees (*guanli fei*) are also assessed, to help underwrite the costs of tents, stalls, and other facilities in the marketplace.

As early as 1956, articles on fairs began to refer to a division of commodities into three categories. Each category of goods was to be subject to a different degree of state control over its purchase and its price, in accord with the significance of that category to the home and export markets. However, it was not until April 1959 that a standardized, formal division of commodities, to apply throughout the nation, was publicized.[8] The relevant directive listed thirty-eight items in the first category, which are goods considered essential to the livelihood of the population. These include grains, edible oils, cotton, salt, sugar, and various metals, and are controlled by "planned purchase." According to this system, the State Planning Commission sets annual compulsory delivery quotas for these products for each province. The government fixes both purchase and retail prices for these goods, which are rationed to consumers. Usually these products have not been allowed on free markets.

Two hundred ninety-three items made up the second category in 1959, and the state purchases these under a system called "unified purchase," again at state-set prices. In this category are iron wire and nails, hemp, wines, cigarettes, eggs, and tea. The Ministry of Commerce sets quotas for the procurement of these products too, but any surplus above that amount can be freely traded. Moreover, these items are not rationed. The great bulk of goods on the free markets have usually been those of the residual, third category, many of which are minor local products and sideline products such as medicinal herbs, scrap metals, poultry, and animal by-products.[9]

Trade within the general scope of these guidelines is considered legitimate rural-fair trade. As distinguished from these fairs, black markets are illicit exchanges which crop up in periods when free markets are not permitted or are heavily restricted; which contain contraband or other

7. *BR*, 24, no. 36 (1981):26, states that at a rural fair on the Huai River taxes and management fees are set at 1 percent for exchanges of more than 100 yuan. Informants in Hong Kong also mentioned taxation of fair trade. The press articles on the fairs of the 1960s discuss taxation procedures, though without specifying the rates.

8. *DGB*, December 4 and 7, 1956; *DGB*, April 4, 1959. See *Zhongguo renmin gongheguo Guowuyuan gongbao* [Bulletin of the State Council of the People's Republic of China], no. 14 (September 5, 1981), p. 452, for a new division into four categories: (1) unified purchase and unified sales; (2) planned purchase; (3) goods placed on order; and (4) select purchase goods. A good discussion of the three categories is found in Robert C. Hsu, "Agricultural Financial Policies in China, 1949–80," pp. 639–40.

9. Audrey Donnithorne, *China's Economic System*, p. 299, cites a 1962 estimate that about 80 percent of the agricultural and sideline products sold at fairs belong to the third category.

goods not allowed in the fairs and of which the government rations are too small; or which sell high-priced and scarce luxury consumer goods, often produced abroad.[10]

Most typically, their publicists attribute one overriding benefit to the fairs: through their reliance on the forces of supply and demand and thus on prices, they expand production in both qualitative and quantitative terms.[11] Heated debate has frequently surrounded this and other claims made on behalf of this trade, as a later section will indicate. Nevertheless, each time that these markets have been reemphasized and encouraged by the leadership—during periods beginning in 1956, in 1959, and in 1978—it has been principally in the name of increased output.

Other crucial aims that partisans hope the fairs will attain include invigorating the overall exchange of goods on all markets in China, facilitating interchange between city and countryside, all in order to satisfy the needs of consumers better; and, through the competition they provide, forcing state trade organs to improve their own management and operations. In the process, they are billed as capable of readjusting supplies and demand between areas, increasing the incomes of participating peasantry, and providing convenience to the people in their purchasing and selling activities. Sometimes, too, a political role is attributed to these markets, expressed as a hope that they will strengthen the alliance between the workers and peasants as goods and cash flow between the two classes.[12]

Many of these advantages that allegedly stem from allowing fairs to run are said to issue from the fact that the trading practices in them are far simpler than those used by state-managed commerce. According to this argument, the reduction in bureaucratic links that comes from letting peasants sell their produce directly themselves (and not through the supply and marketing cooperatives and state companies) saves expenditures, conserves labor time, and preserves the freshness of perishables.[13] Two effects of these savings are that many products not usually produced because they are not easily marketable can suddenly find an outlet, and that raw materials in need can be more conveniently procured.

10. *Guanchajia* [Observer] (Hong Kong) (*GCJ*), no. 9 (1978), pp. 161–62.
11. *ECMM*, no. 64 (1956), p. 28, and *DGB*, February 25, 1961, in *SCMP*, no. 2660, p. 18, are just two examples among hundreds.
12. *DGB*, October 7, 1956, p. 2; March 27, 1961, in *SCMP*, no. 2483 (1961), p. 4; *RMRB*, November 21, 1959, in *SCMP*, no. 2157 (1959), p. 15; and *DGB*, November 20, 1961, are just a few samples of the many articles supportive of fairs which have accompanied the periods of their promotion.
13. *ECMM*, no. 77 (1957), p. 16, and *DGB*, December 1, 1956, in *SCMP*, no. 1447 (1956), pp. 13–16.

The principal theoretical argument used to justify reliance on these peasant markets in a socialist society is that they are "objectively necessary" for economic reasons. Those who put forward this case often begin with the observation that fairs, once closed down, tend to crop up again regardless: "If you control the open ones, others will appear in the dark; if you control the central ones, scattered ones emerge."[14] In this vein the press of the early 1960s (and later of 1980) assured its readers that the existence of this objective foundation for fairs meant they would last a long time, and that they could not be stopped by human will.[15]

At the most general level, this foundation lies in certain basic structural features of the country: its population and territory are large; communications are inadequate; geographical and climatic conditions vary widely among regions; and the economies, products, and customs of different areas are quite diverse, so that only localized markets can truly meet the people's needs.[16] Besides, the practice of trading at close range is one with long roots in Chinese history, "the resultant form of many years," as one source put it.[17] As Lenin realized for Soviet Russia when he introduced the New Economic Policy in the 1920s, the large size of the small-scale peasant-producing sector demanded the application of private market forces after the revolution, in order to get the economy operating again.[18]

Lenin was also aware that the low level of the productive forces in the Soviet Union at that time, and thus the lack of technological sophistication, made it impossible to install a fully planned economy. Therefore, he reasoned, the Russians would have to continue to use a money economy and to rely on regulation by the market.[19] And in China too economic underdevelopment is cited as a reason for holding fairs, in accord with the Marxist dictum that "production [here used to mean the stage of development of the productive forces] determines circulation."[20]

The logic here is that fairs fit the present level and form of development, in which social labor productivity is low. Under such conditions, it is difficult to depend entirely on the collective production sector for

14. *RMRB*, January 31, 1978, p. 3.

15. *Hong Qi* [Red Flag] (*HQ*), no. 31 (November 1, 1980), p. 16, and Che Xinping, *Tan nongcun jishi maoyi* [On rural fair trade], p. 14. That Che's book was written soon after late 1962 is clear from his several references to the then recently concluded Tenth Plenum of the Eighth Central Committee of the Party.

16. *RMRB* editorial of January 27, 1957, in *SCMP*, no. 1467 (1957), pp. 4–6.

17. *ECMM*, no. 42 (1956), p. 29.

18. Wlodzimierz Brus, *The Market in a Socialist Economy*, p. 24; Robert W. Campbell, *Soviet Economic Power*, p. 14.

19. Ibid.

20. As, *DGB*, January 19, 1962.

meeting every kind of need for rural produce. Thus, a system of owner-ship by individual laborers must continue, in the form of private plots and domestic sideline production, for which the fairs are the proper complement and outlet. In sum, since "circulation is the continuation of commodity production," a third trading channel is embodied in the fairs, to supplement the state and cooperative channels, each of which in turn serves its separate ownership system.[21]

Some analyses offer more concrete explanations of the linkage be-tween the low level of economic development and the rural fairs. Such discussions point to the "backward equipment and technique of pro-duction and transportation" in much of the country, which, as one writer prophetically put it in 1958, was "fundamentally unchanged and will remain so."[22] Because of these conditions, free markets have been seen as essential in adjusting circulation to a set of complex and fluctuat-ing circumstances that attend production and consumption in the coun-tryside. Moreover, the storage facilities that would permit more trade of perishables in concentrated, bulk form are lacking as well. In this kind of environment, fairs act as a "technical aid," facilitating sales by requiring only short-distance transport, and cutting back the links in the chain of operations, as goods can be sold near the point of production. Their advocates maintain that the costs thus cut can help to lower prices of goods in the fairs.[23]

From yet another angle, small markets within local regions are espe-cially suited to the sundry nonstaple crops, from fancy fruits to exotic herbs, that dot the Chinese landscape. Here are petty goods in small quantities and of small value, exhibiting a myriad of varieties, scattered in locale, uneven and nonstandardized in quality, perishable and subject to unpredictable changes in natural conditions—features that all make output uncertain and pricing highly variable. These characteristics of such products, which make it impossible to plan their production and exchange, are pointed to when fairs are legitimized.[24]

But these same factors used to justify fairs also lay the foundation for what their opponents see as a "negative potential" lurking in them, as chapter three has shown. That is, the interdistrict and seasonal price

21. Che, p. 4; see also Che, pp. 12 and 20. Also, *DGB*, April 13, 1959, in *SCMP*, no. 2015 (1959), pp. 16–20; *DGB*, November 20, 1961; U.S. *Foreign Broadcast Information Service* (*FBIS*), October 13, 1978, p. E20; *RMRB*, June 20, 1980, p. 5; and *DGB*, January 20, 1964, in *SCMP*, no. 3159 (1964), p. 8.

22. *ECMM*, no. 136 (1958), p. 27. Also see *RMRB*, June 20, 1980.

23. *DGB*, March 27, 1961, in *SCMP*, no. 2483 (1961), p. 6.

24. *SCMM*, no. 372 (1963), p. 6; *SCMP*, nos. 2100 (1959), p. 21, and 2157 (1959), p. 15; and *RMRB*, June 20, 1978.

Peasants proud of their herbs for sale. Free market, June 1983, Wuhan.

differentials, occasioned by local differences in the forces of production and by dependence on nature, respectively, leave loopholes for profiteering. And the leeway given in these markets to forces of supply and demand (as opposed to fixed prices) has, in times of scarcity, resulted in a chance for the entrepreneur to charge prices far higher than the state's, expanding income differentials in the process.[25]

There is one final difficulty to which fairs' advocates allude. This concerns the pernicious side effects of efforts by state trade organs to take over their functions. In the first place, supply and marketing cooperatives on their own simply cannot meet the entire marketing needs of the countryside, for their personnel and depots are too few. But in addition, a host of problems linked to the planned economy plague attempts to substitute public for private traders. As chapter one has shown, the planned economy brings in its wake accumulations of goods in the production area along with sellouts of the same item in the sales district; spoilage of fruits that cannot find a proper market, while city people lack them and prices are high; state-set prices which, by not adjusting to shifts in supply and demand, stymie production increases; and reduc-

25. Che, p. 21.

tion in varieties and quality because of irrational state prices. The far greater directness of the country market, where buyer and seller meet face to face, obviates much of this tangle.[26]

Thus, in allowing this relatively autonomous trading activity among the populace, the Chinese leadership at times comes to terms with an age-old practice, which it hopes will result in enhanced productivity in this socialist state. But even their marketeer publicists insist upon some forms of state regulation of these marts, and turn to Marxist canons to legitimize the fair, this compromise between the dictates of low technology and the goals set by ideological vision.

Changing Policies toward Fairs, and Their Political Contexts

On three occasions since the institution of compulsory purchases in 1953 and the completion of socialist transformation in 1956, temporary victories of those supporting the marketeer philosophy have led to the opening of "free" rural fairs. Each such occasion came at the close of a radical period, during which fairs had been largely shut down. First, the fairs of 1956–1957 followed upon the high tide of socialist transformation. This campaign, coupled with the imposition of retail price controls and compulsory purchase of principal crops by the state, had led to a serious stifling of marketing activity by the spring of 1956.[27]

Then, the opening of markets in mid-1959 (until the middle of the 1960s) succeeded the Great Leap Forward, during which the production of nonstaple foods had been grossly neglected; commune members were forbidden to engage in any private economic activity; barter, local self-sufficiency, and free supply supplanted market exchange; and traditional channels of trade were severely disrupted.[28] And in the third pe-

26. *RMRB*, June 20, 1980, p. 5. Also, *DGB*, November 15, 1956, p. 1; and *SCMP*, no. 1465 (1957), p. 2.

27. Gordon A. Bennett, "Activists and Professionals: China's Revolution in Bureaucracy 1959–1965, A Case Study of the Finance Trade System," pp. 92–93. Skinner (Part III), pp. 365–66; Donnithorne, *China's Economic System*, p. 291; Dwight H. Perkins, *Market Control and Planning in Communist China*, pp. 75, 194. See "State Council Directive on Relaxation of Rural Market Control," in *SCMP*, no. 1408 (1956), pp. 10–11.

28. *DGB*, October 12, 1958, p. 2, for example; Donnithorne, *Economic System*, pp. 293, 303–4, 376; Skinner (Part III), pp. 371–72; and "Communique of the Ninth Plenary Session of the Chinese Communist Party Eighth Central Committee," in Union Research Institute, *Documents of the Chinese Communist Party Central Committee September 1956–April 1969*, vol. 1, pp. 175–76. This communique mentions temporary difficulties in supplying the market caused by poor harvests and a shortage of raw materials for light industry, as reasons for opening fairs.

riod of free trading, beginning in 1978, this activity was promoted in reaction against the highly limited fairs, a reduction in ownership and use of private plots, and tightly controlled prices of the decade of the Cultural Revolution.[29]

Thus, just as in the case of policies toward the distribution of industrial products, those policies toward the management of rural markets have shifted in a cyclical fashion over three decades. There are not three distinct models for handling this arena as there are for industrial output. Nevertheless, the policies approving free markets during the three periods have each contained differential mixes of marketeer and bureaucratic approaches, and the elimination of fairs has generally been inspired by a combination of bureaucratic and radical motivations. Too, as was discussed in chapter five, despite this cycling, there have been secular trends over time in the Chinese experience with free markets under socialism.

The dominant trend over the years, as with the handling of industrial production, has been one in the direction of learning—learning, that is, how to fit the market into a socialist state. Simply put, the fairs of the mid-1950s were loosely defined in scope and haphazardly run. Later, in part out of a sense among the leadership that control over these earlier fairs had been too lax, and also because of what were roundly considered to be dire conditions in the market,[30] much more tightly reined-in

29. All the literature coming from China after the death of Mao charges that the Gang of Four, in closing down fairs, thwarted rural productivity. See, for example, RMRB, November 16, 1977. Under the Gang, the SMCs purchased nearly all produce, as in the well-publicized Haertao commune's "socialist great fair" in Liaoning (RMRB, May 7, 1976). In a more extreme case, the armed forces, public security, and militia, armed with loaded guns, encircled and suppressed village fairs, chasing people away and seizing their goods, in Xiao county, Anhui's "revolution in commerce," according to a later account (RMRB, June 20, 1978). W. L. Parish and M. K. Whyte, in Village and Family in Contemporary China, p. 308, report that in 1975 in North China peasant households' private plots had been abolished or restricted, and that many markets had withered away from lack of activity. This author's interviews in 1979 with ex-residents of Guangdong newly arrived in Hong Kong were full of tales of worker militia confiscating goods sold on the wrong day, or in the wrong place; of secret fairs held at 5 A.M.; and of peasants from the Beijing suburban areas having to ride bicycles into the capital to obtain their vegetables from state-run markets. See also Geng Fu, "Recent Developments and Present Problems in the Free Markets in Guangdong," Dongxifang [East and West] (Hong Kong) (DXF), no. 11 (1979), pp. 24 and 32, on these themes.

30. Chen Yun's assessment of the state of the market in 1962 was the one that gained acceptance by the majority of the leaders making economic policy at that time. He presented it at the Xilou meeting in February of that year, and, as chapter 2 mentioned, by May his writings were published and issued to the whole Party. He noted a decrease in rural production, inflation, currency notes flowing from urban to rural areas as the cities lacked foodstuffs, and speculation developing in the countryside as a result. He suggested a "free market, within a certain scope," as being "good for promoting production." But, "if the peasants get too much cash and we can't get it back," he warned, "there will be no way

markets (the product of an alliance of bureaucrat with marketeer) appeared around 1960. Finally, the twilight of radicalism that began in 1976 made possible the birth of markets whose guidelines merged the looseness of 1956 with the guidance of the early 1960s. A look at the policy documents that directed each episode will illustrate this finding.

At the Eighth Party Congress held in September 1956, several politicians who specialized in economic affairs, notably Chen Yun, Liu Shaoqi, and Li Fuchun, spoke out against the rigidity of the state plan and in favor of a "free market under state leadership." As chapter four showed, Chen had championed caution during the campaign for the socialist transformation of commerce, expressly in the interest of preserving a lively rural market. Now he emerged from this meeting as the new minister of commerce, his appointment preceding by only a few weeks the opening of the first experiment in the use of a free market after the close of that campaign. The free markets he advocated then were clearly marketeer in conception; and the near lack of controls that accompanied their implementation meant that, like the selective purchase experiment of that same period, they quickly got out of control.

The leniency of policy in this first episode appears most markedly in the section on pricing in the State Council's legitimating directive of October 1956. The wording there was extremely vague, and so nearly impossible to enforce:

> For goods that are allowed in the free market, the prices may be *adequately raised* if the former prices were too low. As the prices in the free market may be raised or lowered blindly, control should be imposed when the prices are *beyond the rational standard*. Since the policy of pricing is devised in favor of production development, they should be raised when *production might be affected* as a result of the lower prices. On the other hand, when prices are high enough to be favorable to production and to stimulate production, *excessive rise* in prices as a result of blind competitive purchases in the market must be curtailed by the local government by means of rational valuation and distribution of goods.[31] (Emphasis added to highlight vague phrases.)

---

to get them to sell [their produce] to the state." Thus, "the supply and marketing cooperatives should compete with the speculators and control the free market." See Chen Yun, "Muqian caizheng jingji de qingkuang he kefu kunnan de rogan banfa" [The situation of financial and economic matters at present and certain methods for overcoming difficulties], in *Chen Yun tongzhi wengao xuanbian* [Selected Documents of Comrade Chen Yun] (1956–1962), pp. 157–63, 168.

31. *SCMP*, no. 1408 (1956), p. 11.

Moreover, a few months after the fairs opened, Chen Yun remarked in the same vein on their behalf:

> We ought freely to adopt free trading, and should not worry if prices go up for a time to a certain degree . . . We must avoid that kind of inflation that is due to decreased production. Only increase of production in large amounts can guarantee price stability. . . . Only worry and control prices if they go beyond what is necessary for stimulating production, or if they have risen because of speculation.[32]

This indeterminacy in the approach to price control in these two statements was reinforced in the press in the early months of 1957, when a set of articles revealed that there was a continuing debate over how much guidance to exercise.[33] Another form of this looseness appeared in newspaper articles that indicated a lack of clarity as to what goods could be brought to these markets.[34] That much of this flexibility was deliberate is apparent in the dictum at that time to "fully utilize small merchants and peddlers." It is also clear in the advice that "the key" to solving problems in the markets lay not in any form of control, but in "getting rid of cadres' scruples" (which were manifested in their failure to relax control, out of fear of being unable to manage prices or to get hold of enough goods).[35] As the following discussion will reveal, however, this marketeer thrust in the early months of these fairs led to much disorder, and so was soon checked.

By contrast, the fairs of the early 1960s were much more restricted, at least at the level of policy.[36] A first sort of contrast has to do with the different aims of the 1956 and 1959 fairs. That is, the 1956 guidelines had praised fairs for raising productivity, activating exchange, and, through the competition they provided, promoting state organs to improve their management, all purely marketeer goals. In 1959, though, rural fairs were endorsed because they

> facilitate [the] development [of production], the organization of short-distance transportation, and the control of market prices. They facilitate the exchange of commodities among people. . . . They also help commercial departments locate sources of commodities.

32. *DGB*, November 26, 1956, p. 1, editorial.
33. *DGB*, January 21, February 28, and March 16, 1957.
34. As, *DGB*, November 5, 1956, p. 3; November 9, 1956, p. 2; November 13, 1956; and November 15, 1956, p. 1, editorial.
35. *DGB*, November 3, 1956, p. 3; October 7, 1956, p. 2.
36. See "Directive of CCP Central Committee and State Council on Organization of Rural Fairs," *SCMP*, no. 2108 (1959), pp. 6–9.

Thus, two important new reasons for having fairs were added in 1959, both of which reflected bureaucrats' values: the control of prices and the location of goods by the state. In effect, policy makers hoped this time that state trade organs could use these markets as arenas where they too would participate, so that they could enlarge the range of their own activities.

Moreover, the regulations of the early 1960s set stringent rules, this time explicitly stressing the need for bureaucratic control over prices, as this quotation indicates:

> The *control* over the prices of commodities offered for sale in rural fairs shall be *strengthened* with a view to promoting multiple economic undertakings and *stabilizing* market prices and in accordance with the principle of *centralized leadership* and control at different levels. (Emphasis added.)

More specifically, both first- and second-category goods had now to be sold at state purchase prices, and even principal commodities among materials of the third category were to be "offered for sale normally at prices set by the state." Such orders were absent in the documents of the earlier period.

Whereas the initial directive of September 1959 had allowed first- and second-category goods to come onto the free market, later statements reversed this. Several press articles dictated that surpluses of first-category goods had to be sold to state stores, even after the fixed quota amount had already been delivered to the state.[37] Yet another change from the previous period was the inclusion in the 1959 directive on fairs of a stipulation that county and market-town markets must be governed by market control committees, under the leadership of local Party committees. Such bodies had existed in some places earlier, but their institution had not been decreed in the central-level policy documents of 1956–1957. Their function now was to execute regulations, supervise pricing, ensure "equitable" trading, and prohibit illegalities.

The documents on fairs issued throughout the early 1960s almost uniformly contained injunctions to state commercial departments and SMCs to "strengthen economic leadership."[38] This job was to entail such activities as sending out state cadres to act as peddlers, who would buy for the state at market, not state list, prices; setting up machinery to

---

37. *RMRB*, November 25, 1960, in *SCMP*, no. 2393 (1960), p. 13, and *DGB*, October 18, 1961, in *SCMP*, no. 2614 (1961), p. 18.

38. *DGB*, March 6, 1961, in *SCMP*, no. 2481 (1961), pp. 11–15; *DGB*, April 28, 1961, in *SCMP*, no. 2499 (1961), pp. 1–6; *DGB*, April 17, 1961, in *SCMP*, no. 2499 (1961), pp. 6–10; *DGB*, May 14, 1961, p. 1; and *DGB*, April 9, 1962, editorial, in *SCMP*, no. 2732 (1962), pp. 22–25.

purchase and store peasants' produce left over at the end of market day; organizing under state auspices long-distance interarea purchases; and keeping prices stable by "swallowing and spitting out" (*tun tu*), that is, taking in and later releasing large batches of goods in accord with prevailing conditions of supply and demand. Similarly, many articles spoke of the need to set limits on free bargaining, and enjoined producers to sell only their own produce, consumers to "buy only what one needs."[39] Thus, these carefully managed markets from the start were conceived as far more bureaucratically run bazaars than were their predecessors.

The fairs of the third period first received official approval in early 1978, although the markets did not begin to operate again on a wide scale until about a year later.[40] These fairs were informed by marketeer goals: to better the livelihood of the masses and to promote production.[41] But the earliest pronouncements in the first half of 1978 did list some limitations on them, reflecting the continuing influence of the bureaucratic line in the period before the Third Plenum of the Eleventh Central Committee was held in December. Thus, no "pass-hands" (*zhuan shou*) trade, or reselling, was allowed; only second- and third-category goods could be exchanged; control committees were to set price ranges; and no long-distance trading was permitted.[42]

However, by early 1979 policy had shifted after the Third Plenum, where the marketeer line was clearly triumphant. Then pro-fair literature named "remnant ultra-leftism," or radical opposition to fairs, the present "main problem," just as it had been termed in late 1956 (when the elimination of cadres' fears had been called the key to fair management). At this time sales of grain and oil, those most strategic first-category goods, which central policy generally had not released for free market trade in the past, were authorized, after targets for delivery to the state had been met.[43]

39. *DGB*, December 25, 1961, in *SCMP*, no. 2660 (1962), pp. 18–22; and *Guangming ribao* [Bright Daily] (Beijing) (*GMRB*), March 13, 1961, in *SCMP*, no. 2476 (1961), pp. 4–8.

40. E.g., "Are Trade Fairs Capitalist Free Markets?" *RMRB*, January 31, 1978, p. 3. Premier Hua Guofeng's report to the First Session of the Fifth National People's Congress in February 1978 labeled limited private rural economic activity a part of the Party's rural economic policy (see *Peking Review* [*PR*], 21, no. 10 [1978], 22). But it was the Third Plenum of the Eleventh Central Committee of December 1978 that gave the first real official encouragement to markets in over a decade.

41. Peking Radio, April 28, 1978, in *FBIS*, May 4, 1978, pp. E15–16.

42. Ibid. Also *RMRB*, January 31, 1978, p. 3; June 13, 1978, p. 2.

43. *RMRB*, March 12, 1979; New China News Agency, November 11, 1978; Hefei Radio, January 21, in *FBIS*, January 23, 1979, p. G5; Xining Radio, February 13, 1979, in *FBIS*, February 16, 1979, p. M1. A national conference on fairs in March 1979 approved the sale of collectively produced grain and oil (first-category goods) after targets were met, legitimized urban fairs, and studied the question of long-distance trading (*FBIS*, March 14, 1979, pp. E11–13, and March 28, 1979, pp. L4–5).

*Peddling peasant about to be paid. Free market, May
1983, Wuhan.*

Furthermore, beginning in late 1979 and throughout the summer of
1980, in a sharp reversal of views of the past, a number of articles advocated letting some peasants get rich before others; engaging in commodity production to become prosperous; abolishing the concept of "capitalist spontaneity," a term formerly used to signify the evil tendencies
lurking in the profit-seeking activities of fairgoers; and permitting both
long-distance and "pass-hands" peddling, so long as the only profit
came from interdistrict price differentials, not from exploitation.[44] As
material below will show, this extreme liberalization was checked in the
months that followed, so that the fairs in this third round eventually
received some of the supervision that attended those of the 1960s,
though not nearly to the same extent.

Thus, marketeers in ascendance in late 1956 and late 1978 were able
to carve out rather a broad scope for free trading, in both cases because
immediately preceding radical programs—socialist transformation, the
Cultural Revolution—had severely stifled rural production and ex-

44. Guangzhou Radio, October 3, in *FBIS*, October 5, 1979, p. P14; *RMRB*, May 21,
1980, p. 3; May 16, 1980, p. 3; June 20, 1980, p. 5; August 29, 1980, p. 3; and September
26, 1980, p. 1.

change. In this context, marketeers could produce a consensus for their view that a rapid recovery was required, to be implemented through the agency of a free market exchange. Whereas the leniency of the earlier period was in part the result of unexpected dislocations that issued from too vague guidelines, permissiveness some two decades later was a more carefully crafted policy.

In 1959–1960, however, though many leaders perceived that open markets were needed in the aftermath of the Leap, again to stimulate output, the elite as a whole had become wary of a loss of control (because of their previous experience with fairs and because of havoc arising from the Great Leap's pressures). Therefore the political climate at that time dictated the attaching of caveats to this extra-plan commerce. The most recent phase bears the stamp of learning, as its inspiration blends the flexibility of 1956 with the greater sense of oversight developed in 1960 and thereafter.

Besides this secular change, a second sort of trend in the management of free rural markets in China after 1949 has been common to each episode: an increasing application of bureaucratic fetters on the fairs as concern with corruption and inflation in them has mounted during each period. In 1957, restrictions came abruptly and spelled a total reversal in policy, as new rules nearly closed the fairs altogether in less than one year from the time of their establishment. In the 1960s, however, since the fairs were more circumscribed from the beginning, the addition of extra bureaucratic procedures as time wore on was less obtrusive. And in the late 1970s and early 1980s the restraining measures were added to the original rules, so that fairs could continue, but, according to new laws, they were to be less loosely run than at first.

This trend toward greater use of bureaucratic strategies and rules as each experiment in free marketing unfolded has had several similar manifestations in each era: a tightening of controls over prices; an expansion of state purchases of third-category goods; and a set of institutional arrangements managed by state trade organs to enable them to compete with the fairs for the goods traded in them. These bureaucratic arrangements include state-directed "goods exchange meets," in which mandatory state purchase quotas fixed at higher administrative levels are passed down to lower echelons; where the role of the state trade organs is dominant; and where exchanges are conducted according to a preset plan.[45] Trading at such meets is through the use of contracts, writ-

45. *SCMP*, no. 2024 (1959), pp. 21–23.

ten to connect the plans of local-level agricultural collective production units (brigades, production teams) with state-dictated needs and state-designated purchase plans.[46]

Another part of this process of enhancing state control is the creation of state-run organs modeled on traditional agencies (warehouses, sometimes called "peasant service departments"). These units compete with and attempt to squeeze out private trading for the larger-scale, longer-distance exchanges. They also engage in the storage and wholesaling of extra-quota surpluses, manage business on commission, adjust supplies with demand among localities, negotiate prices with the private sector, and locate goods for the state. And perhaps most typically, restrictions involve expanding or reinstating the duties of the supply and marketing cooperatives as, in effect, they come more and more to vie for goods with the fairs' private-sector patrons.

In the first era of the free market, gradual state encroachment began as early as December 1956, only two months after the State Council's authorizing directive had appeared. State commercial organs in Hubei province began then to increase their purchases and to store surpluses of goods that peasants had brought to the fairs but had not sold. In the same month, SMCs in Jiangxi resumed the practice of finding outlets for peasants' produce and buying their unsold goods, a practice they had discontinued when the fairs first opened. By May 1957, the SMCs in a Hubei *zhen* (township) took over the operation of additional local products, raising the total of varieties of goods they managed from thirty, at the height of the fairs' autonomy, to some three hundred.[47]

Then in August 1957, a mere ten months after the State Council had permitted the fairs to open, that body suddenly decreed the termination of most of the activity. This decision blended bureaucratic wishes for control with radical abhorrence of merchant-class malpractice:

Market control failed to keep pace with the free market, and a number of local merchants, taking advantage of the opening of free markets, started a run on the purchase and arbitrarily raised the purchasing prices and carried on speculation and law-breaching activities. As a result, state purchase of commodities was hampered and some unfavorable effects were

46. *DGB*, April 13, 1959, in *SCMP*, no. 2015 (1959), pp. 16–20, and *SCMP*, no. 2059 (1959), p. 12.
47. *DGB*, December 4 and 12, 1956; and May 11, 1957. See also *ECMM*, no. 77 (1957), pp. 18–19.

produced on the national economy. This state of affairs shows the necessity for the state to strengthen its leadership over the free market.[48]

This first trial of free marketing apparently produced within a short time a backlash of opposition among bureaucrats and radicals. Its conclusion was soon followed by the Great Leap Forward, which continued the clampdown on private trading for several years to come.

A policy permitting fairs again was published in mid-1959. Over the next two years many goods-exchange meets were held, but free-style marketing did not get under way at first.[49] Then, once markets more nearly resembling free fairs began to take place, these state-dominated meets did not convene for a time.[50]

The Eighth Central Committee's Tenth Plenum of September 1962, however, with its stress on class conflict, reawakened concern about possible corruption in the markets and the polarization of income that could accompany it.[51] Besides that plenary meeting, three other political influences had a radicalizing effect on policy toward rural fairs after 1963. These were the "First Ten Points" of May 1963, written by Mao Zedong, which attacked a putative resurgence of commercial speculation and profiteering in the countryside; Liu Shaoqi's wife's findings in 1964 of corruption among basic-level cadres in Taoyuan brigade, of Funing county, Hebei; and Liu's own harsh "Revised Second Ten Points" of September 1964. As a result of these impulses from the capital, local cadres stiffened their hand toward any free economic activity occurring among the peasantry then.[52]

By summer 1963 the goods-exchange meet reappeared. A National Third-Category Goods Fair, sponsored by several state organs, aimed at curtailing, if not replacing, rural fairs, in order to obtain tighter state control over the goods traded in them.[53] At about the same time, many direc-

48. This statement is from *RMRB*, August 18, 1957, editorial, in *SCMP*, no. 1599 (1957), p. 14. See also "State Council Regulations Prohibiting the Flow into the Free Market of Farm Produce on the List of State Planned Purchase and Unified Purchase and Other Commodities," in *SCMP*, no. 1599 (1957), pp. 12–14.

49. *GMRB*, March 13, 1961, in *SCMP*, no. 2476 (1961), p. 5; *SCMP*, no. 2059 (1959), pp. 9–10; *RMRB*, November 24, 1959, in *SCMP*, no. 2157 (1959), pp. 19–23; *SCMP*, no. 2234 (1960), pp. 26–30; and *DGB*, May 7, 1959, p. 3.

50. *Union Research Service*, 33, no. 22 (December 13, 1963): 340–41.

51. Che, *Tan nongcun jishi maoyi*, which opens with a reference to the Tenth Plenum, advocates controls more than do post-Leap documents from before the meeting. See pp. 148 ("we absolutely cannot let buyer and seller freely negotiate") and 149 ("as much as possible, sell to the state").

52. Richard Baum, *Prelude to Revolution: Mao, the Party, and the Peasant Question, 1962–1966*, pp. 21–22, 106.

53. *DGB*, August 12, 1963, and October 6, 1963.

tives handed to SMC workers an important new task: to manage third-category goods, once the stuff of the fairs, to the greatest extent possible. At this point SMCs were also being set up in traditional market towns, rather than just in administrative seats such as counties, as they had been before. The express goal behind this move was to draw peasants' wares into the wagons of the state trade cadres, as this remark justifying the change makes clear: "People are loathe to buy and sell commodities at local SMCs and keep going to the market towns instead."[54]

By the eve of the Cultural Revolution the fairs, while still in existence, were supposed to become sites for carrying out "planned circulation." They were to make possible the incorporation into state plans of diversified farm produce and by-products, through the organizational efforts of state agencies. Such activity was guided by the slogan "The rural market will be occupied by capitalism, if not by socialism."[55] Thus, once again, the cycle leading from stagnant markets (made so by a radical movement) through some leniency for negotiated private exchange and finally back to state control had played itself out.

Although the free markets that followed the 1978 Third Plenum of the Eleventh Party Central Committee went the furthest in their legalized liberalization, the same pattern of gradual restriction marked their progress as well. This is in contradistinction to the fairs of 1956, in which lack of clarity in the initial guidelines and inexperience in designing adequate machinery for control led to a large measure of what the leadership perceived as unintended chaos. Beginning in late summer 1980, a mounting effort commenced to reinsert the basic-level SMCs into the management of petty produce. This switch was introduced under the rubric of allowing many channels of commodity exchange to coexist. The intended effect of this process was to direct more goods into state stores and warehouses, less into private hands.

Graphic examples illustrate the extent to which the state was prepared to go in mid-1980—even to capture seemingly trivial types of goods as its own. In one case, the use of contracts was enforced for trade in grass and mats (both third-category goods) between a Zhejiang production brigade and a local SMC. In another, a new management department, working as an independent accounting unit, was created to link the produce of a production team in Dazhu county, Sichuan, to its basic-level SMC. This department's successful sales work, done through

54. *DGB*, July 13, 1962, in *SCMP*, no. 2792 (1962), pp. 17–19; *DGB*, October 25, 1962, in *SCMP*, no. 2861 (1962), pp. 8–10; *DGB*, January 20, 1964, in *SCMP*, no. 3159 (1964), pp. 8–13; and *DGB*, December 5, 1964, in *SCMP*, no. 3367 (1964), pp. 6–8.

55. *Jingji yanjiu* [Economic Studies] (*JJYJ*), no. 12 (1965), in *SCMM*, no. 536 (1966), p. 23.

the use of a contract, encouraged the team members to sell their produce to the co-op (not at market). Another tale told of an SMC in Guangdong province's Zhongshan county, which "helps peasants get rich" by finding outlets for the output from their privately run plots. At the same time a county-level SMC in Shanxi received permission from its local finance and trade department to handle a greater variety of goods.[56]

A few months later in the year, a meeting of the National Federation of Supply and Marketing Cooperatives stipulated that rural markets ought to be invigorated, but only on the precondition of guaranteeing price stability. At the same time, the *People's Daily* dictated that closer adherence be paid to the plan and required peasants to "sell more of their goods to the state."[57] Then, in early December, the State Council issued a directive calling for stricter supervision of pricing; and, by early 1981, released another, which ordered a crackdown on speculation and smuggling, described as rife. That second decision also banned first-category goods from the fairs (a decision that seems not to have stuck). It also decreed that peasants and peddlers could only bring to market that quantity of goods which they could carry by means of human labor—on a pole, over their shoulder, in a handcart, or on a bicycle.

At that time, despite a continuing official endorsement of the free markets, these were now to "operate under government control and [be] limited in scale."[58] All of these developments point in the same direction— toward a reassertion of state interference in the markets as 1980 wore on. Once again, experiments in free trading clashed with the framework of the socialist state's planned management and with radical ideology.

Thus, the history of the free market in socialist China contains two contradictory stories. On the one hand, the long-term learning trend has permitted the achievement of a balance between liberalization and supervision, so that some measure of relaxation can now persist over time. At the same time, though, each episode has repeated a pattern whereby open trading has had to contend eventually with an incursion of state organs and state power in the marketplace. The following section will examine the roots of this opposition to the free market in China, both on the ideological plane and within society.

---

56. *RMRB,* July 2, p. 2; July 24, p. 1; July 30, p. 1; and October 15, p. 2, 1980.
57. *RMRB,* November 6 and 14, 1980, both on p. 1.
58. *RMRB,* December 8, 1980, p. 1, and *BR,* 24, no. 3 (1981): 3, and no. 7 (1981): 5; and *RMRB,* January 16, 1981, p. 1, and March 7, 1981, p. 4.

Conflict over Free Trading:
Why the Free Markets Are Not Free

Why have recurring restrictions been placed on the free markets following each time that official policy decreed them legitimate? The simplest answer is that these marts occasion a great deal of conflict in socialist China. This part of the chapter addresses this conflict, by examining three central dimensions of the contention: ideologically rooted differences in understandings of the social and economic effects of the free markets; social cleavages laid bare and exacerbated in them; and battles connected with political power over them, between central and local politicians.

CONTROVERSY AMONG THE THREE TENDENCIES
OVER THE EFFECTS OF FAIRS

Radical, marketeer, and bureaucratic tendencies each perceives the social and economic consequences of free markets in fundamentally distinct ways; and each builds its own case by marshaling logic or statistical data, or by appealing to moral values. Five interconnected issues about fairs draw debate between proponents of the three tendencies: Do they breed capitalism? Do they lead to inflation? Do they promote or forestall increases in productivity? Do they hamper or enhance state purchases and the fulfillment of state plans? And, do they increase the income of all the participants? Or do they act to aggravate class polarization?

In a sense, the answer to each of these inquiries about free markets hinges on the judgment one makes about the other questions. To begin with, "capitalism" (in the typical understanding of this term when used about commercial activity in the PRC, i.e., trading done for profit) is most likely to occur when price differentials expand—across regions, seasonally, and between state-set and freely floating prices. For such disparities allow market manipulation and thus profit taking to occur. In this formulation, then, fairs beget capitalism if they generate inflation.

But does this inflation enhance productivity? One answer is that higher prices in free markets (found especially at the onset of a period of intense fair activity, when goods that had been lacking suddenly appear on sale, at first in small quantities) induce more output. The inflation, then, may eventually dissipate, as more goods come onto the market. And state purchases may be facilitated if the existence of the fairs disposes peasants to produce more—so long, of course, as the peasants continue to work for their collective production units as well as on their individual plots. But if producers' interest is diverted by the fairs to

TABLE 7 The Three Tendencies and Disagreements over the Effects of Fairs

Tendency	Issues				
	Capitalism	*Inflation*	*Productivity/Circulation*	*State Purchase/ Plan Fulfillment*	*Income and Class Polarization*
	(Do fairs cause it?)	*(Do fairs cause it?)*	*(Do fairs increase productivity?)*	*(Do fairs increase state purchase?)*	*(Do fairs cause polarization?)*
Radical Marketeer	*Yes** No	*Yes** No, not in the long run	No *Yes!**	No* Yes	*Yes!* Not in any significant way, since everyone is getting richer* Not necessarily*
Bureaucrat	They might,* if not properly run by state organs	They might,* if not properly run by state organs	Maybe,* but often not	Usually *no!**	

NOTE: Italics and exclamation marks indicate the key value for each tendency, the issue that shapes that tendency's overall appraisal of the fairs.
*Indicates agreement between any two tendencies on a given issue.

primarily private transactions, income differentials in the countryside will very likely be widened in the process.

Capitalism

There are three clear positions on the key questions about capitalism and fairs: do fairs cause capitalism to flourish; and, if so, what should be done about it? This three-way split was evident in a series of debates on the nature and role of fairs under socialism which took place among economists and were reported in the press in 1961 and 1962.[59] All participants to the discussion agreed on the necessity for fairs and for state leadership over them. However, at that time a majority took a centrist, bureaucratic view that such markets were "basically [but not fully] socialist"; while two minority opinions flanked that view, a marketeer one from the right and a radical one from the left. The marketeer, rightist perspective saw fairs as completely socialist, "a component part of the socialist market under state direction." In this judgment, the victory in 1956 of socialist transformation produced one single economic structure of socialism in China, whereby capitalism was ipso facto eliminated from the market. Then, on the left, radicals considered fairs to be only remnants of the individual economy, a form of free trading under, but not a part of, the socialist system.

From these basic assessments, marketeer, bureaucrat, and radical took distinct positions on the long-term prospects for this institution under socialism. Marketeers, seeing them as harmless, assumed that fairs would persist even into the communist era. But the radical alternative cried out at the danger they posed of capitalist repercussions, and at most permitted their existence as a "temporary concession." For the bureaucratic middle, free markets would continue during the period of socialist transition, but would disappear along with all other traces of private ownership, with the advent of communism.

In the view of the radicals, rural fairs are a natural outcome of the commodity system, with its exchange by money and its individual production. Because of their association with these practices fairs are tied to profit seeking and, when left to their own course, will inevitably spawn "spontaneous capitalism."[60] Unchecked capitalism, in the radicals' vision,

---

59. These debates were reported in *DGB*, January 20 and July 5, 1961, and January 10 and 19, 1962. Che, p. 18, mentions two views, both of which he terms incorrect, implying the existence of a third, compromise position, which is correct. When fairs were encouraged again in the late 1970s, articles about them contained references to that same inaccurate duality.

60. Articles containing the radical position (either advocating or criticizing it) are in *SCMP*, no. 1465 (1957), p. 4; *DGB*, April 4, 1959, in *SCMP*, no. 2000 (1959), p. 13;

will always be accompanied by cheating with weights and measures, profiteering, adulteration of goods, and price manipulation, as fairgoers seek higher profits. For the rural market, they hold, is an arena of intense class struggle between the bourgeois and proletarian classes, the site of a two-road struggle in which one party must vanquish the other. Calling these fairs a part of the socialist system will only blind policy makers to their pitfalls; policy makers will then fail to manage them properly; and this in turn will allow speculative activity to occur in them. At their most extreme, radicals at times have maintained that state commerce and planning ought to replace these questionable marts altogether.

Marketeers, of course, take a far more sanguine view. According to a Red Guard quotation from Liu Shaoqi, for example, that leader once proclaimed: "The free market must be used for directing us in gaining diversity and flexibility."[61] Marketeers agree with radicals that the fairs are the offshoot of small-scale commodity production; but they claim that they are older than capitalism and different in nature from it. Following Marx, they define the activity in these fairs as a type of simple commodity-exchange performed for the sake of consumption (use value), and not to amass profit (value or surplus value).

Marketeers find other similar arguments for their theoretical justification of free marketing under socialism. For instance, they maintain that state ownership, state management, and planning of the bulk of China's economic activity are the environment in which the fairs exist. Consequently, capitalism (and its concomitants, exploitation and speculation) can be held in check in the larger theater of the economy as a whole, while the backdrop of state direction—through education, regulation, and controls—protects fairs from the intrusion of capitalistic practices. Marketeers also allege that most of the participants are ordinary commune members (90 percent, according to one reckoning);

RMRB, November 21, 1959, in *SCMP*, no. 2157 (1959), p. 18; *RMRB*, May 18, 1954, editorial; *RMRB*, January 27, 1957, editorial, in *SCMP*, no. 1467 (1957), p. 4; Che, pp. 20, 22–23; *DGB*, January 13, 1961, in *SCMP*, no. 2445 (1961), p. 2; *DGB*, October 18, 1961, in *SCMP*, no. 2614 (1961), p. 17; *DGB*, October 24, 1962, in *SCMP*, no. 2863 (1962), pp. 8–10; *DGB*, December 5, 1964, in *SCMP*, no. 3367 (1964), p. 6; *Survey of the People's Republic of China Press (SPRCP)*, no. 6130 (1976), p. 61; *SCMM*, no. 536 (1966), pp. 22–23; *GMRB*, February 1, 1969, in *SCMP*, no. 4363 (1969), pp. 5–6; *Selections from People's Republic of China Magazines (SPRCM)*, no. 831 (1975), pp. 39–44; and *ECMM*, no. 136 (1958), p. 28.

61. *GMRB*, February 1, 1969, in *SCMP*, no. 4363 (1969), p. 5. For articles containing the marketeer's position, see *RMRB*, November 16, 1977, and January 31, 1978, p. 3; *GMRB*, September 16, 1978, in *FBIS*, September 29, 1978, p. E8; and *RMRB*, May 2, 1980, p. 3.

Bargaining over garlic. Free market, May 1983, Wuhan.

while the major part of commodities traded (perhaps as much as 80 percent) are of the third category, with the main products falling under the system of unified purchase by the state, at planned prices.[62] Thus even marketeers (at least after 1956) insist on a certain degree of state involvement in the running of free markets.

A last aspect of the marketeer position holds that China's experience with fairs has revealed that closing markets, not opening them, breeds shortages, which then foster speculation, profiteering, hoarding, black markets, and ultimately capitalism. Thus, in the marketeer's philosophy, fairs should be permitted, a prescription based in part on a perception that they prevent rather than cause capitalism.

The bureaucratic position emphasizes managerial issues in running the fairs, which its adherents are willing to allow only under tight state supervision. For example, they point to such problems associated with free trading as the shortages that occur when demand surpasses supply, shortages which then result in fair prices higher than the state's; and

62. *DGB*, August 24, 1959, in *SCMP*, no. 2100 (1959), p. 23; *DGB*, January 21, 1961, in *SCMP*, no. 2449 (1961), p. 4; *GMRB*, May 22, 1961, in *SCMP*, no. 2524 (1961), pp. 6–7; *SCMP*, no. 1465 (1957), pp. 2–3; *SCMP*, no. 1465 (1957), p. 4; *FBIS*, April 28, 1978, p. E15; *ECMM*, no. 66 (1957), p. 24; and *ECMM*, no. 77 (1957), pp. 14–15.

they call attention to large interdistrict and seasonal differentials that skew fair activity toward speculation in the absence of state guidance. They demand that state trade organs and state-set production and pricing policies be arranged to handle and overcome these difficulties. Thus, in accord with the typical orientation of the bureaucrat, the remedy here is more activity in goods procurement by state offices; restrictions on the free movement of fair prices, with penalties for lawbreaking; and the reduction by fiat of regional price differentials; or, alternatively, the permitting of fairs only at times when supply already meets demand. In short, bureaucrats criticize both what they see as the "overreliance" on fairs and consequent relaxation of leadership of the marketeer, and the "underestimation" of their value, overcontrol, and abolition practiced by radicals.[63]

Thus, radicals, who find fairs ideologically abhorrent, take a hardline stance against them, believing they invariably bode evil and produce capitalism; marketeers, hoping to see them bring the benefits of plenty, leniently look on their brighter side, and build a doctrinal case to deny or play down their capitalistic elements. For the bureaucrats the issue is mainly operational, as they try to compete with and dominate the fairs.

Do fairs "cause capitalism"? Plainly, at least in their initial stages, they do create price increases, which permit those with more means to take advantage of opportunities for profit making. This profit seeking that radicals decry should not in itself, however, be more detrimental to overall livelihood than doing without marketing altogether. Still, for China, the bureaucratic alternative may hit the best balance, in its correction to the marketeer type of commercial free-for-all that characterized pre-1949 society, with its great disparities of wealth and its periodic starvation. For the bureaucratic solution subsumes not simply controls for their own sake, but also state-subsidized prices, efforts at redistribution, and limits on differentials—policies that have improved health and nutrition across the board over three decades.

Inflation

Here again there are two central issues: do fairs cause inflation, and, if so, should this effect be allowed to run its natural course? All parties to the debate do agree that "capitalistic" practices are most likely to occur when the differentials in prices between those set by the state and those obtaining in the fairs are large, a situation that occurs especially under condi-

63. Articles containing the bureaucrats' position are in *DGB*, September 26, 1962; *DGB*, April 4, 1959, in *SCMP*, no. 2000 (1959), p. 16; Xue Muqiao, "The Law of Value and Our Price Policy," *HQ*, nos. 7,8 (1963), p. 7; and *SCMP*, no. 1599 (1957), p. 17.

tions of scarcity. For since fairs operate on the basis of the law of supply and demand, they present a possibility for profit taking, as traders move goods between regions of scarcity and plenty, stock up seasonally specific varieties, and buy at artificially low state-purchase prices in order to sell on the free market. This chance for gain is capitalism to Chinese socialists, but there are three interpretations of what to do about it. As one bureaucratically inclined commentator put it in 1962, "We can neither enforce official prices [in the fairs] [a radical position] nor let prices rise and fall spontaneously [the pure marketeer approach]."[64]

Marketeers oppose prices too rigidly set or too low; these, they say, either will discourage the peasantry from producing and selling, or will induce them to take their goods to the black market to sell.[65] If purchase prices float freely and rise too high, however, complain the bureaucrats, the state's efforts to purchase will suffer, as "certain peasants will throw into the fairs goods they ought to sell and deliver to the state."[66] And the concern of radicals is that no changes at all should be allowed in prices, since such changes give speculators an opportunity and therefore aid the growth of the spontaneous tendency toward capitalism.[67]

Chinese statistics offer little help in determining whether or not fairs inevitably fan up inflation, or whether they fail or succeed to bring prices down again after a time. Generally, journalists choose random data to support their political positions, instead of adducing facts in a systematic manner.

For example, when fairs were soon to be shut down in 1957, the press was full of tales of profiteering, as if to prove that free markets always send all prices shooting upward. The effort in the papers then was to alarm their readers with tales designed to make this point. Thus, while low state-purchase prices made it impossible for those working in state aquatic-products stalls in Shanghai to purchase any fish at all, small-scale mobile peddlers procured a great deal at high rates, which they went on to sell at more than twice the usual market price. If this was indeed the case, consumers with little means must have had to forego the taste of fish. In Beijing peasants entering the city from the suburbs brought in peanuts, which they roasted in some forty or fifty large pots just outside a city gate. They then divided these among several hundred peasants, who set up stalls in the city, where they sold the nuts at some four times the highest state sales price. In Guangdong, the price of non-

64. *DGB*, April 9, 1962, editorial, in *SCMP*, no. 2732 (1962), p. 24.
65. *DGB*, May 12, 1961, p. 3.
66. *SCMM*, no. 372 (1963), p. 10.
67. Ibid.

staple foodstuffs reportedly "rose steadily" between January and May 1957 over the same period in 1956.[68] These stories report on climbing prices months after state policy had first sanctioned fairs.

On the other hand, beginning in 1978, when the leadership line was one of promoting free fair exchange, official press accounts repeatedly told of falling prices. In Sichuan, where liberalization of the economy was pioneered, the encouragement that fairs gave to both collective and private sideline production allegedly brought prices in rural markets down 10–50 percent by late 1978;[69] and in neighboring Guizhou, prices in the fairs in the first half of 1979 fell to 20 percent below those of the same period a year earlier.[70] Nationally, the level of prices in fairs in 1979 fell 1.5 percent as against 1978; at the end of June 1980, prices averaged 5 percent lower than they had been a year earlier, according to official accounts.[71]

Unofficial sources, however, tell a different story. Rather than emphasizing the fall in fair prices after the barren days of the radical Gang of Four, who had practically closed down the markets, such sources compare contemporaneous fair prices with those set by the state. One report from Hong Kong of September 1978 claimed that at that time prices on the free market were from one to five times as high as those set by the state for a range of goods.[72] Although the fairs had not been opened long when that account was written, informants from Guangdong province a year later commented that while prices had dropped since the lenient policies of the post-Gang era were first instituted, they were still running about one and a half times the state prices (probably in part because of state subsidies, in part from the higher quality of what reached the free markets). Under the Gang's reign, though, they reported, when most trading in fairs was banned as illegal, prices were three and four times the official rates.[73]

Although it appears undeniable that fair prices do stay higher than state-set ones even after fairs have been operating for a few years, the

68. *DGB*, April 14, May 23, and June 4, 1957. The Beijing example is from November 22, 1956, also in *DGB*. City officials in Beijing (and a few other places) obviously found fairs offensive earlier than the central government did. See below on Beijing's treatment of fairs in 1957.

69. *Translations on the P.R.C.*, no. 470, in U.S. *Joint Publications Research Service (JPRS)*, no. 72321, November 28, 1978.

70. *FBIS*, June 14, 1979, p. Q2.

71. *RMRB*, March 10, 1980, p. 2; *BR*, 23, no. 32 (1980): 5.

72. Huang Zhongfang, "The Market Situation on the Mainland," *GCJ*, no. 9 (1978), pp. 15–18.

73. Interviews in Hong Kong on October 22 and November 29, 1979.

question remains whether the benefits they offer—more goods of better quality and extra income for those who sell—might not offset this problem. Radicals say no, marketeers say of course, and bureaucrats try to tolerate the elevation in prices, at least for a time. Most crucial in assessing the effect of fairs on welfare, however, is whether the higher prices and hoarding that come in their wake put necessities beyond the reach of the poor; or whether, in inducing more output, they will ultimately mean cheaper food at least somewhat equitably distributed. This query with its long-term implications cannot be definitively addressed at this time.

Productivity and circulation

Since the bond between fairs, inflation, and "capitalistic tendencies" is tightest in times of scarcity, it is crucial to determine whether the presence of fairs provides a significant incentive to induce peasants to increase their productivity substantially and to bring this extra produce to market. In the People's Republic, disagreement on this issue revolves around two, not three, competing positions.

Marketeers insist that, indeed, the existence of free markets does create such an incentive—to grow more, and to trade one's surplus goods. For, they reason, when fairs abound, "those who produce more will retain more and have more to sell." In mid-1959, a writer who wished to promote the fairs reported a most spectacular instance of this phenomenon in Poning county, Guangdong. At that time commune members managed to raise nine thousand chickens in only ten days, once a market was opened.[74] Proponents of fairs also note that when certain small, sundry items are left unpurchased by official trading organs, or when the state offers unreasonably low purchase prices for them, their output drops, unless fairs exist.

Moreover, they hold, closing down fairs wastes and scatters labor power, since people must then travel longer distances to market, and so spend more time finding daily necessities, which subtracts hours from productive activity.[75] Fairs also induce more and different goods to come onto the market, and raise the circulation volume, as statistics garnered in times of fair activity have shown.[76] The new products have

74. *SCMP*, no. 2055 (1959), p. 19.

75. Articles with these arguments are in *DGB*, March 27, 1961, in *SCMP*, no. 2483 (1961), pp. 4–8; *RMRB*, January 27, 1957, editorial, in *SCMP*, no. 1467 (1957), pp. 4–6; *RMRB*, June 13, 1978, p. 2; and *GMRB*, September 16, 1978, in *FBIS*, September 29, 1978, pp. E7–9.

76. E.g., with respect to productivity, in Tianjin the number of subsidiary foods produced increased from 81 to 107 when fairs were opened just after the Great Leap Forward (*SCMP*, no. 2483 [1961], p. 4); in Hochien county, Hebei, more than two times the amount

ranged from crucial goods like eggs and bean products to local specialties and luxury items, such as cane and bamboo products, grass shoes,
herbs, shrimp, duck, and dogmeat.[77]

Arguments that fairs actually lower total productivity contain shades
of both bureaucratic and radical styles of reasoning.[78] The bureaucratic
outlook marks the thinking of "some people [who] ask" this question:
"'Since planned purchasing and marketing can also stimulate production, why are fairs necessary?'" The reporter of one story from 1969
complained that, because the SMC had failed to organize procurement
(but not because of the lack of fairs, also a feature of that period), the
yearly output of grass mats fell in a Guangdong commune.

Bureaucrats, believing that the state procurement system is more
efficient in processing needs than are fairs, have also attacked fairs on
these grounds. In one case in 1956, for example, vegetable-company
cadres left prices entirely to the vicissitudes of the free market, no longer
listing state prices or guiding peasants to plan which vegetables to bring
to market. According to the commentator, the effect was that the quantities on the market were totally inappropriate. This situation induced
petty merchants to take advantage, as they bought cheaply and sold
dear. When the peasantry lost money as a result, producer co-ops

---

of handicraft and other sideline items were produced with the opening of fairs there then
(SCMP, no. 2059 [1959], pp. 11–12); and in another Guangdong commune, 29 percent
more pigs were produced collectively and 32 percent more privately in 1961 than in 1960,
once fairs were operating actively (DGB, March 8, 1962, p. 2). As for goods marketed, the
press claimed, for example, that in a Shandong zhen the number of goods on the market
rose from 38 to 55 with the opening of fairs in 1956 (DGB, May 23, 1957); in a Guangxi
county, four and a half times more products were brought to markets in 1959 than during
the Leap (SCMP, no. 2100 [1959], p. 21); in a Sichuan district in 1961, there was an increase of more than eight times the number of goods on sale than there had been in 1960
(SCMP, no. 2695 [1962], p. 20); and at the Tianjiao Bazaar in Beijing, the volume of
vegetable supply was 200 to 300 percent more than in the past, as of late 1956 (SCMP, no.
1465 [1956], pp. 23–24). Most recently, BR, 23, no. 32 (1980): 5, states that in the first
half of 1980 the number of commodities on sale in urban fairs across the country increased
from 50 to 200. And, with regard to circulation volume, RMRB, March 12, 1979, noted
that in the fourth season of 1978 there was an increase of 30 percent nationally over the
same period in the previous year; this growth continued into 1980, during the third quarter of which, in 70 markets, the total volume of transactions increased 40 percent over the
same period in 1979. Nicholas Lardy, in "Economic Reform in China: Retrospect and
Prospect," Paper prepared for the Luce Seminar in American-Asian Cultural Relations,
University of Chicago, May 30–31, 1980 (draft), reports on p. 20 that the volume of sales
in 1979 was 17 billion yuan, an increase of more than 30 percent over 1978.

77. DGB, October 9, 1956, and GMRB, November 10, 1979.

78. Bureaucratic points of view are from DGB, October 24, 1956; DGB, March 27,
1961, in SCMP, no. 2483 (1961), p. 5; and RMRB, September 18, 1969, in SCMP, no.
4504 (1969), p. 4.

stopped planting certain vegetables altogether. One moral drawn here was that free markets can actually lead to a decrease in supply.

Radical critics agree with bureaucrats, but come at the problem from a different angle. In their eyes, even if fairs induce individuals to produce more goods, collective production suffers during their heyday.[79] Often in times of fair activity one reads charges in the press about peasants who "abandon agriculture for commerce," a proclivity treated by radicals as tantamount to being criminal.[80] The radical press of 1956–1957 in particular reported that where fair regulation was too lax, peasants doing business (and so neglecting farming) accounted for some 60 percent of the merchants in certain localities.

Producer cooperatives (APCs) of that time were busy setting up hotels and beauty parlors in the market towns; joining up with small peddlers in order to use the peddlers' certificates to buy goods from state companies at wholesale prices in the markets; and sending men to buy livestock, hog bristles, and thread from remote localities, or to peddle loganberries and quilts, in the name of "sideline activities." At times the APC members' attendance rates in the fields dropped to 40 percent. In a period of drought in Guangdong, instead of organizing APC members to fight the disaster, some co-ops transferred large numbers of peasants to earn cash through trade. Those who wished to detract from the fairs presented such evidence to prove that this business not only meant a decline in output, but endangered the consolidation of the APC, thereby harming the creation of socialism in China.

If the marketeers' data on sales transactions are combined with the bureaucrats' anecdotes of misfired output quantities and radical tales of abandoned fields, one can conclude that fairs, while enhancing total output and circulation volume, at the same time probably reduce the percentage of produce that can be collectively allocated and redistrib-

---

79. Che, p. 21.

80. Tales of peasants abandoning agriculture for commerce, and of agricultural producer co-ops going into business, were rife in 1956–1957. Examples are in *RMRB*, November 22, 1956, in *SCMP*, no. 1428 (1956), pp. 17–20; *DGB*, November 9 and 14, 1956; *DGB*, December 1, 1956, editorial, in *SCMP*, no. 1447 (1956), pp. 13–16; and *ECMM*, nos. 77 (1957), pp. 14–20, and 84 (1957), pp. 29–30, and 136 (1958), pp. 27–33. Although economic practices of the early and mid-1960s were heavily attacked in the Cultural Revolution, the data on abandoning agriculture found in the Lianjiang documents from that period are far from damning on this score. See *Rural People's Communes in Lien-chiang: Documents Concerning Communes in Lien-chiang County, Fukien Province, 1962–1963*, compiled by C. S. Chen and translated by Charles Price Ridley, pp. 180–81, 184, and 191–92. The documents list, variously, 16 of 224 people in one brigade, or 14 percent; one cadre of 55 brigade and team leaders; 5 of 14 leading brigade cadres; and 2 people from a total of 153 households, who had left agriculture to trade.

uted by the state. This point is underlined in one radical's lament from early 1957: "Even when some cooperatives or members have made some money or temporarily showed some profit, it can by no means offset the loss the cooperatives have sustained."[81]

State purchase, plan fulfillment

The question of whether state purchase and plan fulfillment benefit or suffer from fair activity is connected to this issue of competition between collective and individual production. For it is obviously simpler and more efficient for state purchasing agencies to deal with collective production units than to try to obtain surpluses on a household-by-household basis. Thus, where collectives control output, state procurement must be more nearly assured. Besides, allowing fairs to run is necessarily linked to a policy of allowing more produce to be left in private hands, which is then disposed of at individual (or household) discretion. Under these conditions it seems that it would be difficult for state trade organs to obtain the same proportion of output that they can in the absence of fairs.[82]

Radical, marketeer, and bureaucrat clash again over how each sees the effects that fairs have on state procurement efforts; and they each offer different ways of coping with this issue. Radicals view fairs and state purchasing organs as directly competitive, holding distinctly antagonistic interests, even unable to coexist. In one exemplary article from 1957 written from the radical viewpoint, the writer noted that the Harbin municipal food-products company was able to complete only 24.7 percent of its purchase plan in the first half of 1957 while free markets were in full swing.[83] It is radicals who stress the lure of private profits in producing such an outcome.[84] Both the Great Leap Forward, when fairs were banned altogether, and the Cultural Revolution decade (1966–1976) when their activity was greatly diminished, were products of this radical perspective.

Bureaucrats focus their concerns on the state's loss of command over key commodities, as peasants and collective units choose to fetch the

81. *ECMM*, no. 84 (1957), p. 29.

82. Indications of this problem appeared in the press in late 1981. To cite one instance, on November 26, 1981, *RMRB* carried a report on p. 1 stating that, though the output of many nonstaple agricultural products had increased in Hubei province, there were problems in procuring for the state the amounts of them specified in the plan. Party First Secretary Chen Pixian expressed approval for the policy of economic liberalization, but said that "anarchy" must be overcome and the economy enlivened only under the guidance of the plan. This same Chen figures in accounts about the early 1960s, later in this chapter.

83. *ECMM*, no. 136 (1958), p. 28.

84. *DGB*, August 24, 1959, in *SCMP*, no. 2100 (1959), p. 20.

*No shame left in the thriving free markets of
Central China, mid-1983.*

higher purchase prices the free markets usually offer. The problem of
state-controlled goods entering the fairs has cropped up each time fairs
were in fashion, and has invariably provoked a reaction leading to
restrictions. The bureaucrat charges that fairs "have no unified direction
or planning and will produce confusion in the arrangement of markets."
Those of this persuasion take the position that total relaxation of control would make impossible state guidance over basic construction,
industry, and urban dwellers' livelihood; and that it would upset export
plans. And in terms of social consequences, those taking this stance note
that lack of state direction over important commodities would seriously
inhibit the state's ability to allocate in accord with urgency of need. They
point out that it would also hamper the state's chances for adjusting the
disposal of goods among regions, an adjustment that China's backward
technology and gross geographical disparities require.[85]

Bureaucrats, though, instead of abolishing the fairs (which radicals
do), have official trade organs run commodity-exchange meets as a sub-

85. Editorials on p. 1 of *DGB* for November 15, 1956, December 1, 1956, and August
18, 1957; *ECMM*, nos. 136 (1958), p. 29, and 77 (1957), p. 17; and *RMRB*, August 18,
1957, editorial, in *SCMP*, no. 1599 (1957), pp. 14–16.

stitute for fairs, at which contracts are used to draw secondary products into the orbit of the state plan. At one such meet, officials discovered twenty-two commodities (pine oil, cobalt oxide, and bone glue were a few of these) for which a large gap existed between supply and demand. Subsequently, state trade organs held forums to determine the proper direction for future production, while the State Economic Commission planned to allocate raw materials needed in the production of these items. Bureaucrats also require SMCs to exercise economic control over fairs by participating in them and buying up excesses for the state, to be sold out in times of shortage.[86]

The pure marketeer prescription for procurement has been best realized in the fairs that were sanctioned beginning in 1978, after the Cultural Revolution era. Here the strategy has been to let state organs attend fairs as one competitor among others, while the fairs' successes in promoting transactions prompt state organs to improve their own management. Under such an arrangement, fairs are said actually to help the state organize purchases, even if the official state purchasing stalls may be wanting customers.[87] In the first quarter of 1979 the state managed to purchase 20.6 percent more rural products than in the same period the year before, the marketeer-dominated press of 1979 reported.[88]

Thus, the question whether fairs hinder or facilitate state purchase is contingent on the perspective of the observer and the steps taken to manage fairs in light of that perspective. Radicals believe that fairs encourage individual but thwart collective production, and that because of this their very presence necessarily diverts goods from ever reaching state agencies' warehouses. Both the bureaucratic and marketeer solu-

86. *DGB*, December 25, 1961, in *SCMP*, no. 2660 (1961), pp. 18–22. On exchange meets, see *GMRB*, March 13, 1961, in *SCMP*, no. 2476 (1961), p. 5; *SCMP*, no. 2059 (1959), pp. 9–10; *RMRB*, November 24, 1959, in *SCMP*, no. 2157 (1959), pp. 19–23; *SCMP*, no. 2234 (1960), pp. 26–30; and *DGB*, May 7, 1959, p. 3. *DGB*, June 19, 1963, notes that in the first five months of 1963, 23 percent more in value was purchased by the SMCs than in the same period the year before. *HQ*, no. 7 (1976), on trade in a Gansu county notes with approval that the total volume of state purchases was 59.9 percent greater in 1975 than in 1973.

87. *RMRB*, March 28, 1979, states the official case; Geng Fu (n. 29 above), pp. 24–25, speaks of empty state purchasing stalls.

88. *RMRB*, May 19, 1979. Such comparative statistics always cite improvements over the previous year in terms of value of purchase, but not in terms of relative proportion of output. Nicholas Lardy, in "Chinese Agricultural Development Policy," prepared for the Tenth Sino-American Conference on Mainland China, University of California, Berkeley, June 16–18, 1981, notes on pp. 14–15 that "because of the continuing gap between official and free market prices, the share of cereal output procured by the state has not increased perceptibly since 1977 despite higher prices and greater inducements to market via state channels, such as the increase in overquota prices and the introduction of the still higher negotiated price category." Also, "Procurement in 1979 and 1980, when the new

tions, however, make possible the coexistence of fairs and successful state purchase, by requiring that state organs try either to regulate or to compete in the markets.[89] A synthesis of these views would be that output increases with fairs, but the percentage of that output which goes to the state may decline over time.

Income and class polarization

At the bottom of all the other disagreements about fairs—over their capitalist tendencies, and over their effect on prices, productivity, and procurement—lies the crucial issue of their effect on income inequality. Especially for the radicals, the basic concern is that some will grow rich or richer, while the masses of less well-off peasants will be taken advantage of, and will fall behind. In radicals' eyes, such an outcome would spell the loss of the fruits of revolution.

A radical statement on this matter from 1975 presents this point of view:

> In the rural areas at present a small number of communes and teams are found to ignore the state plans . . . refrain from selling to the state agricultural and subsidiary products in accordance with state regulations and promote the so-called free trade. . . . Failure to struggle against such capitalist tendencies will increase the actual inequalities in the exchange of commodities and widen the differences among the communes and teams and among commune members. And a few rich peasants who reap fabulous profits . . . will turn into new bourgeois elements.[90]

---

marketing incentives were in place and total output was up substantially, was no greater than in 1977 and 1978." "The failure of state procurement to rise is due to a resurgence in private market sales," he concludes. However, *BR*, 24, no. 39 (1981): 3, has a curious statement which makes the phenomenon Lardy chronicles appear to be deliberate: "The amount of grain to be delivered and sold to the state remains the same as for the years 1971–1975." Lardy, in a private communication, speculated that the state purchase price increase of 50 percent for above-quota sales and the even higher negotiated prices (both instituted in 1979) may be designed to get more grain into state hands, even while the basic quota amounts may not have changed, but that this effort may be failing.

89. In 1961, state organs purchased about 10 percent of the products at fairs, calculated in terms of value. Peasants' exchanges accounted for about 70 percent of the value of the fairs' exchanges (Donnithorne, *China's Economic System*, p. 299; and *DGB*, October 18, 1961, in *SCMP*, no. 2614 [1961], p. 17). Presumably the other 20 percent was accounted for by the transactions of collective units.

90. *SPRCM*, no. 831 (1975), p. 41. Also see *DGB*, May 23, 1957, p. 1, and August 31, 1957; *RMRB*, May 10, 1956, editorial, in *SCMP*, no. 1298 (1956), pp. 2–5; *Xuexi* [Study] *(XX)*, no. 1 (1957), p. 25; and *SPRCP*, no. 6130 (1976), p. 61, for other statements of radical views to this effect.

Writers on the Soviet Union have shown that open marketing during the New Economic Policy of the 1920s did indeed lead to a reemergence of class differentiations within the peasantry of that country, differentiations that had begun to disappear under the previous radical policy of war communism.[91]

Neither bureaucrats nor marketeers would be comfortable with fairs if these truly exacerbated the poverty of lower-income groups. And those supporting each of these positions do find this issue of effect on income one that must be addressed. Bureaucrats have sponsored state-led (not "free") fairs of various sorts, which, they claim, can "take good care of the interests and demands of all peasants taking part in market transactions," by curbing speculation, and by forbidding professional [grain] merchants from participating.[92]

Marketeers take a different tack. They neatly sidestep the issue of polarization in their freer-wheeling marts by stressing the generalized benefits of fairs in raising *overall* income. To make this point—a point that obscures both the (probably most significant) interregional and the intravillage income differentials that may arise from fair activities—they present their data exclusively in terms of increases in the *average* income within given regions during periods of free market trading.[93] Those favoring fairs have also pointed to their ability to help poor peasants dispose of surpluses and to aid those in difficulty by enabling them to earn a bit of extra cash.[94] Western observers have made the point that fairs provide an opportunity for the elderly, through their participation in sideline occupations, to help their families earn some additional money.[95]

Thus the Chinese themselves offer little solid evidence that rural markets either heighten existing inequalities or close them as they bring an enhanced standard of living for all. All told, it is probably the bureaucratic point of view that is least questionable—that when the state inter-

91. For example, see R. W. Campbell, *Soviet Economic Power,* p. 20.

92. *RMRB,* June 9, 1954, editorial, in *SCMP,* no. 829 (1954), p. 10, on the state grain markets that followed on the institution of compulsory state purchase of grain.

93. *DGB,* May 11, 1957, states that in a Hubei special district the average income from sideline production turned out to be 11 yuan more from July through October, once fairs opened, than had been projected for the months from July through December. *DGB,* January 15, 1962, in *SCMP,* no. 2672 (1962), p. 14, says that in a Guangdong commune, "the whole commune's income from sideline occupations has increased considerably." And *RMRB,* May 26, 1979, claims that in one year each person's income increased by over 20 yuan, again on the average, in a Zhejiang district since fairs reopened.

94. *XX,* no. 1 (1957), p. 25, and *Shichang* [Market] *(SC),* no. 12 (March 25, 1980), p. 6.

95. Deborah Davis-Friedmann makes this point in chapter 2 of her book, *Long Lives: Chinese Elderly and the Communist Revolution.* Also see Parish and Whyte, *Village and Family in Contemporary China,* p. 76.

venes in the collection and distribution of goods, it should become more nearly possible (at least theoretically) to serve all interests in a roughly egalitarian fashion. And to the extent that state cadres seriously work to realize this objective, bureaucrats' fairs are tightly linked to their vision of socialism, a system of economy managed through state control.

The discussion above has shown how the proponents of three separate stances join battle in China over a set of issues about the effects of the free market under socialism. In addressing these issues, each tendency has developed a critique that includes an assessment of the situation as well as a method for handling that situation in accord with its own values. Radicals' conclusion, that fairs cause class polarization, grows out of their understanding that fairs always will create inflation and profit seeking, and that they invariably divert individual energies away from production or at least from working for collective goals. For these reasons, radicals have tried to shut fairs down.

Bureaucrats allow fairs to exist, just so long as state trade agencies manage to dominate them. This domination includes monitoring the movement of prices in them and trying to procure a large proportion of the goods offered there, in the hope that those who participate in them can all benefit as a result of such interference. Marketeer ideology insists that the increased productivity that fairs occasion will over time bring down any inflation that accompanies their inception; and that not only can the state purchase more (since there is more output) but the lot of all classes will be improved under their reign.

From the perspective of the analyst, it appears that if productivity responded simply to price, the incentive effect of the fairs could work to fulfill the marketeers' vision—one of plenty leading in time to lowered and stable prices in the free markets and a better life for all. But all places, in this largely poor and strikingly diverse country, and all households (with their varying sizes and skills) are far from being equally capable of making this response. Uneven natural—geographical, climatic, soil, locational—and technological conditions throughout China work to create significant interarea and seasonal price differentials. These in turn must sharply skew the experience that individuals and families of differing economic means have in the marketplace. Because of China's level of development, then, radicals' fears of the profiteer are probably often realized; and the state controls preferred by bureaucrats have a definite role in the effort to ensure the achievement of some measure of equity under socialism.

SOCIAL CLEAVAGES

These ideologically based controversies within the political leadership (and among its publicists) over the assessment of fairs reverberate throughout society, as they mirror vital conflicts of material interest among social groups, within the state sector, and between private and public sectors. Through the actual social and political clashes to which they give rise, fairs highlight fundamental issues of distribution and jurisdiction in socialist China. Fairs also illustrate once again the tendency for state ownership and planning to create its own pattern of competition in the market, this time with respect to the products of the countryside.

The competition that turns trading partners into rivals in China grows out of the antagonistic interests of several sorts of actors. Among social groups, the concerns of petty merchants, of the majority of the peasantry, and of city dwellers all diverge in the marketplace. Participation in fairs means quite separate things to those in different social classes and in different regions of the country. Within the state sector, competition pits those working at various governmental levels, in disparate types of organs, and in separate geographical units one against the next. Then, in public-versus-private controversies, state wholesaling companies have become embroiled in disputes with merchants and with peasants, and freely trading peasants have had to contend with state market-management cadres, in both city and countryside.

Social groups

The press of the mid-1950s is particularly rich in stories of conflict between the small professional peddler and the ordinary peasant who is trying to market his or her own produce. Such stories may be instructive in the early 1980s, as policies of economic liberalization again permitted private merchants to practice their craft.

In one case, after the local branch of the state vegetable company paid too little heed to newly opened markets in Xinhui county, Guangdong, merchants took advantage of this lapse in leadership and forced prices down even below the purchase prices the state company had offered. The disgruntled peasantry refused to sell their wares, and instead carted them home to feed the fish or to use as fertilizer. They then went on to cut the sprouts in the ground, and planted yams, which require less care, in their place.[96] In Hubei, peasants entering the cities to sell in the hope of fetching a good price were tricked by merchants bent on engaging in

96. *DGB*, October 28, 1956. A similar tale is in *DGB*, January 21, 1957.

speculation, and by unemployed vagrants trying their luck at trade. These merchants bought the goods at lower prices in the center of town than the peasants could have commanded from ordinary customers in their local markets had they stayed in the suburbs.[97] Presumably, once having transported their products into town, the peasants were compelled to sell them at any price before they spoiled. These stories suggest that the milieu of the marketplace spawns merchants whose financial means and sharp practices can put ordinary peasants at a disadvantage.

Class differences within the ranks of the peasantry may mean they achieve differential outcomes in the market (for instance, some are no doubt better equipped economically to deal with wily merchants). Still, producers as a whole prefer the opportunity to receive the higher purchase prices that fairs generally afford and dislike the typically lower prices that state companies give them. City dwellers, however, while appreciating the better quality, greater quantity, and more copious mix of goods on the markets, have complained at times about the higher prices they must pay there.[98]

But peasants are not always pleased by fairs, nor do city people invariably allow higher prices to dampen their enthusiasm. For urban workers living near fairs have been said to express displeasure when markets are shut down. And the peasantry have often been frightened in China by radicals' propaganda and confiscations of goods bound for market, as they worry that they will later be labeled capitalists if they take part in trading.[99] A description of rural Guangdong from 1956 tells how some peasants felt they had to engage in their business secretly, even after the fairs were officially opened. These people did not dare to admit to the cadres that they were going to the fairs to make sales. Instead, they lied that they were bringing the goods in their arms to market for others, or that these items were gifts for friends or relatives. And some peasants even refused to go to market at all.[100]

Not surprisingly, fairs affect different classes of the peasantry differentially. At first glance, it is difficult to reconcile radical critiques that

97. *DGB*, December 4, 1956.
98. *DGB*, May 20 and June 4, 1957, make these points. In general, city folk seem willing to pay the higher prices to get better produce, at least to the extent of their financial ability.
99. *GMRB*, September 30, 1978, in *FBIS*, October 13, 1978, p. E20, on workers' views; *DGB*, November 9, 1956, and *DGB*, April 17, 1961, in *SCMP*, no. 2499 (1961), p. 7, on peasants'. A report from a Hong Kong journal from late 1979 claims that by that time, though cadres had lingering doubts about fairs, "the peasants are very happy" to see them reopened (Ming Zhu, "A Glance at Rural Fairs in Guangdong," *DXF*, no. 11 [1979], pp. 32–33).
100. *SCMP*, no. 1428 (1956), p. 18.

fairs represent the interests of the bourgeoisie and the rich peasants, on the one hand, with the marketeer assertion that "the masses like fairs."[101] But in fact there is something to the radical judgment; although one may not agree with radicals that fairs should be banned, there does seem to be a richer echelon that benefits more than others do on the free market. An instructive analysis in a Hong Kong journal sheds some light on this:

> The free market is opened for everyone, but the poor come only to buy sweet potatoes to fill their hunger . . . while ordinary people come to buy vegetables, or three to five yuan per *jin* of pork, beef, fish, or shrimp when the state markets are short on goods.

> Peasants selling their rationed grain and oil there are not rich. . . . The majority of them are eating gruel and yams as much as possible, saving their grain to exchange at the fairs for cash, to use for weddings, building houses, times of illness.

Another report told of a poor peasant who sold his rice ration to get a little money to buy salt.[102] These accounts suggest that even if open markets benefit many, they do so while highlighting already existing social cleavages.

Other kinds of differentiation are regionally based. An investigation of several villages in Guangdong province, where many residents have overseas relatives, revealed a proliferation of black markets containing luxury goods in summer 1976. The observer concluded that, because of remittances from their families abroad, a large number of people in this region can afford to pay high black-market prices. Also, the gifts these people receive from visiting relations—tape recorders, jewelry, foreign cigarettes—flow into the free market at exorbitant prices when their recipients need extra cash.[103]

Another type of regional variation derives from the fact that some parts of China are far poorer than others. For example, it is reported that there is no meat in most markets of Guizhou and Yunnan provinces, or in the mountainous areas of Guangdong and Fujian. A vivid illustration of this poverty is a fair frequented mainly by minority nationalities on the outskirts of Guilin City in southwestern Guangxi province. Here

101. *SPRCP*, no. 6130 (1976), p. 61; *GMRB*, November 6, 1970 (this second citation is an attack on the pro-fair policy of Liu Shaoqi), for the radical view; *RMRB*, May 2, 1980, p. 3, for the marketeer position.

102. Huang, "Market Situation" (n. 72 above), p. 16.

103. Elena S. H. Yu, "Overseas Remittances in Southeastern China," pp. 343–46.

thin folk, garbed in clothes with patches over patches and nibbling on bits (of food or herbs?), sell only withered vegetables, herbs, sugarcane, tobacco, and timber, but no meat, eggs, or fish. In the same week and in similar climes, markets on the city streets of Guangzhou (Canton) and Changsha brimmed with lush green vegetables of many varieties, and with several sorts of protein-rich foods.[104]

Under certain conditions, then, markets may align professional peddler against peasant and city dweller against producer. And they offer significantly dissimilar opportunities for different classes of patrons and in different parts of the country. Thus the statement "the masses like fairs," while generally true, covers a range of experiences.

The state sector

Within the state sector, the opening of fairs has usually awakened numerous fears in the hearts of lower-level cadres. Generally speaking, commercial-sector cadres worry about procuring goods for the state when peasants may take their produce to the fairs for higher prices; about meeting their sales targets for the products in which they deal; about inflation in the markets for whose price stability they are responsible; and about an increase in their work load, as they are charged with managing these marts.

Cadres in the agricultural production sector are concerned that fairs will scatter the labor force and so interfere with the filling of production quotas. Those cadres in charge of production co-ops in the mid-1950s opposed free markets, since their presence lured peasants away from membership in the co-op altogether.[105] In short, those whose careers are tied to plan completion and local economic order have always been wary of "spontaneous capitalism" from their own practical, if not ideological, motives. For, as one press article described them, such cadres "rely on control for their livelihood" (*kao tong chi fan*).

Workers in other state departments are less hostile to fairs than are the basic-level cadres in purchasing and production units, and they may support them. For example, in a district in Beijing, managers of a state retail department, a state-run retail shop, a state-managed rice market, and a joint public-private vegetable shop all lamented the shutting down

104. Huang, "Market Situation," p. 16, and observations by the author in Guilin, Canton, and Changsha, November 1979.
105. See Perkins, *Agricultural Development,* pp. 93, 165; and *DGB,* October 9 and 28, 1958; *DGB,* May 20, 1957; and February 18, 1961, in *SCMP,* no. 2476 (1961), p. 1; *DGB,* April 17, 1961, in *SCMP,* no. 2499 (1961), p. 7; *DGB,* November 18, 1961; and *RMRB,* June 13, 1978, p. 2.

of that city's vegetable markets in May 1957, because they all found it easier to get stocks from the small merchants than from state companies. Also, they preferred the better quality of the produce that higher prices on the free markets attracted.[106]

Another sort of conflict within the bureaucracy has been one between cadres at the very lowest levels and those situated above them. In one account, lower-level cadres were said to feel that their flexibility was restricted whenever markets opened, as they had to continue to fulfill a plan issued from above, written in terms of volume of turnover. But as peddlers and peasants cornered the market in popular goods, basic-level state commercial workers could no longer use these "hot items" to force buyers to purchase slow-moving products by coupling them with the "hot items" in making sales.[107] Here the split was one between higher-echelon officials, content to see additional sales activity going on which perhaps would stimulate output and in turn more sales, and those at the grass roots who were worried about the loss of their ability to monopolize the market.

Additionally, when local trade was taxed in the fairs of the early 1960s, tax-organ cadres probably found the fairs to be a welcome source of revenue.[108] And a last category of cadre appreciative of free markets consists of those who participate in them. Such individuals have been known to sell off their goods a bit more cheaply than others doing business. For, in the fear of being observed in action by a fellow worker, who would certainly subject them to heavy criticism, they conclude their transactions in haste. Cadres who are customers at the black markets, even including those placed in charge of enforcing laws against them, are reportedly loathe to close them down.[109]

Fairs also complicate interregional relations, since they have always coexisted in China with sales and purchase plans designed for implementation by (and within) localities. In every era of free marketing, there have been cases of local cadres complaining of the outflow of commodities to other areas where prices are higher, since this affects the fulfillment of their own purchase task. In a recent case, officials in Guangxi province chose to ration pork, rather than permit sellers from neighboring Hunan to bring in cheap fresh meat.[110] In this episode,

106. *DGB*, May 20, 1957.
107. *DGB*, May 11, 1957.
108. Donnithorne, *Economic System*, p. 377.
109. Huang, "Market Situation," p. 16.
110. *SC*, no. 27 (November 10, 1980), p. 1. See also *DGB*, May 23, 1957, p. 1; and January 15, 1962, in *SCMP*, no. 2672 (1962), p. 10.

Guangxi officials probably worried about meeting their own sales targets, and about finding a market for home-grown products if the local people spent too much of their cash on Hunan's meat.

Each sort of cadre then, whether purchasing agent, brigade leader, shop manager, tax official, or regional representative, interprets the worth of the fairs in terms of the yield to his own unit's interest. And it is socialist institutions and practices—specifically, planned quotas and geographically delimited areas for legitimate exchange—that structure this form of competition.

Public versus private traders

A final kind of contention centered around fairs is between the public and private sectors. In the fairs of the mid-1950s, when peddlers had relatively more free rein than they did later, state companies saw these individuals as their main competitors for goods. As one account put it, cadres thought that "once the markets were open, hot items will be snatched up by the merchants and peddlers, and cold items will pile up in the [state's] warehouses." Because of this problem, they favored first putting on the free market products hard to sell or those causing them to lose money.[111]

This tension over getting control of commodities in demand has often led commercial cadres to impose restrictions on the merchants.[112] Two and a half decades later state fruit and noodle shops found not their goods but their business stolen by fairs. Since the fairs operate through direct dealings between producer and consumer, trade there does not involve multiple transfers of goods among bureaucratic offices. One result is that prices of some items in the fairs may be lower than in state shops, as transport costs and losses from spoilage can be avoided.[113]

Disputes have developed over prices between state company representatives and the peasantry. In one instance in 1957, the management of a Tianjin vegetable company decided to release all control over prices, hoping thus to please the peasants. But free market prices shot upward as a result, and the producers stopped trying to fulfill the terms of sales contracts signed earlier with the companies.[114] It is out of a concern over such problems that state commercial cadres have lobbied their local Party financial committees for increases in state pro-

111. *DGB*, November 13, 1956.
112. *DGB*, October 28, 1956; April 14, 1957, and May 11, 1957. See Wädekin, pp. 137–38, for a discussion of the same phenomenon in the Soviet Union in the mid-1960s.
113. *SC*, no. 22 (July 25, 1980), p. 6.
114. *DGB*, June 4, 1957.

curement prices for the goods in which they deal, in order to win goods away from the free markets.[115]

Commercial management personnel have tried in various ways to intervene in free-market activity, with uneven success. In one colorful episode in early 1957, peasants from various parts of Hunan were transporting hogs to the Jiangxi border in droves, since prices were far better there. When Hunan cadres tried to interfere, peasants ganged up with clubs in their hands and the cadres hastily backed off.[116]

More recently, in Yuncheng prefecture, Shanxi, once the national newspapers and magazines began to print reports approving fairs in 1978, more and more people started to attend them. These people ignored the propaganda conducted by local industrial and commercial departments on the "benefits" of closing trade fairs, and they refused at first to respond to the cadres' persuasion that they depart. Finally, the state management cadres found they could only disperse the traders by using force.[117]

In the cities, pressure against peasant traders has been more effective, perhaps because here the peasants operate in alien territory, cut off from kin and local ties. In mid-1980 a peasant woman in Hebei journeyed to the city, where she tried to sell eggs from a small basket, but was fined two yuan, which was more than the worth of her wares. In Tianjin, a market-management cadre forced a peasant to pay both a "management fee" (*guanli fei*) and a tax on a sofa even before he sold it. When the peasant complained, the official ordered, "Go away if you won't pay."

In many cities, several different departments—including urban construction, public security, transportation, and environment and sanitation—each took a cut from private sales transactions, as they collected monthly management fees from peddlers for using the streets. These fees sometimes cost a peddler as much as ten yuan a month.[118] In this situation, cadres in these urban departments resent the fairs, because their presence in the cities complicates the cadres' work; but at the same time they are also quick to grab the opportunity for squeeze that fining the fairs' patrons affords.

Free markets illuminate distinctions between class and region, and sharpen conflicts of authority within Chinese society. The principal

115. Bennett, "Activists and Professionals," p. 100.

116. *RMRB,* January 26, 1957.

117. *GMRB,* August 18, 1978, in *FBIS,* August 31, pp. E10–11, and September 16, 1978, in *FBIS,* September 29, 1978, pp. E7–9.

118. *SC,* nos. 22 (August 25, 1980), p. 2, and 26 (October 25, 1980), p. 2.

cleavages in the private sector, among social groups—merchant and peasant, peasant and worker, peasant and peasant—are related to price, as in any marketplace. But within the state sector and between state and societal groups, contention grows out of competition for the control of goods and from rivalry for a greater volume of business, with each publicly managed unit vying to meet its planned obligation to the state. Thus, in socialist China there is a definite constituency within society for closing fairs, and its principal members are the functionaries who staff certain offices of the bureaucracy.

POLITICAL POWER: CENTRAL AND LOCAL POLITICIANS

Battles about power over free markets—and, of course, over control of the goods traded in them—are joined by politicians in the provinces. The ideological disagreements about the nature of fairs and the social cleavages underlined in them which were described above inform these political conflicts as well. In each era of the free market there has been at least one dramatic publicized case of provincial-level contravention of official central policy.

In the first period, as early as December 1956, a number of provinces had begun to strengthen controls over their local fairs: by specifying clearly which goods could be traded, by setting price ranges within which bargaining must take place, and by urging SMCs to become more involved.[119] A month later, however, the central government was still holding firm to its policy of relaxation: a *People's Daily* editorial in late January 1957 admitted to problems of adulteration and profiteering, but at the same time proclaimed the necessity for fairs, and criticized the error of imposing too rigid control over them. The day before, the same paper chastised some places in Hebei for forbidding trading, and some in Guangdong for confiscating goods not produced by the seller.[120]

But the most arresting step in this epoch was taken by the mayor of Beijing, Peng Zhen. This man had recently received a setback at the September 1956 Eighth Party Congress. There he had been demoted from seventh to tenth place in the leadership lineup. Variously described as a "bully" and a "hard-liner," Peng had already taken the lead in late 1955 in propelling Beijing toward a rapid socialist transformation campaign, as chapter four noted.[121]

119. *DGB*, December 4 (Hubei, Jiangxi), December 7 (Sichuan), and December 12 (Jiangxi), 1956.

120. *RMRB*, January 27, 1957, in *SCMP*, no. 1467, pp. 4–6. See also *RMRB*, January 26, 1957.

121. Roderick MacFarquhar, *The Origins of the Cultural Revolution*, pp. 145, 203, and 280.

Perhaps in an effort to recoup lost standing, but also in keeping with his preference for a firm hand against the private sector, Peng began to curtail his city's free markets in March 1957.[122] At the time the city set up a network of market control committees, strictly banned all speculation by merchants operating without a license, mobilized peddling peasants camped in the city to return home, and organized itinerant peddlers under state markets. Meanwhile, a month later, by contrast, Shanghai reported that its free markets were still "developing normally."[123]

Though Shanghai also had a problem with growing numbers of unorganized merchants, its leadership chose to adopt less drastic measures as a solution: It set down fixed areas for trading, and its market control committees busied themselves with managerial business activities— weighing produce, calculating prices, writing invoices, supplying beds, and establishing state-run warehouses to do business on commission. Beijing's market committees, on the other hand, were punitive bodies: they were charged with investigating the type of goods brought to market, the prices asked, and the work style of the traders, and with meting out penalties for disobedience of rules.

The major showdown, however, came in May.[124] Suddenly, on the twentieth, the key economic newspaper, *Da Gong Bao*, carried a lead article which told readers in large headlines that Beijing had altogether abolished its vegetable markets earlier in the month. A small box accompanying the article clearly bore the information that the central government disagreed with Beijing City on this issue. "The center says don't control the markets," it read; yet the local vegetable companies, under local Party leadership, were compelled to implement the orders laid down by the Beijing Party committee and the city government.

Beijing City's explanation for its act centered around the view that free markets were "not suitable" for the capital. Inflation had resulted, the city leadership claimed, because of outside peasants and unlicensed peddlers flocking into town. Ordinary bureaucratic methods would suffice to supply the city's vegetable needs, local leaders believed: "The vegetables coming from outside could be brought in by [state-managed] vegetable companies or by signing [state-supervised] contracts with outside places." Other suggested solutions were for more local production, better techniques in state-run trade, and more state-operated sales points.

122. *DGB*, March 18, 1957, p. 1. Although Peng's name was not mentioned in the article, as MacFarquhar put it, Peng Zhen was running Beijing from 1951, and "it was not easy to do anything in the capital against his wishes" (p. 204).

123. *DGB*, April 14, 1957.

124. This incident and its aftermath are noted in *DGB*, May 20 and 23, 1957.

Besides openly exposing the provincial-central conflict to the paper's readership, *Da Gong Bao* used three other methods in attempting to demonstrate the wrongheadedness of Beijing City's leaders. First, it published a survey of the views toward this measure held by local producers, consumers, and suppliers, the great majority of whom were shown to be dissatisfied with the long queues, poor quality, and short supplies that followed quickly on the fairs' closing. Then, within a few days the paper published a front-page editorial under the title, "Free Markets Can Be Controlled Well," in which it pointed out several other reasons, besides the fairs, that had led to rising prices.

And third, over the next two weeks it printed reports from three other jurisdictions—a township in Shandong and one in Shanxi, and Tianjin City—in all of which free markets, under appropriate regulation, were successfully promoting production, meeting needs, and leading new products onto the market.[125] The article on Tianjin explicitly applauded the accuracy of the center's policy, and found as many as six different reasons why vegetables cost more in 1957, of which the free market was said to be only a minor one.

Peng won his point soon after in the radicalizing atmosphere that led up to the Great Leap Forward. Three months later, in early August 1957, a severe ruling by the State Council prohibited all private sales of goods that were part of the state's purchase plan, and stipulated that state trade organs must even handle a certain proportion of those commodities that were permitted in the fairs (chickens, ducks, eggs, herbs).[126] Despite this eventual concurrence within the national leadership on closing fairs, it seems that this king of the capital had made his move from the motives of a local bureaucrat, one who wished to enforce order, control over goods, and price stability within his domain, even if the populace there ate less well as a result.

Another episode of regional rebellion in a time of central-level endorsement of fairs came in the early 1960s. Fairs were clearly legalized at a Ministry of Commerce conference and in a State Council directive in mid-1959.[127] The Ninth Plenum of the Eighth Party Central Committee,

125. *DGB*, May 23, p. 1, and June 4, 1957.
126. See *SCMP*, no. 1599 (1957), pp. 12–14, for the State Council regulations, and pp. 14–16 for a *People's Daily* editorial on the decision. Donnithorne, *Economic System*, p. 296, reports that many markets ceased operating after this directive was issued.
127. Donnithorne, p. 297, has a reference to a conference of the Ministry of Commerce of June and July 1959 which proclaimed the "need to restore basic-level rural markets to widen the exchange of commodities and stimulate the growth of production." Also see *SCMP*, no. 2108 (1959), pp. 6–9, for the State Council directive of September on organizing the fairs.

held in January 1961, also approved the policy of activating primary markets; and the "Sixty Articles on Commune Management" of 1961–1962 continued to sanction this institution.[128] Moreover, *Da Gong Bao* ran several pieces reporting on debates over fairs in 1961 and early 1962, in which all parties to the discussion agreed on the objective necessity for fairs, at least for the present.[129] Thus, official policy favored fairs in the early 1960s.

Among the leadership even Chairman Mao, who had not long before initiated the radical Leap, admitted in mid-1959 that "we have to restore the primary market in the rural areas." Within two years, however, Mao seems to have changed his mind, for he wrote then in criticism of the freedom in Soviet collective farm markets, and emphasized the need for a form of state leadership and control over them that would go beyond mere price adjustment.[130] Other leaders, though, including Liu Shaoqi, Zhu De, and Tao Zhu, expressed unrestrained approbation for fairs in these years, both at central Party work conferences and in the provinces, according to materials publicized in the Cultural Revolution.[131]

Perhaps the best documented case of provincial-level contravention of this near central-level consensus on holding fairs appeared in a Red Guard attack on Chen Pixian. Chen was then a Shanghai official who often acted for Ke Qingshi, Shanghai Party Committee's first secretary, when Ke was out of town.[132] Chen had attempted to enforce central policy by permitting free trading in Shanghai in the early 1960s, against the wishes of Ke. Thus, in effect, the Cultural Revolution attack on Chen for his fairs amounted to an admission that Ke had gone against official plans of that period ("Liu Shaoqi said that free markets were okay," the Red Guards charged in disapproval; "Ke Qingshi opposed him," they noted in commendation).

Chen's methods were to wait for those occasions when Ke left Shanghai, and then to open the markets. At one point in early 1961 he and the

---

128. See n. 28, above; Richard Baum, *Prelude to Revolution*, p. 162.

129. *DGB*, July 5 and November 20, 1961, and January 19, 1962.

130. Mao Tse-tung, "Several Important Instructions," June 29 and July 2, 1959, p. 183; and Mao Tse-tung, *A Critique of Soviet Economics*, pp. 89, 96.

131. *Survey of China Mainland Press-Supplement (SCMPS)*, no. 180 (1967), p. 14; *SCMP*, no. 4083 (1967), pp. 1–3; and *SCMPS*, no. 172 (1967), p. 23, for example.

132. *GMRB*, July 21, 1967, in *Current Background*, no. 836 (1967), pp. 31–37; and *Caimao zhanshi* [Finance and Trade Warrior], February 18, 1967 (a Red Guard tabloid reproduced in *Red Guard Publications, Part I: Newspapers*). George N. Ecklund, "Protracted Expropriation of Private Business in Communist China," pp. 247–48, mentions that free markets did "spring up" in a few large cities in late 1960, but "apparently were closed several weeks later"; and that free markets were reintroduced in Shanghai in 1962, with prices considerably above those in the state markets. He published this in 1963.

city's mayor, Cao Diqiu, wrote a document on their own authority, permitting the fairs to be held in Shanghai. According to criticisms of Chen and Cao in the Cultural Revolution, even grain and daily-use industrial products entered these markets, which were attended by some ninety thousand people. Whenever Ke returned home, though, Chen was compelled to close fairs down again.

In this case, Ke, a radical official, appalled by what he considered to be chaotic conditions, by speculation, and by black marketeering, chose to suffocate free trading, despite the judgment of his local colleagues then that "free markets can't be effectively banned." Unlike Peng Zhen, whose protective attitude toward his domain drew principally on bureaucratic motives, Ke based his purism on his ideological perspective.

In the third period Guangxi province was the scene of local opposition to free marketing. An incident here was considered important enough to merit top billing on page one of the fortnightly journal *Market*.[133] In reporting on it, the paper castigated the provincial leadership ("We don't know what, after all, Guangxi's attitude is toward the policy of economic liberalization and activating the market").

In this episode, a group of cadres was carting local sideline products out of Guangxi to a "sales exhibition" in Beijing. These people were representatives of a new form of business operation, the "integrated enterprise," a concern that combines in one work unit the functions of agricultural and industrial production and of trading. Such enterprises keep independent accounts, are free to market and process their own output, and can retain some profits.[134] En route, armed militia detained these cadres, snatched their goods (which included cinnamon and fennel oil), threatened them with gunshots, and bound up the escorts. Thereafter, the finance and trade leadership at the basic level praised the militia; and the Guangxi provincial leadership ordered: "Agricultural sideline products must all be sold only by the [state] grain, supply and marketing, commerce and foreign trade departments."

Later, when the Guangxi provincial reclamation bureau requested permission to attend the national exhibition, it was allowed to bring only a small amount of products, was forbidden to sign contracts with other provinces, and had to accept certain limits on the type of goods that its workers could carry out of provincial boundaries (sugar was disallowed, while less-vital products, such as anise and cassia bark, could

133. *SC,* no. 27 (November 10, 1980), p. 1.
134. For information on these complexes, see *BR,* 23, no. 31 (1980): 20–26, and *JJYJ,* no. 7 (1980), pp. 42–47.

go). Here provincial officials limited marketing activity through their "localism"—by hoarding native specialties, and by preventing unplanned exchange outside administrative boundaries by units not a part of the normal bureaucratic system.

These three episodes, then, illustrate three separate reasons that politicians responsible for large jurisdictions have had for working against free trading: a preference for maximum bureaucratic order, ideological distaste, and a desire for control over local produce. In each case, marketeer politicians in power in Beijing have been countered in their efforts to open markets, at least in these localities. Thus, political strains in central-local relations—strains that attend the implementation of many sorts of policies in this formally unitary but extremely diverse socialist state—infringe upon the operation of the free market too. Indeed, they act as a third force—along with ideology and social cleavages—accounting for opposition to this form of economic liberalization.

Limits on the freedom in free markets—from those with either radical or bureaucratic outlooks, and from the provinces—represent one aspect of an internal dynamic in Chinese socialist commerce that repeatedly to date has pressed economic policy and practice toward the left, and in extreme cases the far left. Though there was some movement toward greater liberalism in the fairs of the late 1970s than in earlier ones, this trend toward increasing controls with time still followed its typical course.

This chapter has shed light on the forces that propel marketeer policies to recede and submit to restrictions. The data here can be fitted into the same framework used to analyze the other issues addressed in this volume. Thus, it is crucial in this case too to consider the effects on fairs of technology and level of economic development, the fact of the planned economy, and the strong ideological commitment to socialism in which both the leadership and the populace have been schooled.

Technological factors are important, first in that they make fairs necessary, but also in that they limit the efficiency of marketing in China and cause the large price differentials that permit speculative activities. Consequently, the underdeveloped economy lays fairs open to charges of having caused corruption, as they tend to breed unlawful practices which then make them easy targets for attack. As illegalities multiply, leftists and ultraleftists who oppose fairs can win a hearing for their views.

The planned economy is significant because it gives its officials and its offices certain set tasks to perform, tasks with which fairs interfere in many cases. Therefore the existence of the plan creates an array of individuals whose vested interests pit them against the fairs. The bureaucrats whose positions are threatened hold power in their domination of the bulk of the economy. Therefore their distaste for markets carries real weight in policy councils when inflation occurs, or when the state has serious difficulty in obtaining the goods it requires.

Finally, loyalty to the socialist values that the Chinese revolution was waged to realize still inspires many officials, and no doubt finds sympathy among those within the population who continue to place their hopes for a better life in collective production and state-directed distributional schemes. Any class polarization that issues from fairs, and any opportunities fairs seem to offer for enriching the wily few, make them vulnerable to attack by those devoted to a more egalitarian China.

Conclusion:

The Pattern, Shape, and Dilemmas of Chinese Business under Socialism

In early 1981, in the wake of restrictions then recently placed on a policy of economic liberalization, a policy just over two years old at that time, a commentator in Hong Kong referred to a "vicious circle" in economic policy making in the PRC. Observers, he said, described this circle as follows: "Unification leads to stifling, stifling calls forth crying out, crying out promotes liberalization, liberalization produces chaos, and chaos directs back again to unification."[1] The present study has also identified a cyclical process in Chinese commercial policy, and it has presented this pattern analytically in terms of a conflict among three lines.

This pivotal finding of a "three-line struggle" formed the foundation for a range of insights into policy making in this one-party state. First of

1. Jiang Yi, "Can Chen Yun's Scheme Resolve the Difficult Problems in the Economy?" *Zheng Ming* [Contend] (Hong Kong), no. 41 (March 1981), p. 43.

all, the investigation uncovered a sequence to the conflict. That is, bureaucratic approaches have repeatedly been followed by marketeer policies, which were then succeeded by radical initiatives. These in turn have
been righted (in a double sense) by a return to bureaucratic modes. Second, it has shown that the dominant strategy, at which the system has
repeatedly come to rest, is the bureaucratic one, despite frequent experiments to its left and right. And third, it has revealed that not just cyclical
but also secular change, involving some learning, has occurred, from the
perspective of the Chinese elite.

The cycling among three competing strategies for commercial work
delineated here (as opposed to a simple alternation of "right" and "left"
lines) is far more than just a battle over power between contending elites.
Instead, the switches from one approach to another—as, in policy toward the private sector, from controls to liberalization and then to elimination; or, toward free markets, from restrictions to openness and then
to abolition; or again, with respect to the products of light industry,
from planned procurement to a degree of selective purchase, and then to
the predominance of mass production over trade—are grounded as well
in a clash between generally shared values, as the policy making elite
constantly reassesses its tactics in light of feedback from the economy.

From the viewpoint of the observer, the pursuit of these shared values—egalitarianism, order, and productivity—has entailed the sequen-
tial use of incompatible policies. Maximum concentration on productivity often requires incentives that give short shrift to egalitarianism; and
it also demands a flexibility for the play of market forces, which runs in
the face of tight planning. Though egalitarianism and order are not in-
herently contradictory, one important Chinese approach to the promotion of equity, through mass movements and disregard for centralized
plans, has spawned much disorder; whereas more orderly, bureaucratic
solutions tend to enhance the power of those at the upper levels, at a
distance from the lives of ordinary people, and thereby to reduce equal-
ity. Thus, the single-minded pursuit of any one of these ideals, which has
generally been the style of politics in China, almost necessarily occurs to
the detriment of the other two values.

The economic results of the separate strategies dictated by each value,
when that value is pursued to its extreme, have been at least as important
a factor in reorienting policy as has been squabbling that is purely politically generated. Most simply, the chaos that has always resulted from
radicals' promotion of a "spontaneous" production zeal and from their
iconoclastic disregard for structures has made necessary the retighten-
ing of the sinews of the plan and its centrally dictated norms.

But the rigidities, waste, inefficiency, and inability to serve demand effectively which characterize bureaucratic business, plus the tendency to play down material incentives (an approach that bureaucrats share with radicals), have several times paved the way for the release of some market forces. Finally, however, to complete the cycle, the illicit profit-seeking and price increases that have accompanied this market-type release then provoke and legitimize once again the radical profession of egalitarian ideals. This history shows that Chinese socialism encompasses three often contradictory values, and that when each value is carried out to its limit, the economic consequences trigger an elite reaction which leads to policy shift.

Although this particular sequence has recurred several times, there has also been a tendency for a return over and over to planned, bureaucratically organized marketing. For, from the point of view of most Chinese socialists, an excessive reliance either on market forces or on mobilization politics produces chaos, and so calls, in time, for the reimposition of structure. For this reason, although there is scope for experimentation within the system, sometimes inspired by a concern for dearth, sometimes by a commitment to redistribution, a choice for stability and control has often emerged in policy councils as the most comfortable form of compromise. Consequently, the periods of bureaucratically run business were by far the most lengthy in the first three decades of the PRC.

The study also exposed a principal locus within society that underpins this recurrent and abiding elite commitment to the planned economy: the lower-level cadre in the commercial bureaucracy. For the fact of the plan in China has created a set of vested interests, dependencies, and habits oriented toward meeting its targets, in short, a corps of officials who, in the Chinese expression, *kao tong chi fan* (rely on control for their livelihood).

There is an irony suggested in this study which grows out of this reliance on control. That is, in principle a leadership-designed plan may be essential to the achievement of the goals of socialist distribution: equity, price stability, the provision of basic necessities for all at affordable prices. And yet, such a plan has to be effected by real human beings, through commands whose fulfillment entails rewards. In their ardor to meet these commands, these workers engage in a range of competitive behaviors that entail bribery, privilege and perquisites, hoarding and diverting goods, hamstringing free markets, forcing the sale of shoddy merchandise, and placing shackles on or otherwise shortchanging whatever portion of the private sector happens to be legitimately operating at the moment. Thus, the very effort to actualize socialist values leads the individuals charged with this task to distort the operation of those values.

Are we to conclude then that "socialist commerce," at least as practiced in the PRC, just does not work? Indeed, much of the analysis in this volume has underscored the grave difficulties in putting its ideals into practice. A number of aspects of marketing in China over the three decades examined here bear the unhappy brand of failures in planning, or of excessive and damaging radical zeal. For instance, radically inspired attempts to stamp out entrepreneurship, to impose uniformity on the commodities that appear in the marketplace, and to dismantle commercial organs have frequently impoverished the people's livelihood in the process. Meanwhile, bureaucratic procedures have produced stockpiles and sellouts, waste, queues, and inefficiency. Often the results of these two strategies were severe disincentives for the peasantry, as high procurement quotas incited state purchasing agents in the countryside to buy up so much that even the most productive lost their drive.

Moreover, problems come to mind also in regard to this commerce's record in addressing the three social issues connected with capitalist commerce which were identified in the Introduction to this study. And yet these issues—where, when, and for whom—are the very ones that socialist commerce was designed to resolve. For though the plan seeks to "balance" supplies and redistribute them on a national scale, bureaucratic barriers between regions have sometimes led to such absurdities as those that occurred when marketing cadres in Guangxi province preferred to ration pork, rather than to "import" it from neighboring Hunan, since that would have interfered with their ability to fulfill local sales and purchase quotas.

As for the issue of when, certainly national unification has done away with the rampant warlordism and civil wars of earlier years in the century; the creation of national power has made foreign invasion a thing of the past; and the leadership's choice to shelter the Chinese market (sometimes excessively so) has protected producers from the vagaries of international prices. But radical experiments—the Leap, the Cultural Revolution—introduced perhaps nearly as much unpredictability over time for the folk who expect to engage in exchange.

Third, the question for whom is one that is not easily answered. A major difficulty here lies in the nature of the data publicized by the press in the PRC. From years of reading Chinese papers, this researcher is convinced that information—both statistical and anecdotal—is garnered and presented to support currently legitimized policies. Therefore it is difficult to assess the extent to which the socialist system, and in particular its trade and distribution networks, has resulted in greater equity than a market would for the populace taken as a whole.

If purchase by plan is so fraught with confusion and disorder, would greater reliance on the market be more efficacious? After all, this study has demonstrated that the style of trading in the PRC is in some ways not so different from business as it is known in capitalist environments. Here one can point to the omnipresence of competition, a trait that China's socialist commercial system shares with commerce in capitalist countries. The only difference is the arena—the most significant competition does not take place within the private sector, but is structured instead by the state plan, which sets sector against sector, and which also motivates state trade cadres to push petty private merchants from the scene.

Looking at the second feature of the framework used in this book, policy conflict, one finds here that leaders have time and again settled— at least temporarily—on market-type strategies in times of extreme dearth, when the most pressing concern has been to stimulate production. Thus, the forces of supply and demand have a place in Chinese commerce (if within the strictures of the plan), although the choice to rely on them has always been the product of heated debate.

And third, just as under capitalism, loopholes in the system encourage profit seeking. In China, however, these loopholes are linked to scarcity and underdevelopment, and often arouse a more ideologically based ire than corruption does in bourgeois contexts. In short, each of the three factors that have shaped Chinese domestic trade in recent decades—the plan, politics, and the level of development—also bears the stamp of business practices under any regime. Given these similarities, can one simply conclude that the free market should fit neatly enough into Chinese society, as well as better serve its needs?

I hesitate to resolve the issue so simply. Perhaps the problems would be worse under the reign of the free market. In prerevolutionary days the free market in poor and populous China (features which, of course, still mark the place today) meant a freedom to buy opium, to sell children, to become a prostitute, to purchase basic foodstuffs at skyrocketing prices, to trade at a loss with clever businessmen after trekking miles over mountainous terrain. Thus, there are costs either way, and the repeated debate over plan versus market in China (and, indeed, in all socialist states) is in fact one between two imperfect systems, the ideal model of each of which is subject to distortion when put into practice.

As of the early 1980s, there is a trend both within China and among many of its observers to compare the market as an ideal, the market as it works at Adam Smith's best, on the one hand, with the failures of the plan as it has actually been implemented, on the other. But this study suggests that further experimentation with market-like policies will be likely to reveal that the market in its model form cannot be realized in China, given that country's crude technologies; its intractable inequalities among regions and households and between urban, periurban, and rural places; and its uneven topography and climes. There are trade-offs and unintended consequences in relying on the market, as in the case of any policy. It remains to be seen at the time of this writing whether further and untrammeled use of the market in post-1949 China would re-create the social injustices the revolution managed to mitigate; or whether that revolution built a base on which a more circumscribed and so a more humane market can now exist.

Besides, it is also true that the income polarization, higher prices and wild inflation, gaping disparities among regions in levels of consumption and incidence of starvation (disparities far from abolished even now), elitism and profit chasing that could (and do) crop up in the wake of the abandonment of the tenets of socialist commerce, have been muted under its regime.

What has the Chinese leadership itself concluded about how best to operate trade in its socialist country, as of the early 1980s? Insofar as any consensus has been reached, it is one in favor of combining the two systems while keeping the plan dominant. This brings the discussion to the point made above about secular change in the form of long-term learning in the fashioning of socialist commerce in the PRC. The material presented in this study has highlighted the fact that the market reforms of the late 1970s in procuring light industrial products and in running free markets were more judiciously designed than those of the 1950s, and yet more openly geared to promoting growth attuned to popular needs than those of the early 1960s.

The occasion for this learning to be put into effect came soon after the death of Mao Zedong in 1976. For the discrediting of radicalism that followed permitted the flowering of ideas only tentatively tested in earlier periods, or whose implementation had quickly petered out in the past. In this instance, political factors as well as learning led to the changed shape of policy in the late 1970s. For this leader's passing facilitated the formation of political coalitions supportive of or at least tolerant toward responding to scarcity through the use of material incentives, as it enhanced the legitimacy of appealing to segments of the population better poised to act on and benefit from economic liberalization. Thus, learning, economic effects, and politics have each had their role to play in shifting the course of commercial as well as other policies in the PRC.

Because of the limitations of this study—only domestic and not foreign trade was considered; mainly the commercial, but not other sectors of the economy, formed the focus; only a few top leaders at several crucial junctures received attention—it is impossible to use its findings to determine decisively what all the roots have been of either the cyclical or the secular change described here. Undoubtedly, each of the factors that were ignored—foreign trade and the world economy; other aspects of economic development and policies toward and the behavior of other branches of the economy; and the activities and beliefs of many other members of the elite—would have its explanatory power, its contribution to make in the analysis.

Nevertheless, it is possible to discuss the future of Chinese socialist commercial policy through the use of the variables and findings of this research. Here two broad conclusions emerge: in the first place, the three organizing principles of the study—the plan, political conflict, and the low level of technology for marketing—are all unlikely to undergo significant alteration in China in the near future. The commitment to the planned economy is fundamental. It has again and again outlasted even the most enthusiastic efforts to base growth principally on economic incentives. Political debates and disagreements over the role of the market in Chinese socialism proceeded apace in the wake of the much heralded reforms put forward by the Third Plenum of the Party's Eleventh Central Committee in December 1978, and have not yet silenced all opposition. And the underdeveloped infrastructure for trade has not been significantly remolded in thirty years, a fact which in itself does not bode well for the immediate future.

Given the intractability of these parameters, then, a second conclusion follows as a corollary: some learning may have occurred to date and may continue to occur; and the passing of the man whose person served as the principal rallying point for radicalism may mean that policy will never again veer as far to the left as it has in the past. Still, Chinese business under socialism should remain largely what it has been heretofore—an essentially state-run affair, engaged in an uneasy rivalry with age-old Chinese entrepreneurial instincts, and striving at times to achieve ideals of equity.

APPENDIX A:

Rationing

The administration of rationing takes place at the municipal level, with individual cities having their own different arrangements.[1] In Changsha, for example, the Second Commercial Bureau, which handles foodstuffs, has under it a "coupon and certificate office" (*piao zheng bangongshi*); in Guilin, where there is only one commercial bureau, rationing is managed by that bureau's coupon and certificate group (*piao zheng zu*). The goods that are rationed vary from city to city, but always include grain, cotton, oil, and pork. In Guilin, for instance, soybean cake and sugar are rationed only when production output is low.[2]

Piao, or coupons, are used for items strictly and always rationed. Each individual receives a certain number of *piao* per month for each rationed item (about six *piao* per person was the average for pork in Guangzhou in late 1979). Each *piao* represents a certain quantity of the product and must be accompanied by a certain amount of cash. *Piao* are numbered, and each month only those *piao* bearing certain numbers may be used in the market. Both the price and the amount of the goods in question, which are represented by one *piao*, vary with the supply of

1. The material that follows was supplied by a municipal-level commercial official in Guilin in November 1979; by an interview in Hong Kong on November 12, 1979; by workers at a state-run vegetable and pork market in Guangzhou in November 1979; and by a Beijing tourist official in Changsha, January 1979.

2. William Parish shared with me a 22-item chart used in his refugee interviewing, which sought to discover which items were rationed and how, in various Guangdong counties. Presumably material gleaned from analysis of this instrument will appear in his forthcoming study of urban China, jointly authored with Martin King Whyte.

the item available on the market at any time. The quantity of grain one receives as a ration depends on one's job, with army personnel receiving most, then workers and intellectuals, followed by office employees and students. The cotton ration differs for a given consumer in accord with the climate of the city in which that consumer lives.[3]

Gouhuo zheng, or certificates for buying goods, are used only when supplies of certain items are temporarily insufficient in a particular locality. In Guilin certificates have been used for soap, wine, and sugar, all of which are combined in one certificate. These too are used with money, and each household is issued one certificate per month. These certificates are printed in the form of charts, and the name of the item purchased is checked off by officials when one buys, unlike the practice in the case of the *piao,* a small ticket which one hands over in purchasing.

3. In Tianjin and Beijing, the following were reported by a tour guide in Changsha to be the rations as of late 1978: cloth: 17.3 feet per person per year; oil: ¼ kilogram per month per person; grain: 16 kilograms per person per month for light office workers; 25–30 kilograms per person per month for those engaged in heavy work. Cotton rationing was terminated, at least temporarily, as of the end of 1983. See *FBIS,* November 23, p. K9. Also, pork rationing seems to have ceased in many cities as pork appeared more and more commonly in free markets after 1980.

APPENDIX B:

A Comparison of the Organizational Outcomes of the Socialist Transformation Campaign in Various Economic Sectors

In comparison with agriculture, industry, and large-scale capitalism, smaller retail trade was dealt with later in time; the percentage of firms converted at the end of socialist transformation (late 1956) was lowest in this sector; and those firms that were labeled as having been converted when the transformation period had come to an end experienced far less reorganization than those in the other sectors.

Agriculture's cooperativization received its impetus in July 1955 when Mao delivered his mobilizational speech. Although the speech was not officially endorsed by the Party Central Committee until October, a policy of consolidation which had preceded the speech was effectively undone then, and cadres at the lower levels began at that point to organize peasants at a more rapid tempo and, by year's end, into larger units.[1] To give one example, in Henan province, a front-runner in the socialization campaign on all fronts, Xinxiang special district reported at the end of December that over 80 percent of the rural households had "basically" become semisocialized. Only 42 percent of the merchants there at the time, however, had been through their socialist transformation.[2]

It was not until the Party leadership agreed that Mao had made his case on the benefits of agricultural collectivization that, in October 1955 at the Sixth Plenum of the Seventh Party Central Committee, the Party

1. See Kenneth R. Walker, "Collectivisation in Retrospect: The 'Socialist High Tide' of Autumn 1955–Spring 1956," pp. 29–34, and Mark Selden, "Cooperation and Conflict: Cooperative and Collective Formation in China's Countryside."
2. *Da Gong Bao* (*DGB*), December 30, 1955.

began to accelerate the transformation of capitalist industry and commerce.[3] However, even though this was a move for dealing henceforth with these two sectors in tandem, and although the phrase used to refer to this campaign always joined the two together, two qualifications are in order. First of all, industry's conversion had begun much earlier than that in commerce. And second, only the very largest of the commercial firms were handled in the same extreme way as industrial firms were.

Some of the larger industrial companies had already been converted into joint public-private enterprises in 1949, and by 1954 one thousand of these companies had gone through this transition.[4] Among commercial, catering and service establishments, by contrast, only 137 had been brought under joint operation before 1955.[5] Moreover, by the second half of 1955, once the process had gotten under way, more than half of major capitalist industry (as based on property valuation), but only about 30 percent of capitalist commerce, as measured by business turnover, had come under joint operation.[6] These figures pertain to large retail trade, as wholesale trade was in the main nationalized and replaced by state-owned monopoly companies soon after 1949.[7] Thus, for agriculture, industry, and wholesale trade, the process of transformation began earlier and achieved results more rapidly than it did for retail commerce.

As for comparisons of the end-product, according to data compiled by the State Statistical Bureau, at the end of 1956 agricultural cooperativization was basically completed: 96 percent of rural households were part of cooperatives, and 88 percent had already joined the higher-level co-ops, or collectives.[8] Private industry, too, had been basically changed into joint enterprises: seventy thousand firms had been converted from private ownership in 1956 alone, and their output represented 99.6 percent of the total output of what had originally been private industry. Also, 99 percent of the staff and workers of the original private industrial concerns were then working in joint enterprises.

The transformation of commerce, however, was only cited in this report as having "obtained a great victory." Only 85 percent of the personnel from once-private commerce now served in state capitalist firms, and the total volume of retail sales by the newly reorganized firms in 1956

3. Roderick MacFarquhar, *The Origins of the Cultural Revolution*, pp. 19–20.

4. George N. Ecklund, "Protracted Expropriation of Private Business in Communist China," pp. 242–43.

5. Kuan Ta-t'ung, *The Socialist Transformation of Capitalist Industry and Commerce in China*, p.77.

6. *Extracts from China Mainland Magazines* (ECMM), no. 35 (1956), p. 5.

7. Kuan, p. 67. See also chapter 4, note 2, and appendix C, on wholesale trade.

8. The material that follows comes from *Xuexi* [Study] (XX), no. 20 (1957), p. 21.

TABLE B-1 Comparison of Socialist Transformation in
Industry and Commerce, 1955–1956
(percentages)

		Industry		Commerce	
		1955	1956	1955	1956
Firms	Joint Public-Private	34.73	95.73	24	66.8
	Private	65.27	4.27	76	33.2
Employees	Joint	37.51	98.73	28.9	72.9*
	Private	62.49	1.27	71.1	27.1

SOURCE: *Da Gong Bao* (Beijing), December 26, 1956.
*Unaccountably, this figure differs from the one given in footnote 8 (see text).

represented an increase of only 15 percent over that conducted by firms that were transformed as of the year before.

More important, however, than either the differential pace at which transformation took place in the various sectors or the percentages cited as achievements at the conclusion of "high tide," was the fact that only a very small proportion of the firms said to have been converted in commerce had actually undergone any significant degree of change in their operations or form of ownership by the end of 1956. Thus, although the firms which had been transformed in this sector amounted to 82.2 percent of original private firms, only 16.5 percent of the total original number were in joint enterprises (64.23 percent of all industrial firms were in this form at the same time), and only 11.6 percent of the total were being operated in full accord with the principles of such enterprises. Another 59.6 percent of the total were in various types of cooperatives, but only 24 percent (of the total) were members of cooperative stores, in which profits, losses, sales, and purchases were managed collectively.[9] In sum, these figures show that only about two-fifths of all private commercial enterprises were truly collectivized (the 16.5 percent in joint enterprises plus the 24 percent in co-op shops). So, as many as 17.8 percent of these firms remained unorganized at the end of transformation, as against .87 percent of industrial enterprises, according to this account.

The analytic factors used throughout chapter four can help to account for these differential outcomes. First of all, technological consid-

9. Zhongguo shehui kexue yuan, jingji yanjiuso [Chinese Academy of Social Sciences, Economic Research Institute], *Zhongguo ziben zhuyi gongshangye de shehui zhuyi gaizao* [The socialist transformation of China's capitalist industry and commerce] (CASS), pp. 228–29. See chapter 4, p. 191.

erations seemed then to dictate a different outcome for the three sectors. In agriculture, according to Walker and Shue, there was an economic case to be made for cooperativizing: larger units and unified management promised greater efficiency of resource use, a higher rate of capital formation, and a greater chance to incorporate production into the state plan.[10] Similarly, in industry, mergers and reorganization were seen as a means of reducing difficulties in production and management, and of raising efficiency.[11] Only in small trade was a case made for maintaining its traditional organizational forms.

The consumers of industrial and agricultural output would be unaffected in the main, or at least only indirectly affected by a change in the organization of productive relations. The customers of the rural peddlers and the urban shops and stalls, however, would be greatly disadvantaged by the dispossession or gross rearrangement of ownership and management in the small, scattered businesses they patronized. Furthermore, in terms of their numbers, small merchants were too many to replace, given the scarcity of trained state personnel.[12] And since the work of the merchants was best done in widely dispersed locales, it would have been ineffective to employ state cadres to supervise groups of merchants (as they supervised industrial capitalists and peasants) working jointly.

The extinction of large wholesale trade, and the takeover through mergers into state-supervised joint enterprises of the more substantial urban retail firms, was for each a far greater organizational change than was the transformation of the small merchants and peddlers. As in the case of industry and agriculture, their clients were less specific than were those of the smaller-time businessmen, while the economic activity in which they engaged would be less likely to be upset by mergers and reorganization than would that of the tiny shops' owners and pole-bearers. Also, the smaller numbers of wholesale firms made them easier to replace, whereas the larger retailers, also far fewer than the small traders and more concentrated in the larger cities, were relatively easy to dominate and oversee, compared with peddlers.

Besides these economic reasons for the less thorough reorganization of small trade, class factors also came into play. Because their assets were

10. Walker, p. 6; Vivienne Shue, *Peasant China in Transition: The Dynamics of Development toward Socialism, 1949–56*, pp. 281–82.

11. *Renmin ribao* [People's Daily] (*RMRB*), editorial, November 22, 1955, in *Survey of the China Mainland Press* (*SCMP*), no. 1178 (1955), p. 13.

12. See chapter 4, note 10.

far smaller in amount than were those of the more wealthy capitalists, and because they existed mainly from the proceeds of their own labor, it was possible to categorize them as "commercial laborers." One opinion even held that, being workers, they need not be transformed at all.[13] From another angle, some cadres, focusing on these traders' negative features, lacked confidence in their own ability to transform them, or feared to associate too closely with what they took to be representatives of the bourgeoisie.[14] The upshot of these two views amounted to a kind of leniency for the traders, in contrast with what peasants experienced, for example: "Commerce is behind the other sectors ... some SMC cadres have not seen favorable conditions. Feeling anxiety and hesitation, they wonder if all the requisite conditions are present."[15]

In contrast, the wholesalers and the owners of large retail concerns, being either members of the middle or of the upper bourgeoisie, called forth none of this ambivalence in the minds of policy makers and cadres. As a result, these groups were definitely seen as the proper object for transformation, compared with their petty-bourgeois and semiproletarian confrères.

A last point concerns the relative costs and benefits to the state which a large-scale transformation would entail. The bigger farms that collectivization in agriculture would create, it was expected, would yield larger crop deliveries to the state, as taxation and compulsory purchase became easier to manage. Also, this world could be largely self-supporting, and so mergers would not present any burden to the state. In agriculture, then, amalgamation was to yield benefits, but no costs, to the state.

In the case of the national bourgeoisie, whether in industry or in big retail business, the worth to the state of the transformed enterprises must have far outweighed the costs of providing the fixed interest, welfare, pension, and sick leave benefits that the capitalists received as members of the joint enterprises.[16] And according to Xu Dixin, then director of the State Council's Central Administrative Bureau of Indus-

13. *Jingji yanjiu* [Economic Studies], no. 5 (1955), p. 13.
14. *DGB*, December 18, 1955; Ezra Vogel, *Canton Under Communism*, p. 163.
15. *DGB* editorial, December 28, 1955, in *SCMP*, no. 1210 (1956), pp. 13–16.
16. The only relevant figures I was able to uncover provide a basis for comparing the costs the state paid out in fixed interest with what it took in through transforming larger-scale capitalist industry and commerce into joint enterprises. That is, according to *Beijing Review* no. 17 (1980), p. 20, the state paid out 120 million yuan per year in fixed interest to the capitalists beginning in 1956. Over ten years (that is, up to the time these payments were terminated in the Cultural Revolution), this came to 1,200,000,000 yuan. CASS, p. 228, states that, as of the end of 1956, the total value of industry brought into joint enterprises amounted to 7,237,000,000 yuan, by contrast.

try and Commerce, the costs of "squeezing out" altogether the capitalist industrialists and businessmen seemed prohibitive in terms of the responsibility that would fall upon the state of finding new jobs for the one million staff and workers in their firms and for dealing with the certain bankruptcy of several million large and small capitalists and their dependents.[17]

The peasantry, then, were thrown back upon their own resources, while ex-capitalists were appeased with an annual dividend of 5 percent and the fringe benefits noted above. For the small merchants with their far larger numbers, however, neither could the state afford to guarantee this array of benefits, nor would the returns from their small capital holdings have been worth the cost of doing so.[18]

17. *XX*, no. 1 (1956), p. 48.
18. Vogel, pp. 171–73.

Forms and Procedures in the Transformation of Wholesale and Large Retail Trade

The socialist transition of retail trade, both large and small, to "state capitalist" forms (that is, various agent and commission arrangements between the state and the private sector and joint state-private operations, all of which enabled the state to limit the amounts and types of, the prices charged for, and the profits taken from the goods sold by the private sector) rested on the prior takeover of the large wholesale firms. That takeover got under way almost immediately after communist victory, as the state began at once to collect taxes in kind; to buy up from the capitalists stockpiles (particularly of grain and cotton) they had been hoarding in the hopes of dumping; to sign contracts with private factories, by means of which the state supplied raw material and the enterprises fulfilled orders to the state for finished products; and to purchase agricultural goods from the countryside.[1] Once the government had managed to wrest key commodities from the hands of the producers, its own wholesale monopoly companies were in a position to replace the private wholesalers.

A Chinese chronicler of this transformation termed the conversion of private wholesaling, which began on a large scale in 1953, "a precondition for stabilizing the market and strengthening the leadership of the socialist sector."[2] For once the goods and the capital originally controlled by these firms were in the state's possession, it became possible

1. Hsueh Mu-chiao [Xue Muqiao], *Peking Review (PR)*, no. 49 (1977), pp. 4–8.
2. Kuan Ta-T'ung, *The Socialist Transformation of Capitalist Industry and Commerce in China*, p. 65.

313

for the state to dominate the disposal of goods to the retail sector and to regulate prices according to its own priorities.[3] In a typical example, one state-operated wholesaler, the Tianjin General Goods Company, placed such huge orders with local private factories that the factories were unable at the same time to fill orders from private retail firms. As a result, all retail shops were forced to buy their provisions from the state firms.[4]

By the end of 1952, the private wholesalers, along with other capitalist businessmen, had been steadily subjected for three years to a whole array of restrictions with regard to rate of profits and dividends, the prices they could charge, and the wages they must pay, and through taxation policy.[5] They were also one group among the victims of a massive campaign against capitalists in the first half of 1952, the *wu fan* (five antis), which struck severe blows at the economic power of many of them.[6] However, it was not until the second half of 1953 that particular measures were set in motion specifically to bring the economic life of the wholesalers entirely to a close.[7]

The first steps in this final process were to control wholesalers' business on credit and their use of promissory notes; to step up the processing by and ordering from private industry by the state; and to restore a business tax on wholesalers' undertakings, which had been rescinded earlier in the year. Then, in 1954, as the state grasped control of more raw materials, it began to force the closing of the private concerns, to induce their owners to invest in other businesses, and to absorb their personnel into state organs.[8] By the second half of the year when only small products of secondary importance remained outside state control, the firms were categorized into three groups, according to the type of commodity in which they dealt and the size of the firm.

3. Ezra Vogel, *Canton Under Communism*, pp. 158, 168.

4. *China News Analysis (CNA)*, no. 19, (1954), p. 7.

5. George N. Ecklund, "Protracted Expropriation of Private Business in Communist China," *Pacific Affairs*, 36, no. 3 (1963):240–41. Kuan, p. 44; *CNA*, no. 15 (1953); Mao Tse-tung, *Report to the Second Plenary Session of the Seventh Central Committee of the Communist Party of China*, p. 11.

6. John Gardner, "The *Wu-fan* Campaign in Shanghai"; Hsueh Mu-chiao, *PR*, no. 50 (1977), p. 15; Kenneth G. Lieberthal, *Revolution and Tradition in Tientsin, 1949–1959*; and Li Choh-ming, *The Economic Development of Communist China*, p. 6.

7. The discussion that follows is drawn from Zhongguo shehui kexue yuan, jingji yanjiuso [Chinese Academy of Social Sciences, Economic Research Institute], *Zhongguo ziben zhuyi gongshangye de shehui zhuyi gaizao* [The socialist transformation of China's capitalist industry and commerce] (CASS), pp. 174–78. See also *Renmin ribao (RMRB)* editorial, October 9, 1954, in *Survey of China Mainland Press (SCMP)*, no. 916 (1954), pp. 17–19.

8. According to *Da Gong Bao* [Impartial Daily], May 15, 1955, in 1954 state commercial departments absorbed more than 42,000 private wholesale merchants. At the same time some individual private retail merchants and some small merchants and peddlers joined state commerce and cooperative commercial work organs.

Firms in the first of the categories were "left alone" (*liu*) or allowed to continue in operation, but as state agents. Such an arrangement was considered to be a middle-level form of state capitalism, and was used for firms dealing in such goods as wine and tobacco whose consumption was widely scattered and which had many retail outlets. Second, a few large firms were permitted to *zhuan*, or change over to other trades, where they would then undergo transformation. As for a third group, which had no way to carry on, as state commerce had already totally invaded their field of operations, their personnel were simply absorbed into state-run concerns (*bao*).

Meanwhile, traveling merchants engaged in wholesale work were "plugged up" so they could not engage in purchases and sales outside a given area; and brokers were eliminated and replaced by state trust service organs and SMCs. At the end of 1954 private wholesalers were responsible for only 10.2 percent of the total volume of business on the market; by 1955, the percentage had fallen to 4.4.[9] At this stage, the first battle in the transformation of the ownership system of private commerce was considered concluded, and the regime was prepared to move on to the more finely honed process of interposing its business forms between the consumers and their accustomed salespeople. The beginning of change in retailing took place among the more sizable urban firms.[10]

Because of the sensitive nature of this transition, a process called "arrangement" (involving the state's allocation of goods, setting of prices, and locational redistribution of commercial outlets within areas) was combined from the start with the change in ownership and management structure of the firms. During the period of national economic recovery (1949–1952), elementary and middle-level forms of state capitalism were already instituted in the urban retail sector, all of which amounted in one way or another to forcing the firms to serve as agencies for state-operated commercial concerns, and all of which were of a temporary nature.

After 1953, however, once private wholesale trade was well on the road to extinction, four forms developed quickly for private retail firms: first, *pigou* (*lingxiao*), in which private merchants bought commodities in bulk from the state with cash and then sold these on a retail basis, according to a price set by the state or negotiated with state offices, and obtained the differential between the wholesale and retail prices as profit. In this arrangement, the private personnel could still obtain a substantial amount of the same type of commodities on the free market.

9. CASS, p. 177.
10. The material that follows is taken from CASS, pp. 193–216.

Under the second form, *jingxiao*, agency sales, the state assigned commodities to the private purchaser, who bought these with cash in accord with the state's supply plan. The purchaser would then sell these goods at a fixed price, in line with a supply method designated by the state. Here again the merchant earned his income from the wholesale-retail differential.

Daixiao, commission sales, a more advanced form, entailed state commerce's entrusting commodities to the private operator to sell, again according to the state supply plan and state-fixed prices. The difference between this form and the previous one is that this type of agent, more closely linked to the state trade organs that supplied him, was required to deposit his cash with that organ, and was paid by the state organ on a commission basis.

Finally, *zhuanye daixiao*, specialized commission sales, the most advanced form, stipulated that a private firm must obtain all of its goods from state commercial organs; here the private enterprise's sales plan was completely dominated by the state commercial plan.

Throughout 1953, these forms served as the basis for experimentation. With the institution of state-planned purchase and supply, first of grain in November 1953 and then of cotton in September 1954, all grain and cotton merchants were compelled to become agents of the state, as they lost total control over their commodities.[11] Several lessons garnered from that experience were later extended to other trades: for example, the organization of all shops dealing in a given line of goods in one city into companies, within which compulsory mergers and relocations were organized by state offices, and supplies and the work force were redistributed, to eliminate imbalances in profits and losses among firms; and the creation of new management systems, such as liaison personnel sent from state firms to oversee the converted shops' business practices, and centralized state-run wholesale suppliers for the retailers.

Within a short time, retailers in the pork, tobacco, tea, salt, wine, coal, and general-goods trades were similarly turned into state agents by whole trades. By August 1955, 23.7 percent of all private retail firms in China had been converted into some form of agency trade. At this point, however, only 1.0 percent of the private retail sales volume was generated by the more advanced joint public-private enterprises, and 1.9 percent by the somewhat more advanced cooperativized commerce.

This process, of course, entailed far more than the smooth shepherding of willing or even docile firms into arrangements that took from

11. See *RMRB*, November 23 and 27, 1955.

them their right to control commodities. Many among the wholesalers, watching the extinction of their businesses, adopted an attitude of passive resistance, some preferring to allow their own capital to become depleted; others, dreaming of a return of past days, pulled out some capital to invest elsewhere before applying to close down their firms; while yet others, taking advantage of the still lively free market, even became small merchants and peddlers rather than submit to entry into the state firms.[12]

Retailers, perhaps more skilled at adapting to a changing market, chose to turn to commodities not yet under state operation; or attempted to bypass the agency system by going to other cities where transformation was not yet so far under way as in their own, or by working directly with the producers. Others, once they had begun to act as agents, resorted to various tricks, manipulating prices or selling shoddy goods to destroy the state's prestige; or used the agency name as a cover for their own speculation and embezzlement.[13] For both groups, however, the effort at opposition was largely stifled by the growing economic power of the state as it laid its hands on a steadily greater proportion of goods.

With the nationwide speedup in transformation of all kinds in late October 1955, some of the larger retail businesses, along with the bulk of industrial firms, were pushed onto the path of joint public-private operation. As was noted above, at summer's end in 1955, only a miniscule fraction of private retail trade had been converted into enterprises jointly managed with the state. Even within another year's time, only 11.6 percent of all private commercial firms were in full-fledged joint enterprises; and about another 5 percent had been organized into less advanced joint enterprises, which did not provide fixed interest payments to their former owners.[14] These two groups of firms together amounted to only one-sixth of all private retail firms.

In the elementary, jointly operated firms—although the state had already invested capital and goods and assigned its personnel to share in management—capitalists still had some control over their own profits. Firms under this arrangement found their only constraint in the fact that the state set a formula to be followed in capitalists' division of the firm's profits.[15] At this point contradictions still existed within a trade between

12. CASS, p. 178.
13. CASS, p. 195.
14. CASS, p. 229.
15. The formula was this: 35% went to the state as income tax, 15% went to the workers' welfare fund, 30% went to the enterprise accumulation fund, and 20% could be used for dividends. In *Beijing Review*, no. 17 (1980), p. 19.

firms that had been converted to the joint enterprise form and those that had not. Once the advanced form of joint operation was instituted in the late fall and mid-winter of 1955–1956, all the firms in a given trade could be supervised and reorganized jointly by the state, under the control of the state trading companies.[16]

At that time, capitalists' profits were no longer under their own control, and a fixed annual interest was given them instead (a procedure termed "buying out"). The rate of this interest was first set at from 1 to 6 percent of the valuation of their holdings, and later was unified at 5 percent.[17] Also, specialized trade corporations were created to manage each trade. While capitalists were placed in positions generally at the same level as they had worked at previously and were paid a far higher salary than state cadres,[18] tensions ran high between ex-capitalists and state cadres in these enterprises, as the capitalists were forced to work as state employees, offering advice but exercising no authority.

The state was able to use this arrangement to reallocate equipment and labor power between enterprises and regions within a trade, and also to elevate the status of workers relative to their former bosses. Thus, this higher and final level of joint operation was aimed at consolidating the state's planning control over the once-private commercial sector of the economy, as the means of industrial production also came under state domination.

16. Kuan, pp. 72–90. See also *Jingji yanjiu* [Economic Studies], no. 2 (1956), pp. 40–47; and *RMRB*, December 14, 1955, in *SCMP*, no. 1196 (1955), pp. 3–6.

17. A State Council decision of February 8, 1956 (in *RMRB*, February 11) set the rate of annual interest at from 1 to 6 percent; in a later directive in July 1956, following a suggestion by Chen Yun at the Third Session of the First National People's Congress in June 1956 (in *Current Background*, no. 393 [1956], p. 17), fixed interest was unified for all firms at 5 percent a year (see *SCMP*, no. 1346 [1956], p. 7).

18. Barry M. Richman, "Capitalists & Managers in Communist China," p. 60, notes that in 1966 a capitalist was being paid 380 yuan per month, while both the Party secretary and the state-appointed director of the factory earned only 110 yuan.

APPENDIX D:

Forms and Procedures in the Transformation of Small Retail Trade

Unlike the large private wholesalers (who were altogether replaced by state trading companies into which they were by and large absorbed), and unlike the wealthy urban retailers (who were forced to become reorganized under "state capitalist" ownership forms, and whose businesses were "bought out" through fixed annual interest payments, high salaries, and at least nominal positions as advisers within their own former firms), the small businessmen—owners of husband-and-wife shops, stall-keepers, and mobile vendors in the cities; the owners of little stores in the market towns; and the peddlers of the rural areas—were "transformed," to the extent that they were, through cooperativization.[1] The entire process was marked, at least at the level of policy, by meticulous care in trying to specify precise and subtly differentiated forms for the myriad types and sizes of small firms.[2]

---

1. *Jingji yanjiu* [Economic Studies] (*JJYJ*), no. 2 (1956), p. 47; Zhongguo shehui kexue yuan, jingji yanjiuso [Chinese Academy of Social Sciences, Economic Research Institute], *Zhongguo ziben zhuyi gongshangye de shehui zhuyi gaizao* [The socialist transformation of China's capitalist industry and commerce] (CASS), p. 235. See Lynn T. White III, "Low Power: Small Enterprises in Shanghai, 1949–1967," pp. 45–76, for a detailed account of the process of socialist transformation as it pertained to the small shops and vendors in that city.

2. Articles on the forms used in the transition for small business are in *Da Gong Bao* [Impartial Daily] (*DGB*), February 18, 1955, in *Survey of the China Mainland Press* (*SCMP*), no. 999 (1955), pp. 7–11; *DGB*, April 15, 19, and 22, 1955; and September 8, 1955, in *SCMP*, no. 1134, pp. 32–36; and *SCMP*, no. 1191, p. 8; *Renmin ribao* [People's Daily] (*RMRB*), March 10, 1955, May 15, 1955, and December 14, 1955; *Xuexi* [Study] (*XX*), no. 6 (1955), pp. 11–13; *Xinhua yuebao* [New China Monthly] (*XHYB*), no. 6

The main early, lower-stage forms used to transform these merchants in the early 1950s—*pigou lingxiao, jingxiao* and *daixiao*—were the same ones that were used for larger retail trade before the mass campaign to merge stores and buy out their owners in late 1955. *Pigou lingxiao,* buying in bulk and selling in small amounts, was meant for those handling less important commodities, and merchants who used this form could set their own prices.[3] The *jingxiao* form, for commercial capitalists (those whose scale of business was somewhat larger), was considered to be appropriate for a group of these wealthier merchants dealing in approximately the same trades, and entailed little change in the ownership system.[4] Dealing gingerly with these bigger businessmen at first, the state merely subjected their businesses to some planning and price controls through the use of contracts; and they were even permitted to obtain some of their goods on the free market. Just so long as they got at least 60 percent of their stock from the SMC, merchants qualified for this form.[5]

Daixiao was used in the countryside with the smaller-scale merchants, especially itinerant peddlers, and was more restrictive. It was meant for those whose capital was quite limited, but who could contribute either labor power or business skills. Some sources claim that those using this form could deal on the free market, but other sources do not. But all sources agree that the trader was required to deposit the bulk of his capital with the SMC. Since the products circulated in this arrangement belonged to the SMC, this form entailed a change in ownership system. According to one formula, if the merchant engaged in any operations on his own, the arrangement in his case was considered to be semisocialist. If not, those partaking in the *daixiao* form were treated like other work personnel of the SMC, with the sole difference being the form of their compensation: where SMC cadres received fixed wages, the merchants got a commission, justified as being akin to a piecework wage.[6]

(1955), pp. 133–35; *Xinhua banyuekan* [New China Semimonthly], no. 3 (1956), pp. 53–54; *DGB*, January 29, 1956, in *SCMP*, no. 1229 (1956), pp. 14–17; *DGB*, March 3, 1956, in *SCMP*, no. 1254 (1956), pp. 11–15; *RMRB*, April 14, 1956, in *SCMP*, no. 1288 (1956), p. 12, and April 28, 1956, in *SCMP*, no. 1288 (1956), pp. 14–17; *DGB*, August 2, 1956; in Kuan Ta-t'ung, *The Socialist Transformation of Capitalist Industry and Commerce in China*, pp. 60–61; and CASS, p. 235.

   3. *RMRB*, May 15, 1955.

   4. *RMRB*, May 10 and September 8, 1955; *DGB*, April 26, 1955.

   5. *XX*, no. 6 (1955), pp. 11–13; *XHYB*, no. 6 (1955), pp. 133–35.

   6. *RMRB*, March 10 and May 15, 1955; *XHYB*, no. 6 (1955), pp. 133–35; *DGB*, April 15, 1955, and January 29, 1956.

Other, less commonly used early forms included the joint operation group, whose member firms kept their capital and business calculations separate, though they pooled labor, a form used for those operating fragmentary miscellaneous items that the SMC did not deal in;[7] *jingpi* and *daipi*, for small rural wholesalers, in the first of which the commodities entrusted to the trader by the state were not necessarily all state-controlled, but in the second of which they were;[8] *daigou*, commission purchasing, whereby state trade or SMC organs designated the types, specifications, amounts, and procurement prices that were to govern a purchase, and then delegated private merchants to order imports from foreign firms or to buy agricultural products domestically;[9] and the most advanced form, public-private joint purchase, organized by the state companies, in which the state companies and the private side both invested and together purchased goods at production sites.[10]

As of the end of 1954, according to national-level reckoning, only 200,000 rural merchants had been organized into any transformation form.[11] As 1955 progressed, and the larger retail firms moved on to public-private joint operation, three more forms for transformation came into use for the smaller traders: the cooperative team, the cooperative shop, and joint operation. The first two of these new forms merged the operations of some three to ten firms, and it was stipulated that the small merchants organized in them should invest all of their commercial capital in these mergers, including their fixed assets. The fixed assets were assessed by converting them into their value as capital investment or by considering them to be rented or on loan from the merchants.[12]

By early 1955, both the cooperative teams (for firms with more scattered operations, mainly in the rural areas) and cooperative shops (for more fixed firms, in the cities) were forced to engage in unified planning and accounting for all their member firms, and to set aside a proportion of their profits for joint reserve funds. With time the percentage of earnings going to this fund was to increase, while the amount going to dividends would decline.[13] Ultimately, these units were to be converted into retail outlets for their local SMCs. Later in the year, one article specified that those working in the vegetable, slaughtering, and restaurant trades

7. *XHYB*, no. 6 (1955), pp. 133–35.
8. *RMRB*, May 15, 1955.
9. Ibid.
10. Ibid.
11. *RMRB*, March 10, 1955.
12. *DGB*, September 8, 1955, in *SCMP*, no. 1134, pp. 32–36.
13. *DGB*, February 18, 1955, in *SCMP*, no. 999 (1955), pp. 7–11.

were mainly small merchants and peddlers with very little capital, and that their firms could be formed into cooperative shops,[14] and that stall merchants could be formed into teams.[15] Thus this directive indicated that the cooperative store was more suitable for fixed merchants, whereas the team best fit mobile traders.

The third new form, joint operation, was a semisocialist form, meant for use with commercial capitalists working in the rural areas and market towns, whose capital and business turnover were on a larger scale and whose firms did processing or other work of a more technical nature. To these firms the SMC delegated a few cadres and sometimes invested some capital in them; on occasion the SMC incorporated the firm as its outlet. Soybean factories, specialized medical salesmen, and some restaurants fell into the category that might become joint enterprises, and the arrangement provided the SMC with an opportunity to utilize talent, facilities, and capital that it would not otherwise have had at its command. Regulations required firms in this group to divide up their profits according to a fixed formula.[16]

Just for a moment, at the peak of the "high tide" (from mid-December 1955 to mid-January 1956), a glimmer of radicalism appeared in policy toward transforming small merchants. Even then, for the most part this did not entail gross changes for the small merchants immediately, but at least presaged them in the offing.[17] Thus, the *People's Daily* anticipated that when more private urban stores had been converted into agents for the state (through the *dai* form), "after a certain period these stores will change into state stores with the state leasing their common equipment and employing their personnel." Some few cotton-cloth, hardware, and general-goods shops were converted into joint public-private enterprises; in Beijing, for example, 800 of the city's 42,000 private retail outlets (only 2,600 of which employed even two or more workers) had come under joint operation, only 500 of them being bigger shops.[18]

And some stall merchants were organized into cooperative teams, which "after a certain time" would be changed into being shop assistants of state commerce or would act as state stall merchants. But even at

14. *XX*, no. 6 (1955), pp. 11–13.
15. *RMRB*, December 14, 1955, in *SCMP*, no. 1196, pp. 3–6.
16. *DGB*, April 22, 1955; *RMRB*, April 14, 1956, in *SCMP*, no. 1288 (1956), p. 12. Profits were to be divided as follows: reserve fund, 50%; welfare fund, 5%; bonus fund, 5%; construction, 10%; education, 10%; and dividends, 20%.
17. *RMRB*, December 14, 1955, in *SCMP*, no. 1196 (1955), pp. 3–6. A report from Shanxi province at this time directed that by the end of 1956, 90 percent of private commerce would enter cooperative shops and teams (*DGB*, December 12, 1955).
18. *SCMP*, no. 1201 (1955), pp. 19–20.

this time of heady radicalism, a few groups—principally floating food-stalls and scattered stalls dealing in odd commodities—were to be left alone entirely.

Because of massive dislocations and confusion occasioned by the zealous spirit of the "high tide," Chen Yun was able to apply brakes to the process within a month's time.[19] The *dai* form, in which merchants operated independently and only "*mainly* do not participate in the free market" (emphasis added), which had not even been mentioned at the height of the "high tide" in December, was once again promoted, and it was now to exist on a large extent and for a long period. Those who had been merged into teams continued to use unified plans and to replenish their stocks jointly, but they now handled their accounts separately.

By early March, talk of cooperatives had disappeared altogether from the press, as more backpedaling occurred.[20] At that time small merchants demanding to enter into joint operations were told that their applications could be approved, but that they should go on at the present simply working through *dai* and *jing* forms; and that they should continue making procurements on their own.

Then, in April, small stores dealing in daily necessities in fragmentary quantities and travelling peddlers were enjoined to remain indefinitely in the early *dai* and *jing* forms, as were small stores in larger and medium-sized cities. Personnel in such stores, wishing no doubt to obtain the welfare and fixed-wage benefits enjoyed by those in the larger joint enterprises, were assured that *jing* and *dai* operations were "a form of joint public-private operation." They were told, too, that they might put up a signboard indicating that they were joint stores, despite being unable to obtain the perquisites that accompanied this label for their bigger competitors.

At the same time, widely scattered food-stalls and small merchants and peddlers who changed their trade with the seasons (e.g., trading in melons and vegetables part of the year, fans and straw hats at other times, and sometimes collecting scrap metals) were merely asked to register. These traders were vaguely informed that "when necessary," they would be organized into mutual aid teams (for sharing labor, but not

19. *DGB*, January 29, 1956, in *SCMP*, no. 1229 (1956), pp. 14–17.
20. *DGB*, March 3, 1956, in *SCMP*, no. 1254 (1956), pp. 11–15. A good editorial on small urban stores and how to merge them from this period is in *DGB*, March 21, 1956. According to this article, stores were treated in terms of the type of commodities in which they dealt. Also see *DGB*, March 29, 1956, p. 2 (editorial), for a detailed description of the proper forms to use for commercial establishments in the rural areas at this time.

accounts). By this time, the joint-operation form was to be extended to only a very small number of commercial capitalists.[21]

Finally, in late summer 1956, as the "high tide" subsided entirely, an order went out to organize cooperative teams among that 52 percent of all merchants and peddlers who were then operating in the *jing* and *dai* modes.[22] Such teams were to be composed of ten to twenty firms, which would jointly organize their intake of goods, although each firm would remain responsible for its own individual profits and losses. Cooperative stores, the most advanced form of transformation, would be put into effect for only some 30 percent of the rural merchants—those owning and working in small shops in market towns, as well as for some fixed-stall vendors. Such stores were to be created from those already practicing unified accounting within cooperative teams. These shops, considered semisocialist, involved the investment of capital shares by participating firms, the building of reserve and welfare funds, and the payment of less than 20 percent of earnings as dividends to the merchants.

Even the final goal at the end of socialist transformation, then, was to involve substantial reorganization for less than one-third of all small merchants, who were to join into a full-fledged cooperative. Far greater numbers, of course, were left basically unorganized, as those working in the rest of the economy underwent a much more extensive transition to socialism.

21. *RMRB* editorial, April 14, 1956, in *SCMP*, no. 1288 (1956), p. 12. Perhaps an indication of some controversy, this editorial states that the major portion of small merchants, along with some fixed traders in market towns and rural areas, should merge into cooperative stores; whereas an editorial two weeks later (*RMRB*, April 28, 1956) says that small stores in large and medum-sized cities, and small, scattered rural stores should continue in the *jing* and *dai* forms. Merging was said to be suitable only for stores of a similar trade in small cities having populations under 50,000.

22. *DGB*, August 2, 1956. By year's end, 32 percent of the firms were in co-op stores and 46 percent in co-op teams. See CASS, p. 235.

APPENDIX E:
Vicissitudes of Socialist Commerce, 1950–1980

Year	Retail Sales Volume	Number of Commercial Workers[a]	Number of Shops, Restaurants, Commercial Centers
	(in billion yuan)		
1950	17.6[b]	6,850,000[b]	
1951		9,000,000[b]	
1952	27.68[b]		
1957	47.42[b]		1,000,000[g] (under commercial departments, in urban and industrial and mining areas)
			2,820,000[f,j] (commercial centers and shops for commerce, food, and service trades)
1958	54.8[b]	6,400,000[b]	
1965	67.03[c]		
1978 (before the 3d Plenum of the 11th Party Congress)	155.86[c]	2,900,000[i]	180,000[g] (under commercial departments, in urban and industrial and mining areas)
			1,300,000[f] (commercial centers and shops)
			1,077,000[g]
1979	175.3[d]		
1980	214[e]	5,230,000[i]	790,000[h] (urban, above the level of county towns: state-operated, cooperative, individual, and enterprises not managed by commercial departments)
			1,205,000[h] (rural: SMCs, their branches, commission shops, cooperative stores and groups, and individual firms)
			1,210,000[i] (commercial centers and shops)
			1,340,000[i] (commercial centers)

(continued on following page)

APPENDIX E (continued)

SOURCES: [a]These figures are somewhat, but not greatly, different from those calculated by J. P. Emerson, in *Non-Agricultural Employment in Mainland China, 1949–58* (Washington, D.C.: U.S. Bureau of the Census, 1965), p. 128.

[b]Yao Yilin, "Ten Years of Commercial Work," *Renmin ribao (RMRB)*, September 28, 1959, p. 10.

[c]*Beijing Review (BR)*, no. 48 (November 29, 1982), p. 18.

[d]*BR*, no. 38 (September 22, 1980), p. 34.

[e]*BR*, no. 20 (May 18, 1981), p. 17.

[f]*BR*, no. 22 (June 1, 1981), p. 21.

[g]*Guangming ribao* [Bright Daily], February 9, 1980, p. 4.

[h]*RMRB*, April 19, 1981, p. 2.

[i]*BR*, no. 22 (June 1, 1981), p. 22.

[j]*Jingji yanjiu* [Economic Studies], no. 5 (May 20, 1980), p. 33.

APPENDIX F:

Prices (in *yuan*) for Items of Daily Life in Six Provinces, Early 1975

Commodity	Gansu	Qinghai	Heilongjiang	Xinjiang	Hebei	Sichuan
Basin	2.00	2.50		2.00	.30	.60
Battery	.24	.17–.25				.18
Bicycle	140.00	160.00–180.00	154.00–175.00	160.00	130.00–150.00	170.00–180.00
Blanket	17.00	5.00–13.00		5.00	15.00	20.00
Chopsticks		.02–.50		.02 (10 prs.)	.02 (1 pr.)	.02 (1 pr.)
Cigarettes		.20–.50 (for 20)	.30–.41 (for 20)	.25 (for 20)	.10–.60 (for 20)	.30 (for 20)
Clock		8.00–16.00		28.00	8.00–15.00	9.00–30.00
Cloth (cotton)	.30–.40/meter	.90–4.00/meter		1.70/meter	2.00/meter	1.00/meter
Comb	.18	.20–.60		.60		.06
Eggs	.03 each	.10 each	.95/catty	.08 each	.87/catty	
Flour (rationed)	.20/catty	.17/catty	.175/catty	.32/catty	.18/catty	
Fruit	.32/catty	.30/catty	.50/catty		.30/catty	.20/catty
Ink	.26/bottle	.25/bottle		.70/bottle	.20/bottle	.32/bottle
Oil (rationed)	.75/catty	.80/catty	.84/catty	1.70/catty	.80/catty	
Pen	1.60	3.00–7.00		1.00	3.00–5.00	5.00
Pencil	.04	.05		.09	.05	.06
Pork (rationed)	.84/catty	.92–1.00/catty	.93/catty	1.50/catty	1.00/catty	
Radio		50.00–60.00		100.00	50.00–100.00	40.00–130.00
Salt	.12/catty	.13–.14/catty	.17/catty	.20/catty	.20/catty	
Sauces	.90/catty	.26–.29/catty	.12/catty	.50/catty	.18/catty	
Shoes (leather)	11.50/pr.	15.00–24.00/pr.		18.00/pr.	5.00–15.00/pr.	16.00/pr.
Toothpaste	.34/tube	.40/tube	.35/tube	.50/tube	.70–1.00/tube	.55/tube
Towel	.70	.42–.80		.30		.22
Trousers	5.00	6.00–7.00		12.00	7.00	6.00
Vegetables	.05/catty	.10–.20/catty	.05/catty	.10/catty	.20/catty	
Watch	100.00–120.00	120.00–200.00	120.00	120.00	110.00–500.00	100.00–300.00

SOURCE: *China News Summary*, issues from March and April, 1975.
NOTE: A catty is equal to ½ kilogram or 1.1 pounds.

Ministers of Commerce, 1949–1982:
Relevant Biographical Data

Minister and Dates in Office	Background
Chen Yun (November 1956– September 1958)	Director, special office for managing and coordinating financial and economic affairs in the Shen-Gan-Ning and the Shansi-Suiyuan Border Regions, 1940–1945 Head, Party Central Committee's Finance and Economics Department, 1940–1945 Chairman, Finance and Economics Committee of the Northeast Administrative Committee, 1946–1949 Chairman, Finance and Economics Committee of the Government Administrative Committee, 1949–1954
Cheng Zihua (September 1958– February 1960)	Vice-Chairman, Provisional Board, All-China Federation of Cooperatives, 1952, and Acting Chairman, 1952–1953 Director, Central Cooperative Enterprises Administration, 1950 Member, Finance and Economics Committee, Government Administrative Council, 1950–1954 Chairman, All-China Federation of Supply and Marketing Cooperatives, 1954–1963 Vice-Chairman, State Council's Finance and Trade Office, 1959–1961

Minister and Dates in Office	*Background*
Fan Ziyu (ca. 1972–1977)	Worked in the Department of Supplies, 2d Front Army during Long March Head (Major General), 2d Section of Materials, PLA General Logistics Department, August 1964 Carried out the work of "three supports and two militaries" in Ministry of Commerce during the Cultural Revolution
Jin Ming (February 1979– September 1979)	First Deputy Minister of Finance, 1953–1961 Specialized mainly in economic construction work Criticized and dismissed in the Cultural Revolution for favoring the "capitalist road"
Wang Lei (March 1978– August 1978) (September 1979– March 1982)	Director, Trade Department, Southwest Military Administrative Committee, 1951–1953 Member, Preparatory Committee, All-China Federation of Industry and Commerce, June 1952 Vice-Minister of Commerce, 1954–1958; 1967 Director, Political Department, Ministry of Commerce, February 1966 Accused of being a "counterrevolutionary revisionist" April 1967
Yao Yilin (February 1960– ca. 1967) (August 1978– February 1979)	Head, Industry and Commerce Department, and member, Finance and Economics Committee, North China People's Government, 1949 Vice-Minister of Trade, 1949 Member, Provisional Board of Directors, All-China Federation of Cooperatives, 1950; Standing Committee member, 1950– (later, the All-China Federation of Supply and Marketing Cooperatives) Member, China Democratic National Construction Association, 1950–1952; Member, Central Committee, CDNCA, 1955– Vice-Minister of Commerce, 1952–1960 Deputy Director, Finance and Trade Office of the State Council, 1959 Deputy Director, Party Central Committee's Finance and Trade Work Department, 1959 Director, Central Committee's Finance and Trade Political Department, 1964

Minister and Dates in Office	*Background*
Ye Jizhuang (September 1949– August 1952)	Red Army's foremost logistics specialist from early 1930s until 1949 Leading expert in foreign trade, 1949–1967 (year of his death) People's commissar of trade for Chinese Soviet Republic's government, 1931 Director and political commissar of the General Supply Department of the First Front Army Director, Supply Department for the First Front Army on the Long March Manager of the official trading company for the Shen-Gan-Ning Border Region, 1945 Head, Rear Services Department, Northeast PLA, 1949 Director, Northeast Administrative Committee's Finance and Commerce Department, 1949 Director, Foreign Trade Department, Northeast People's Government, 1949 Director, Board of Supervisors, All-China Federation of Cooperatives, 1950–1954 Member, Finance and Economics Committee of the Central People's Government, 1949
Zeng Shan (August 1952– November 1956)	Member, North China People's Government's Finance and Economics Committee, 1948–1949 Head, East China Branch, People's Bank of China, 1949–1950 Head, East China Finance and Economics Committee, 1949–1954 Member and later Vice-Chairman, Government Administrative Council's Finance and Economics Committee, 1949–1954 Member, National Committee, All-China Federation of Supply and Marketing Cooperatives and head of its Supervisory Committee, 1954 Deputy Director, Fifth Staff Office, State Council (the office concerned with finance and trade)

GLOSSARY

Beijinglu Huaqiao Shangpin Gongying Shangdian	Beijing Road Overseas Chinese Commodities Supply Store	北京路华侨商品供应商店
Bu lao er huo	Reap without sowing	不劳而获
Ceng ceng sung li	Present a gift at every level	层层送礼
Changsha Baihuozhan Lingshou (Zhuan) Dian	Special Store for Retail Sales of the Changsha General Goods Station	长沙百货站零售（专）店
Changsha Erqinggongyeju Chanpin Fuwubu	Products Service Unit of the Changsha Second Bureau of Light Industry	长沙二轻工业局产品服务部
Chen Yun	Minister of Commerce, 1956–1958	陈云
Cheng Zihua	Minister of Commerce, 1958–1960	程子华
Chuli shangpin	Goods sold at reduced prices (usually leftover stocks or damaged goods); goods for disposal	处理商品

Da shou	Great procurement	大收
Dai	Underwriting sales, sales commission agent	代
Daigou	Commission purchasing	代购
Daipi	Form of socialist transformation for wholesalers	代批
Daixiao	Purchase and sales done, and prices set, according to state sales plan; income from commission; leaves security deposit with state organ	代销
Daixiao dian	Shop that sells on commission	代销店
Ding gou	Fixed purchase	定购
Disi Fuzhuangchang Zhongxin Menshibu	Central Retail Outlet of the 4th Clothing Factory	第四服装厂中心门市部
Fan Ziyu	Minister of Commerce, 1972–1977	范子瑜
Gongren chaduei	A form of worker militia in Cultural Revolution days	工人察队
Gouhuo zheng	Certificate for buying goods	购货证
Guan	Barrier	关
Guan er bu si, huo er bu luan	Under control but without being suffocated, alive but without chaos	管而不死，活而不乱
Guanli fei	Management fee	管理费
Guanxi	Relationship, personal connections	关系
Gui bin shi	Distinguished-guest lounges (sections of department stores with special high-class goods for upper-level cadres)	贵宾室

Guilinshi Jiaoqu Chuanshan Gongxiaoshe Zhongxin Menshibu	Central Retail Outlet of the Supply and Marketing Cooperative of Guilin Municipality's Suburban District, Chuanshan	桂林市郊区穿山供销社中心门市部
Guilinshi Liangyou Gongÿing Gongsi	Guilin Municipal Grain and Oil Supply Company	桂林市粮油供应公司
Guilinshi Tangyanjiu Gongsi Daixiaodian Zhengyang Menshibu	Zhengyang Retail Outlet of a Commission Shop of the Guilin Municipal Sugar, Tobacco, and Wine Company	桂林市糖烟酒公司代销店正阳门市部
Guojia shangye bumen	State commercial departments	国家商业部门
Hezuo dian	Cooperative shop	合作店
Hou men	Going through the back door (getting things done by connections)	后门
Jianxin Guopin Hezuo Yidian	Shop One of "Build-the-New" Fruits Cooperative	建新果品合作一店
Jin	Catty, equal to ½ kilogram (1.1 pounds)	斤
Jin Ming	Minister of Commerce, 1979	金明
Jing	Consignment deals, agent, retail distributors	经
Jingpi	Form of socialist transformation for wholesalers	经批
Jingxiao	Purchase and sales done, and prices set, in accord with state sales plan; income from price differentials	经销
Jiti	Collective	集体

Kao tong chi fan	Rely on control for their livelihood	靠统吃饭
Li	Chinese unit of length, equal to ½ kilometer	里
Liang	A unit of weight, equal to 50 grams	两
Liu, zhuan, bao	Terms referring to the treatment of wholesale firms in socialist transformation, meaning, respectively, left alone, changed over to a different line of work, absorbed by another firm	留，专，包
Menshibu	Retail outlet	门市部
Pai gou	Administratively assigned purchase	派购
Piao	Ration coupons or tickets	票
Piao zheng bangongshi (zu)	Office of (group for) ration tickets and certificates	票证办公室（组）
Pigou (lingxiao)	Bulk purchasing from the state; profit from price differential; commodities not controlled (socialist transformation form)	批购（零销）
Renminbi	The Chinese unit of money or dollar (see Yuan)	人民币
Rongchang Tangyanjiu Hezuo Jiufendian	Branch Shop Nine of the Rongchang Sugar, Tobacco, and Wine Cooperative	荣昌糖烟酒合作九分店

San, wu fan	Three and five "antis," campaigns to rectify the bureaucracy and begin the socialization of the bourgeoisie, respectively (1951–1952); 3 "antis" opposed corruption, waste and bureaucracy; 5 "antis" opposed bribery of government workers, tax evasion, theft of state property, cheating on government contracts, and stealing economic information for private speculation	三，五反
Shangyebu	Ministry of Commerce	商业部
Shougou shangdian	Shop that buys used goods from owners and sells them for the owner (in the manner of a pawn shop)	收购商店
Tongchou jiangu, quanmian anpai	The policy of overall arrangement and all-around consideration	统筹兼顾，全面安排
Tonggou baoxiao	Unified purchase and guaranteed sales	统购包销
Tongxiao	Unified purchase	统销
Touji daoba	Profiteering and speculation	投机倒把
Tun tu	Swallow and spit out (refers to taking in and releasing goods to regulate prices)	吞吐
Wang Lei	Minister of Commerce 1978, 1979–1982	王磊

Weituo	Trust, as in a shop that holds goods on trust	委托
Wu fan	See *San, wu fan*	五反
Wu jin	Hardware	五金
Wuze diaoji shangdian	Shop for exchanging goods (in the manner of a pawn shop)	物资调剂 商店
Xi Lou	Western Chamber, where a crucial Politburo meeting was held in 1962	西楼
Xian	County	县
Xiang	Township	乡
Xinhua Shudian Keji Menshibu	Scientific and Technical Retail Outlet of the New China Bookstore	新华书店科技门市部
Xintuo shangdian	Shop that holds goods on trust (in the manner of a pawn shop)	信托商店
Xuangou	Selective purchase	选购
Yao Yilin	Minister of Commerce 1960–1967, 1978–1979	姚依林
Ye Jizhuang	Minister of Trade, 1949–1952	叶季壮
Yiyao Daixiaodian	Medical Products Commission Sales Shop	医药代销店
Yuan	Chinese unit of money or dollar, equivalent to about $.67 U.S. to 1980	元
Zeng Shan	Minister of Commerce, 1952–1956	曾山
Zhen	Town	镇
Zhuan shou	"Pass hands," or resale of goods for a profit	转手
Zhuanye daixiao	All of a firm's goods are obtained from state commerce (socialist transformation form)	专业代销

BIBLIOGRAPHY

The bibliography is divided into three sections: English-language works, English-language serials, and Chinese-language books and periodicals. The first section includes books, journal articles, and book chapters in English. The second section lists a number of translation series, primary materials (such as radio broadcasts, reviews of the Chinese press), and periodicals containing analyses of current Chinese events of which an entire series (or, in a few cases, selected issues) was consulted in the research for this book.

The third section contains Chinese books used in the research, as well as newspapers and journals in Chinese. Rather than listing separately every one of the literally thousands of articles used here, I have chosen instead simply to note the years covered for those papers and journals that were researched for a set block of time; and to indicate where only selected issues were used in the other cases. The footnotes in each chapter are more specific.

I have relied on the *pinyin* system of romanization for transliterating Chinese publications and their authors, except in cases where English-language translations from before 1979 use the Wade-Giles system.

ENGLISH-LANGUAGE WORKS

Ahn, Byung-joon. *Chinese Politics and the Cultural Revolution.* Seattle: University of Washington Press, 1976.

Balazs, Etienne. *Chinese Civilization and Bureaucracy.* New Haven: Yale University Press, 1974.

Bates, Robert. *Markets and States in Tropical Africa.* Berkeley: University of California Press, 1981.

Baum, Richard. *Prelude to Revolution: Mao, the Party, and the Peasant Question, 1962–66.* New York: Columbia University Press, 1975.

Beals, Ralph L. *The Peasant Marketing System of Oaxaca, Mexico.* Berkeley: University of California Press, 1975.

Belshaw, Cyril S. *Traditional Exchange and Modern Markets.* Englewood Cliffs, N.J.: Prentice-Hall, 1965.

Bennett, Gordon A. "Activists and Professionals: China's Revolution in Bureaucracy, 1959–1965: A Case Study of the Finance-Trade System." Ph.D. dissertation, University of Wisconsin, 1973.

———. *China's Finance and Trade: A Policy Reader.* White Plains, N.Y.: M. E. Sharpe, 1978.

———. *Huadong: The Story of a Chinese People's Commune.* Boulder, Colo.: Westview Press, 1978.

Bernstein, Thomas P. "Cadre and Peasant Behavior Under Conditions of Insecurity and Deprivation." In *Chinese Communist Politics in Action*, pp. 365–99. Edited by A. Doak Barnett. Seattle: University of Washington Press, 1969.

Bettelheim, Charles. *Class Struggles in the U.S.S.R.: First Period: 1917–1923.* New York and London: Monthly Review Press, 1976.

———. *Class Struggles in the U.S.S.R.: Second Period: 1923–1930.* New York and London: Monthly Review Press, 1978.

———. *Economic Calculation and Forms of Property: An Essay on the Transition between Capitalism and Socialism.* New York and London: Monthly Review Press, 1975.

———. *The Transition to Socialist Economy.* Atlantic Heights, N.J.: Humanities Press, 1975.

Blaustein, Albert P. *Fundamental Legal Documents of Communist China.* South Hackensack, N.J.: Fred B. Rothman and Co., 1962.

Bowie, Robert R., and Fairbank, John K. *Communist China 1955–1959: Policy Documents with Analysis.* Cambridge: Harvard University Press, 1962.

Brus, Wlodzimierz. *The Market in a Socialist Economy.* London and Boston: Routledge & Kegan Paul, 1972.

Bucknall, Kevin. "Capitalism and Chinese Agriculture, 1960–66." *Australian Journal of Chinese Affairs*, no. 1 (1979), pp. 69–90.

Butterfield, Fox. *China: Alive in the Bitter Sea.* New York: New York Times Books, 1982.

Campbell, Robert W. *Soviet Economic Power.* 2d ed. Boston: Houghton, Mifflin Co., 1966.

Chang, Parris. *Power and Policy in China.* University Park: Pennsylvania State University Press, 1975.

Chao Kuo-chün. *Economic Planning and Organization in Mainland China: A Documentary Study (1949–1957).* Cambridge: Harvard University Center for East Asian Studies, 1960.

Chen, C. S., comp. *Rural People's Communes in Lien-chiang: Documents Concerning Communes in Lien-chiang County, Fukien Province, 1962–1963.* Translated by Charles Price Ridley. Stanford: Hoover Institution Press, 1969.

Chen, Nai-ruenn. "China's Inflation, 1979–82: A Quantitative Assessment." Draft, February 15, 1983.

Chinn, Dennis L. "Research Note: Basic Commodity Distribution in the People's Republic of China." *China Quarterly*, no. 84 (December 1980), pp. 744–54.

Chou, Yu-min. "Wholesaling in Communist China." In *Comparative Marketing*, pp. 253–69. Edited by Robert Bartels. Homewood, Ill: Richard D. Irwin, 1963.

Cohen, Stephen F. *Bukharin and the Bolshevik Revolution: A Political Biography.* New York: A. A. Knopf, 1973.

Cunningham, W., D.D. *The Growth of English Industry and Commerce During the Early and Middle Ages.* New York: Augustus M. Kelley, 1968.

Cyert, Richard M., and March, James G. *A Behavioral Theory of the Firm.* Englewood Cliffs, N.J.: Prentice-Hall, 1963.

Davis, William G. *Social Relations in a Philippine Market.* Berkeley: University of California Press, 1973.

Davis-Friedmann, Deborah. *Long Lives: Chinese Elderly and the Communist Revolution.* Cambridge: Harvard University Press, 1983.

Dernberger, Robert F. "P.R.C. Industrial Policies . . . Goals and Results." Paper for presentation at the Tenth Sino-American Conference on Mainland China, Berkeley, California, June 16–18, 1981.

Dewey, Alice G. *Peasant Marketing in Java.* New York: The Free Press of Glencoe, 1962.

Donnithorne, Audrey. *Centre-Provincial Economic Relations in China.* Canberra: Contemporary China Centre, Research School of Pacific Studies, Australia National University, 1981.

———. *China's Economic System.* London: George Allen and Unwin, 1967.

———. "Organizational Aspects of the Internal Trade of the Chinese People's Republic with Special Reference to 1958–1960." In *Symposium on Economic and Social Problems of the Far East*, pp. 55–71. Edited by E. F. Szczepanik. Hong Kong: Hong Kong University Press, 1962.

Ecklund, George N. "Protracted Expropriation of Private Business in Communist China." *Pacific Affairs*, 36, no. 3 (1963): 238–49.

Eckstein, Alexander. *China's Economic Revolution.* Cambridge: Cambridge University Press, 1977.

Eighth National Congress of the Communist Party of China, Volume I: Documents. Peking: Foreign Languages Press, 1956.

Eighth National Congress of the Communist Party of China, Volume II: Speeches. Peking: Foreign Languages Press, 1956.

Elvin, Mark. *The Pattern of the Chinese Past.* Stanford: Stanford University Press, 1973.

Engels, Frederick. *Anti-Dühring*. Peking: Foreign Languages Press, 1976.

Etzioni, Amitai. *A Comparative Analysis of Complex Organizations*. New York: Free Press, 1961.

Falkenheim, Victor C. "Political Reform in China." *Current History*, September 1982, pp. 259–63, 280–81.

Felker, Jere L. *Soviet Economic Controversies: The Emerging Marketing Concept and Changes in Planning, 1960–1965*. Cambridge: M.I.T. Press, 1966.

Feuerwerker, Albert. *The Chinese Economy, ca. 1870–1911*. Ann Arbor: University of Michigan, Center for Chinese Studies, Michigan Papers in Chinese Studies, No. 5, 1969.

———. "Economic Conditions in the Late Ch'ing Period." In *Modern China*, pp. 105–25. Edited by Albert Feuerwerker. Englewood Cliffs, N.J.: Prentice-Hall, 1964.

First Five Year Plan for the Development of the National Economy of the People's Republic of China in 1953–1957. Peking: Foreign Languages Press, 1956.

Fitzgerald, C. P. *The Tower of the Five Glories*. London: Cresset Press, 1941.

Fried, Morton H. *The Fabric of Chinese Society*. New York: Praeger, 1953.

Friedman, Edward. "Maoism, Titoism, Stalinism: Some Origins and Consequences of the Maoist Theory of the Socialist Transition." In *The Transition to Socialism in China*, pp. 159–214. Edited by Mark Selden and Victor Lippit. Armonk, N.Y.: M. E. Sharpe, 1982.

Frolic, B. Michael. *Mao's People*. Cambridge: Harvard University Press, 1980.

Gamble, Sidney D. *Ting Hsien: A North China Rural Community*. Stanford: Stanford University Press, 1954.

Gardner, John. "The *Wu-fan* Campaign in Shanghai: A Study in the Consolidation of Urban Control." In *Chinese Communist Politics in Action*, pp. 477–539. Edited by A. Doak Barnett. Seattle: University of Washington Press, 1969.

Garvy, G. "The Monetary System and the Payments Flow." In *Socialist Economics: Selected Readings*, pp. 275–306. Edited by Alec Nove and D. M. Nuti. Harmondsworth and New York: Penguin Books, 1972.

Geertz, Clifford. *Peddlers and Princes*. Chicago: University of Chicago Press, 1963.

Goldman, Marshall I. *Soviet Marketing: Distribution in a Controlled Economy*. New York: The Free Press of Glencoe, 1963.

Good, Charles M. *Rural Markets and Trade in East Africa: Study of the Functions and Development of Exchange Institutions in Ankole, Uganda*. Department of Geography, Research Paper No. 128. Chicago: University of Chicago, 1970.

Gras, N. S. B. *The Evolution of the English Corn Market from the 12th to the 18th Century*. New York: Russell and Russell, 1967 [reissued].

Griffiths, Franklyn. "A Tendency Analysis of Soviet Policy-Making." In *Interest Groups in Soviet Politics*, pp. 335–77. Edited by H. Gordon Skilling and Franklyn Griffiths. Princeton: Princeton University Press, 1971.

Grossman, Gregory. "The 'Second Economy' of the USSR." *Problems of Communism*, no. 9–10 (1977), pp. 25–40.

————. "The 'Shadow Economy' in the Socialist Sector of the USSR and Eastern Europe." Paper presented to conference on The CMEA Five-Year (1981–1985) Plans in a New Perspective: Planned and Non-Planned Economies, NATO-Economics Directorate, Brussels, March, 1982.

Grove, Linda. "Treaty Port and Hinterland: Revolution in a Semi-Colonial Society." Paper presented to the Workshop on Rebellion and Revolution in North China, Late Ming to the Present, Harvard University, July 27–August 2, 1979.

Hanson, Philip. *Advertising and Socialism*. White Plains, N.Y.: International Arts and Sciences Press, 1974.

Ho P'ing-ti. *The Ladder of Success in Imperial China*. New York: Columbia University Press, 1964.

Hodder, B. W., and Ukwu, U. I. *Markets in West Africa*. New York: Africana Publishing Corporation, 1969.

Höhmann, Hans-Hermann; Kaser, Michael; and Thalheim, Karl C., eds. *The New Economic Systems of Eastern Europe*. Berkeley: University of California Press, 1975.

Horvat, Branko. *The Yugoslav Economic System*. White Plains, N.Y.: International Arts and Sciences Press, 1976.

Howe, Christopher. *China's Economy: A Basic Reader*. New York: Basic Books, 1978.

Howe, Christopher, and Walker, Kenneth. "The Economist." In *Mao Tse-tung in the Scales of History*, pp. 174–222. Edited by Dick Wilson. Cambridge: Cambridge University Press, 1977.

Hsiao, Kung-ch'üan. *Rural China*. Seattle: University of Washington Press, 1960.

Hsu, Robert C. "Agricultural Financial Policies in China, 1949–1980." *Asian Survey*, 22, no. 4 (1982): 638–58.

Huang, Ray. *Taxation and Governmental Finance in 16th Century Ming China*. New York: Cambridge University Press, 1974.

Hughes, T. J., and Luard, D. E. T. *The Economic Development of Communist China 1949–1958*. London: Oxford University Press, 1959.

Jasny, Naum. *The Socialized Agriculture of the U.S.S.R.: Plans and Performance*. Stanford: Stanford University Press, 1949.

Jones, Susan Mann. "Trade, Transport, and Taxes: The Decline of a National Medicine Fair in Republican China." In *Political Leadership and Social Change on the Local Level in China, 1850–1950*, No. 2, pp. 112–42. Edited by Tang Tsou. Chicago: University of Chicago Center for Far Eastern Studies, 1980.

Klein, Donald W., and Clark, Anne B. *Biographic Dictionary of Chinese Communism, 1921–1965*. Cambridge: Harvard University Press, 1971.

Kuan Ta-t'ung. *The Socialist Transformation of Capitalist Industry and Commerce in China*. Peking: Foreign Languages Press, 1960.

Lange, Oskar, and Taylor, Fred M. *On the Economic Theory of Socialism*. Edited by Benjamin Evan Lippincott. Minneapolis: University of Minnesota Press, 1938.

Lardy, Nicholas R. "Centralization and Decentralization in China's Fiscal Management." *China Quarterly*, no. 61 (March 1975), pp. 25–60.

_____ . "Chinese Agricultural Development Policy." Paper prepared for the Tenth Sino-American Conference on Mainland China, University of California, Berkeley, June 16–18, 1981.

_____ . *Economic Growth and Distribution in China*. New York: Cambridge University Press, 1979.

_____ . "Economic Reform in China: Retrospect and Prospect." Paper prepared for the Luce Seminar in American-Asian Cultural Relations, University of Chicago, May 30–31 (draft).

Lardy, Nicholas, ed. *Chinese Economic Planning*. White Plains, N.Y.: M.E. Sharpe, 1978.

Lee, Hong Yung. *The Politics of the Chinese Cultural Revolution*. Berkeley: University of California Press, 1978.

Lele, Uma J. *Food Grain Marketing in India: Private Performance and Public Policy*. Ithaca, N.Y.: Cornell University Press, 1971.

Lewin, Moshe. *Political Undercurrents in Soviet Economic Debates*. Princeton: Princeton University Press, 1974.

Lewis, John Wilson. "Commerce, Education and Political Development in Tangshan, 1956–1969." In *The City in Communist China*, pp. 153–79. Edited by John Wilson Lewis. Stanford: Stanford University Press, 1971.

Li Choh-ming. *The Economic Development of Communist China*. Berkeley: University of California Press, 1959.

Li, Lillian M. "Introduction" to "Food, Famine, and the Chinese State—A Symposium." *Journal of Asian Studies*, 41, no. 4 (1982): 687–707.

Liao, T'ai-ch'u. "The Rape Markets on the Chengtu Plain." *Journal of Farm Economics*, 28, no. 4 (1946): 1016–24.

Lieberthal, Kenneth. "Beijing's Consumer Market." *China Business Review*, September-October 1981, pp. 36–41.

_____ . *Revolution and Tradition in Tientsin, 1949–1959*. Stanford: Stanford University Press, 1980.

Lin, Cyril Chihren. "The Reinstatement of Economics in China Today." *China Quarterly*, no. 85 (March 1981), pp. 1–48.

Lin Zili. "Initial Reform in China's Economic Structure." *Social Sciences in China*, no. 3 (1980), pp. 172–94.

Lindblom, Charles E. *Politics and Markets*. New York: Basic Books, 1977.

Lippit, Victor D. *Land Reform and Economic Development in China*. White Plains, N.Y.: International Arts and Sciences Press, 1974.

Lopez, Robert S., and Raymond, Irving N., eds. *Medieval Trade in the Mediterranean World*. New York: W. W. Norton and Co., 1967.

Lowenthal, Richard. "Development vs. Utopia in Communist Policy." In *Change in Communist Systems*, pp. 33–116. Edited by Chalmers Johnson. Stanford: Stanford University Press, 1970.

MacFarquhar, Roderick. *The Origins of the Cultural Revolution 1: Contradictions Among the People 1956–1957*. New York: Columbia University Press, 1974.

Mandel, Ernest. *An Introduction to Marxist Economic Theory.* 2d ed. New York: Pathfinder Press, 1973.

———. *Marxist Economic Theory.* Translated by Brian Pearce. New York and London: Monthly Review Press, 1968.

Mann, Susan. "The Order of the Marketplace in Agrarian China." Manuscript in progress, forthcoming.

Mao Tse-tung. *A Critique of Soviet Economics.* Translated by Moss Roberts. New York and London: Monthly Review Press, 1977.

———. "On the Policy Concerning Industry and Commerce." Peking: Foreign Languages Press, 1968.

———. *Report to the Second Plenary Session of the Seventh Central Committee of the Communist Party of China.* Peking: Foreign Languages Press, 1968.

———. "Several Important Instructions," June 29 and July 2, 1959. In "Miscellany of Mao Tse-tung Thought (1949–1968)," Part I. *Joint Publications Research Service,* no. 61269-1 (February 20, 1974).

———. *Selected Works.* Vol. 5. Peking: Foreign Languages Press, 1977.

Marx, Karl. *Capital.* Vol. 3. Moscow: Foreign Languages Publishing House, 1962.

———. *A Contribution to the Critique of Political Economy.* Translated from the German edition by N. I. Stone. Chicago: Charles H. Kerr and Co., 1918.

Metzger, Thomas A. "The State and Commerce in Imperial China." *Asian and African Studies,* no. 6 (1970), pp. 23–46.

Milenkovitch, Deborah D. *Plan and Market in Yugoslav Economic Thought.* New Haven and London: Yale University Press, 1971.

Mintz, Sidney W. "The Role of the Middleman in the Internal Distribution System of a Caribbean Peasant Economy." *Human Organization,* 15, no. 2 (1956): 18–23.

Montias, J. M. "Planning with Material Balances in Soviet-Type Economies." In *Socialist Economics: Selected Readings,* pp. 223–51. Edited by Alec Nove and D. M. Nuti. Harmondsworth and New York: Penguin Books, 1972.

Morse, H. B. *The Trade and Administration of the Chinese Empire.* Taipei: Ch'eng-wen Publishing Co., 1966.

Myers, Ramon H. *The Chinese Peasant Economy: Agricultural Development in Hopei and Shantung, 1890–1949.* Cambridge: Harvard University Press, 1970.

———. "Customary Law, Markets, and Resource Transactions in Late Imperial China." In *Explorations in the New Economic History,* pp. 273–98. Edited by Roger L. Ransom, Richard Sutch, and Garmy M. Walton. New York: Academic Press, 1982.

Neuberger, Egon, and Duffy, William. *Comparative Economic Systems.* Boston: Allyn and Bacon, 1976.

New China's Economic Achievements 1949–1952. Compiled by the China Committee for Promotion of International Trade. Peking: Foreign Languages Press, 1952.

Nove, Alec. *An Economic History of the U.S.S.R.* London: The Penguin Press, 1970.

_____. "Economic Reforms in the USSR and Hungary, a Study in Contrasts." In *Socialist Economics: Selected Readings,* pp. 335–62. Edited by Alec Nove and D. M. Nuti. Harmondsworth and New York: Penguin Books, 1972.

_____. "The Liberman Proposals." *Survey,* no. 47 (April 1963), pp. 112–18.

_____. *Political Economy and Soviet Socialism.* London: George Allen and Unwin, 1979.

_____. *The Soviet Economic System.* London: George Allen and Unwin, 1977.

Nove, Alec, and Nuti, D. M., eds. *Socialist Economics: Selected Readings.* Harmondsworth and New York: Penguin Books, 1972.

Ortiz, Sutti. "Colombia Rural Market Organization: An Exploratory Model." *Man,* N.S. 2 (1967): 393–414.

Parish, William L. "Egalitarianism in Chinese Society." *Problems of Communism,* no. 1–2 (1981), pp. 37–53.

Parish, William L., and Whyte, Martin King. *Village and Family in Contemporary China.* Chicago: University of Chicago Press, 1978.

Pejovich, Svetozar. "The End of Planning: The Soviet Union and East European Experiences." In *The Politics of Planning: A Review and Critique of Centralized Economic Planning,* pp. 95–113. San Francisco: Institute for Contemporary Studies, 1976.

Pepper, Suzanne. *Civil War in China.* Berkeley: University of California Press, 1978.

Perkins, Dwight H. *Agricultural Development in China 1368–1968.* Chicago: Aldine Publishing Co., 1969.

_____. *Market Control and Planning in Communist China.* Cambridge: Harvard University Press, 1966.

Pirenne, Henri. *Early Democracies in the Low Countries.* New York: Harper Torchbooks, 1963.

_____. *Medieval Cities.* Princeton: Princeton University Press, 1969.

Posner, Richard A. "Theories of Economic Regulation." *Bell Journal of Economics and Management Science,* 5, no. 2 (1974): 335–58.

Prybyla, Jan S. "Key Issues in the Chinese Economy." *Asian Survey,* 21, no. 9 (1981): 925–46.

_____. *The Political Economy of Communist China.* Scranton, Pa.: International Textbook Company, 1970.

Red Guard Publications, Part I: Newspapers. Reprinted by Center for Chinese Research Materials, Association of Research Libraries, Washington, D.C., 1975.

Richman, Barry M. "Capitalists & Managers in Communist China." *Harvard Business Review,* January–February 1967, pp. 57–78.

_____. *Industrial Society in Communist China.* New York: Vintage Books, 1972.

Rodrik, Dani. "Rural Transformation and Peasant Political Orientations in Egypt and Turkey." *Comparative Politics,* 14, no. 4 (1982): 417–42.

Rozman, Gilbert. *Urban Networks in Ch'ing China and Tokugawa Japan.* Princeton: Princeton University Press, 1973.

Sabatier, Paul A. "Regulatory Policy-Making: Toward a Framework of Analysis." *Natural Resources Journal,* 17, no. 3 (1977): 415–60.

Schram, Stuart, ed. *Chairman Mao Talks to the People.* New York: Pantheon Books, 1974.

Schran, Peter. *Guerrilla Economy.* Albany, N.Y.: SUNY Press, 1976.

Schurmann, Franz. *Ideology and Organization in Communist China.* Berkeley: University of California Press, 1966.

———. *The Logic of World Power.* New York: Pantheon Books, 1974.

Schwartz, Charles A. "Corruption and Political Development in the U.S.S.R." *Comparative Politics,* 11, no. 4 (1979): 425–43.

Selden, Mark. "Cooperation and Conflict: Cooperative and Collective Formation in China's Countryside." In *The Transition to Socialism in China,* pp. 32–97. Edited by Mark Selden and Victor Lippit. Armonk, N.Y.: M.E. Sharpe, 1982.

———. *The Yenan Way.* Cambridge: Harvard University Press, 1971.

Shiba, Yoshinobu. *Commerce and Society in Sung China.* Translated by Mark Elvin. Ann Arbor: Center for Chinese Studies, Michigan Abstracts of Chinese and Japanese Works on Chinese History, No. 2, 1970.

Shue, Vivienne. *Peasant China in Transition: The Dynamics of Development Toward Socialism, 1949–1956.* Berkeley: University of California Press, 1980.

———. "Reorganizing Rural Trade: Unified Purchase and Socialist Transformation." *Modern China,* 2, no. 1 (1976): 104–34.

Šik, Ota. *Plan and Market Under Socialism.* Prague: Academia, 1967.

Sjoberg, Gideon. *The Preindustrial City: Past and Present.* New York: The Free Press, 1960.

Skinner, G. William. "Cities and the Hierarchy of Local Systems." In *The City in Late Imperial China,* pp. 275–351. Edited by G. William Skinner. Stanford: Stanford University Press, 1977.

———. "Marketing and Social Structure in Rural China, Part I." *Journal of Asian Studies,* 24, no. 1 (1964): 3–43.

———. "Marketing and Social Structure in Rural China, Part III." *Journal of Asian Studies,* 24, no. 3 (1965): 363–99.

———. "Vegetable Supply and Marketing in Chinese Cities." *China Quarterly,* no. 76 (December 1978), pp. 733–93.

Skinner, G. William, and Winckler, Edwin A. "Compliance Succession in Rural Communist China: A Cyclical Theory." In *A Sociological Reader on Complex Organization,* pp. 410–38. 2d ed. Edited by Amitai Etzioni. New York: Holt, Rinehart and Winston, 1969.

Smith, Hedrick. *The Russians.* New York: Ballantine Books, 1977.

Solinger, Dorothy J. "Economic Reform via Reformulation in China: Where Do Rightist Ideas Come From?" *Asian Survey,* 21 no. 9 (1981): 947–60.

———. "Minority Nationalities in China's Yunnan Province: Assimilation, Power, and Policy in a Socialist State." *World Politics,* 30, no. 1 (1977): 1–23.

_____. *Regional Government and Political Integration in Southwest China, 1949–1954.* Berkeley: University of California Press, 1977.

_____. "Some Speculations on the Return of the Regions: Parallels with the Past." *China Quarterly*, no. 75 (September 1978), pp. 623–38.

Stalin, Joseph. *Economic Problems of Socialism in the U.S.S.R.* Peking: Foreign Languages Press, 1972.

Tawney, R. H. *Land and Labor in China.* Boston: Beacon Press, 1966.

Tilly, Charles. "Food Supply and Public Order in Modern Europe." In *The Formation of National States in Western Europe*, pp. 380–455. Edited by Charles Tilly. Princeton: Princeton University Press, 1975.

Twitchett, Denis. "The T'ang Market System." *Asia Major*, N.S. 12, part 2, pp. 202–48.

Union Research Institute. *Documents of the Chinese Communist Party Central Committee September 1956–April 1969*, vol. I. Hong Kong: Union Research Institute, 1971.

_____. *Hierarchies of the People's Republic of China, March 1975.* Hong Kong: Union Research Institute, 1975.

Usher, Abbott Payson. *The History of the Grain Trade in France, 1400–1710.* Cambridge: Harvard University Press, 1913.

Van der Sprenkel, Sybille. "Urban Social Control." In *The City in Late Imperial China*, pp. 609–32. Edited by G. William Skinner. Stanford: Stanford University Press, 1977.

Vogel, Ezra. *Canton Under Communism.* Cambridge: Harvard University Press, 1969.

Wädekin, Karl-Eugen. *The Private Sector in Soviet Agriculture.* Edited by George Karcz. Berkeley: University of California Press, 1973.

Wakeman, Frederic, Jr. *The Fall of Imperial China.* New York: The Free Press, 1975.

Wang, Tong-eng. *Economic Policies and Price Stability in China.* Berkeley: University of California Press, Center for Chinese Studies, Chinese Research Monograph No. 16, 1980.

Walker, Kenneth R. "Collectivisation in Retrospect: The 'Socialist High Tide' of Autumn 1955–Spring 1956." *China Quarterly*, no. 26 (June 1966), pp. 1–43.

Ward, Benjamin N. *The Soviet Economy.* New York: Random House, 1967.

Wheelwright, E. L., and McFarlane, Bruce. *The Chinese Road to Socialism.* New York and London: Monthly Review Press, 1970.

White, Lynn T. III. "Low Power: Small Enterprises in Shanghai, 1949–1967." *China Quarterly*, no. 73 (March 1978), pp. 45–76.

Wiles, P. J. D. *The Political Economy of Communism.* Cambridge: Harvard University Press, 1962.

Williamson, Oliver. *Markets and Hierarchies: Analysis and Antitrust Implications.* New York: The Free Press, 1975.

Wilson, James Q. "The Politics of Regulation." In *Social Responsibility and the*

Business Predicament, pp. 135–68. Edited by James W. McKie. Washington, D.C.: the Brookings Institution, 1974.

Wong, R. Bin. "Food Riots in the Qing Dynasty." *Journal of Asian Studies*, 41, no. 4 (1982): 767–88.

Wortzel, Larry M. "Incentive Mechanisms and Policies of the Eleventh Central Committee." *Asian Survey*, 21, no. 9 (1981): 961–76.

Yahuda, Michael. "Political Generations in China." *China Quarterly*, no. 80 (December 1979), pp. 793–805.

Yang Ching-kun. *A North China Local Market Economy*. New York: Institute of Pacific Relations, International Secretariat, 1944.

Yu, Elena S. H. "Overseas Remittances in Southeastern China." *China Quarterly*, no. 78 (June 1979), pp. 339–50.

Zauberman, Alfred. "The Soviet Debate on the Law of Value and Price Formation." In *Value and Plan*, pp. 17–35. Edited by Gregory Grossman. Berkeley: University of California Press, 1960.

ENGLISH-LANGUAGE SERIALS

Beijing Review (Beijing), 1979–1981.

China News Analysis (Hong Kong), 1953–1979.

Extracts from China Mainland Magazines (Hong Kong), 1955–1959.

Foreign Broadcast Information Service, 1977–1979.

Issues & Studies (Taipei). Selected issues.

Peking Review (Beijing), 1970–1978.

Union Research Service (Hong Kong), 1955–1973.

U.S. Consulate General. *Current Background* (Hong Kong), 1950–1977.

———. *Selections from China Mainland Magazines* (Hong Kong), 1960–1973.

———. *Selections from People's Republic of China Magazines* (Hong Kong), 1974–1977.

———. *Survey of the China Mainland Press* (Hong Kong), 1950–1973.

———. *Survey of the China Mainland Press-Supplement* (Hong Kong). Selected issues.

———. *Survey of the People's Republic of China Press* (Hong Kong), 1973–1977.

U.S. *Joint Publications Research Service*. Selected issues.

CHINESE-LANGUAGE BOOKS AND PERIODICALS

Caijing yanjiu [Financial Research] (Beijing). Selected issues.

Che Xinping. *Tan nongcun jishi maoyi* [On rural fair trade]. Beijing: Renmin chubanshe, n.d.

Chen Yun tongzhi wengao xuanbian [Selected Documents of Comrade Chen Yun] (1956–1962). N.p.: Sichuan renmin chubanshe, 1981. (Neibu faxing [Internal publication].)

Chengdu ribao [Chengdu Daily] (Chengdu). Selected issues.

Changjiang ribao [Yangtze River Daily] (Hankou). Selected issues.

Da Gong Bao [Impartial Daily] (Beijing). Selected issues, 1956–1965.

Da Gong Bao [Impartial Daily] (Tianjin). Selected issues, 1950–1955.

Ding Wang, ed. *Zhonggong wenhua da geming zeliao huibian* [Compilation of materials from China's Great Cultural Revolution]. Hong Kong: Ming bao yuekan, 1967.

Dongbei ribao [Northeast Daily] (Shenyang). Selected issues.

Dongxiang [Trend] (Hong Kong). Selected issues.

Dongxifang [East and West] (Hong Kong). Selected issues.

Gongren ribao [Worker's Daily] (Beijing). Selected issues.

Guanchajia [Observer] (Hong Kong). Selected issues.

Guangdong Sheng zhexue shehui kexue yanjiuso. Jingji yanjiu shi bian [Guangdong Province Philosophical Social Science Research Institute. Economic Research Office, ed.]. *Shangpin zhidu he huabi jiaohuan* [Commodity system and monetary exchange], rev. ed. Guangdong: Renmin chubanshe, 1976.

Guang jiaojing [Wide Angle] (Hong Kong). Selected issues.

Guangming ribao [Bright Daily] (Beijing). Selected issues.

Guangxi ribao [Guangxi Daily] (Guilin). Selected issues.

Guangzhou ribao [Guangzhou Daily] (Guangzhou). Selected issues.

Hong Qi [Red Flag] (Beijing), 1958–1981.

Jianguo shinian 1949–1959 [10 Years of National Construction]. Hong Kong: Jiwen chubanshe, 1959.

Jiangxi ribao [Jiangxi Daily] (Nanchang). Selected issues.

Jihua jingji [Planned Economy] (Beijing). Selected issues.

Jing bao [Mirror] (Hong Kong). Selected issues.

Jingji yanjiu [Economic Studies] (Beijing), 1955–1965, selected issues; 1978–1981.

Lou Yunlin, ed. *Sichuan fensheng dizhi* [Sichuan's geography]. Kunming: Zhonghua shuju, 1942.

Nanfang ribao [Southern Daily] (Guangzhou). Selected issues.

Qing bao [Intelligence] (Hong Kong). Selected issues.

Quanguo caimao xue daqing xue dazhai huiyi dianxing cailiao xuanbian [Selected model materials from the National Finance and Trade Conference to Study Daqing and Dazhai]. Beijing: Zhongguo caizheng jingji chubanshe, 1978.

Renmin ribao [People's Daily] (Beijing). Selected issues, 1949–1980.

Renmin shouce [*People's Handbook*] *1957*. N.p.: Da gong bao she, 1957.

Shanghai Shi shangye gongzuo huiyi bian [Shanghai Municipality commercial work conference, ed.]. *Shangye zhanxian qixiang xin* [A new atmosphere on the commercial front]. Shanghai: Renmin chubanshe, 1974.

Shangye kuaiji bian xie zu [The compilation group for *Commercial Accountant*]. *Shangye kuaiji* [Commercial Accountant]. Shanghai: Shanghai renmin chubanshe, 1977.

Shichang [Market] (Beijing), 1979–1980.

Sichuan ribao [Sichuan Daily] (Chengtu). Selected issues.

Xin Gong Shang [New Industry and Commerce] (Beijing). Selected issues.

Xinhua banyuekan [New China Semimonthly] (Beijing), 1956–1959.

Xinhua ribao [New China Daily] (Chongqing). Selected issues.

Xinhua yuebao [New China Monthly] (Beijing), 1949–1955.

Xuexi [Study] (Beijing). Selected issues.

Xuexi yu pipan [Study and Criticism] (Shanghai), 1973–1976.

Yangcheng wanbao [Yangcheng Evening News] (Guangzhou). Selected issues.

Zhang Xiaomei. *Guizhou jingji* [The Economy of Guizhou]. N.p.: Zhongguo guomin jingji yanjiuso, 1939.

Zheng Ming [Contend] (Hong Kong), 1979–1981.

Zhongguo renmin gongheguo Guowuyuan gongbao [Bulletin of the State Council of the People's Republic of China] (Beijing). Selected issues.

Zhongguo shehui kexue yuan. Jingji yanjiuso [Chinese Academy of Social Sciences. Economic Research Institute]. *Zhongguo ziben zhuyi gongshangye de shehui zhuyi gaizao* [The socialist transformation of China's capitalist industry and commerce]. Beijing: Renmin chubanshe, 1978.

Zhonghua renmin gongheguo fagui huibian [Chinese People's Republic Compendium of Laws and Regulations]. Beijing: Falu chubanshe, 1956, 1962.

INDEX

Accounting units, 187, 189, 197, 199
Administrative zones, and circulation of
   commodities, 51
Advertising, 50
Age, and attitudes toward markets, 75–76
Agency sales, 316, 317
Agricultural producer cooperatives
   (APCs), 275. *See also* Agriculture
Agricultural productivity, effect of rural
   fairs on, 273–276
Agricultural products, distribution of, 34,
   45. *See also* Fairs; Vegetables
Agriculture: abandoned by peasants for
   commerce, 275; by-products from, 236;
   central planning for, 21–22, 23–24;
   cooperativization of, 24, 89–90, 180,
   181, 307–308, 310; labor by small
   merchants for, 197; private plots for,
   251, 254n, 264; role in the Chinese
   economy, 16–17. *See also* Grain
Ahn, Byung-joon, 61n
All-China Federation of Supply and
   Marketing Cooperatives, 33, 34n, 45n,
   235n. *See also* Supply and marketing
   cooperatives
All-China General Goods Company, 224n
All-circles' people's representative
   conference, 147
Alliances: of bureaucrats and radicals, 74,
   164, 167, 254, 261–262, 299; of
   marketeers and bureaucrats, 108–109,
   112, 122, 228, 255; of merchants,

133, 137, 142–147; of radicals and
   marketeers, 73, 74, 100–101, 236, 268
Anhui province, 233
Animal by-products, 248
Anise, 293
Anshan steel works, 75n
Antagonism between industry and
   commerce, 206–242; models of policy
   approaches to, 215–242; structural
   causes of, 207–215
Antimarket ideology, 58, 65–66, 113,
   167, 241. *See also* Market forces
Antirightist rectification campaign, 196
"Arrangement" policy, 173–179, 180,
   186, 187, 188; attitudes of commercial
   cadres toward, 174–176; defined,
   173–174, 315
Associational and political resources of
   merchants, 137, 142–144, 153

Bachman, David, 80n
"Back-doorism," 56, 120, 127
"Balance" principle, 79n42, 98
Banking system: centralized financial
   transactions in, 20, 22–23; and loans to
   merchants, 177–178, 203, 205; loan
   quotas in, 144
Bargaining, 55–56, 138; at fairs, 258.
   See also Barter; Bribery
Barter, 12, 16, 31; and commercial
   corruption, 125, 127; by individuals,